Literary Research: Strategies and Sources
Series Editors: Peggy Keeran & Jennifer Bowers

Every literary age presents scholars with both predictable and unique research challenges. This series fills a gap in the field of reference literature by featuring research strategies and by recommending the best tools for conducting specialized period and national literary research. Emphasizing research methodology, each series volume takes into account the unique challenges inherent in conducting research of that specific literary period and outlines the best practices for researching within it. Volumes place the research process within the period's historical context and use a narrative structure to analyze and compare print and electronic reference sources. Following an introduction to online searching, chapters will typically cover these types of resources: general literary reference materials; library catalogs; print and online bibliographies, indexes, and annual reviews; scholarly journals; contemporary reviews; period journals and newspapers; microform and digital collections; manuscripts and archives; and Web resources. Additional or alternative chapters might be included to highlight a particular research problem or to examine other pertinent period or national literary resources.

1. *Literary Research and the British Romantic Era* by Peggy Keeran and Jennifer Bowers, 2005.
2. *Literary Research and the Era of American Nationalism and Romanticism* by Angela Courtney, 2008.
3. *Literary Research and American Modernism Era* by Robert N. Matuozzi and Elizabeth B. Lindsay, 2008.
4. *Literary Research and the American Realism and Naturalism Period* by Linda L. Stein and Peter J. Lehu, 2009.
5. *Literary Research and Irish Literature* by J. Greg Matthews, 2009.
6. *Literary Research and the Literatures of Australia and New Zealand* by H. Faye Christenberry and Angela Courtney, 2011.
7. *Literary Research and British Modernism* by Alison M. Lewis, 2010.
8. *Literary Research and the British Renaissance and Early Modern Period* by Jennifer Bowers and Peggy Keeran, 2010.
9. *Literary Research and the Victorian and Edwardian Ages, 1830–1910* by Melissa S. Van Vuuren, 2011.
10. *Literary Research and Canadian Literature* by Gabriella Natasha Reznowski, 2011.
11. *Literary Research and Postcolonial Literatures in English* by H. Faye Christenberry, Angela Courtney, Liorah Golomb, and Melissa S. Van Vuuren, 2012.
12. *Literary Research and the British Eighteenth Century* by Peggy Keeran and Jennifer Bowers, 2013.

Literary Research and the British Eighteenth Century

Strategies and Sources

Peggy Keeran
Jennifer Bowers

Literary Research: Strategies and Sources, No. 12

THE SCARECROW PRESS, INC.
Lanham • Toronto • Plymouth, UK
2013

Published by Scarecrow Press, Inc.
A wholly owned subsidiary of The Rowman & Littlefield Publishing Group, Inc.
4501 Forbes Boulevard, Suite 200, Lanham, Maryland 20706
http://www.scarecrowpress.com

10 Thornbury Road, Plymouth PL6 7PP, United Kingdom

British Library Cataloguing in Publication Information Available

Library of Congress Cataloging-in-Publication Data

Keeran, Peggy, 1959–
  Literary Research and the British Eighteenth Century : Strategies and Sources / Peggy
Keeran, Jennifer Bowers.
      pages cm. — (Literary Research: Strategies and Sources ; No. 12)
  Includes bibliographical references and indexes.
  ISBN 978-0-8108-8795-4 (pbk. : alk. paper) — ISBN 978-0-8108-8796-1 (ebook)
  1. Literature—Research—Methodology. 2. Criticism—Authorship. I. Bowers,
Jennifer, 1962–. II. Title.
  PN73.K44 2013
  807'.2—dc23   2012041411

Contents

Acknowledgments vii

Introduction ix

1 The Basics of Online Searching 1

2 General Literary Reference Sources 19

3 Library Catalogs 53

4 Print and Electronic Bibliographies, Indexes, and Annual Reviews 81

5 Scholarly Journals 113

6 Eighteenth-Century Books, Periodicals, and Newspapers 135

7 Contemporary Reviews 163

8 Archives and Manuscripts Collections 181

9 Web Resources 207

10 Researching a Thorny Problem 255

Appendix 267

Bibliography 291

Index 295

About the Authors 313

Acknowledgments

We would like to thank Martin Dillon, our editor at Scarecrow Press, for his valuable recommendations regarding this book and for the Literary Research: Strategies and Sources series. The authors of the other volumes in the series inspired us, and we challenged ourselves to meet the high quality of their work. We'd also like to thank Kellie Hagan, our production editor, and Barbara Berliner, our indexer for the series.

Michael Levine-Clark and Christopher C. Brown provided us with feedback about the content of the book, as well as expert advice when we needed to clarify certain details.

Finally, we'd like to thank Dean Nancy Allen for granting us time to work on the project, and our colleagues for allowing us to discuss aspects of the content with them. We truly appreciate the encouragement, patience, and support of our families, friends, and colleagues throughout this process.

Introduction

Each literary period offers unique research opportunities and challenges for scholars. The eighteenth century was a "commercial age, an era in which the processes of production and exchange had dramatically increased the wealth, improved the living standards, and transformed the mores of western societies."[1] In Britain, citizens were living longer, becoming more educated, and growing wealthier. Literacy rates, particularly for women, increased throughout the century. But the eighteenth century in Britain was also a long transition period for literature. Patronage, either a benefactor or through subscription, lingered, even as the publishing and bookselling industries took hold and blossomed.[2] The practice of reviewing books was thoroughly established as part of the literary marketplace during the second half of the century, with the first review periodical in 1749. For the literary scholar, these gradual changes mean that different search strategies may be required to conduct research into primary source material across the era that, in turn, vary from search techniques to find secondary academic sources. The current availability of print and manuscript content in digital forms presents opportunities to access texts that do not have modern editions or reprints, but there are searching and retrieval challenges caused by the lack of standard spelling, the printing practices of the era, and the handwriting in manuscripts.

The purpose of this volume is to describe standard and specialized print and electronic reference sources for eighteenth-century literary scholars and best practices for conducting research. This book details various search techniques and strategies for building effective, efficient skills conducting eighteenth-century literary searches. Throughout this text, we point out the challenges that may be encountered and how to overcome them, if possible. Scholars who have solid search skills and a good understanding about the types and purposes of the range of reference tools and collections available will be more confident and effective researchers. We intend graduate students to be our primary audience, but advanced undergraduates, academic librarians unfamiliar with eighteenth-century literature, and professors teaching literary research methods classes will find this volume helpful as well.

Although we cover Scottish, Welsh, and Irish examples throughout the text, our focus is primarily English literary authors and works. We discussed whether we should expand our time frame to include the long eighteenth century, stretching from the Restoration through the Romantic eras; however, since our first volume in the series focuses on the Romantic era and we included the Restoration as part of the early modern period, we decided to focus on the century itself. Our searches in most electronic databases are limited to the years 1700 to 1800, but, since trends and changes in literature don't adhere to the absolute boundaries that demarcate centuries, we may at times push these dates a bit, back to 1695 and the expiration of the Licensing Act, which required that all printed materials be examined and approved prior to publication, and with the Stationers' Company loss of the monopoly on printing, which permitted printing to expand outside London, Cambridge, and Oxford, up to the turn of the nineteenth century with the launch of the *Edinburgh Review* and the abandonment of eighteenth-century review practices. The century itself isn't a cohesive literary movement, but it can be divided into Augustan, Johnson, Sensibility, Romantic, and Enlightenment ages. When necessary, we are fluid about the borders of the century.

The eighteenth century experienced the progression of a robust literary marketplace and the development of such genres as the novel, newspaper, magazine, book review, dictionary, and encyclopedia. The lapse of the Licensing Act opened the doors to publishing opportunities and the growth of the industry during the century. Even so, the government continued to try to censor content, including the use of blasphemy, profanity, obscenity, and seditious libel through laws and enforcement, although these gradually eased over the century.[3] The first daily newspaper was established in 1702; by 1790, London alone had one evening and thirteen morning dailies.[4] Three common forms of periodicals emerged: Essay periodicals on politics, literature, and moral affairs were the standard in the first decades; in 1731, the *Gentleman's Magazine*, a compendia-style monthly, was established, with imitators soon following; and review periodicals initially appeared in 1749.[5] Habits shifted from intensive to extensive reading, with individuals reading more broadly rather than reading one text repeatedly.[6] Books dealing with secular topics, especially novels, were available to an increasingly literate, wealthier population with more leisure time.[7]

Charles Rivington and Thomas Longman, owners of major publishing firms at the end of the century, started as booksellers/publishers in 1711 and 1724, respectively.[8] In England, improvements to the transportation system, the building of the infrastructure to print and distribute printed matter, and the establishment of such financial institutions as banks to provide funds to commercial enterprises all enabled the rapid growth of print as a commodity.[9] Oddly enough, the one advancement that did not occur until the beginning of the nineteenth century was the process of printing itself, which meant that the "transformation of the book trade into a contemporary consumer industry had been achieved within the technological constraints of the handpress."[10]

The population that could read also grew, with the reading public expanding from 1,267,000 readers in 1700 to 2,928,000 readers in 1800.[11] Reading became part of the daily culture of eighteenth-century life, and the choices of subjects and literary genres expanded to meet the tastes and interests of the wider audience. Books, promoted by publishers and booksellers as fashionable commodities, were expensive, as were newspapers due to taxes levied through the Stamp Act of 1712.[12] Circulating and subscription libraries and book clubs, emerging in the late 1730s, provided broader access to books, periodicals, and newspapers.[13] Coffee houses had long been established as public spaces where reading materials could be shared, and they continued to play this role throughout the century.[14] The literary marketplace, consisting of publishers, booksellers, distributors, reviewers, and readers, was firmly established by the end of the century.

The transitions and changes that occurred during the century initiated some of the challenges that affect the current literary research process. Although printing flourished overall, newspapers and periodicals frequently went out of business quickly, especially after the Stamp Act of 1712,[15] and, although we refer to newspapers and periodicals as two types of publications, definitions were not that concrete in the eighteenth century; thus making such distinctions problematic. Characteristics of fictional storytelling, too, were fluid; the word "'novel,' in fact, is only one of the many names floating around in the discourse of writers and readers during those years for prose narratives of various kinds, which were just as often called by other names such as 'romance' or 'history,' or most confusingly 'true history' or 'secret history.'"[16] Book reviewing didn't exist for the first half of the century, making assessment of contemporary reputation during those decades difficult, if not impossible. The fonts used in handpress printing were nonstandard, creating obstacles for effectively searching the modern digital collections of eighteenth-century works. Throughout the following chapters, we provide guidance for navigating around such challenges.

This volume is intended to be read as a narrative, for we have woven the parts into a tale about the research process, but it can be consulted as a reference tool to identify and understand sources. We begin with the basics of searching, including standard techniques that can be used across a variety of online research tools, and more specialized strategies necessary for digital collections containing publications with poor-quality typeface. Throughout the following chapters, we offer examples of how to search effectively in specific databases. In chapter 2, we describe recommended standard and specialized reference tools, for example, literary dictionaries, companions, encyclopedias, and, in chapter 4, we discuss scholarly literary indexes and bibliographies. We present an overview on library and union catalogs in chapter 3, and explain how and why traditional library catalogs are changing. Other chapters cover the important literary scholarly periodicals for this era; digital and microform collections of eighteenth-century books, periodicals, and newspapers; manuscript and archival research; and quality academic websites. In chapter 10, we explore a thorny problem to illustrate how all the information in the prior chapters comes together when researching a lesser-known author. And, finally, we've included an annotated bibliography of research tools from other disciplines for scholars pursuing interdisciplinary topics. Throughout the book, we provide access dates to freely available websites, to differentiate them from subscription databases, which do not contain access dates.

We hope that our readers will benefit from the literary research sources and strategies we offer. Research can be rewarding and frustrating, as will be observed in the following chapters. For scholars working on traditionally canonical figures, there will be a plethora of materials, while for authors who have not been as studied, there may be few sources. In both situations, help may be necessary to narrow or broaden the search, and the reference librarian is there for you to consult. As reference librarians, teaching research methods and engaging with research on behalf of others is central to our profession. We encourage all scholars to seek advice from reference librarians at any point during the process when help is needed. Although we intend for this book to provide a solid foundation, everyone has times when they require research guidance, even us. Literary reference librarians have their own online network, and they confer with one another daily to answer difficult questions, so if your librarian doesn't know the answer, he or she will have access to a wealth of collective knowledge for assistance.

NOTES

1. Paul Langford, *A Polite and Commercial People: England, 1727–1783* (New York: Oxford University Press, 1989), 2.

2. Dustin Griffin, "The Rise of the Professional Author?" in *The Cambridge History of the Book in Britain*, vol. 5, 1695–1830, ed. Michael F. Suarez and Michael L. Turner (New York: Cambridge University Press, 2009), 133; Michael F. Suarez, "Publishing Contemporary English Literature, 1695–1774," in *The Cambridge His-*

tory of the Book in Britain, vol. 5, 1695–1830, ed. Michael F. Suarez and Michael L. Turner (New York: Cambridge University Press, 2009), 659.

3. Mark Rose, "Copyright, Authors, and Censorship," in *The Cambridge History of the Book in Britain*, vol. 5, 1695–1830, ed. Michael F. Suarez and Michael L. Turner (New York: Cambridge University Press, 2009), 127–31.

4. Bob Harris, "Print Culture," in *A Companion to Eighteenth-Century Britain*, ed. H. T. Dickinson (Malden, MA: Blackwell, 2002), 286–87.

5. Harris, "Print Culture," 287–88.

6. James Van Horn Melton, *The Rise of the Public in Enlightenment Europe* (New York: Cambridge University Press, 2001), 92.

7. John Richetti, "Introduction," in *The Cambridge Companion to the Eighteenth-Century Novel*, ed. John Richetti (Cambridge, UK: Cambridge University Press, 1996), 6; Michael F. Suarez, "Introduction," in *The Cambridge History of the Book in Britain*, vol. 5, 1695–1830, ed. Michael F. Suarez and Michael L. Turner (New York: Cambridge University Press, 2009), 8–9.

8. Suarez, "Introduction," 32.

9. Suarez, "Introduction," 12–35.

10. James Raven, "The Book as a Commodity," in *The Cambridge History of the Book in Britain*, vol. 5, 1695–1830, ed. Michael F. Suarez and Michael L. Turner (New York: Cambridge University Press, 2009), 87.

11. Suarez, "Introduction," 11.

12. Raven, "The Book as a Commodity," 108; Uriel Heyd, *Reading Newspapers: Press and Public in Eighteenth-Century Britain and America* (Oxford, UK: Voltaire Foundation, 2012), 14.

13. Harris, "Print Culture," 290.

14. Suarez, "Introduction," 12.

15. Alvin Sullivan, ed., *British Literary Magazines*, vol. 1, *The Augustan Age and the Age of Johnson, 1698–1788* (Westport, CT: Greenwood, 1983), xvi.

16. Richetti, "Introduction," 1.

Chapter One

The Basics of Online Searching

In this chapter, our goal is to provide an overview of the types of search techniques that are most commonly used to conduct academic research in online databases and explain how electronic content is searched and how to search effectively. A wide variety of online resources and digital collections are introduced in this volume that require understanding the basics covered in this chapter. In addition to such traditional electronic reference tools as catalogs, indexes, and bibliographies are full-text book, newspaper, periodical, and manuscript collections with content from the eighteenth century; there are challenges associated with searching the nonstandard typeface used during that era, and we offer best practices for doing so.

The philosophies about and protocols for online searching in electronic library resources are in transition, for we are moving away from complex searches that can retrieve as much information as possible on a topic toward single-search box "discovery tools" intended to find something on a topic, not everything. To be effective researchers, scholars need to understand the strengths and weaknesses of both and learn how to recognize the different environments. In addition to these challenges, Web pages are prone to change appearance to keep them fresh and inviting, and electronic reference tools are no different. These changes to the look of the search interface may disorient researchers familiar with a certain resource. Also, various vendors may offer the same database, for example, *MLA International Bibliography* (*MLAIB*), so that the interface to the same content may differ significantly from one library to another. And, finally, if a database publisher is bought out by another company, the content of the database may get incorporated into another resource; this happened when the Research Libraries Group union catalog *RLIN* was purchased by the Online Computer Library Center (OCLC), and its contents absorbed into *WorldCat*. The online environment, much like the publishing industry at the beginning of the eighteenth century, is changing and adapting to the power of this Web-based form of access and distribution.

We hope to demystify the search process by breaking it down into practical steps so that our readers can approach research comfortably and knowledgeably. We explain how a basic library catalog record is organized and how the search interface works in a Web-based catalog to retrieve relevant materials using information extracted from that record. We describe effective techniques and strategies in various database environments. This chapter is intended to serve as the foundation for the rest of this volume, and we will assume a certain level of knowledge and understanding when we delve more deeply into specific electronic resources later on. To begin the process, we, of course, first need to have a question to research.

STEP 1: WRITE THE RESEARCH QUESTION AS A TOPIC SENTENCE

Once you have identified a topic you want to explore, it is helpful to write out the research question as a topic sentence to identify the main concepts. These concepts are necessary for brainstorming keywords to create effective search strategies that will find relevant materials. For example, if interested in how the elite or upper classes were depicted in British fiction during the course of the century, you would write "I want to research how the elite, or the upper classes, were depicted in the novels of the eighteenth century." If the topic were about British travel writing, the sentence might read, "I want to research the development of British travel writing during the course of the century." For a more robust statement, you would complete these statements by explaining what you want to find out and why it is important for your audience to understand, but for the purposes of this chapter we will stop with these brief sentences.

STEP 2: BRAINSTORMING KEYWORDS

Next, identify the main concepts in the sentence so that you can generate other terms and phrases that describe your topic. By developing the vocabulary for the topic, you can try different words until you find the right combination to retrieve relevant materials. Later in this chapter, we will discuss subject headings, also known as descriptors and controlled vocabulary, which are assigned to books and articles by indexers and catalogers. Subject headings, however, are not always obvious, for example, the Library of Congress

Table 1.1. Keywords for the Topic Travel Writing across the Eighteenth Century

Concept #1	Concept #2	Concept #3	Concept #4
travel	writing	British	eighteenth
Grand Tour	letters	English	century
	diaries	Scottish	18th century
	narratives	Irish	Georgian
	memoirs	Welsh	Augustan
			Enlightenment

subject heading for the American Revolution, which is "United States—History—Revolution, 1775–1783," so almost every research process will start with keywords and phrases. For depictions of the upper class in novels, synonyms, alternate words, and broader concepts could include *elite, aristocracy, social classes, landowners*, and *landed society*, while novels may also be referred to as *fiction* or *romance*, Britain as *England, Wales, Scotland*, and *Ireland* (or the nationalities *British, English, Welsh, Scottish*, and *Irish*), and the eighteenth century as *18th century* or *Augustan* or *Georgian* or *Enlightenment*. For the development of travel writing, other concepts could be *Grand Tour, narratives, letters*, and *diaries*.

Creating a table with the terms helps sort the terms into categories, and this method is utilized later when Boolean operators are explained. In table 1.1, the main concepts appear across the top, and the related words are listed underneath. By breaking *travel* into its own concept, we can later combine it with the various types of writing in a more complex search.

STEP 3: THE STRUCTURE OF
ELECTRONIC RECORDS: THE MARC EXAMPLE

Before moving to search strategies, let's first discuss one method used to organize and identify elements of a database record, in this case a typical library catalog record that describes a book. In online catalogs, the results retrieved will differ depending upon which elements are searched, namely title, author, keyword, or subject; as mentioned above, we are in a transition period, so in a "discovery"-type library catalog, results can be restricted to specific elements after the search is executed rather than up front.

In the 1960s, the Library of Congress developed a standard, called MARC (Machine Readable Cataloging), which sets rules for capturing, sharing, and displaying bibliographic information in an online environment.[1] Catalogers essentially assign certain standard numeric, letter, and symbol codes, called

MARC field tags, to identify each field (author, title, publication information) found in a bibliographic record. Libraries that use MARC can contract
with commercial vendors that offer library automation systems compatible
with the standard, for example, Innovative Interfaces Inc., Ex Libris, or
SirsiDynix. Library automation systems help manage the data and allow records to be read and displayed in different indexes (title, author, subject, and
so forth) through the use of MARC fields and field tags: The bibliographic
information for the publication is entered into the MARC fields, the MARC
field tags are used to identify each field numerically, and these are then managed through indexing rules as defined by librarians in the library automation
system. Records can be searched in the online library catalog, shared with
other libraries that also use MARC, and pooled into "union catalogs" so that
holdings of several libraries can be searched at once (more about this in chapter 3). These types of conventions, whereby each field representing a piece
of bibliographic data is coded with a field tag, enable researchers to execute
searches that will bring consistent results within library catalogs and scholarly indexes; this is not true of a discovery-type catalog, which isn't intended
for precision searching.

To understand how MARC fields and field tags work, let's analyze records
for a book and for a periodical. Figure 1.1 is the MARC record for the scholarly edition of Alexander Pope's poetry. The brief numbers are the field tags
that mark each field, such as author field with the field tag 100, the title field
with the field tag 245, the tables of contents field with the field tag 505, and
subject field with the field tag 650. The numeric field tags that identify the
field names as containing the author, title, subject, or other data, are associated with the relevant indexing rules within the library automated system, so
that the data in that field can be searched and the record retrieved (see table
1.2 for sample MARC field names, tags, and indexes). Therefore, a search
in the author index on *pope, alexander* will retrieve all the books by, but not
about, the poet, because the author field name is associated with the field tag
100, not 650, in the indexing rules. If the numeric field tags for the author,
title, contents, and subject fields are all included in the keyword index, then
the bibliographic data in those fields can all be searched at the same time
when a keyword search is executed.

Libraries may choose to have a separate periodical title index to make
searching for this type of serial publication (scholarly journals, magazines,
newspapers) easier. The title in the MARC record for the electronic version of
the scholarly journal *Eighteenth-Century Studies*, seen in figure 1.2, contains
not only the 245 field for the title, but also a 222 field. In this library catalog,
the 222 field is associated in the indexing rules table with the periodical title
index, so that a search on the periodical title using the periodical title index

```
090      PR3621|b.B82
100 1    Pope, Alexander,|d1688-1744.
245 00   Poems.
250      [Twickenham ed.|bGeneral editor: John Butt.
260      London :|bMethuen;|aNew Haven :|bYale University Press,
         |c1951-1969; v. 1, 1961]
300      11 v. in 12 ;|c23 cm.
500      Each volume has also special t.p.
505 0    v. 1. Pastoral poetry, and An essay on criticism.--v. 2.
         The rape of the lock, and other poems.--v. 3. i. An essay
         of man. ii. Epistles to several persons (Moral essays)--v.
         4. Imitations of Horace, with An epistle to Dr. Arbuthnot
         and Epilogue to the satires.--v. 5. The dunciad.--v. 6.
         Minor poems.--v. 7-8. Translations of Homer: The Iliad.--
         v. 9-10. Translations of Homer: The Odyssey.--v. 11.
         Index.
650 0    English poetry.
740 0    Pastoral poetry, and An essay on criticism.
740 4    The rape of the lock, and other poems.
740 3    An essay of man.
740 0    Epistles to several persons (Moral essays)
740 0    Imitations of Horace, with An epistle to Dr. Arbuthnot and
         Epilogue to the satires.
740 4    The dunciad.
740 0    Minor poems.
740 0    Translations of Homer: The Iliad.
740 0    Translations of Homer: The Odyssey.
```

Figure 1.1. Modified MARC record for Alexander Pope's poems, with fields 100, 245, 505, and 650 highlighted. *Source:* University of Denver Penrose Library classic catalog.

will retrieve the record for the publication. A library with a separate periodical title search option would associate the 222 field tag with the periodical title index, and the 245 field tag with the title index, so the publication is discoverable in both indexes. If the desired publication isn't retrieved using

Table 1.2. Simplified Indexing Rules Table: Selected Field Tag/Field Index Association

MARC Field Name	MARC Field Tag	Index
Personal Author	100	Author
Corporate Author	110	Author
Conference Author	111	Author
Title Proper	245	Title
Uniform Title	240	Title
Contents Note	505	Note
Summary Note	520	Note
LCSH	650	Subject

the periodical title search, the next step is to try a basic title search in case the 222 field is missing from the MARC record.

The 650 field, containing the subject data, also highlighted in figure 1.2, is another common search option found in online library catalogs. This journal has two Library of Congress subject headings assigned to it: "Arts—Periodicals" and "Civilization, Modern—18th Century—Periodicals"; in many library catalogs these are clickable links to find other items with that particular heading. As we will see in the keyword and subject heading discussion that follows, we don't always recommend clicking on the subject-heading hyperlink unless it describes exactly what you need. Other fields that often have their own indexes are the ISSN with the 022 field tag and the publisher with the 260 field tag. As previously mentioned, the keyword index frequently contains all field tags for the elements that are searchable, which, in addition to the title, author, contents, and subjects, could also include alternate titles, the ISSN, the publisher, and the publication date. Keyword and subject searching is discussed further later in this chapter and in chapter 3. Generally, the physical description fields with tags in the 300s are not indexed, but if you are interested in retrieving, for example, books that have maps, and only the 300 field contains that information, ask the reference librarian if a list can be generated by searching the data through the back end of the library's cataloging system.

Although MARC tags are invaluable for field searching, which is discussed next, more libraries are transitioning to discovery tools: *Summon* from Serial Solutions, *Primo Central* from Ex Libris, *EBSCO Discovery Service* (*EDS*) from EBSCO, and *WorldCat Local* from OCLC allow the library catalog and

```
130 0   Eighteenth-century studies (Online)
210 0   Eighteenth-century stud.|b(Online)
222   0 Eighteenth-century studies|b(Online)
229   0 Eighteenth-century studies|b(Online)
245 10 Eighteenth-century studies|h[electronic resource].
260     Baltimore, Md. :|bJohns Hopkins University Press
310     Quarterly
362 1   Print began fall 1967.
506     Access restricted to subscribing institutions.
530     Also available in print.
538     Mode of access: World Wide Web.
550     Issued on behalf of: American Society for Eighteenth-
        Century Studies.
650   0 Arts|vPeriodicals.
650   0 Civilization, Modern|y18th century|vPeriodicals.
```

Figure 1.2. Modified MARC record for *Eighteenth-Century Studies*, with fields 222, 245, and 650s highlighted. *Source:* University of Denver Penrose Library classic catalog.

articles in e-journal collections to be searched together, while *Encore* from Innovative Interfaces Inc. is an example of a discovery-type library catalog, also sometimes called a next-generation catalog. These types of interfaces can be used to search the library's holdings and, in some cases, articles. Discovery tools frequently offer a one-search box, with results narrowed and limited after executing the search by clicking on multiple facets, for example, author, title, subject, format (book, periodical, video), publication date, and language. To differentiate between the traditional catalog, which employs field searching up front, and the discovery catalog, the former is generally referred to as the "classic catalog." Understanding a standard like MARC, however, is still valuable, for most scholarly bibliographic databases function similarly to the classic catalog. Next, we will examine how data is extracted from a database when different searches are executed.

STEP 4: CREATING SEARCH STRATEGIES

Field Searching

As previously noted, searching by fields is a more traditional strategy, as the researcher tells the system where in the bibliographic record to look to find relevant resources. The most logical fields are title, author, and subject, but these can also include periodical title, genre, call number, standard number (ISBN, ISSN, OCLC), publication date, language, abstract, or full text. Keyword is the default in most classic catalogs and may search all the fields mentioned. There are two variations of field searching: anchored and keyword. In left-anchored searches, for example, an author field search will require that the last name be typed in first, and the title field will require that the title to be entered exactly. In keyword field searching, the system will still search the specific field, but, in these cases, the author's name or words from the book's title can be entered in any order. The help screens can assist in determining if word order is important in field searching. Generally, a drop-down menu next to the search box displays the list of fields that can be selected and searched. The advantage of field searching is that it is more precise than discovery tools.

Boolean Searches

Online classic catalogs and scholarly subject-specific bibliographies typically offer Boolean operators as a means of searching. George Boole, a nineteenth-century mathematician and logician, developed a theory now called Boolean logic, that later became important in computer programming during the

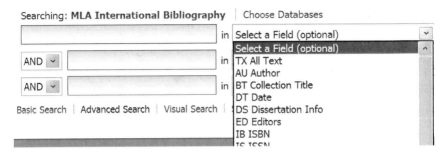

Figure 1.3.   Advanced-search screen *MLAIB* via EBSCOhost. *Source: MLAIB*, via EBSCO-host.

twentieth century. Boolean operators, *and*, *or*, and *not*, are often used in re-search databases to allow results to be narrowed or broadened; some systems require that the operators be capitalized (*AND, OR, NOT*). Most one-search box discovery tools do not normally allow Boolean operators, but instead treat *and*, *or*, and *not* the same as any other word. In this transition time, understanding and knowledge of Boolean operators, and how to use them effectively, is vital to the scholarly researcher. Database help screens will indicate if the operators are used, or the advanced search screen will explicitly provide search boxes with the operators available in drop-down menus. The advanced search screen for *MLAIB*, seen in figure 1.3, illustrates both Boolean operators and the fields that can be searched. We will use the concepts and keywords in table 1.1, generated for eighteenth-century travel writing, to explain how Boolean operators can be used to combine these words to find relevant resources.

1. The Boolean Operator "And"

The *and* operator narrows a search by finding records that include all the keywords searched. Our topic sentence has three concepts: *travel writing*, *british*, and *eighteenth century*. To find books, book chapters, articles, dissertations, and more in *MLAIB*, type *and* between each word, as follows:

*travel writing **and** british **and** eighteenth century*

The overlapping shaded area in the Venn diagram in figure 1.4 illustrates how *and* narrows the search to retrieve records that have all of the terms present.

The search retrieved the record seen in figure 1.5 from *MLAIB*, with the keywords highlighted. Note in the "Subject Terms" field that the phrase is ac-

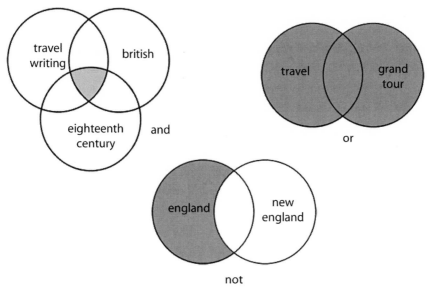

Figure 1.4. Boolean operators.

Age of Peregrination: **Travel Writing** and the Eighteenth-Century Novel

Authors:	Bohls, Elizabeth
Source:	pp. 97-116 IN: Backscheider, Paula R. (ed.); Ingrassia, Catherine (ed. and introd.); A Companion to the Eighteenth-Century English Novel and Culture. Malden, MA; Blackwell; 2005. (xiii, 550 pp.)
ISBN:	9781405101578
Series:	Blackwell Companions to Literature and Culture (Blackwell Companions to Literature and Culture): 30
General Subject Areas:	*Subject Literature:* **British** and Irish literatures *Period:* 1700-1799 *Genre:* novel
Subject Terms:	genre conventions ; relationship to **travel** literature ; literary historical approach
Document Information:	*Publication Type:* book article *Language of Publication:* English

Figure 1.5. Modified record from *MLAIB* using Boolean *and* to combine concepts. Source: *MLAIB*, via EBSCOhost.

tually *travel literature.* Using keywords to find subject headings is discussed in a later section.

2. The Boolean Operator "Or"

The *or* operator, on the other hand, broadens the search, so that all the words in table 1.1 listed under one concept can be searched together to find resources that contain any of the words.

*travel **or** grand tour*

The corresponding Venn diagram in figure 1.4 shows that the circles are completely shaded, for the search will retrieve all records that have any of the words.

3. The Boolean Operator "Not"

The *not* operator is trickier to use, for it excludes concepts; thus it should be used sparingly. This operator is generally used to eliminate records that contain words that muddy the results. For example, if doing literary research on England, and the results include a great many records for New England, *not* can remove any records with the word *new* in them, as illustrated in figure 1.4. The danger with such a search is that a record using *new* in another sense, such as a new genre or a new book, will not be retrieved. In this case, to avoid that from happening, use *not* in the following way:

*england **not** new England*

Truncation/Wildcards

This technique allows symbols to be used, either at the end of a word to find the stem of the word and all variant endings (truncation, sometimes called wildcard), or to place a symbol within a word to find variant or additional letters (wildcard). Help screens in databases will indicate if these strategies are offered, and, if so, which symbols to use. Most typically, the truncation symbol is an asterisk (*). When looking for materials about travel writing and diaries, *diaries* can be either singular or plural. Instead of conducting two separate searches to find both, the word can be truncated, or shortened, at the "r" to find either: *diar** finds *diary, diaries,* and *diarist* and *travel** retrieves *travel, travels, traveling, travelers,* and so on. To find *theatre, theater,* or *theatrical,* the word should be truncated after the second "t," so that both the British and American spellings of theater can be found. Internal wildcard symbols, which are not as frequently available as truncation, are used to substitute letters in a word. EBSCOhost has two wildcard symbols: the question mark (?) to replace one letter (*wom?n* to retrieve *woman* and *women*) or the pound symbol (#) to find extra letters (*colo#r* to find *color* or *colour*). In some databases, the search system has been designed to automatically find these variants.

OCR and Fuzzy Searching

Optical Character Recognition (OCR) technology is frequently used in full-text digital projects. OCR allows for the recognition of print text characters in the digital environment, so that the scanned image of a text doesn't have to be rekeyed or transcribed to be searchable online. But this technology can be problematic for eighteenth-century literary researchers, because of the sometimes poor quality of the print and the variety of fonts used by eighteenth-century printers. In these cases, the fuzzy search option, which retrieves near matches to the word or phrase being searched, may be offered to counter the limits of the OCR'd text.

In his article "'The New Machine': Discovering the Limits of *ECCO*," Patrick Spedding illustrates some of the challenges of searching a digital database like *Eighteenth Century Collections Online* (*ECCO*), which has been created from a microfilm collection and uses OCR and fuzzy searching.[2] The fact that microforms are a step away from the original may cause issues, for, in the digital environment, much depends upon the quality of that copy. As *ECCO* does not offer the behind-the-scenes OCR'd text for viewing, Spedding examined a passage from Eliza Haywood's *Female Spectator*, found in Google Books and Internet Archive, in which the OCR'd text can be displayed to determine the drawbacks of eighteenth-century OCR'd texts. In comparing the OCR'd documents and the actual text, he found the error rate average at more than 150 typos per 2,000 characters, making parts of the text unreadable. For example, the long "s" was interpreted as an "f" in both, "theiefined tall" for "the refined taste," and "t:ut: uifimguilhes" for "taste distinguishes." Spedding points out that "it should also now be clear why the fuzzy search option on *ECCO* is of limited usefulness. While it seems able to resolve 'prefs' and 'press' or 'molt' and 'most,' it does not stand a chance against 'fubjr&s,' 't:ut:' or 'mofr.' And even 'low'-level fuzzy searching tends to vastly increase false returns."[3]

Spedding's topic, condoms, added a further difficulty to successfully discovering relevant texts in *ECCO*. The word *condom* had different spellings throughout the century, and it had other meanings as well, which were difficult to eliminate even using the Boolean *not*. Printers would substitute such common yet euphemistic words as *sheath*, *implement*, *armour*, and *machine*, or they frequently dashed the word out of the text completely. According to Spedding, "They wanted these passages, in particular, to be invisible to guardians of public morality. It is not clear how well they succeeded in this aim, but they certainly succeeded in making their texts invisible to modern users of *ECCO* and other text-bases."[4] In terms of the dashes, "while the reader may 'readily guess' the author's meaning, *ECCO* not only can't guess, it offers no way of searching for such meaning-laden dashes."[5]

In chapters 6 and 7, we describe strategies for searching digital collections effectively, but OCR technology is not yet at the point where we can rely on technology to interpret text, and, as we will see, searching digital facsimiles of eighteenth-century books, pamphlets, newspapers, and periodicals can be frustrating and time consuming.

Nesting

Nesting allows more complex and powerful searches, whereby two, or even all three, of the Boolean operators can be employed in a single search. Parentheses are used to "nest" synonyms or like terms together through the use of the *or* operator, and then the separate concepts combined using *and*. The individual concepts and keywords from table 1.1 can be searched separately, as follows:

> *travel **and** writing **and** british **and** eighteenth century*
> *travel **and** letters **and** british **and** 18th century*

Or they can be searched together by enclosing the synonyms or like terms in parentheses (*writing or letters*; *eighteenth century or 18th century*) using nesting, as follows:

> *travel **and** (writing **or** letters) **and** british*
> ***and** (eighteenth century **or** 18th century)*

The advantage of nesting terms into a single search is that the results won't have duplicate records, whereas conducting the two separate searches may retrieve some of the same records. Nesting streamlines searching.

Phrase Searching/Proximity Operators

Even databases that allow the use of Boolean operators may automatically employ the *and* as the default, thus treating all keywords in a search as independent concepts. If the search includes a phrase, such as *eighteenth century* or *18th century*, enclosing the words with quotation marks will tell the system that these are phrases, not separate concepts: *"eighteenth century"* or *"18th century."*

Proximity operators offer a more complex method for searching words in a record or in full text, by instructing the system how far apart the words should be, and in which order they should appear. Proximity operators are important when searching the full text because they reduce false drops, which are items that have all the words but aren't relevant. For example, the word *travel* may be the first word of a 5,000-word chapter in a book, and *writing* the last word, but the terms have no relationship to one another. Most commonly, the operators are *w* (with) and *n* (near), although others, for example, *adj* (adjacent), may be used instead. The operator is then followed by a number, *wn* or *nn*, to indicate the number of words apart they are in the text. The *w* operator is used for searches where one word must follow another within a certain number of words, and the *n* is used to indicate that the words are near one another but can be in any order. For example, in *Annual Bibliography of English Language and Literature (ABELL)*, the *near* proximity operator should be used when searching names of authors to retrieve both first name or last name coming first: *richard near sheridan* retrieves Richard Sheridan, Richard Brinsley Sheridan, and Sheridan Richard.

In his quest for relevant sources in *ECCO*, Spedding also tried, although still unsuccessfully due to the various previously described challenges, to use proximity operators because they facilitate context searching. He tried "'cundum W3 machine' and 'cundum N3 machine' . . . for instances where the second term either follows within three words of the first, or appears within three words before or after it."[6] We, too, have difficulties effectively using proximity searches in the full-text eighteenth-century digital collections to narrow searches down to relevant results, so, although we still promote their use, be cognizant that results may contain innumerable false drops.

Subject versus Keyword Searches

As previously mentioned, brainstorming terms helps identify potential keywords that can be used in a variety of search strategies. Once relevant records are found, the next step is to examine the subject headings field (also called controlled vocabulary or descriptors) to determine the standard vocabulary employed within that database to describe that subject. Generally, a subject heading can offer multiple concepts in a single heading, while descriptors are typically single-notion terms, but they both serve the same function. Most academic libraries in the United States use Library of Congress subject headings for books, while *MLAIB* and *ABELL*, discussed in detail in chapter 4, both have their own controlled vocabularies. Each item found in a library catalog or scholarly subject-specific database has been examined by a knowl-edgeable cataloger or indexer, who decides what it is about and then assigns appropriate subject headings or descriptors. It is common to have several headings or descriptors assigned to a single piece to more fully describe the content.

Returning to the *travel writing* sample search executed earlier, we note in figure 1.5 that the descriptor in *MLAIB* is "travel literature." Executing the same search in a library catalog retrieves a potentially useful title, *Travel Writing and Empire: Postcolonial Theory in Transit*, edited by Steve Clark. The record reveals that the Library of Congress offers two useful headings for this subject: "Travel writing" and "Travelers' writings, English." The second heading informs us that we should truncate both *travel* and *writing* to expand our search (*travel* writing**), and that we should broaden our search to in-clude *english* as well as *british*. In Web-based catalogs and bibliographies, subject headings tend to be clickable links, but be cautious about doing so if the heading is too broad. Whereas clicking on the "Traveler's writings, Eng-lish" heading leads to publications on this genre in terms of English writings, "Travel writing" would cover all travel writing, not just English. As a best practice, examine the subject headings for vocabulary to add to your list of keywords and then reexecute the search incorporating those terms and trun-cating specific words as necessary.

Relevancy Searching

While classic catalogs most frequently display results by date, author, or title, discovery tools and some subject-specific scholarly databases display by relevancy, whereby the system, based upon the search executed, ranks the results using internal criteria to determine the item's relevancy. Each system has its own method for determining relevance, but some factors that rank certain results over others may include the location of the words in the item (title, first paragraph, abstract, subject field), the frequency of the occurrence of the keywords, and the proximity of keywords to one another. A keyword search, *travel and letters*, in *ECCO*, retrieved more than 32,500 items; when sorted by author, many were irrelevant to the topic, but when sorted by relevance, the 500 results were much more relevant to the topic, with fewer false drops.

Limiting/Modifying

Limiting and modifying are both ways to narrow a search by selecting specific values assigned to every record as part of the search (e.g., date, language, document type), or by selecting the values after a search has been executed. To further modify the results, *ECCO* offers the option to search for keywords within results. *MLAIB* via EBSCOhost allows limiting up front, by publication type (e.g., book, book chapter, journal article, etc., or to exclude dissertations), peer-reviewed publication, publication date, language, genre, and period, so that the search executed returns results with the selected values. The search can also be limited after the fact by using the facets. The digital collections *17th & 18th Century Burney Newspapers*, *Eighteenth Century Journals*, and *British Periodicals* can be limited to include or exclude advertisements. Early in the research process, it is best to limit after the search, but once familiar with results, it may prove useful to employ the limiters from the start.

STEP 5: DATABASES VERSUS VENDORS VERSUS INTERFACE PLATFORMS

The next step is to begin searching, but there is one more piece of background information to impart before selecting a library catalog or database to search. Commercial vendors that provide interface platforms to search the content of a database are not necessarily responsible for the content in that database. Researchers often confuse the prominent branding of the vendor with the name of the database being searched. EBSCO, Cengage Learning/Gale, ProQuest, and other vendors offer access to a wide variety of databases, and their respective interface platforms search the data, but neither the vendor nor the interface are the databases themselves.

The contents of the two most prominent literary databases, *MLAIB* and *ABELL*, are the responsibility of the Modern Language Association and the Modern Humanities Research Association, respectively. Electronically, *ABELL* is available through ProQuest/Chadwyck Healey via its interface platform *Literature Online*, while *MLAIB* is available from EBSCO via its interface EBSCOhost, Cengage Learning/Gale via *Literature Resource Center*, and ProQuest/Chadwyck-Healey via *Literature Online*. The interface for the database will determine how results will be retrieved, so it is best to read the help screens or "Frequently Asked Questions" section for searching advice, including whether Boolean operators are necessary, if truncation and wild-card options are offered, how to search by phrase or proximity, how results are displayed (author, title, date, relevancy), how to mark and export your results, and how to download and print. Because vendors may change the way an interface searches, it is best to review the help screens periodically. For example, in recent years, EBSCOhost began to automatically find the singular and plural forms of words, making truncation no longer necessary in those cases. Truncation, however, is still necessary to search other variant endings: While *diary* will retrieve *diaries* in *MLAIB* via EBSCOhost, it won't retrieve *diarist*.

STEP 6: GOOGLE

Google has had a significant impact on the development of search interfaces for library catalogs and subject-specific scholarly databases. Discovery tools for academic research are incorporating some of the more popular elements of a Google search, including the single-search box and relevancy ranking. As with other Web-based search interfaces, inspect the help screens in Google for tips. Basic keyword searching, excluding stop words, is recommended, while the advanced search offers the ability to search all the words (Boolean *and*), any of the words (Boolean *or*), none of these words (Boolean *not*), the exact phrase (phrase searching), and limiting (language, region, reading level, usage rights, domain). Stop words such as "the" can be searched by highlighting them or putting them into quotation marks. Google doesn't use truncation, but instead "stems" the word automatically, so that records with that stem are all retrieved. Results can be limited to specific types of domains using the command *site:.edu* (or *.gov* or *.ac.uk*). According to Steve Lohr in the *New York Times*, Google is constantly adjusting its algorithm. The "algorithm is a tightly guarded trade secret, but it relies heavily on linking search terms to noun phrases in a Web page—as well as the popularity of a site and how often other sites link to it."[7] Google had a major overhaul in 2011, to improve the quality of search results.

In addition to searching the Web itself, Google also has been working with partners to build quality online collections. Google Books provides full-text access to public domain, pre-1923 publications, and, depending upon their agreement with the publisher, either previews or snippets of copyrighted works. Titles with no e-book available will not display any content, and the full text is not searchable. In a controversial collaboration, HathiTrust partnered with Google to scan copyrighted materials from participating library collections. The intent was to allow the content to be searched, working much as an index would, but with the full text not visible. This would allow scholars to determine whether their key terms were present in the text before seeking out the print copy. Other Google partnerships include publishers of scholarly journals, which are searchable via *Google Scholar*, and museums, for images in *Google Art Project*. It has translation options for Web pages or for text. Google has illustrated the potential Web searching has to offer, but, as with any resource at the beginning of the twenty-first century, it is difficult to know what lies ahead during this incredible shift from print to digital.

CONCLUSION

Revising and refining search interfaces to effectively search Web-based resources is ongoing, and as computers and software become more sophisticated, technology will become more capable of retrieving relevant information for researchers. At present, software such as OCR cannot crack the meanings found in eighteenth-century texts, for it is unable to interpret the subtle references and coded language used in that era. The fact that such rich digital collections from the eighteenth century are available for research is heartening, but the fact that searching them online is frequently no easier than visiting the library that holds the printed copies, then scouring them for relevant references, is frustrating. It is hoped that, as technology improves, digital texts will become easier to search. Whether the OCR'd documents from microfilm will have to be rescanned from the originals to at least allow for greater searching success, or whether the technology can be improved to get better results from these collections, remains unknown.

To fully appreciate the strategies and techniques presented in this chapter, we recommend that you practice to master them. We will go into more detail about specific types of searches in the chapters to come, and we advise that you try the examples we describe to see which results you get. Our hope is that you will become effective, knowledgeable, efficient searchers, especially with the eighteenth-century digital collections. You will ultimately be able to provide librarians with strategies that work for you in your particular era and subject area, and offer publishers of these resources feedback that could immensely help improve their power.

NOTES

1. Betty Furrie, "What Is a MARC Record, and Why Is It Important?" in *Understanding MARC Bibliographic: Machine-Readable Cataloging* (Washington, DC: Library of Congress), www.loc.gov/marc/umb/um01to06.html (accessed 23 July 2012).

2. Patrick Spedding, "'The New Machine': Discovering the Limits of *ECCO*," *Eighteenth-Century Studies* 44, no. 4 (2011): 437–53.

3. Spedding, "'The New Machine,'" 440.

4. Spedding, "'The New Machine,'" 443.

5. Spedding, "'The New Machine,'" 445.

6. Spedding, "'The New Machine,'" 63n.

7. Steve Lohr, "Google Schools Its Algorithm," *New York Times*, March 6, 2011, p. 4, www.nytimes.com/2011/03/06/weekinreview/06lohr.html?pagewanted=all&_r=0 (accessed 20 August 2012).

Chapter Two

General Literary Reference Sources

General literary reference sources serve an important purpose in the research process. Such tools as literary encyclopedias, dictionaries, and companions can answer specific factual inquiries and provide background or contextual information about authors and their works, literary movements, the development of particular genres, and literary themes for a given time period or country. Biographical resources are central not only for presenting an overview of an author's life and literary career, but also, frequently, for verifying titles or specific editions and including details about the locations of manuscripts and archival material. Other types of general literary reference tools, like chronologies or concordances, perform very specific functions, whether to outline dates for literary or other cultural and historical events, or to demonstrate the way in which an author uses language in his or her writings. And research guides, like this one, are valuable for compiling and recommending a range of reference sources to direct the literary scholar. Think of general reference sources as laying a foundation from which to initiate your research, to be further shaped by your existing knowledge and interests.

British literature of the eighteenth century has long been an area of scholarly study and, as such, is well represented by general reference resources. These resources offer snapshots of the primary authors and topics of the field at the time that they were written. Older (but still standard) reference tools that address this period, for example, often focus on traditionally canonical authors and subjects, whereas newer tools are likely to take a more inclusive approach, typically incorporating more female and/or lesser-known authors, broader conceptions of the "literary," and current theoretical methodologies. Although the scope of this research guide is the eighteenth century from 1700 to 1800, reference works may examine the period through the lens of the long eighteenth century, from the Restoration in 1660 to the end of the century, or through that of the Enlightenment or the Romantic period straddling the nineteenth century. This chapter also presents resources that cover British literature from even wider perspectives, especially for resources about Welsh, Irish, and Scottish literature, or those about the Gothic genre. When you use a reference tool, be sure to read the introduction to determine the scope and general purpose of the resource and understand how it will serve your specific research needs. This chapter introduces you to the standard general reference formats so you will know what to expect.

Literary scholars will find that reference sources, much like many books, journals, and other types of material, are migrating to an electronic environment as more publishers choose this format. Online reference tools have the advantage of being searchable and updated more easily, they don't take up shelf space, and they are accessible by multiple people from any computer; for these reasons, they are the preferred choice of many libraries. As a consequence, the traditional reference collection may now be primarily online rather than in a dedicated area in the library. Many standard reference tools, however, are still available only in print, so you should expect to use a combination of print and electronic reference resources for your research. This chapter discusses recommended general reference sources for conducting eighteenth-century literary research, presents a selection of the types of resources that are available for the period, and recommends strategies for finding additional resources. Your reference librarian can also help you stay informed about new editions or recent publications in the reference collection that may be relevant for your particular project.

RESEARCH GUIDES

Bracken, James K. *Reference Works in British and American Literature*, 2nd ed. Englewood, CO: Libraries Unlimited, 1998.

Harner, James L. *Literary Research Guide: An Annotated Listing of Reference Sources in English Literary Studies*, 5th ed. New York: Modern Language Association of America, 2008.

Marcuse, Michael J. *A Reference Guide for English Studies*. Berkeley: University of California Press, 1990.

For many years, graduate students and other literary scholars have depended on the expert guidance of James Harner's ***Literary Research Guide: An Annotated Listing of Reference Sources in English Literary Studies***. Now in its fifth edition, *Literary Research Guide* features lively, evaluative discussions of 1,059 print and electronic handbooks, dictionaries, encyclopedias, bibliographies, surveys of research, indexes, biographical sources, Web resources, and specialized reference tools for researching English and American literatures, as well as the literatures of Ireland, Scotland, Wales, other literatures in English, and foreign-language literatures. Published by the Modern Language Association, Harner's work is considered an indispensible resource for identifying a vast range of reference sources for any period of literary study, and for understanding the strengths and limitations of those sources and how to get the most from them. As comprehensive as the guide is, however, Harner does not cover resources for individual authors or literary works, or scholarly journals and background studies. It is advisable to use the *Literary Research Guide* in concert with this volume for additional recommendations, especially for sources about Irish, Scottish, and Welsh literatures or for guidance with general literary sources.

Organized first by chapters on specific types of reference sources, including chapters on libraries and library catalogs, guides to manuscripts and archives, guides to dissertations and theses, periodicals, and genres, the guide then presents chapters on the national literatures and other literatures previously described, as well as concluding chapters on comparative literature and literature-related topics and sources. This last chapter ranges widely from sources for the study of literature and art, film, folklore, linguistics, medicine, music, philosophy, religion, science, history and other social sciences, and women, to the book trade and history of the book, cultural studies, GLBT studies, literary criticism and theory, and scholarly writing and publishing. Each chapter is referenced by letter (from A to U), and each source is assigned a separate entry number, preceded by the letter of the chapter in which it is discussed. Within individual chapters, sources are grouped by type of reference tool and, in the case of English and American literature, also by time periods. The "Restoration and Eighteenth-Century Literature" section found in "M. English Literature," for example, covers histories and surveys, literary handbooks, dictionaries and encyclopedias, and bibliographies for the period in general, followed by histories and surveys, guides to primary works, guides to scholarship and criticism, and biographical dictionaries for the period, as well as for periodicals, fiction, drama and theater, poetry, and prose. The "Restoration and Eighteenth-Century Literature" section also contains discussions of selected text archives, *Eighteenth Century Collections Online* and *Eighteenth-Century Fiction*, and some bibliographies of eighteenth-century British history. Each annotation outlines the source's scope and organization; evaluates the tool; compares it to related sources; notes earlier editions; cites reviews, if available; and sometimes provides "see also" references to other relevant sections and works within the guide. Sources listed in the volume may be accessed by consulting the pertinent section or by using the name, title, and subject indexes. The *Literary Research Guide* is also available online by subscription, and although the fifth print edition comprises sources published through October 2006, the electronic guide is updated on an ongoing basis. Harner's work maintains its highly regarded reputation for good reason—it excels in the knowledgeable, authoritative selection of key reference resources essential to literary study.

Complementing Harner's *Literary Research Guide*, James Bracken's **Reference Works in British and American Literature** is solely focused on sources of individual authors. Bracken describes more than 1,500 reference works and typically provides the following for each author: one or several bibliographies; a dictionary, encyclopedia, or handbook; an index and concordance; and a journal relevant for studying the author, depending on availability. Canonical authors are more likely to be represented by several reference works in each category, whereas other author entries may contain only a bibliography or refer to *The New Cambridge Bibliography of English Literature* (described in chapter 4). Bracken states in his introduction that rather than compiling a comprehensive listing, the reference works were instead chosen for their importance and usefulness, and they include English-language sources published through 1996, with some 1997 titles. Entries are arranged alphabetically by author's last name, with British and American writers from all time periods mixed together throughout the volume. Each reference source for the author receives either a brief (a few sentences) to a more detailed description (a long paragraph), with the scope and comparable sources noted. If you are not searching for a known author but want to browse for period writers, the chronological appendix enables you to identify those authors born in the seventeenth and eighteenth centuries, who can be confirmed as British in the nationality appendix. The subject index can lead you to relevant author-specific reference works for eighteenth-century English literature, poetry, and drama, as well as to works for Irish, Scottish, and Welsh literatures by century and genre. *Reference Works in British and American Literature* is a helpful tool for the initial identification of twentieth-century print bibliographies and other reference works devoted to authors of the period.

Although dated, Michael Marcuse's *A **Reference Guide for English Studies*** still offers valuable guidance to older reference works for eighteenth-century literary research. This standard resource regrettably has not been revised since its original publication in 1990, and so its strength lies in its evaluative annotations to print reference tools published before that date. Marcuse's guide is arranged in twenty-four sections, each assigned a letter, that cover specific types of publications or resources (e.g., national bibliographies, serial publications, libraries, archives, manuscripts), national languages and literatures, periods of English literature, genres (e.g., poetry, performing arts, prose fiction and nonfictional prose, theory, rhetoric, composition, bibliography), and the profession of English. Section P, "Literature of the Restoration and Eighteenth Century," describes period-specific serial and monograph bibliographies, scholarly journals in Restoration and eighteenth-century studies, recommended criticism, and bibliographies, checklists, and other reference sources for period poetry, drama and theater, prose fiction, and prose and criticism. Unlike Harner's guide, Marcuse provides a listing of reference sources for forty-four English and Irish authors to be found in subsection "M-60, Guide to Major-Author Reference Works," including newsletters and journals, primary and secondary bibliographies, handbooks and indexes, standard editions (which may be outdated), concordances, and biographies. Traditional in its approach, eighteenth-century authors accorded this treatment are Jane Austen, William Blake, James Boswell, Samuel Taylor Coleridge, Henry Fielding, Samuel Johnson, Alexander Pope, Sir Walter Scott, Jonathan Swift, and William Wordsworth. Given the extensive range of this work, it is essential to consult the "Index of Subjects and Authors as Subjects," so that relevant sources that might be listed in other sections are not overlooked. For example, the index entry for James Boswell leads to a description of special collections held at Yale University Libraries (B-21), and a guide to Boswell's private library (Y-69). Additional access to the content is facilitated by the "Index of Authors, Compilers, Contributors, and Editors" and the "Index of Titles." Marcuse's guide should be used to supplement the resources described in this volume and in Harner's *Literary Research Guide*.

EIGHTEENTH-CENTURY ENCYCLOPEDIAS, DICTIONARIES, AND COMPANIONS

Backscheider, Paula R., and Catherine Ingrassia, eds. *A Companion to the Eighteenth-Century English Novel and Culture.* Malden, MA: Blackwell, 2005.

Black, Jeremy. *Eighteenth-Century Britain, 1688–1783*, 2nd ed. New York: Palgrave Macmillan, 2008.

Brackett, Virginia, ed. *The Facts on File Companion to British Poetry: 17th and 18th Centuries.* New York: Facts on File, 2008.

Cambridge Collections Online. West Nyack, NY: Cambridge University Press, 2006– . cco.cambridge.org.

Chisick, Harvey. *Historical Dictionary of the Enlightenment.* Lanham, MD: Scarecrow Press, 2005.

Delon, Michel, ed. *Encyclopedia of the Enlightenment.* 2 vols. Chicago, IL: Fitzroy Dearborn, 2001.

Gerrard, Christine, ed. *A Companion to Eighteenth-Century Poetry.* Malden, MA: Blackwell, 2006.

Johnson, Clifford R. *Plots and Characters in the Fiction of Eighteenth-Century English Authors.* Hamden, CT: Archon Books, 1978.

Keymer, Thomas, and Jon Mee, eds. *The Cambridge Companion to English Literature, 1740–1830.* New York: Cambridge University Press, 2004.

Kors, Alan Charles, ed. *Encyclopedia of the Enlightenment.* 4 vols. New York: Oxford University Press, 2003.

Langford, Paul, ed. *The Eighteenth Century, 1688–1815.* New York: Oxford University Press, 2002.

Moody, Jane, and Daniel O'Quinn, eds. *The Cambridge Companion to British Theatre, 1730–1830.* New York: Cambridge University Press, 2007.

Probyn, Clive T. *English Fiction of the Eighteenth Century, 1700–1789.* New York: Longman, 1987.

Richetti, John, ed. *The Cambridge Companion to the Eighteenth-Century Novel.* New York: Cambridge University Press, 1996.

———. *The Cambridge History of English Literature, 1660–1780.* New York: Cambridge University Press, 2005.

Sitter, John, ed. *The Cambridge Companion to Eighteenth-Century Poetry.* New York: Cambridge University Press, 2001.

Womersley, David, ed. *A Companion to Literature from Milton to Blake.* Malden, MA: Blackwell, 2000.

Yolton, John W., Roy Porter, Pat Rogers, and Barbara Maria Stafford, eds. *The Blackwell Companion to the Enlightenment.* Cambridge, MA: Blackwell, 1991.

Zwicker, Steven N., ed. *The Cambridge Companion to English Literature, 1650–1740.* New York: Cambridge University Press, 1998.

Although there is often ambiguity between literary encyclopedias, dictionaries, and companions, since these terms may be used interchangeably to describe the same type of reference resource, in general, dictionaries offer brief definitions of figures and topics, encyclopedias give a more detailed treatment of similar subjects, and companions feature scholarly essays about authors, genres, literary movements, and time periods that can resemble a monograph more than a reference book. No matter what the format, however, all of these sources are important for obtaining factual information about literary subjects and understanding the literary and historical context for individual authors and genres. This section covers encyclopedias and other reference sources that address the eighteenth century broadly, including those devoted to particular genres (fiction, poetry, drama). For sources specifically concerned with the Romantic period, including the *Encyclopedia of the Romantic Era, 1760–1850* and *An Oxford Companion to the Romantic Age: British Culture, 1776–1832*, please see chapter 2 in *Literary Research and the British Romantic Era: Strategies and Sources* for descriptions and other recommended sources.

Part of a well-regarded series, John Richetti's ***The Cambridge History of English Literature, 1660–1780*** is representative of the narrative companion, designed to be read as a historical survey of literary topics for the period, but also to be consulted for the individual critical essays on specific subjects. This substantial volume (at more than 900 pages with supplementary material and indexes) offers thirty essays by recognized scholars in the field organized in the following six parts: "Literary Production and Dissemination: Changing Audiences and Emerging Media," "Literary Genres: Adaptations and Reformation," "Literature and Intellectual Life: The Production and Transmission of Culture," "Literature and Social and Institutional Change," "Literary Genres: Transformation and New Forms of Expressiveness," and a conclusion that addresses literary change in the mid-eighteenth and late eighteenth century. Each essay typically ranges from twenty to thirty pages and covers such topics as publishing and bookselling, authorship, the novel and the marketplace, women writers, the rise of national literary history, and Augustan England and British America. Many of the essays are concerned with genres, including drama, poetry, and the novel, but also the periodical essay, sentimental fiction, personal letters, political pamphlets, diaries and autobiography, and travel literature, among others. The volume concludes with a chronology of literary and historical events from 1660 to 1793; a list of bibliographies for each chapter, most with primary and secondary sources; and an index.

Cambridge University Press also publishes *The Cambridge Companions to Literature* series, which comprises individual monograph collections of scholarly essays on specific British literary periods, genres, and authors, as well as on other national literatures. Organized in a similar fashion, the Cambridge companions feature ten to twenty essays, typically ranging from twenty to thirty-five pages in length, that introduce the major themes and provide the reader with a solid grounding in the cultural and historical context. They also usually contain a brief chronology and bibliographies for further reading. The eighteenth century is covered in two volumes. The first, Steven Zwicker's ***The Cambridge Companion to English Literature, 1650–1740***, begins with the Cromwellian Protectorate and traces literary culture from that time onward, concluding with the major authors and issues of the Augustan period. Seven essays focus on contextual and generic topics, whether examining historical and political events, theatrical culture, the flourishing of satirical works, relationships between gender and literature, translations of classical texts, or lyric poetry. The second half of the companion offers seven more essays devoted to selected writers, including "Swift, Defoe, and narrative forms" and "Alexander Pope, Lady Mary Wortley Montagu, and the literature of social comment." In addition to the notes, each essay also has a tailored bibliography of recommended sources for further investigation. Scholars will find the chronology useful for quick reference to dates for historical events and texts, as well as a chronologically arranged "Contemporary Lives" section, which lists authors and notable period figures with their birth and death dates.

Bridging the eighteenth and nineteenth centuries, Thomas Keymer and Jon Mee's *The Cambridge Companion to English Literature, 1740–1830* deliberately emphasizes the continuity and ongoing development of literary culture during the period, rather than drawing a line between the traditional categories of Enlightenment and Romantic. Arranged in two parts, the first section, entitled "Contexts and Modes," features seven essays about the relationship between readers, writers, reviewers, and the professionalization of literature; criticism and aesthetics; the role of literature and politics; national identity and empire; sensibility; theatrical culture; and the Gothic. Part two, "Writers, Circles, Traditions," presents nine essays focused on individual and groups of authors, including Samuel Richardson, Henry Fielding, Sarah Fielding, Samuel Johnson, James Boswell, Laurence Sterne, William Blake, Anna Barbauld, Mary Robinson, Charlotte Smith, William Wordsworth, Samuel Taylor Coleridge, Jane Austen, John Clare, and the later Romantics. Unlike most volumes in the series, this particular one does not have a chronology, and, rather than a general bibliography for further reading, each chapter concludes with a list of recommended books. These more general volumes are complemented by companions concerned with the novel, poetry, and theatre during the century.

Also by Richetti, *The Cambridge Companion to the Eighteenth-Century Novel*, employing a social and political historical approach, "seeks to show that the novel is not defined primarily by its realism of representation, but by the new ideological and cultural functions it serves in the emerging world of print culture" (i). Following an introduction, eleven chapters address the novel and social and cultural history, women writers, sentimental novels, Gothic fiction, and works by Daniel Defoe, Jonathan Swift, Samuel Richardson, Henry Fielding, Laurence Sterne, Tobias Smollett, and Burney.

Concerned less with individual authors, John Sitter's *The Cambridge Companion to Eighteenth-Century Poetry* presents thematic essays entitled "Political Passions," "Questions in Poetics: Why and How Poetry Matters,"

"The Return to the Ode," and "Creating a National Poetry: The Tradition of Spenser and Milton," in addition to chapters on publishing, women poets and readers, nature poetry, images of the city, and the poetry of sensibility, among others.

The sixteen essays in *The Cambridge Companion to British Theatre, 1730–1830*, edited by Jane Moody and Daniel O'Quinn, are grouped into sections on "Performance," "Genres," "Identities," and "Places of Performance," and they include such topics as performance and theatrical geography, spectatorship, race and profit, the actress, private theatricals, opera, the Irish theatre, and theatre and empire. The genre essays specifically cover comedy, tragedy, pantomime, and Romantic melodrama. A final chapter, "Reading Theatre, 1730–1830," is a narrative bibliography that includes a section on reference works and bibliographic tools, as well as one on recent editions and anthologies. The detailed chronology, which outlines historical events, theatrical performances in London, theatrical events in London (e.g., strikes, riots, tours, actors' debuts), theatrical performances and events outside of London, related publications, and births and deaths, is especially helpful.

The Cambridge companions can be searched and accessed online through the subscription resource *Cambridge Collections Online*. Scholars can browse specific volumes or search either the entire collection of companions, or the individual subcollections, the *Cambridge Companions to Literature and Classics*, the *Cambridge Companions to Philosophy, Religion, and Culture*, or *Shakespeare Survey*. The advanced search option enables you to search within the full-text of the volumes or by author or editor, title, volume, subjects, year of publication, ISBN, text of an extract or abstract, and article type (e.g., critical essay, book review essay, interview). A full-text search for Mary Leapor, for example, finds her mentioned five times in *The Cambridge Companion to Eighteenth-Century Poetry*, specifically within chapters on eighteenth-century women poets and readers, publishing and reading poetry, nature poetry, and couplets and conversation, and also in supplementary material (in this case, the chronology), as well as in a chapter on spectacle, horror, and pathos from *The Cambridge Companion to English Restoration Theatre*, and within a chapter on John Clare and laboring-class poets in *The Companion to English Literature, 1740–1830*. The relevant chapters can be viewed in PDF (with or without search terms highlighted), and the "My Collections" feature allows users to create a password-protected account to run recent or saved searches, write notes on specific saved chapters, or create workgroups for shared access. Whether you prefer the print or online versions, these companions are extremely useful for surveying the principal authors and works, and for placing literary movements and genres within a cultural and historical context.

Blackwell offers a similar set of companions to eighteenth-century literary culture and genres, as part of its *Blackwell Companions to Literature and Culture* series. David Womersley's *A Companion to Literature from Milton to Blake* addresses the long eighteenth century. At nearly 600 pages, this impressive collection of essays covers contextual investigations of specific topics, including literature and nationhood or the book trade; individual readings of authors' literary works; surveys of literature within particular time periods (1701–1713, 1733–1742, 1757–1776); and essays devoted to genres. These include pamphlets; political, philosophical, historical, and religious writing; the novel; and poetry. Thirty-five essays are concerned with analyzing specific works, and twenty-two of these are focused on authors who published during the eighteenth century, ranging from Jonathan Swift's *A Tale of a Tub* to Eliza Haywood's *Fantomina*, and from Samuel Johnson's *The Vanity of Human Wishes* to James Macpherson's *Poems of Ossian*. Each essay finishes with a list of references and sources for continued study, and one index gives access to authors, titles, and subjects.

Scholars interested in period novelists will find Paula Backscheider and Catherine Ingrassia's *A Companion to the Eighteenth-Century English Novel and Culture* valuable for its discussions on formative influences, the social context, and the eighteenth-century novel's modern legacy. Essays about early influences explore such topics as translations, travel writing, the poetics of ecstasy, the oriental tale, and British seduction stories, whereas those examining the world of the eighteenth-century novel investigate literacy, fictions of population, female novelists and book reviews, women and old age, and joy and happiness, among other subjects. The modern legacy section presents essays on print culture, "Queer Gothic," racial legacies, representations of poverty, the Gordon Riots, and the "Novel Body Politic," as just a few examples.

A Companion to Eighteenth-Century Poetry, edited by Christine Gerrard, contains forty-one shorter essays (about fifteen pages) arranged into the categories "Contexts and Perspectives," "Readings," "Forms and Genres," and "Themes and Debates." These essays place poetry within the contexts of politics, empire, science, religion, the visual arts, and popular culture; center on such poetic forms as blank verse and rhyming couplets, verse satire, the ode, and the georgic; and examine the sublime, constructions of femininity, classical inheritance, cartography, and rural poetry. The "Readings" section contains critical readings of specific works by Gay, Pope, Swift, Lady Mary Montagu, Thomson, Duck, Collier, Leapor, Akenside, Johnson, Collins, Gray, Smart, Goldsmith, Cowper, and Burns. References and a bibliography of recommended texts for further reading conclude each essay and provide the scholar with an initial list of sources for the topic.

Representing one of the volumes in the Longman Literature in English Series, Clive Probyn's *English Fiction of the Eighteenth Century, 1700–1789* fulfills a similar purpose—to introduce the major literary genres and place them within their historical and cultural context. This companion offers seven essays on works by Daniel Defoe, Samuel Richardson, Tobias Smollett, and Laurence Sterne, as well as novels and readers and one entitled "Transition and Transformation: Society, Sentiment, and the Self in the Novel, 1764–1789." A chronology covers fiction, other works, and cultural events from 1700 to 1789. And bibliographies list relevant titles for the topics of history and criticism; historical, intellectual, and cultural background; bibliographies and reference guides; forms and subgenres; themes; and individual authors (biography, major works, criticism). Other series volumes of potential interest include *English Poetry of the Eighteenth Century, 1700–1789*; *English Drama: Restoration and the Eighteenth Century, 1660–1789*; *English Prose of the Eighteenth Century*; and *The Eighteenth Century: The Intellectual and Cultural Context of English Literature, 1700–1789*.

Clifford Johnson's *Plots and Characters in the Fiction of Eighteenth-Century English Authors* serves as a guide to scholars needing more detailed plot overviews and extensive character descriptions than those provided in the general encyclopedias and literary companions, such as the *Oxford Companion to English Literature*. Volume 1 treats the fiction of Jonathan Swift, Daniel Defoe, and Samuel Richardson, whereas volume 2 covers Henry Fielding, Tobias Smollett, Samuel Johnson, Laurence Sterne, and Oliver Goldsmith. In total, forty-seven works and 3,370 characters are described. The character lists are arranged alphabetically and give textual references for the first appearance of the character, variant names (if any), and sometimes symbolic references, as in the example of Betty Pippin from *Tom Jones*, where it is noted that the word *pippin* means a "seedling apple." Two chronologies, of events (1707–1791) and of publications (1728–1780), add value to this reference work.

The Facts on File Companion to British Poetry: 17th and 18th Centuries is part of a four-volume set that surveys British poetry from the earliest times to the present. Edited by Virginia Brackett, this volume comprises alphabetically arranged entries about period English, Scottish, Welsh, and Irish poets and their individual poems, in addition to poetic themes, genres, forms, and literary movements pertinent to the two centuries. Some poets whose work bridges the eighteenth and nineteenth centuries are also covered. Entries are sometimes longer than a typical encyclopedia essay, especially for canonical figures and works, but even those for less-studied authors like Sarah Fyge Egerton, John Dyer, and Anna Hunter Seward span a full one to two pages, and all conclude with a bibliography. Discussions of individual poems provide a critical overview of the piece and its place in literary history and are enriched with excerpts; some examples are Sir Charles Sedley's "Phillis Is My Only Joy," Alexander Pope's "Eloisa to Abelard," and James Thomson's "A Hymn on the Seasons." Appended material includes a glossary of poetic terms and a general bibliography of books relevant for studying poetry of the period, as well as English literature in general.

Although not concerned directly with literature, the following two companions to history of the period are helpful in understanding the broader contexts for literature written during this time. Paul Langford's *The Eighteenth Century, 1688–1815*, part of the Short Oxford History of the British Isles series, compiles essays on political and religious movements, government structure, economics, the "culture of improvement," and imperial warfare. Like other companions, this one also offers a chronology, a bibliography, and, in this case, maps of the turnpike road network, the canal system, and England's empire in 1689 and 1815.

Jeremy Black's *Eighteenth-Century Britain, 1688–1783* provides more of a social analysis of the period, with chapters on life and death, agriculture, industry, society, towns, enlightenment and science, culture and the arts, politics, comparisons with the Continent, and the empire, among others, and it concludes with a chronology and brief thematic bibliographies.

As the major intellectual movement of the eighteenth century, the Enlightenment has many reference books devoted to its impact on European society and culture. The *Encyclopedia of the Enlightenment*, edited by Alan Charles Kors, is a wide-ranging examination of the Enlightenment, not only in England, Scotland, France, English-speaking North America, and other northern European countries, but also in Spain, Russia, Greece, eastern European countries, and Jewish cultures. Four volumes present nearly 700 individually authored entries, some running several pages, and all with concluding bibliographies. Illustrating the scope covered by the encyclopedia, the topical outline groups articles into the following subject categories: definitions and interpretations of the Enlightenment (e.g., Enlightenment studies, feminist theory, poststructuralism, postmodernism); political geography (e.g., historical events, nations and states, cities, universities, demography, colonialism); agencies and spaces (e.g., the world of print, media of diffusion, education); and thought and eighteenth-century culture (e.g., philosophy, aesthetics and the arts, human nature, natural philosophy and science, political philosophy, religion). This latter, broader category also lists each biographical entry, including those for many eighteenth-century British authors. Scholars will find the essays in the "Agencies and Spaces of the Enlightenment" category especially relevant, since they address specific literary genres, authors and copyright, censorship, salons and clubs, libraries, literacy, representations of reading, coffee houses, and print culture, among other subjects. The *En-*

cyclopedia of the Enlightenment is an excellent resource for understanding the literature of this period in its European intellectual and cultural contexts.

Originally published in French as the *Dictionnaire européen des Lumières*, and edited by Michel Delon, the similarly titled ***Encyclopedia of the Enlightenment*** features 350 signed essays on countries and cultural regions; scientific and artistic disciplines; political, economic, legal, and cultural institutions; philosophical, aesthetic, and religious topics; and anthropological subjects, including love, the body, and work. Although there is some overlap in categories with Kors's Enlightenment encyclopedia, many entries here are unique (e.g., Japan), and the same subject categories should be consulted, as they will likely offer a distinct perspective and references (e.g., Jansenism).

The Blackwell Companion to the Enlightenment, edited by John Yolton and colleagues, focuses more narrowly on the years 1720 to 1780, but it nevertheless takes an interdisciplinary approach to the period. Following an introductory overview of the movement, entries range from short, unsigned paragraphs to two- to three-page signed essays on the major figures; countries and places; and political, philosophical, scientific, religious, social, and cultural components of the Enlightenment. Entries on Amerindians, collections, honour, women in literature, homosexuality, "orang-utan," quackery, skepticism, and wild men are found among entries on human nature, materialism, natural philosophy, and the novel. The longer essays typically conclude with a brief bibliography, and black-and-white illustrations are presented throughout.

Harvey Chisick's ***Historical Dictionary of the Enlightenment*** also provides shorter entries on the principal people, places, historical events, institutions, and literary output of the European Enlightenment between 1687 and 1789. In addition to the entries, the dictionary includes a chronology arranged by "Main Figures," "Politics and Society," and "Science, Arts, and Letters" categories from 1605 to 1801, and a fifty-five-page introductory essay to the Enlightenment addressing the paradigms of Enlightenment thought, key values and assumptions, the social dimensions, and the movement of ideas. An extensive bibliography lists reference and general works; important primary works; anthologies; and sources about religion, society, economy, politics, institutions and education, print culture and the book trade, science, and art.

GENRE AND GENERAL BRITISH LITERARY ENCYCLOPEDIAS AND COMPANIONS

Birch, Dinah, ed. *The Oxford Companion to English Literature*, 7th ed. New York: Oxford University Press, 2009.

Bomarito, Jessica, ed. *Gothic Literature: A Gale Critical Companion.* 3 vols. Detroit, MI: Thomson Gale, 2006.

Hahn, Daniel, and Nicolas Robins, eds. *The Oxford Guide to Literary Britain and Ireland*, 3rd ed. New York: Oxford University Press, 2008.

Head, Dominic, ed. *The Cambridge Guide to Literature in English*, 3rd ed. New York: Cambridge University Press, 2006.

Hogle, Jerrold E., ed. *The Cambridge Companion to Gothic Fiction.* New York: Cambridge University Press, 2002.

Jarvis, Branwen, ed. *A Guide to Welsh Literature c. 1700–1800.* Cardiff: University of Wales Press, 2000.

Loeber, Rolf, and Magda Loeber, with Anne Mullen Burnham. *A Guide to Irish Fiction, 1650–1900.* Portland, OR: Four Courts, 2006.

Mulvey-Roberts, Marie, ed. *The Handbook to Gothic Literature.* New York: New York University Press, 1998.

Punter, David, ed. *A Companion to the Gothic.* Malden, MA: Blackwell, 2000.

Royle, Trevor. *The Mainstream Companion to Scottish Literature.* Edinburgh: Mainstream Publishing, 1993.

Spooner, Catherine, and Emma McEvoy, eds. *The Routledge Companion to the Gothic.* New York: Routledge, 2007.

Welch, Robert, ed. *The Oxford Companion to Irish Literature.* New York: Oxford University Press, 1996.

The reference sources in this section are comprised of companions and encyclopedias as well; however, rather than focusing on the eighteenth century specifically, these works either cover a particular genre throughout time (e.g., the Gothic) or are devoted to a national literature. These tools are useful in checking references to individual authors, works, events, and literary movements, or placing eighteenth-century works and themes in their broader context.

Emerging in the latter part of the eighteenth century with the publication of Horace Walpole's *The Castle of Otranto*, in 1764, the Gothic novel became a dominant genre of the period. Several reference works address the Gothic tradition, typically ranging from its beginnings in the eighteenth century through the twentieth and twenty-first centuries. Edited by Catherine Spooner and Emma McEvoy, ***The Routledge Companion to the Gothic*** assumes this broad approach by examining the Gothic in distinct centuries (eighteenth through twentieth); in specific settings or regions, for example, Gothic locations and cities, or American, Scottish, Irish, Canadian, Australian Gothic and empire, more generally; and by thematic concepts, including the uncanny, abject and grotesque, hauntings, Gothic femininities and masculinities, queer

Gothic, and children. A final collection of essays focuses on Gothic culture and media in the late twentieth and early twenty-first centuries as manifest in theatre, film, television, graphic novels, music and subcultures, and the Internet. Although the signed essays tend to be brief (two to ten pages), they offer a works cited list for further investigation.

In a similar fashion, Jerrold Hogle's *The Cambridge Companion to Gothic Fiction* spans 250 years to investigate the Gothic tradition from its origins in England, France, and Germany, and explore its development in Ireland and Scotland, the United States, and the Caribbean. Fourteen signed chapters treat specific subjects, including English Gothic theatre, Gothic film, and video and computer games, in addition to those that look at Gothic fiction in historical contexts. The concluding bibliography covers principal Gothic texts, anthologies, major studies of the genre, collections of criticism, and bibliographies; the companion is also enhanced by a filmography and a chronology of literary and selected cultural and historical events from 1750 to 2001.

David Punter's *A Companion to the Gothic* brings together twenty-four essays about Gothic backgrounds; early works; nineteenth- and twentieth-century versions; and Gothic theory and genre (criticism, psychoanalysis, comic Gothic). A section entitled the "Continuing Debate" features essays on the Gothic heroine, queer Gothic, madness, counterfeit in the tradition, and magic realism in contemporary Gothic.

The Handbook to Gothic Literature, edited by Marie Mulvey-Roberts, serves as more of an encyclopedic collection of brief, signed essays on a wide range of Gothic topics. Arranged in two sections, "Gothic Writers and Key Terms" and "Gothic Specialisms," the first section provides entries for thirty-five authors (or author groups, like the Brontës); national and regional Gothic movements (e.g., American, Australian, English-Canadian, German, Irish, Russian, Scottish, Welsh, San Franciscan, Southern); concepts (e.g., the demonic, occultism, madness, horror, terror, the sublime, zerrissenheit); genres, including ghost stories, drama, film, novel, and roman noir; and such subjects as penny dreadfuls, vampires, the hero-villain, graveyard school, postcolonial Gothic, and the Wandering Jew. The "Gothic Specialisms" section offers shorter entries (typically a few paragraphs) on cyberpunk, golem, Gothic parody, Jacobean tragedy, lycanthropy, Illuminati novels, Sturm und Drang, and transgression, to name a few examples. A short bibliography concludes the handbook; however, the lack of an index or bibliographies for the entries detracts from this source.

Although designed for undergraduate audiences, scholars may want to consult Jessica Bomarito's *Gothic Literature: A Gale Critical Companion* for its general overviews and compilations of excerpted, selected literary works and

criticism for thirty-seven authors from the eighteenth through the twenty-first
centuries and the following topical sections: Gothic literature; society and
culture; Gothic themes, settings, and figures; the performing arts; and the
visual arts. Each section also ends with a list of recommended bibliographies
and/or criticism for further reading, which could prove useful as a starting
point for more in-depth investigations.

Arranged in dictionary format, *The Oxford Companion to English Literature* has long been a standard source for concise, factual overviews of
authors, works, genres, movements, places, critical theory, terminology,
and other topics associated with British literary culture, including selected
coverage of authors and works from the United States, Canada, Europe, and
Asia that have impacted British literary tradition. Now in its seventh edition
and overseen by Dinah Birch, this version incorporates more contemporary
authors and has enhanced its coverage of children's literature, black British
writing, postcolonial literature, science fiction, travel writing, and fantasy,
as well as the relationship between literature, film, and television. In fact,
the companion begins with four introductory essays, "Literary Culture and
the Novel in the New Millennium," "Cultures of Reading," "Black British
Literature," and "Children's Literature," which the editor identifies as areas
of "particular interest" (ix) for this moment in English literary study. Entries
representative of eighteenth-century literary topics range from those about
the Grand Tour, circulating libraries, the epistolary novel *The Spectator*, and
the Rhyming Weavers, to entries for authors Christopher Smart, Olaudah
Equiano, Susanna Centlivre, Stephen Duck, and Voltaire, among many others canonical and less well-known. Author entries typically provide birth and
death dates, occupation, and a brief discussion of the author's literary career
and major works, whereas entries for specific works discuss the genre, plot,
reception, and publication history. An appended chronology guides the reader
to principal literary works and related historical and cultural events from c.
1000 to 2008. The eighteenth century opens with Congreve's *The Way of
the World* (1700) and is accompanied by notes on John Dryden's death and
James Thomson's birth, as well as the Act of Settlement and the beginning of
the War of Spanish Succession (1701). Additional appendixes outline poets
laureate, children's laureates, and literary awards. The final index identifies
new and heavily revised entries by contributor.

The Cambridge Guide to Literature in English performs a similar function to *The Oxford Companion to English Literature* by featuring single to
several paragraph entries about English-language literature worldwide, from
the Anglo-Saxon period to the present day. Subject matter covers writers,
individual works, literary groups and movements, genres, poetic forms, critical concepts, rhetorical terms, literary magazines, theatres, and related topics,

with eighteenth-century British material represented throughout. Dominic Head's third edition places a greater emphasis on contemporary literature by adding significantly more entries for living authors. Eighteenth-century authors include such well-known figures as Samuel Johnson, as well as the less-familiar, like John Byrom. Both the *Cambridge Guide to Literature in English* and *The Oxford Companion to English Literature* provide basic factual information about literature and literary topics of any period.

Scholars researching authors from Scotland, Ireland, or Wales will find the following national literature reference sources helpful for placing these authors in the context of their distinctive literary traditions, and also for potentially finding information about authors not necessarily covered in reference sources with a more pronounced English bias. Trevor Royle's *The Mainstream Companion to Scottish Literature* offers concise biographical entries about Scotland's poets, novelists, playwrights, and critics, as well as authors of history, philosophy, religion, and other prose forms from the beginnings through the twentieth century. The authors addressed wrote in either English, Scots, or Gaelic, and were born and raised in Scotland, were Scottish through parentage, or resided in Scotland long enough to have made a significant contribution to its literature. These author entries typically provide the birth and death dates, occupation, a brief summary of his or her life, and major publications, followed by a list of works, editions, and sometimes principal biographical or critical studies. To illustrate the range of entries for the eighteenth century, the companion covers Robert Burns, James Boswell, Henry Mackenzie, Allan Ramsay, Joanna Baillie, Robert Fergusson, and Sir Walter Scott, but also includes entries for John Moore, William Tytler, Iain MacCodrum, Alison Cockburn, the Scottish Enlightenment, and *The Lounger*, as well as for genres, individual literary works, societies, places, and historic events. The companion's value would be greatly enhanced with a chronology outlining authors' works and historical events, and either a topical compilation of entries or a subject index. As it stands, this source works best as a tool for looking up known people or topics more than a discovery tool about the time period.

Much like the other Oxford companions, Robert Welch's *The Oxford Companion to Irish Literature* features encyclopedic entries for Irish authors, literary works, movements and genres, historical events and people, and additional Irish subjects relevant to the study of its literature into the twentieth century. The authors included in the companion wrote in English, Gaelic, Latin, or Norman French. Such well-known eighteenth-century authors as Laurence Sterne, Oliver Goldsmith, Richard Sheridan, and Jonathon Swift receive detailed coverage, with cross-references to entries about individual works or named individuals. Additional material includes a chronology of historical events (6000 BCE–1994 CE), a general bibliography, and maps of Ireland and Dublin depicting places of literary interest.

Operating under a very different organizing principle, Rolf and Magda Loeber's *A Guide to Irish Fiction, 1650–1900*, written with Anne Mullen Burnham, is not exclusively concerned with Irish authors, but also with those works of fiction in English "dealing with Irish matters," (xv) regardless of the authors' nationality. Nearly 6,000 titles and 1,455 authors from Ireland and other countries are represented in alphabetically arranged entries that succinctly describe the author's life and list the relevant titles with bibliographical details and primary library locations in Ireland, Britain, and North America, and sometimes a brief summary of the work. Anonymous works and authors are also addressed. The introduction provides an interesting survey about literary production during the period and uses the data gathered to examine gender, religious background, and social status, in addition to trends regarding illustrations, popularity, the market, and the prevalence for particular genres. Five indexes offer access to the entries by person (author, dedicatee, editor, illustrator, pseudonym); book title, historic period, theme and setting (1750s to 1790s, legends, courtship novel, moral fiction, poverty, working women), publisher, and places mentioned in the author biographical sketches.

Although this volume emphasizes literature in English, scholars working on comparative projects or investigating eighteenth-century Welsh authors will want to consult Branwen Jarvis's *A Guide to Welsh Literature c. 1700–1800*, the fourth volume in a series examining literature in Welsh from the sixth through the twentieth century. Featuring thirteen scholarly essays, the guide covers such topics as historical writing, Celticism and Pre-Romanticism, anterliwt (or interludes), and folk poetry, as well as individual authors of prose and poetry, including Ellis Wynne, the Morris brothers, Goronwy Owen, Williams Pantycelyn, and Iolo Morganwg. The concluding bibliographies for each chapter present sources in Welsh and English.

Edited by Daniel Hahn and Nicolas Robins, *The Oxford Guide to Literary Britain and Ireland* specifically focuses on the places associated with British and Irish writers and their works. Arranged by nine geographical regions, encompassing South West England, South East England, London, East of England, Midlands, North of England, Wales, Scotland, and Ireland, this guide features entries for cities, towns, villages, houses, taverns, theatres, chapels, castles, colleges, parks, lakes, islands, hills, and more. The "Index of Writers" enables readers to identify all the places affiliated with a particular author. The entry for Samuel Johnson, for example, lists numerous sites, from his place of birth (Lichfield), education at Oxford (Pembroke College), and holidays at Tissington, to the London streets where he frequented coffee houses and clubs, travels in Scotland, and his burial place in Westminster Abbey. Illustrated with color and black-and-white photographs and sketches, as well as city maps, the guide will enhance both biographical and textual studies.

CHRONOLOGIES

Cox, Michael, ed. *The Oxford Chronology of English Literature.* 2 vols. New York: Oxford University Press, 2002.

Chronologies of literature are primarily designed to help scholars determine when a particular work was published and to place that work within the context of contemporary texts, or to assess the literary output of a certain year or years. *The Oxford Chronology of English Literature*, discussed here, is the main chronological resource for achieving these goals; however, there are many period-specific chronologies with a literary or historical focus that may also be relevant. Several of these have been described in the preceding sections as appended materials in *The Cambridge Companions to Literature* series, in other literary companions or encyclopedias, or in historical resources. It may be helpful to consult either a period-, genre-, or author-specific chronology in concert with the more general literary chronology discussed in this section.

One important factor to keep in mind when working with dates during the eighteenth century is the necessity of understanding the different dating systems employed during that time. At the beginning of the eighteenth century, Britain used the Julian calendar, also known as "Old Style" or "Lady Day dating." This particular calendar marked March 25 (the Feast of the Annunciation, or Lady Day) as the start of the new year, rather than January 1. In fact, it wasn't until 1752 that Britain switched to the Gregorian calendar (or "New Style dating") and recognized January 1 as the official and legal new year. When examining printed materials or manuscripts written before 1752, it is necessary to be aware of the difference in dating practices. Likewise, when consulting a reference work, especially a chronology, it is important to determine how the author or editor is accommodating or adjusting the dates between January and March and if he or she is changing the original date to match our current calendar year.

Edited by Michael Cox, ***The Oxford Chronology of English Literature*** records literary achievements from 1474 to 2000, beginning with William Caxton's *The Recuyell of the Historyes of Troye* and ending with Jeanette Winterson's *The Powerbook*. Focusing only on printed works, this chronology comprises entries for approximately 30,000 texts, with more than 11,000 titles identified as fiction, almost 6,000 as poetry, 2,500 as dramatic works, and more than 6,500 as works of nonfiction, namely biographies, letters, criticism, historical and literary scholarship, and reference works. The primary emphasis is on works written in English by British authors and published in Britain, but it does include some foreign authors who resided in Britain or colonial authors who published with British presses. Selected translations of classical and European titles, some significant periodical publications, and works for children are also covered. Texts that were published between January 1 and March 24 during the Julian calendar are listed under the corresponding Gregorian date. The entries are arranged by year of imprint (or actual year of publication), and then alphabetically by the author's last name. If several works by one author were published within a year, the entries are listed alphabetically by title. Each entry typically contains the author's birth or flourish date; the title; title-page matter; imprint details; and notes, including serialization details, the illustrator, dates of succeeding editions, contextual information, and cross-references to related titles. To the left of each entry, an abbreviation indicates whether the work is fiction, verse, prose satire, drama, nonfiction, or other categories (the complete list is in the "Abbreviations" guide). Although the work certainly covers the major authors of the eighteenth century, an effort was also made to address those writers who were not necessarily part of the formal literary canon. Rather, the editors attempt to represent English literature broadly, with more than 4,000 authors in total whose works span the full range of both elite and popular literary expression. The chronology contains works by major figures, but also Jane Holt's *A Fairy Tale* (1717), Edward Jerningham's *The Nunnery, An Elegy in Imitation of the Elegy in a Churchyard* (1762), and Ann Gomersall's *The Disappointed Heir; or, Memoirs of the Ormond Family, A Novel* (1796), as some examples. The second volume is devoted entirely to author, title, and translated authors indexes, along with a guide to using the indexes.

BIOGRAPHICAL SOURCES

Dictionary of Literary Biography. Detroit, MI: Gale, 1978– . Also available online as *Dictionary of Literary Biography Complete Online* and as part of *Gale Literary Databases*, www.gale.cengage.com.

Hager, Alan, ed. *Encyclopedia of British Writers*. 4 vols. New York: Facts on File, 2005.

Highfill, Philip H., Jr., Kalman A. Burnim, and Edward A. Langhans. *A Biographical Dictionary of Actors, Actresses, Musicians, Dancers, Managers and Other Stage Personnel in London, 1660–1800*. 16 vols. Carbondale and Edwardsville: Southern Illinois University Press, 1973–1993.

Matthew, Henry C. G., and Brian Harrison, eds. *Oxford Dictionary of National Biography*, rev. ed. (in association with the British Academy). 61 vols. New York: Oxford University Press, 2004. www.oxforddnb.com.

McGuire, James, and James Quinn, eds. *Dictionary of Irish Biography from the Earliest Times to the Year 2002*. 9 vols. Cambridge, UK: Cambridge University Press, 2009. Available online at dib.cambridge.org.

Todd, Janet, ed. *A Dictionary of British and American Women Writers, 1660–1800*. Totowa, NJ: Rowman & Allanheld, 1985.

Although many of the sources previously described provide factual, biographical information about eighteenth-century authors, the two major reference works discussed here, the *Oxford Dictionary of National Biography* and the *Dictionary of Literary Biography*, have more detailed and enhanced biographical profiles. The term *dictionary*, in this case, is somewhat misleading, since you can expect surveys of the person's life and literary career that might sometimes span many pages, depending on the perceived influence or significance of the figure to British history, or availability of source materials (*Oxford Dictionary of National Biography*), or to the literary canon (*Dictionary of Literary Biography*). *A Dictionary of British and American Women Writers, 1660–1800* conforms more to the standard dictionary format, with brief entries, but it is also valuable for its attention to female authors of the period.

Representing a significant achievement, the ***Oxford Dictionary of National Biography (ODNB)***, edited by Henry Matthew and Brian Harrison, features more than 57,000 biographies of deceased individuals and selected families or groups that were important to the history of Britain from the fourth century B.C. to the twenty-first century. Scholars will find not only people born in the British Isles or its territories, but also foreigners whose lives impacted the trajectory of British history.

Comprised of sixty volumes, the 2004 print edition revises and brings together the original *Dictionary of National Biography (DNB)*, published between 1885 and 1900, and its supplements published from 1901 to 1996. The *ODNB* aims to reflect current scholarly assessments by rewriting all of the essays published in the *DNB* and its supplements and by adding another 16,500 essays, not only to extend its coverage of all time periods and professions, but especially to strengthen previously neglected areas, notably that of women and twentieth-century subjects. The essays themselves have been written by more than 10,000 contributors, including many well-known literary scholars. The online version has the advantage of being updated three times a year; more than 2,000 additional biographies were added between 2005 and 2010, as well as new thematic feature essays (see the following description).

Each biography follows a similar format, with a chronological overview of the person's life and (in the case of authors) a survey of his or her literary career and reputation. The amount of information in and details of the essay vary from individual to individual. Canonical authors typically have longer essays, many of which are divided into several thematic subsections. Samuel Richardson's biography, for example, contains subsections on the following topics: "Early Years and Education, 1689–1706," "Apprenticeship and Freedom, 1706–1721," "Early Printing Business and Politics," "Richardson's First Anonymous Publications," "Printing and Editing in the 1730s," "Pamela," "Clarissa," "Sir Charles Grandison," "Richardson's Last Literary Activities," and "Reputation and Influence." This last essay is accompanied by a list of sources, the location of important archival collections, likenesses, and wealth at death (14,000 pounds). If desired, the scholar can also link to the Samuel Richardson biography originally published in the *DNB*, in 1896, for comparison. The most recent essay's archival information may be especially useful for identifying major holdings. According to the *ODNB*, Richardson's letters and literary drafts are dispersed among Harvard University, Rice University, the British Library, Victoria and Albert Museum National Art Library, and the Bodleian Library, Oxford.

In sharp contrast, however, Mary Leapor's biography consists of five scant paragraphs, despite the claims of the concluding sentences, "Leapor's verse, largely in the style of Pope, achieves a considerable range of feeling and forcefully displays an individual voice. After renewed interest in her work she is counted one of the leading women poets of her century."[1] Granted, she lived a short life, and her work was published posthumously (Samuel Richardson published the second volume of her poetry in 1751, five years after her death), and there may not be many surviving documents to provide biographical information. In fact, although a few sources conclude the essay, there are no likenesses or listing of any archival holdings; she received a one-paragraph essay, however, in the *DNB* published in 1892. Some biographies may also provide "see also" references, with hyperlinks to entries for related people, or to related thematic essays. Sarah Fielding's essay links to that of her brother, Henry Fielding, and also to the essay about the Bluestocking circle, as an illustration of these features.

The *ODNB* presents several ways to search the entries, including a quick search for people who have biographies or for keywords within the entries, and complex search interfaces for people, full-text searching within all or specific parts of the text (e.g., statement of occupation, name of a place, source, archive), references, contributor, and images. Name searches can be conducted first name followed by last name (e.g., *mary leapor*), but when searching by last name and first name, be sure to separate the last and first name with a comma, or no results may be returned (e.g., *leapor, mary*). Also, be aware that alternative spellings of names may be used, rather than the Library of Congress spellings with which you may be most familiar, so it is important to try all known versions of your author's name. The "People" search can be used to identify figures that match certain desired criteria, since you can limit by fields of interest (e.g., literature, journalism and publishing, theatre and live entertainment, travel and exploration); sex; life dates; places, dates, and life events (e.g., birth, education, residence, burial); religious affiliation; presence of an image; or by a text search. For example, if you want to identify Scottish female writers active during the eighteenth century, you can select *literature, journalism and publishing* as the field of interest, *female* as the sex, active during 1700 to 1800 as the life dates, and *Scotland* as the place. This search finds fifty-eight women who meet these parameters, including poets, playwrights, novelists, letter writers, literary patrons, and diarists, and the list can be arranged either alphabetically or by birth or death date order.

The *ODNB* also offers thematic essays on subjects integral to British history, essays on groups of people, or reference lists (usually by occupation or achievement), which can be browsed by field of interest or type. The "Arts and Culture" category, for example, contains a feature essay on "Early Modern Women: The Rediscovery of Public and Private Life"; essays on the Scriblerus Club, the Nonsense Club, the Rainbow Coffee House group, and the Ivy Lane Club, among others; and reference lists for poets laureate (1668–2006) and principal librarians and directors of the British Museum (1756–2006). The *ODNB* can be counted on for its authoritative, introductory biographical essays, but the dictionary is equally important as a tool for identifying relevant archival repositories, noteworthy secondary works, and image resources for many eighteenth-century British authors.

Concerned with eminent Irish figures from all of Ireland, the ***Dictionary of Irish Biography from the Earliest Times to the Year 2002*** (***DIB***), edited by James McGuire and James Quinn, provides biographical profiles for more than 9,000 individuals who were either born in Ireland or had noteworthy careers in the country. As indicated by the title, the coverage spans from prehistory through the early twenty-first century, with the eighteenth century well represented. The print edition comprises nine volumes and is arranged alphabetically; however, the online version features access to the content by multiple fields. It is possible to search the essays by name; gender; birth, death, or flourish dates; places (e.g., Belfast, Irish counties, foreign countries); religion (e.g., Anglican, Buddhist, Catholic, Jewish, Methodist, Quaker, Unitarian, other Protestant nonconformist); occupation or field of interest, including literature; contributor's name; and keywords in the text. A search for females born between 1700 and 1780, limited to Ireland and the literature category, and using the keyword *poet*, retrieves 114 matches. Although not all of the results are poets (since *poet* can be mentioned in any context within the essay), this search does find interesting individuals the likes of poet and dramatist Charlotte Brooke, who is known for her collection *Reliques of Irish Poetry, Consisting of Heroic Poems, Odes, Elegies and Songs Translated into English Verse, with Notes Explanatory and Historical and the Originals in Irish Character, to Which Is Subjoined an Irish Tale, by Miss Brooke* (1789), as well as Eibhlín Dhubh Ní Chonaill, who composed the lament "Caoineadh Airt Uí Laoghaire" for her husband, who was shot and killed on May 4, 1773. Each signed essay concludes with a list of sources that are helpful in obtaining further information about the person in question. The *DIB* is a collaborative venture of Cambridge University Press and the Royal Irish Academy and received the 2010 Information Services Group Award for an Outstanding Work of Reference.

The **Dictionary of Literary Biography (DLB)** is an ongoing series devoted to individual authors and thematic author groups, typically focused on genres (e.g., prose writers, poets, dramatists, short story authors, travel writers, philosophers, historians); nationality (e.g., primarily British and American, but also European and other regions or countries, including Brazil, Denmark, Japan, China, Australia, South Africa, Southeast Asia, Arab countries, the Caribbean); time period; and special topics related to literature, including booksellers and collectors, the book trade, publishers, and periodicals, as just a few examples. The series features more than 360 volumes, which are available either in print or in the online database of the same name, offered as part of Gale's *Literature Resource Center* or *Literature Criticism Online*. Several volumes are concerned with eighteenth-century British literary topics, including *Eighteenth-Century British Poets*; *British Novelists, 1660–1800*; *British Prose Writers, 1660–1800*; *Restoration and Eighteenth-Century Dramatists*; *The British Literary Book Trade, 1700–1820*; *Eighteenth-Century British Literary Biographers*; *Eighteenth-Century British Literary Scholars and Critics*; *British Philosophers, 1500–1799*; *Eighteenth-Century British Historians*; and *Pre-Nineteenth-Century British Book Collectors and Bibliographers*. For research interests having to do with the latter part of the century, the British Romantic-era volumes are very useful. It is important to note that some specific titles are published in multiple series, with different content available in each one. The *Eighteenth-Century British Poets* volume, for example, has thus far been published in two series, in 1990 (*First Series*) and 1991 (*Second Series*) with no overlap of authors covered. The *Second Series* volume contains an essay about Mary Leapor that greatly elaborates on the information provided in the *ODNB*, with almost five pages rather than five paragraphs examining her life and literary works.

The value of this biographical resource lies in the attention paid to the literary career of the profiled author or figure. Each biographical essay, written by a scholar in the field, traces the development of the person's life and literary accomplishments, and places that career within the larger context of contemporary literary culture. As a result, some essays may offer discussion of individual works, outline the author's critical reception, and provide an assessment of the author's current (at time of publication) reputation. Each essay begins with a list of the author's works (for authors covered in multiple volumes, this list corresponds to the thematic focus of the volume, with references to the other pertinent volumes) and concludes with important publications. Examples include letters, bibliographies, and biographies; holding institutions for the author's papers; and the references for the essay. Consulting these bibliographies can assist in quickly identifying important reference tools that can be updated by searching *WorldCat*. The essays in the print volumes are also frequently enhanced with portraits, photographs of places associated with the author, or reproductions of manuscript or print publications, which are missing from the *Literature Resource Center* online version, but are reproduced in *Literature Criticism Online* (since the latter version of the *DLB* provides digital images of the print series). The Oliver Goldsmith biography in the *Restoration and Eighteenth-Century Dramatists, Third Series* print volume, for example, contains a character sketch by Henry Bunbury, his portrait by Benjamin West, a photograph of his statue outside Trinity College, pages from a letter to David Garrick, *She Stoops to Conquer*, a playbill for the same play, and a page from the playhouse copy of *The Grumbler*.

The online *DLB* offers the easiest access to relevant entries, since the advanced search interface enables searching by author's name, title of a specific work, birth and death years, nationality, subject or genre, essay topic, ethnicity, gender, specific volume title, or within the full text. Limiting *oliver goldsmith* to the author name field finds six biographical essays in volumes devoted to period British novelists, dramatists, poets, prose writers, literary biographers, and historians (with one false hit to a Canadian author with the same name); however, a search for his name in the full text retrieves 189 results, including an essay about George Newnes Limited, which published cheap classics in its *Penny Library of Famous Books* series, which includes works by Goldsmith. Such full-text search options and the various field limiters allow the researcher to explore the *DLB*'s content at a deeper level and pick up references that would be missed by only consulting the individual author essays. Searching for an author's name or title of a specific work, for example, may be useful for tracing literary influences, publishing history, or critical reputation beyond that featured in the main author essays. Other search options, like those for gender, genre, and nationality, enable the identification of such targeted groups as female Welsh poets, leading to the discovery of Hester Lynch Thrale Piozzi, who not only composed poetry, but who is also known for her biography of Samuel Johnson, letters, diary, and works of European history and English grammar. The print volumes, on the other hand, give author access in the cumulative index, or you can search for thematic or period titles by keyword in the library catalog. An additional advantage to the online version is the hyperlinks within each essay to cross-referenced authors and/or other people, so that within the Piozzi essay, you can quickly link to *DLB* essays about James Boswell, James L. Clifford, Boethius, Sir Joshua Reynolds, Edmund Burke, Horace Walpole, Hannah More, and David Garrick, among others. Whether your access is to the print or online volumes, the *DLB* is a foundational reference work that serves as a useful springboard for many kinds of literary investigations.

Arising out of feminist revisions to the traditional literary canon in the 1970s and 1980s, Janet Todd's *A Dictionary of British and American Women Writers, 1660–1800* aims to redress the women authors missing from standard biographical reference books. As stated in the preface, she writes that the "two major purposes of this book are to illuminate the forgotten writers—aristocratic, middle, and working class—and to represent the major or accepted ones in the light not only of new scholarship but of new consciousness" (xvii). Although newer reference books now incorporate some of these authors, this work still remains useful for its biographical profiles, lists of known works, brief discussions of the author's style, critical assessments, and overviews of themes and major genres—many for authors not discussed elsewhere. The signed entries range in length from a paragraph to a few pages, following the dictionary, alphabetically arranged format, and cover more than 500 published and unpublished authors who are listed under their most commonly used names, titles, or professional names, with cross-references to married or family names. To supplement the known biographical facts, many entries also include excerpts from the author's own writing or prefaces, in addition to obituaries and contemporary or later critical commentary. Unfortunately, none of the entries provide a bibliography or details about the works cited other than title and date.

The *Encyclopedia of British Writers*, edited by Alan Hager, is a four-volume endeavor to describe significant and less-familiar authors from the sixteenth through twentieth centuries; volume 2 is devoted entirely to the eighteenth century. Although the emphasis is on British figures, selected individuals from Europe and America are covered if they were deemed influential to British literature. Authors are defined broadly so that novelists, poets, and dramatists are included, along with diarists, cookery writers, conduct writers, and authors of other nonfiction. Each entry presents a brief biography and literary career overview, noting works by the author, as well as a selected work or two about the author, if available. Longer treatments for some major figures feature a critical analysis of themes and particular works. A few entries are about topics, such as the Graveyard School, conduct books, the Augustan age, and the Celtic Revival movement. Volume 2 of this encyclopedia will be valuable to scholars wishing to survey a broad range of eighteenth-century British literary figures.

For those with a particular interest in eighteenth-century theatre, *A Biographical Dictionary of Actors, Actresses, Musicians, Dancers, Managers and Other Stage Personnel in London, 1660–1800* may be particularly useful. This massive, sixteen-volume work by Philip H. Highfill Jr., Kalman A. Burnim, and Edward A. Langhans comprises biographical profiles for more than 8,500 individuals who were involved professionally with a wide range of London theatrical entertainments during the period. In addition to the types of participants enumerated in the title, the volumes also cover singers, scene painters, machinists, prompters, acrobats, contortionists, pyrotechnists, magicians, dwarfs, freaks, animal trainers, strong men, public orators, mimics, dressers, callers, and concessionaires, among other occupations, as well as the monkey General Jackoo, Moustache the Marvelous Poodle, and Nippotate the Tame Hedgehog. Most entries contain birth, death, or flourish dates; occupation or position; and an overview of facts known about the person's life and career or relationship to the theatre. Consequently, some entries are only one sentence or a few sentences in length, while others span several pages. Black-and-white portraits and other illustrations accompany several of the profiles. Unfortunately, few references are given for the biographical information, which Harner calls the "only major flaw and one that will not be rectified by a bibliography volume" (297).

INDIVIDUAL AUTHOR SOURCES

Battestin, Martin C. *A Henry Fielding Companion*. Westport, CT: Greenwood, 2000.

Berry, Reginald. *A Pope Chronology*. Boston: G. K. Hall and Co., 1988.

Degategno, Paul J., and R. Jay Stubblefield. *Critical Companion to Jonathan Swift: A Literary Reference to His Life and Works*. New York: Facts on File, 2006.

Lynch, Jack, ed. *Samuel Johnson in Context*. New York: Cambridge University Press, 2012.

Rogers, Pat. *The Alexander Pope Encyclopedia*. Westport, CT: Greenwood, 2004.

Sabor, Peter, ed. *The Cambridge Companion to Frances Burney*. New York: Cambridge University Press, 2007.

Shinagel, Michael, ed. *A Concordance to the Poems of Jonathan Swift*. Ithaca, NY: Cornell University Press, 1972.

Reference works devoted to individual authors are common for firmly established canonical authors, but they are less likely to be available for authors outside of or newly incorporated into the English literary tradition. This is especially true for women authors of the period. The first place to check for author-specific reference tools is Bracken's *Reference Works in British and American Literature*, the *New Cambridge Bibliography of English Literature*, and Marcuse's *A Reference Guide for English Studies*. The *Cambridge Companions to Literature* series covers individual authors, as well as literary time periods and genres (as previously described). To date, volumes have been published for the following eighteenth-century authors: Frances Burney, Daniel Defoe, Henry Fielding, Samuel Johnson, Alexander Pope, Laurence Sterne, Jonathan Swift, and Mary Wollstonecraft, in addition to Jane Austen and the Romantics. These volumes feature similar collections of scholarly essays and typically include a chronology and bibliography.

Aside from these sources, local or union library catalogs can be useful in locating author-specific reference works. This can be done by searching with the author's name and the type of resource, for example, typing in the search string *pope and concordance** or *johnson samuel and companion**. The following is a selection of Library of Congress subject headings to illustrate the range and format typical of author reference sources that can be used to construct targeted searches. Please note that companions are not designated as such with their own subject heading, but are usually assigned the general subheading "Criticism and Interpretation"; therefore, to find companions for an author, it is necessary to conduct a keyword rather than a subject heading search.

Johnson, Samuel, 1709–1784—Encyclopedias
Gray, Thomas, 1716–1771—Concordances
Pope, Alexander, 1688–1744—Chronology
Defoe, Daniel, 1661?–1731—Handbooks, manuals, etc.

Keyword searches for author chronologies are valuable for retrieving chronologies published as a separate chapter or appended material in an author bibliography, anthology, or critical study. These "inserted" chronologies may be found if the book's contents are indexed, but wouldn't necessarily be retrieved from a subject heading search. For example, a search for *eliza* *haywood and chronolog** retrieves *Fantomina and Other Works* (Alexander Pettit, Margaret Case Croskery, and Anna C. Patchias, eds., 2004), which contains a brief (five-page) chronology from 1693 to 1788, outlining Haywood's publications and selected life events. Since this title is a collection of Haywood's writings, it doesn't have any associated reference-type subject headings, but instead has the assigned subject headings "Imaginary Conversations," "Love-Letters," and "Love." For many eighteenth-century female and noncanonical authors, it may be necessary to rely on the period and general reference sources discussed earlier to find concise biographical and other factual information, in the instance that a specific reference source cannot be identified for a particular author.

This section provides examples of the type of author-centered reference sources available, with a primary focus on encyclopedias, companions, chronologies, and concordances. Author-centered bibliographies are discussed in chapter 4.

Designed to compile the "material facts" about the author in a single volume, Pat Rogers's *The Alexander Pope Encyclopedia* offers an alphabetical presentation of 342 brief entries (ranging from one paragraph to several columns in length) about Pope's prose and verse, life, correspondence, people central to his life, literary themes and techniques, and selected contextual historical topics. Works are defined not only as all major publications, but also many shorter poems, books that he either edited or contributed to, and collaborative endeavors. *The Rape of the Lock* and *The Dunciad* receive extended treatments; *The Dunciad* entry, for example, addresses composition, publication history, literary sources and models, narrative analysis, targets of the satire, contemporary response, and critical history. The majority of entries (more than 300 of them) are devoted to biographical profiles for figures Pope knew or wrote about, as well as entries for nonliving critics and scholars who have made significant contributions to Pope literary scholarship. Living critics and scholars are featured in the general "reputation" entry. Sample topical entries range from accidents, Bedlam, gardening, health, and manuscripts, to pamphlet attacks, the Scriblerus Club, stock quotations, and wit. Most entries contain a brief reading list, primarily of recommended books. Additional material includes a succinct chronology arranged by year, Pope's age, and events in his life from his birth in 1688 to 1745, the year after Pope's death, in which Jonathan Swift and Robert Walpole died, and a selected bibliography covering reference works, editions, biography, and criticism (with subcategories for specialized topics, feminist issues, books and publishing, style, reputation and afterlife, studies of individual works, local studies, and background and comparison). This encyclopedia is a helpful, go-to compendium for quick reference regarding Pope.

Reginald Berry wrote a detailed, book-length chronology of Alexander Pope's life to make it easier for scholars to quickly access factual information about his life and career. *A Pope Chronology* presents entries about Pope's literary endeavors and publications; correspondence; critical reception; pamphlet attacks; travels; biographical information on meetings of the Scriblerus Club, illnesses, and social engagements, among others; and selected events from the careers of Gay, Arbuthnot, and Swift. These entries are arranged by year, month, and day from 1688 to 1744; some years begin with a headnote to indicate events that transpired throughout or were ongoing during that time, such as the note for 1723, in which Berry states, "During this year AP continues his work on the Shakespeare edition and the *Odyssey* translation. Unlike in recent years, he makes frequent visits to London, where he now customarily stays with Lord Peterborough" (48). Since Pope lived during the time England used the Julian calendar (or Old Style calendar), the chronology maintains the Old Style dates, except that it begins the year on January 1 rather than March 25. Additional material includes an overview of principal people mentioned in the chronology, with brief biographical notes, a list of the main places referred to with descriptions (e.g., Chiswick, Grub Street, Haymarket Theatre), and a concise bibliography of sources used to compile the chronology. The index facilitates identifying relevant sections of the chronology for particular publications, people, and other topics.

Organized thematically, Martin Battestin's *A Henry Fielding Companion* serves as a quick reference to Fielding's residences, members of his family and household, figures whom Fielding knew and also the authors he read, works known to have been written by Fielding (journalism, legal and social works, miscellanies, miscellaneous prose, plays, poetry, prose fiction, puppet theatre, translations), anonymous works attributed to Fielding, letters, manuscripts, themes and topics, and characters in the plays and fiction. Within these categories, entries range from a few sentences to more developed descriptions of one or several paragraphs. The "Themes and Topics" section covers adultery, charity, comic prose epic, deism, good nature, honor, Latitudinarians, marriage, masquerades, the passions, providence, and the ridiculous, among others, which Fielding explored in his writings. Much of the information in the companion is drawn from Martin and Ruthe R. Battestin's *Henry Fielding: A Life* (1993), which is a good resource for more developed background and context. Names and subjects that appear in bold throughout the companion refer to distinct entries, but readers must guess the appropriate section or consult the index to find the entry itself. A detailed chronology outlines events and publications from Fielding's birth in 1707, to the performance of his lost comedy, *The Fathers: or, The Good-Natured Man*, in 1778, and both the works cited list and extensive bibliography lead to reference works, editions, and scholarship, as well as film and television adaptations.

The Cambridge Companion to Frances Burney, edited by Peter Sabor, offers ten individually authored chapters that address specific works (*Evelina, Cecilia, Camilla,* and *The Wanderer*); Burney's family, journals and letters; her role as a dramatist; and thematic examinations of Burney and politics, gender, society, and the literary marketplace. The final chapter presents an overview of her reputation and critical heritage from the earliest criticism through the beginning of the twenty-first century. Like other volumes in *The Cambridge Companions to Literature* series, this title provides a chronology of Burney's life from 1752 to 1846 (the year her niece edited *Diary and Letters of Madame d'Arblay*) and a bibliography of recommended biographies, a monograph bibliography, and books and journal articles of criticism to accompany the final chapter's critical heritage assessment.

Arranged in separate thematic parts, Paul Degategno and R. Jay Stubblefield's ***Critical Companion to Jonathan Swift: A Literary Reference to His Life and Works*** has entries about Swift's poetry and prose, the individuals and events associated with his life, and the "topics and places of biographical or literary significance in Swift's writing" (v). Beginning with a biographical profile, the main body of the companion (nearly 300 pages) is devoted to Swift's 280 poems and almost all of his prose works. Each of these entries gives composition and/or publication information, a description of the content, and context of the work, often with references to related entries. Some entries are brief, like the one for "On Burning a Dull Poem," which follows the publication date with the sentence, "It describes the speaker's negative response to a poem so bad it could only have come from a brainless 'ass's head'" (243). Many of the entries also present a synopsis and commentary of major works, for instance, *Gulliver's Travels,* and contain entries for individual characters and a bibliography. The *Gulliver's Travels* entry serves as a good example of the detail to be found for principal texts; covering sixty-three pages, the synopsis is divided by individual parts and chapters, and characters, places, ships, and terms are also described separately. The last section of the companion gives brief entries for the people, locations, and subjects related to Swift's life and works, including literary and ecclesiastical colleagues, political friends and enemies, publishers and printers, and intimates and relatives. Of added value are the many black-and-white illustrations featured throughout the text, such as drawings by Arthur Rackham and Thomas Morten and reproductions of title pages, frontispieces, and portraits of Swift and his contemporaries. Finally, the appended material comprises a chronology of Swift's life, a bibliography of modern editions, bibliographic works, biographies, criticism, and a works cited list of books and journal articles referenced in the volume.

Functioning as a companion to the author and his cultural milieu, ***Samuel Johnson in Context*** presents forty-seven brief chapters addressing Johnson's life, critical heritage, and eighteenth-century world. Written by leading scholars in the field and edited by Jack Lynch, this work can be used as a reference tool to obtain biographical details, information about Johnson's publications, notes about editions and translations, and a survey of his critical reception and reputation throughout time. The main body of the volume concerns cultural and historical contexts. Thirty-eight essays review literary topics, including authorship, biography, the book trade, dictionaries, essays, fiction, journalism, literary criticism, poetry, Shakespeare, theatre, and women writers; social issues like clubs, conversation, domestic life, mental health, money, slavery and abolition, social hierarchy, and travel; other disciplines, from anthropology, education, and history, to law, medicine, philosophy, science and technology, and visual arts; such religious contexts as Anglicanism and sermons; and historical themes, including America, empire, nationalism, politics, and war. A chronology of Johnson's life traces events from 1709 to 1796, and a list of recommended references and other books, arranged by chapter, guides scholars to additional resources.

A concordance acts as an alphabetical index to all the words used in an author's corpus, an individual work, or selected works (e.g., poems or letters), or for texts with multiple or unknown authors, for instance, the Bible, the Torah, the Qur'an, the Dead Sea Scrolls, the Nayakas, the inscriptions of Palenque, or even medieval English recipes. This listing typically shows the words in context, so that the scholar can determine the sense or meaning of the word as it was used. Since the specific text (or texts) consulted to create the concordance is crucial in determining the content, it is important to note which particular edition(s) were referenced. *A Concordance to the Poems of Jonathan Swift* is based on Sir Harold Williams's second edition of *The Poems of Jonathan Swift*, published in 1958. The concordance's editor, Michael Shinagel, decided to modify the content by including all the poems supposedly by penned Swift, but also indicating with a prefatory "D" those that there is doubt about Swift being the author. Shinagel excludes all the poems that Williams listed as attributed to Swift (at the end of volume 3), and he excludes Swift's Latin poems, but includes all foreign words and phrases that Swift used in his English poems. Reading Shinagel's preface is key in understanding the reasons behind these decisions, as well as being apprised of the omitted word list (with their frequencies) and the abbreviated poem titles. What remains are 13,660 word entries ranging from the terms *a-dream'd* to *dean*, to *fancy* to *smoak*, to *whimsyes* to *zounds*, making this a substantial guide to Swift's poetic vocabulary. For each word listed, the corresponding contextual poetic line is given, along with the page number in Williams's edition, the poem title, and the line number. Variant spellings are cross-referenced, so that *again* also leads to entries for *agayne* and *agen*. This cross-referencing only occurs, however, when the variant terms are more than half a page apart in the concordance, and it is not carried out for variants created by the use of an apostrophe. Browsing through the concordance can present interesting opportunities for close readings or critical study, as particular words delight, intrigue, or jump off the page. Since the contextual lines and poem reference are provided, you can quickly obtain a preliminary understanding of Swift's facility with a particular word. The concordance concludes with a list both of index words and omitted words in order of frequency. Among Swift's most frequently used words, you will find *he* (1,119), *she* (456), *wit* (176), *think* (155), *time* (118), and *true* (111). Although it is now often possible to search a digitized version of a text to determine the context and frequency of distinct words (by using the Web browser's find command or an entire document keyword search in a subscription database, like *Eighteenth Century Collections Online*), the traditional concordance offers the valuable opportunity to survey an author's entire vocabulary and possesses the advantage of careful scholarly selection, cross-referencing of variant spellings and related terms, and an understanding of the ways in which an individual word is used (for interpreting and organizing the word list). For scholars studying authors that do not have a published concordance to their works, however, digitized texts offer an alternative and still very useful means of analyzing an author's vocabulary to the same effect.

CONCLUSION

Although the ways in which scholars access general reference sources have changed significantly in the past few years, the type of content and the value of these tools remains the same. Online reference tools are becoming the norm, as libraries and publishers both invest in digital publications. Scholars are now just as likely to use an online dictionary, encyclopedia, or companion as they are to rely on a print reference book, and this trend will only continue to shift in favor of the online environment. In fact, it can be argued that online reference tools have increased their usefulness to the research process by providing, in some cases, searchable access to their information, content that is not fixed, but updated as needed, to reflect changes in the field, and often links to outside sources, including relevant images, journal articles and books, or archival material. These features only serve to enhance the traditional value of a quality reference tool that offers authoritative content written by subject specialists and is overseen by an editor or editorial board. Whether in print or online, general reference sources give researchers the means to answer factual or introductory inquiries about literary authors, works, genres, periods, and themes; identify important bibliographies or secondary scholarship; and place literary investigations within the larger national, cultural, or historical context. And, as such, they will continue to play a viable role in the research process.

NOTE

1. Stuart Gillespie, "Leapor, Mary (1722–1746)," in *Oxford Dictionary of National Biography*, online edition ed. Lawrence Goldman (Oxford, UK: Oxford University Press, 2004), www.oxforddnb.com/view/article/16246 (accessed 28 July 2012).

Chapter Three

Library Catalogs

In the past, the catalog was the central gateway to the library's collection. Through the catalog, the scholar could discover what books and other items were part of the collection, finding these materials through their surrogate library records. The traditional print card catalog provided access by author, title, and limited subjects, whereas the online catalog not only maintained these access points, but added the ability to search by keywords throughout selected fields in the bibliographic record (as described in chapter 1). Although the library catalog still functions in its gateway role to a large degree, these days it faces some stiff competition from Internet resources like Google and *WorldCat.org*.

In response to this trend, efforts have been made to transform the catalog so that it better suits the needs of contemporary library users. The next-generation catalog aims to be more Google-like in appearance and search capabilities. Your university or college catalog most likely features a single search box and the opportunity to narrow results by facets, including by location, format, date, and collection, and by tags (either composed of Library of Congress subject heading stems or words assigned by library users). Many catalogs now offer a single interface for combined searching of books, journals, and newspapers, as well as other content in their collections and subscription databases, sometimes across the full text of these materials, so that searching the library's print collection and online subscription content occurs simultaneously. The current inclination is to make searching easier for students and to enable them to identify a larger range of materials at once, rather than having to go through separate resources. Traditional search strategies, including knowledge of Boolean operators and Library of Congress subject headings, are less relevant in this new catalog environment, since students can begin with keywords and use the facets and tags to refine or narrow their searches.

Despite the benefits of simpler, Google-like access, it is important to remember that searching by traditional means may still be the most effective way to conduct a comprehensive review of the library's collection. For this reason, many libraries have maintained some version of a standard library catalog interface, which may be referred to as the classic catalog, or another similar term, for advanced searches. The classic catalog interface supports field searching, including author, title, and periodical or series title; Library of Congress subject heading; ISBN/ISSN or additional fields; and advanced keyword construction with Boolean operators and nesting. The next-generation catalog interfaces typically do not permit searches with Boolean operators and nesting of alternative terms or synonyms, since all words entered are treated as terms to be found within a bibliographic record; however, you may have limited field-search capabilities.

Not only is the library catalog search interface changing, but the nature of the collections is transforming as well. Libraries have provided access to digital content through their catalogs for several years now, but the practice of including proprietary and freely available digital titles has recently exploded. The academic catalog is likely to lead you not only to print and electronic books, periodicals, and other items, but also to digitized books in the public domain, including those scanned by the HathiTrust Digital Library, digitized archival material (either available freely on the Web or through the library's subscription databases), image collections, video or sound archives, and government documents, as just a few examples. This trend means that the catalog no longer only acts as the gateway to those items physically held or purchased by the library, but also to a range of sources that might be located in other libraries or collections, if available in analog format, or that exist only virtually, if born digitally.

In addition to your local catalog serving as a portal to this broader range of materials, you probably also have access to union catalogs, which enable you to search consortial collections at the local, regional, state, national, or even international levels. Indeed, the principal union catalog is the subscription database *WorldCat*, which provides the opportunity to identify items in collections held by libraries around the world. Since many libraries, especially those in North America, the United Kingdom, and other English-speaking countries, follow the guidelines outlined in the *Anglo-American Cataloging Rules* (*AACR*, *AACR2* for the second revised edition), catalog records will be fairly consistent in terms of their bibliographic and physical descriptions. Although you will certainly encounter variations, usually in the details, the *AACR2* means that you will find standard bibliographic elements in each record, which, together with the Machine Readable Cataloging (MARC) record structure (discussed in chapter 1), ensures consistency across library catalogs.

Even though libraries continue to purchase print monographs, the recent trend is certainly to acquire more electronic books for their collections. And while electronic books have the advantage of being accessible by multiple readers simultaneously and don't require precious shelf space, it is also true that their bibliographic records in the library catalog are often incomplete, usually lacking assigned Library of Congress subject headings. Scholars need to be aware of this practice and the impact it has on searching the library's book holdings, since these books will not be found by a traditional subject heading field search but must be identified through keyword, title, or author searches instead.

Another trend impacting libraries and their collections is the current practice of moving many of the library's lesser-used print and microformat materials to off-site or closed-stacks storage facilities. In this environment, the library catalog becomes even more central to the process of identifying and accessing the library's collection, because material may no longer be discovered by browsing the stacks in person. Online browsing tools re-create some of the characteristics of scanning the library's collection in a specific call number range, but most do not offer (at this stage anyway) the ability to review each book's index or examine the full contents, although many libraries feature a link to Google Books previews for selected titles. Without the ability to browse an entire book online, scholars will need to rely more than ever on searching the catalog effectively to find all materials that could be of potential relevance for their research and then request those items to be delivered for further inspection.

This chapter recommends strategies for searching the library catalog, with emphasis placed on author, title, and Library of Congress subject heading field searches. We also cover best practices for conducting keyword searches, which can be employed in either next-generation or traditional catalog environments. Recognizing the opportunities to access collections more widely, the chapter discusses the role of union catalogs and guides you to the important national and international catalogs central to research in eighteenth-century British literary studies. Throughout the chapter, we address the impact of current library trends, so that you can be mindful of how they influence your catalog searches and proceed accordingly. Extensive changes, like those currently under way in libraries, can be exhilarating, frustrating, unsettling, exciting, and challenging to varying degrees. We aim to lead you through the current uneven terrain, so that you can use the catalog to your advantage.

AUTHOR SEARCHES AND EVALUATION OF RESULTS

To find works by eighteenth-century British authors, begin with an author field search in your library catalog. In the context of this volume, works are defined as writings created by one or more authors, or attributed to a particular author, that may or may not have been published. The eighteenth century holds forth a rich variety of potential texts to investigate, from novels, poems, plays, essays, and devotional tracts, to advice books, commonplace books, pamphlets, letters, diaries, speeches, and more, all of which can be considered a work, either as a single or collected endeavor. For many canonical authors of the period, an author field search will be a straightforward process of entering the author's last name, followed by the first name. Even this simple search may present problems, however. If we enter the author search *boswell james* in our regional Prospector union catalog, for example, we would retrieve the results displayed in figure 3.1.

Here we see multiple author headings for James Boswell, several of which might represent the author we intended to locate. This search illustrates the importance of determining the authoritative Library of Congress author heading, in this case, "Boswell, James, 1740–1795." The Library of Congress author headings are one of the standardized headings, more broadly referred to as authority records. Authority records exist for names, titles, and subjects, so that access is consistent across library catalogs. Since the purpose is to aid in identifying the correct person, the authoritative author heading will most likely include the author's birth and death dates, an especially crucial component in cases where an author has a common name. Once identified, researchers can use the official heading to retrieve most works by the author, since catalogers assign the authoritative heading to works that are published or written under variant names, married names, royal or honorific titles, multiple surnames, and unknown or unattributed authorship, thus bringing together most anomalous author variants under one searchable standard. The

| AUTHOR | boswell james | | System Sorted | Sort | Search |

Save Marked Records		Save All On Page		
		AUTHORS (1-7 of 7)		
1	☐	Boswell James		7
2	☐	Boswell James 1740 1795		412
3	☐	Boswell James 1745 1795		2
4	☐	Boswell James 1778 1822		4
5	☐	Boswell James 1906 1971		2
6	☐	Boswell James D	1969	1
7	☐	Boswell James Jr		2

Figure 3.1.   Author field search of *boswell james*. *Source*: Prospector classic catalog.

first entry for Boswell, without the dates, is retrieved because he is listed as an author within an anthology of travel writing, but he is not the assigned author for the published book. Author headings without dates often lead to anthologized or collected works, thus you may want to review these entries, as well as those listed under the official author heading, to ensure that you are finding all potentially relevant works. The Boswell entry with the dates 1745–1795 affirms the necessity of knowing the biographical details about your particular author. Does this entry represent our James Boswell or another contemporary? Is the birth date 1745 a mistake, or was there a different Boswell born in that year who also died in 1795? Be sure to consult the *Oxford Dictionary of National Biography* (*ODNB*), the *Dictionary of Irish Biography* (*DIB*), or the *Dictionary of Literary Biography* (*DLB*) (discussed in chapter 2) to confirm important facts about your author, so that you can find the correct heading. Besides birth and death dates, biographical information can help pinpoint married names, honorific titles, and publication dates that might all be valuable for searching library catalogs comprehensively.

Women authors can pose a particular challenge when searching for their works in the catalog. A female author from the eighteenth century may have written or published under her maiden and/or married name, or she may have published under a pseudonym, alternative name, or anonymously. Eliza Haywood serves as an example of an author who employed many of these tactics, publishing under Mrs. Eliza Haywood, Mrs. E. Haywood, Mrs. Haywood, "Justicia, the author of the masqueraders, or fatal curiosity," "By the author of Miss Betsy Thoughtless," Explorabilis, "a celebrated author of that country," anonymous, Mrs Prattle, and Mira, among them. These variants are all drawn together by searching the authoritative heading, "Haywood, Eliza Fowler, 1693?–1756"; however, she also has works listed in our catalog under "Haywood, Eliza," "Haywood, Eliza, 1693–1756," and "Haywood, Eliza, 1693–1755." Although the authoritative heading may redress many of these challenges, you may still find that you will need to search by all potential variants to find works in anthologies or collections, or other examples where the author is not the primary attributed creator.

To further complicate matters, not every author from the eighteenth century will have an authoritative heading. Many of the lesser-known or recently rediscovered authors may only be found through a keyword search in the library catalog. If you are unsuccessful searching for your figure in the author field, try this strategy to identify works embedded in anthologies or collections where the author is listed in the table of contents. An author search for *dixon sarah* in our catalog obtains five works, all collected in *Eighteenth-Century Poetry: An Annotated Anthology* (2004), but a keyword search *"sarah dixon" or "dixon sarah"* in *WorldCat* retrieves additional work in anthologies, including *Eighteenth Century Women Poets: An Oxford Anthology* (1989), picked up through the contents. We could also expand our search by removing the quotes and employing a proximity operator instead. Although an author keyword search will inevitably retrieve irrelevant titles, it can still be used effectively to find texts that have been included in thematic anthologies or literary collections.

To conduct the broadest review possible, you can also try searching for period anthologies that might contain relevant works by your author, even if the contents aren't listed, by using keyword strategies like *antholog* and poet* and eighteenth*, as one example. The compilation *British Women Poets of the Long Eighteenth Century: An Anthology* (2009) displays contents by genre or subject matter (e.g., friendship poems, religious poetry, poetry of war, poems on the public sphere, poems on pain and illness), rather than by poet, as shown in figure 3.2. You would need to examine this title to determine if it contained relevant work by a specific author. Other search terms that may be used in this manner include *literary collections*, *correspondence*, or *sources*, and *Augustan, Georgian, Enlightenment, Romantic, Britain*, or *England*, which, used in different combinations, identifies such works as *Restoration and Augustan British Utopias* (2000) or *Eighteenth-Century Coffee-House Culture* (2006), with four volumes devoted to Restoration and eighteenth-century satire, drama, science, and history writings. For some lesser-known authors, you will need to be a detective and try all possible avenues for finding their works in the catalog.

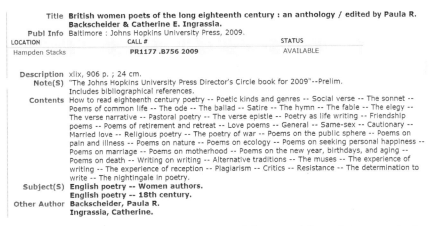

Figure 3.2. Contents of *British Women Poets of the Long Eighteenth Century: An Anthology*. *Source*: University of Denver Penrose Library classic catalog.

Once you have conducted your author search, the next step is to evaluate the results so that you can select the best sources for your research. If you are lucky, you will have a wide range of material from which to choose. Researchers working with canonical authors will typically have the most options, and those titles that have been standard elements of the university curriculum will be represented in numerous editions and formats. You might discover that a title you want to investigate is available in the catalog in scholarly critical editions, facsimile, digital reproductions, or microform formats. Be sure to search not only your local catalog, but also regional or international union catalogs to draw upon the collections of other institutions that might hold a particular copy that would be of value for your research. This will be especially true for scholars studying lesser-known authors whose works may not have been published in a modern edition, or whose work is not held by a local library.

If you are preparing an academic journal article or researching your dissertation, you will want to use the latest scholarly edition of the eighteenth-century text. Both Michael Marcuse's *A Reference Guide for English Studies* and the *Dictionary of Literary Biography* (*DLB*) list standard editions for individual authors. Marcuse notes editions for Blake, Boswell, Coleridge, Fielding, Johnson, Pope, Swift, and Wordsworth; however, some of these titles may have been superseded by new editions. Likewise, although the *DLB* offers better coverage of female and less-familiar authors, you will need to check the publication date of the biographical essay and determine if it is still a relevant recommendation. For example, the essay about Eliza Haywood lists editions for twelve of her works, including the 1979 Garland edition of *The History of Miss Betsy Thoughtless*. Published in *DLB*, volume 39, *British Novelists, 1660–1800*, in 1985, it may be likely that a newer edition is now the one preferred by current scholars. If the standard edition recommendation is older, you should review the bibliographies in recent academic books and journal articles to assess whether that edition is still used by scholars, or if they rely on a more recently published source. Keep in mind, however, that a particular edition can remain the standard for many years, so an older publication date doesn't necessarily make it an invalid choice. If you do not require a standard edition, or if one is not available for your author, you should consider the following elements when evaluating a text: the authority of the publisher and editors, the currency or relevance of the publication date, and the place of publication.

If your research requires consulting the original text rather than a reprint, or if you are unable to find a modern edition, you can alternatively look for a digital facsimile, like those available in *Eighteenth Century Collections Online* (*ECCO*), or another digital collection. See chapter 6 for details about digital collections important to eighteenth-century literary study. Micro-form or print facsimile formats are other viable options, and best practices for working with these formats are also discussed in this chapter. If these surrogate formats won't work for your project, you can identify copies of the original manuscript or publication either through *WorldCat* or the sources recommended in chapter 8 about primary source research. Original eighteenth-century publications and manuscripts will probably be held in special collections or archives with restricted access, so you will need to plan your research accordingly.

TITLE SEARCHES

Just as author searches aren't always necessarily straightforward, the same can be true for title searches. In general, a title field search will retrieve all items in the catalog corresponding to the information entered. In the case of canonical authors, the results might represent the title in numerous formats (as previously noted), ranging from scholarly editions, digital reproductions, and facsimiles, to theatrical or film adaptations, selected or entire works in anthologies, and microform copies. If the list of titles is too overwhelming, you can refine your search by combining an author and title field search, which will help narrow the results to just the versions that are by your par-ticular author.

Some eighteenth-century works are notorious for their descriptive titles, which may not be consistent throughout each published version. Defoe's *Moll Flanders* sports the full title *The fortunes and misfortunes of the famous Moll Flanders, &c. Who was born in Newgate, and during a Life of continu'd Variety for Threescore Years, besides her Childhood, was Twelve Year a Whore, five times a Wife (whereof once to her own Brother) Twelve Year a Thief, Eight Year a Transported Felon in Virginia, at last grew Rich, liv'd Honest, and died a Penitent, Written from her own memorandums*. The novel *Robinson Crusoe* was published as *The life and strange surprizing adventures of Robinson Crusoe, of York, mariner: who lived eight and twenty years, all alone in an un-inhabited island on the coast of America, near the mouth of the great river of Oroonoque; Having been cast on Shore by Shipwreck, wherein all the Men perished but himself. With An Account how he was at last as strangely deliver'd by Pyrates. Written by himself.* Since books are typically cataloged using the information from the title page, you may discover that one work can actually be represented by slightly different titles.

A uniform title, another type of Library of Congress authority record, serves to counter this dispersal by bringing together variant titles, editions, translations, and facsimiles under one standard appellation. The uniform title is indicated in the 240 field within a MARC record, and it may be necessary to choose the MARC record display option if the uniform title isn't noted in the regular catalog record. A preliminary search for Henry Fielding's novel *The History of Tom Jones*, for example, shows that several titles are listed in this manner, but others have added *A Foundling*, and sometimes the author's name and volume information to the title (see figure 3.3).

Searching further reveals that other versions possess the title *Tom Jones*. If we look at the MARC record for *Tom Jones: An Authoritative Text, Contemporary Reactions, Criticism*, illustrated in figure 3.4, we learn that the uniform title is *History of Tom Jones*, which should retrieve most versions of the work published under these variant titles.

In addition to reading the catalog record to determine whether there is a uniform title for your work, the description, series, and notes fields may impart valuable clues about that specific edition or version of the work that can help determine if it is suitable for your research project. Look in these fields for information about whether the work is a facsimile, and the source text (or even sometimes specific copy, such as the British Library copy) used for

Title	history of tom jones	Penrose Library	System Sorted	Sort

☐ *Limit search to available items*

[Search]

Save Marked Records   Save All On Page   Add Marked to My Lists

Num	Mark	Title (1-23 of 23)	Year	Entries 146 Found
1	☐	History Of Tom Jones		67
2	☐	History Of Tom Jones A Foundling -- 24 entries		24
3	☐	History Of Tom Jones A Foundling Abridged From The Works Of Henry Fielding Esq Adorned With Cuts : Fielding, Henry,	1797	1
4	☐	History Of Tom Jones A Foundling By Henry Fielding Esq		9
5	☐	History Of Tom Jones A Foundling By Henry Fielding Esq In Four Volumes		3
6	☐	History Of Tom Jones A Foundling By Henry Fielding Esq In Six Volumes : Fielding, Henry,	1789	1
7	☐	History Of Tom Jones A Foundling By Henry Fielding Esq In Three Volumes		2
8	☐	History Of Tom Jones A Foundling By Henry Fielding Esqr In Three Volumes : Fielding, Henry,	1780	1
9	☐	History Of Tom Jones A Foundling By Henry Fielding Esquire : Fielding, Henry,	1792?	1
10	☐	History Of Tom Jones A Foundling By Henry Fielding Esquire In Three Volumes : Fielding, Henry,	1775	1
11	☐	History Of Tom Jones A Foundling In Four Volumes : Fielding, Henry,	1780	1
12	☐	History Of Tom Jones A Foundling In Four Volumes By Henry Fielding Esq		8
13	☐	History Of Tom Jones A Foundling In Six Volumes By Henry Fielding Esq		2
14	☐	History Of Tom Jones A Foundling In Three Volumes By Henry Fielding Esq		3
15	☐	History Of Tom Jones A Foundling Vol Ii : Fielding, Henry,	1765	1
16	☐	History Of Tom Jones A Foundling With The Life Of The Author By Arthur Murphy In Three Volumes By He : Fielding, Henry,	1766	1
17	☐	History Of Tom Jones French		12

Figure 3.3.   Catalog title search for *History of Tom Jones*. *Source*: University of Denver Penrose Library classic catalog.

```
LEADER 00000cam a2200301I  4500
001    402360
003    OCoLC
005    19810521171204.0
008    720818s1973    nyu       b   |000 1 eng
010    72007320
020    0393043592
020    0303093938 (pbk)
035    fb100061967
040    DLC|cDLC|dm.c.|dDVP
049    DVPP
090    PR3454.T65 1973
100 1  Fielding, Henry,|d1707-1754.
240 00 History of Tom Jones.
245 10 Tom Jones:|ban authoritative text, contemporary reactions,
       criticism,|cedited by Sheridan Baker.
250    [1st ed.]
260    New York :|bNorton|c[1973]
300    viii, 934 p. ;|c23 cm.
490 0  A Norton critical edition.
504    Bibliography: p. 933-934.
700 1  Baker, Sheridan Warner,|d1918-2000.
919    MARCIVE|dSpring 2011
```

Figure 3.4. Modified MARC record for *Tom Jones: An Authoritative Text, Contemporary Reactions, Criticism* highlighting the 240 and 490 fields. *Source*: University of Denver Penrose Library classic catalog.

either print or digital reproductions. Different source texts can produce different content, even though the actual titles may be identical. Because many eighteenth-century titles were published in numerous editions following their initial release, be sure to educate yourself about the scholarly reputation and distinguishing characteristics of particular editions if these details are crucial for your project.

The series note in figure 3.4 indicates that this is a *Norton Critical Edition*, which is often assigned for university courses given its contextual framing, and further searching shows that a second edition was published in 1995. Marcuse recommends the *Wesleyan Edition of the Works of Henry Fielding*, of which *The History of Tom Jones* comprises two volumes of the multivolume *Works*. Since both of these editions are fairly dated, however, you may want to check the bibliographies from current scholarly journal articles and books to identify a more recent standard edition. Conduct a "Primary Subject Work" field search with the terms *tom jones* in *MLA International Bibliography* (described in chapter 4) or use the Library of Congress subject heading "Fielding, Henry, 1707–1754. History of Tom Jones" to search for works of criticism in the library catalog. Many journal articles found with this search cite either the British edition (1974), the Wesleyan edition (1975), or the Modern Library edition (2002), all edited by Fredson Bowers, with an introduction and commentary by Martin C. Battestin, who, notably, wrote the 2004 *ODNB* essay about Fielding. If you come across an unfamiliar edition, you can assess its authority by reading reviews in the literature. Choosing a recent edition published by a university or reputable academic press is also a good strategy for finding a scholarly edition.

If you are unsuccessful in locating a particular work by title after searching your local library, as well as union catalogs, you can try a keyword search with the title words instead. This strategy is usually more effective for shorter works, for instance, poems, that are likely to be anthologized; however, full-length novels and plays may also be reproduced. Searching *duck and thresher's labour*, for example, retrieves the poem in *The Writing of Rural England, 1500–1800* (2003), as well as in an anthology of eighteenth-century poetry, neither of which are found with a title search.

In addition to books, title field searches can be used to locate a specific journal or identify a series. Through a title search, you can determine if your library subscribes to the scholarly journal *Eighteenth-Century Fiction*, or if it has online, print, or microform access to the popular eighteenth-century periodical *The Spectator*. Individual titles from a series, like *AMS Studies in the Eighteenth Century* or *Cambridge Studies in Eighteenth-Century English Literature and Thought*, can be reviewed with a title field search by scanning the results. Depending on the indexing capabilities of your library catalog, you may be able to search series and journal title fields directly, as described in chapter 1. If this is not an option, however, or if you don't see what you are looking for with a periodical title or series title search, try again with a title field search to account for all possibilities. Title searches can also be employed to find materials beyond books and journals, including DVDs, videos, images, databases, Web resources, music, maps, government documents, and archival materials.

SUBJECT SEARCHES

Subject searches enable you to pinpoint materials on specific topics, for instance, the figure of the rake in eighteenth-century literature, female dramatists, the reception of Sterne's *Tristram Shandy*, or imperialism and period travel writing. Subject searches can usually be conducted in two ways: as a keyword search or subject heading search. A keyword search will find books and other materials on a topic based on a match with the terms entered in the search query. This strategy will execute a broad search, since the terms may be present in the author, title, series title, publisher, contents, notes, or subject heading fields within the record. Keyword searches are excellent ways to begin looking for a topic in the library catalog, and you can use the most relevant results to identify the best subject headings affiliated with your topic. Check the records for the books that match your topic most closely, and scan their assigned subject headings, noting those that mirror the subject of your research.

For example, a keyword search of *rake* and literature* retrieves books with the following potentially useful subject headings: "Libertinism in literature," "Libertines in literature," "Seduction in literature," "Characters and characteristics in literature," "Masculinity in literature," and "English literature—18th century—History and criticism." Although any one of these subject headings by itself may be too broad for investigating the rake specifically in the eighteenth century, they can be used in combination with additional keywords for the period (eighteenth, Georgian, Augustan), nationality (British, English, Scottish, England, Scotland, Great Britain), or specific author (Davys, Fielding, Richardson) to refine the search to achieve the desired results. Alternatively, you could simply restructure your keyword search by accounting for the related terms *libertine** or *seduc** or *masculin**.

Keyword searches may also be employed to identify specific types of resources, including criticism, bibliographies, correspondence, biographies, concordances, or diaries. To find particular material types for your author or subject, combine the terms as required: *wollstonecraft and bibliography*, *montagu and correspondence*, *samuel and richardson and biography*, *fielding and diar**, or *bluestocking* and criticism*. The most relevant results from these searches will guide you to the pertinent subject headings for your author or topic: "Wollstonecraft, Mary, 1759–1797—Bibliography," "Montagu, Mary Wortley, Lady, 1689–1762—Correspondence," "Richardson, Samuel, 1689–1761," "Fielding, Henry, 1707–1754—Diaries," "Feminism and literature—Great Britain—History—18th century," "Women and literature—Great Britain—History—18th century," and "Women intellectuals—Great Britain—Biography," among many others. You will note that the Richardson subject heading does not contain a subheading for biography, whereas the "Women intellectuals" subject heading does possess this subheading. Cataloging practices change throughout time, and although older author subject headings may have the biography subheading, more recent biographical works will be listed under the general author subject heading, in addition to, or instead of, a topical biographical designation (e.g., English poets, Scottish novelists, women intellectuals). If you are specifically looking for an author or period figure biography, check the listings under the general heading and, if it exists, biography subheading. To find criticism about a particular author or work, use the standard subheading "Criticism and interpretation" (e.g., "Pope, Alexander, 1688–1744—Criticism and interpretation").

The pattern, and best practice outlined thus far in this section, is to begin with a keyword search and then use the results to help identify the relevant authoritative subject headings for your topic. In contrast to a keyword search, which is dependent on a match with the specific search terms you select, a subject heading search allows you to bring together many of the materials on that topic, since the cataloger has identified the subject content for you through the official headings. If you only searched with the keywords *letters and swift jonathan*, for example, you would miss those relevant works that don't contain the word letters in the record. Conducting a subject heading search instead, however, with "Swift, Jonathan, 1667–1745—Correspondence" or "Swift, Jonathan, 1667–1745—Correspondence—Early works to 1800" will guarantee that you find most works about or collections of his correspondence.

Since subject headings are fairly standardized, you will be able to employ them effectively in many library catalogs, including the union catalog *WorldCat*, described later in this chapter. Keep in mind, however, that you may encounter subject heading variations outside those countries that use *AACR2* standards, or in older records. Subject headings have become more precise and detailed as cataloging practices have evolved over time. Many older works may not even have an assigned subject heading or may have been cataloged with such simple headings as "Criticism," "Women authors," or "Poets, English." Works of fiction typically do not have assigned subject headings, and electronic book catalog records are often missing them as well. Despite these exceptions, subject heading searches remain an effective way to identify resources for literary research. The following is a representative selection of Library of Congress subject headings for eighteenth-century British literature:

English poetry—18th century—History and criticism
English literature—18th century
English fiction—18th century
Women and literature—England—History—18th century
Literature and society—Great Britain—History—18th century
Literature—Societies, etc.—History—18th century
Scriblerus Club
Periodicals—Publishing—Great Britain—History—18th century
Gothic revival (Literature)—Great Britain
Horror tales, English—History and criticism—Theory, etc.
Sentimentalism in literature
Poets, English—18th century—Biography
Women poets, English—18th century

Novelists, English—18th century—Diaries
Novelists, Scottish—18th century
Novelists, Irish—18th century
Authors and readers—Great Britain—History—18th century
Authors and publishers—Great Britain—History—18th century
English drama—18th century
Theater—Great Britain—History—18th century
Theatre—England—History—18th century—Sources
Authors, English—18th century—Correspondence
Montague, Mary Wortley, Lady, 1689–1762
Haywood, Eliza Fowler, 1693?–1756—Bibliography
Richardson, Samuel, 1689–1761—Parodies, imitations, etc.
Swift, Jonathan, 1667–1745—Manuscripts

As you conduct your research, pay attention to and create a list of those subject headings that are relevant for your area of investigation. Familiarize yourself with the standard subject headings and subheadings for your author(s) and topic(s). You can tailor many of the subheadings and formatting practices illustrated in the preceding list and in the examples throughout this chapter to suit your own focus. If certain books are crucial to your research, use their assigned subject headings to find similar works in your library catalog, as well as in the holdings of libraries both nationally and internationally. Browsing the subject heading index for a particular author can be especially informative and is highly recommended. Just as many authors have an authoritative author heading, they may also be assigned a Library of Congress subject heading. These headings typically contain the author's birth and death dates, as well as married names or titles. Author subject headings are employed to search for the author as the principal subject of a work. Not only will the author subject heading display show you the assigned subheadings for your author, enabling you to find bibliographies, correspondence, diaries, criticism, and so forth, it will also reflect the most common areas of research investigating your author and his or her works.

In figure 3.5, the subject heading index is displayed for Tobias Smollett. From the results in this library catalog, we learn that his official heading is "Smollett, Tobias George, 1721–1771." We also discover that areas of concern include several character studies; his knowledge of art, medicine, and literature; and investigations of his style and technique. Conducting a similar search in a union catalog would give us a more accurate representation of the full range of Smollet's subheadings and would be advisable to do for your own author. As you progress with your research, subject headings will be instrumental in helping you conduct a thorough literature review.

| LC Subject Heading ⌄ | smollett | Penrose Library ⌄ | System Sorted ⌄ | Sort |

☐ *Limit search to available items*

〔Search

 Save Marked Records Save All On Page Add Marked to My Lists

Mark	LC Subject Headings (1-21 of 21)	Year	Entries 52 Found
☐	**Smollett T Tobias 1721 1771**		18
☐	**Smollett T Tobias 1721 1771 Aesthetics** : Gibson, William,	c2007	1
☐	**Smollett T Tobias 1721 1771 Bibliography**		4
☐	**Smollett T Tobias 1721 1771 Characters Artists** : Gibson, William,	c2007	1
☐	**Smollett T Tobias 1721 1771 Characters Men** : Skinner, John,	c1996	1
☐	**Smollett T Tobias 1721 1771 Characters Women**		2
☐	**Smollett T Tobias 1721 1771 Correspondence** : Smollett, T.	1766	1
☐	**Smollett T Tobias 1721 1771 Criticism And Interpretation**		7
☐	**Smollett T Tobias 1721 1771 Criticism And Interpretation History 18th Century** : Donoghue, Frank,	1996	1
☐	**Smollett T Tobias 1721 1771 Expedition Of Humphry Clinker** : Sekora, John.	c1977	1
☐	**Smollett T Tobias 1721 1771 Knowledge Anatomy** : Douglas, Aileen,	1995	1
☐	**Smollett T Tobias 1721 1771 Knowledge Art** : Gibson, William,	c2007	1
☐	**Smollett T Tobias 1721 1771 Knowledge Literature** : Basker, James G.	c1988	1
☐	**Smollett T Tobias 1721 1771 Knowledge Medicine** : Douglas, Aileen,	1995	1
☐	**Smollett T Tobias 1721 1771 Portraits**		3
☐	**Smollett T Tobias 1721 1771 Style** : Grant, Damian.	c1977	1
☐	**Smollett T Tobias 1721 1771 Technique** : Skinner, John,	c1996	1

Figure 3.5. Modified catalog record for Smollett as the Library of Congress subject heading. *Source*: University of Denver, Penrose Library classic catalog.

CALL NUMBERS AND THE (CHANGING) ART OF BROWSING

Much in the manner of subject headings, Library of Congress call numbers can also help you identify books on similar subjects. In fact, the classification system is designed to facilitate this very process by grouping books and other materials about like subjects together. You've probably noticed that when you retrieve a book from the library shelf, the books surrounding your desired title address the works by the same author, or congruent themes. If you have been studying British literature for some time, you are already aware that English authors and literary subjects are classed in the PRs, with different call number ranges assigned to specific authors. Canonical authors, in particular, were originally awarded generous call number ranges when the classification outline was developed, whereas newer figures of literary attention may be squeezed in to narrower perimeters.

For example, Henry Fielding is given the range PR3450.D62-3458, but his sister, Sarah Fielding, PR3459.F3. The *Library of Congress Classification Outline* is available online at www.loc.gov/catdir/cpso/lcco. Language and literature is assigned to class P, while PN covers literature generally, PR is for English literature, and PS is for American literature. You may want to take some time to review the classification outline specifically for PR, so that you are familiar with the ranges assigned to literary time periods, with PR441-449 for the eighteenth century and PR3291-3785 for the seventeenth and eighteenth centuries, and to genres, by period and generally. Other areas might also be relevant, both within literature and in other subjects, including philosophy, history, social history, music, art, or science, depending on your individual research project. Although Library of Congress classification is the predominant classification scheme used by academic libraries in the United States, you may also encounter Dewey Decimal classification, in which literature is found in the 800s.

Any time you find a relevant book, it will also be worthwhile to browse the shelf for other potentially relevant titles. Browsing is an important part of literary research, and it can be just as fruitful as searching in a catalog or database. Sometimes the shelf holds an incredibly pertinent book that was missed in your initial online search. Browsing the library shelves offers the additional advantage of being able to examine the books more closely than is possible through the library catalog. You can check the table of contents, thumb through the pages, look for specific references in the index, and review the notes and bibliography, options that might not be possible in the library record.

As libraries are challenged by space restraints and thus are storing more books in closed stacks or off-site facilities, and as they incorporate more electronic books into their collections, the nature of browsing the shelves is in transition. Humanities scholars, in particular, are noted for their preferences for browsing through collections, and so libraries are responding with alternative browsing options that take into account the search techniques of different disciplines. Many library catalogs feature the opportunity to browse by call number online, so that you can still scan the titles shelved adjacently. Some catalogs also provide links to Google Books, so that you can preview the contents of books online, although at this time it is not possible to view the index. In many ways, virtual browsing presents a truer picture of the collection than going to the physical shelves, since it can represent those titles that are currently checked out or are in electronic format or microformat, neither of which would actually be on the shelf if you went to the stacks. Browsing is an integral part of the research process, and it should be employed both by accessing the physical shelves, if possible, and by using the newer browsing capabilities of online catalogs, so that the entire collection is available for you to discover.

UNION CATALOGS

Center for Research Libraries. www.crl.edu (accessed 27 August 2012).
Copac. www.copac.ac.uk (accessed 24 August 2012).

Library of Congress and the National Union Catalog Subcommittee of the Resources Committee of the Resources and Technical Services Division, American Library Association. *National Union Catalog, Pre-1956 Imprints: A Cumulative Author List Representing Library of Congress Printed Cards and Titles Reported by Other American Libraries.* 754 vols. London: Mansell, 1968–1981.

WorldCat. OCLC. www.oclc.org/worldcat.

WorldCat.org. www.worldcat.org (accessed 24 August 2012).

A union catalog represents the collective holdings of multiple participating libraries, often either at the local, state, regional, national, or even international levels. Many scholars are familiar with online union catalogs, since it is increasingly common for libraries to form consortia within their state or region to make their collections available to a wider audience. Indeed, the advantage of consulting a union catalog is that you can search numerous bibliographic records through one interface and identify potentially relevant items for your research from collections beyond that of your own library, including many significant national, university, and special library holdings. Although most researchers likely already have some experience with an online local or regional union catalog, there are also print union catalogs that may still be essential for some literary projects; the main one described here is the *National Union Catalog, Pre-1956 Imprints.*

WorldCat is probably the best-known and certainly the largest union catalog. This subscription database, developed by the Online Computer Library Center (OCLC), currently boasts more than 1 billion items cataloged by 72,000 member libraries from around the world. *WorldCat* includes books, journals, newspapers, musical scores, DVDs, archival material, microforms, maps, sound and video recordings, electronic resources, websites, and digital objects, among many other formats, in more than 470 languages and dialects. Continually growing, *WorldCat* is the powerhouse resource for leveraging the collections of libraries worldwide. Even given its impressive size, however, it is important to note that it only represents reported holdings from its member libraries, but not every item in their individual collections.

WorldCat was designed as a tool for cooperative cataloging, and this initial purpose is reflected in the advanced search interface, which presents an extensive range of field options. For example, the author field can be further specified as author phrase, corporate and conference name or phrase, and personal name or name phrase. In addition to author, you can search by keyword, access method, accession number, language phrase, material type, musical composition, notes/comments, publisher, publisher location, standard number, subject, title, or series title. The subject field is another that contains specific designations, including subject phrase, descriptor, genre/

form, geographic coverage, named corporation and conference, and named person. Searches can then be limited by year, language, number of holding libraries, material type (e.g., books, serial publications, archival materials, Internet resources), and availability. Such control over your search allows you to construct very specific queries. If you wanted to create an initial list of eighteenth-century serials published in Edinburgh, you could select Edinburgh as place of publication and limit to serials as the material type, with a publication date between 1700 and 1800. This search retrieves 638 records, beginning with the *Transactions of the Royal Society of Edinburgh* as the most widely held, and proceeding to such titles as *The Scots Magazine*, the *Edinburgh Weekly Review*, *The Weekly Magazine*, or *Edinburgh Amusement*, *The Lounger*, and the *Caledonian Mercury*.

Although this list would be a good start, chapter 6 gives further advice on how to identify period journals and newspapers. You may see separate bibliographic records for items that appear to be the same in your results. This often happens because one library has cataloged the item slightly differently than another. Search results are normally displayed in order of items held by the most libraries, but you can change the display to a relevance, date, or accession number ranking instead.

Searching the numerous records available through *WorldCat* enables you to conduct the widest survey possible through one interface for resources about particular authors and subjects, as well as for identifying variant editions and formats of the same work. These latter searches can be conducted up front with an author and title search, or you can use the "Find Related" feature from a specific bibliographic record, which offers a link to search for alternative versions. For example, a search for *pix* as author and *double distress* as title finds eighteen records for different formats of Mary Pix's play *The Double Distress. A Tragedy*, published in 1701, including microform, book, and electronic versions.

Daniel Defoe's successful novel *Robinson Crusoe* appeared in four editions between April and August of 1719.[1] If you wanted to compare the print originals of these different editions, you would search for *defoe* as author, *robinson crusoe* as title, limit to the year *1719*, check "Books," and select "not Microform" from the "Subtype limits" drop-down format options. Since the sequel *Farther Adventures of Robinson Crusoe* was also published in August of that year, you can refine your search by adding "not" to the interface and typing *farther* in the title field if you want to exclude the sequel from your results. Figure 3.6 illustrates a record for the third edition, containing important details for this type of textual investigation. You will notice that the edition is listed in the main citation, as well as in the "Publication" field. The "Note(s)" field provides information about the engraving and reveals

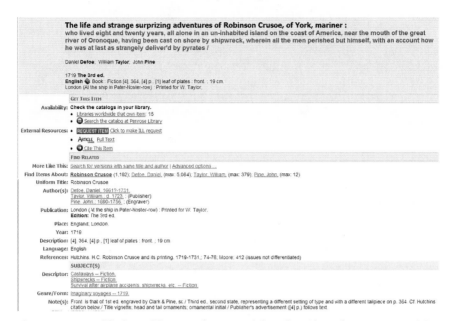

The life and strange surprizing adventures of Robinson Crusoe, of York, mariner :
who lived eight and twenty years, all alone in an un-inhabited island on the coast of America, near the mouth of the great river of Oronoque, having been cast on shore by shipwreck, wherein all the men perished but himself, with an account how he was at last as strangely deliver'd by pyrates /

Daniel **Defoe**; William **Taylor**; John **Pine**

1719 **The 3rd ed.**
English 🌐 Book : Fiction [4], 364, [4] p. : [1] leaf of plates : front. ; 19 cm.
London (At the ship in Pater-Noster-row) : Printed for W. Taylor.

GET THIS ITEM
Availability: **Check the catalogs in your library.**
  • Libraries worldwide that own item: 15
  • 🔍 Search the catalog at Penrose Library
External Resources: • **REQUEST ITEM** Click to make ILL request
  • ARTICLE Full Text
  • ⊙ Cite This Item

FIND RELATED
More Like This: Search for versions with same title and author | Advanced options...
Find Items About: **Robinson Crusoe** (1,192); Defoe, Daniel. (max: 5,084); Taylor, William. (max: 379); Pine, John. (max: 12)
Uniform Title: Robinson Crusoe
Author(s): Defoe, Daniel, 1661?-1731.
  Taylor, William ; d. 1723. ; (Publisher)
  Pine, John ; 1690-1756. ; (Engraver)
Publication: London (At the ship in Pater-Noster-row) : Printed for W. Taylor.
  Edition: The 3rd ed.
Place: England; London.
Year: 1719
Description: [4], 364, [4] p. ; [1] leaf of plates : front. ; 19 cm.
Language: English
References: Hutchins, H.C. Robinson Crusoe and its printing, 1719-1731.; 74-76; Moore; 412 (issues not differentiated)
SUBJECT(S)
Descriptor: Castaways -- Fiction.
  Shipwrecks -- Fiction.
  Survival after airplane accidents, shipwrecks, etc. -- Fiction.
Genre/Form: Imaginary voyages -- 1719.
Note(s): Front. is that of 1st ed. engraved by Clark & Pine, sc./ Third ed., second state, representing a different setting of type and with a different tailpiece on p. 364. Cf. Hutchins citation below./ Title vignette; head and tail ornaments; ornamental initial / Publisher's advertisement ([4] p.) follows text

Figure 3.6. Modified WorldCat catalog record for *The Life and Strange Surprizing Adventures of Robinson Crusoe, of York, Mariner,* 1719, 3rd edition. *Source*: WorldCat, via FirstSearch.

that this copy represents the second state (of the third edition) with a different type and tailpiece. References to Hutchins's study on the printing history of *Robinson Crusoe* from 1719 to 1731 could be valuable for your research, and searching Google for this title shows that it is available online via HathiTrust Digital Library. The "Find Related" section lets you look for other resources about the book, author, publisher, or engraver, essentially conducting a subject search on these topics.

Although there are fifteen libraries that hold copies of this particular book, it is unlikely that they would lend the work through interlibrary loan. If you are unable to travel to any of the holding libraries, then you may want to consider changing the search query so that microform and digital formats could be identified as surrogates, as well as checking *ECCO* directly. Chapter 6 describes the principal digital and microform collections available for eighteenth-century British literature and offers specific search strategies for finding works in these formats. For books whose access isn't restricted to special collections, you can use the interlibrary loan link to have them delivered to your home library. Finally, the "Accession number" field gives a unique OCLC number that will enable you to get back to this particular record again—a sometimes problematic feat since, as previously mentioned, slight variations in cataloging can result in different records for the same title. *WorldCat's* extensive collections, multiple index fields, and detailed search interface offer the researcher an unparalleled resource that will be instrumental in supporting both broad literature reviews, as well as in identifying specific titles for eighteenth-century literary projects.

As of summer 2012, *WorldCat* has announced plans to change its search interface. Be sure to check the *WorldCat* website or consult with your reference librarian to stay informed about developments that may impact searching this important resource.

If your institution doesn't subscribe to *WorldCat*, however, you can still use the publicly available version known as ***WorldCat.org***. Designed primarily to bring an awareness of library collections to Internet searchers, *World-Cat.org* features basic and advanced search interfaces that have fewer options than those found in the subscription database. The "Advanced Search" offers searching by keyword, author, title, subject, journal source, ISBN/ISSN, and accession number, with limits by year, audience, content, format, and language. Once you have conducted your search, the resulting records will be in abbreviated form compared to the detailed subscription *WorldCat* record. Nevertheless, many of the fields may still be present. Figure 3.7 shows that the *WorldCat.org* record for the 1719 third edition of *Robinson Crusoe* still contains the valuable notes, but not the references field. You will notice that this record also provides a link to search for the book in a local area library by entering your zip code, with suggested libraries displayed in descending

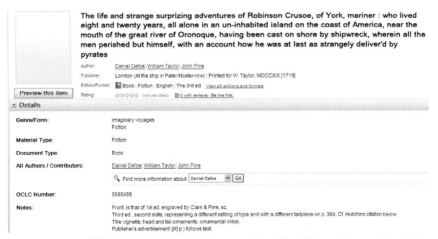

Figure 3.7.   Modified WorldCat.org catalog record for *The Life and Strange Surprising Adventures of Robinson Crusoe, of York, Mariner*, **1719, 3rd edition.** *Source*: **WorldCat .org.**

proximity. Be aware that only libraries that maintain a current subscription to *WorldCat* will have their holdings displayed. *WorldCat.org* also promotes access to its collections through a mobile phone app. Although *WorldCat.org* can be used effectively for scholarly research, it does not have the sophisticated search capabilities and detailed bibliographic records of the subscription version.

Copac serves as the online union catalog to many of the national and university library collections, and to some special library collections in the United Kingdom. This freely available catalog currently comprises 36 million records drawn from the British Library; the National Library of Scotland; the National Library of Wales; university libraries at Cambridge, Oxford, Aberdeen, Birmingham, Bristol, Cardiff, Durham, Edinburgh, Glasgow, Leeds, Liverpool, Manchester, Newcastle, Nottingham, St. Andrews, Sheffield, Southampton, Trinity College Dublin, University College London, and Warwick; and such special libraries as the Guildhall Library, the Imperial War Museum, Royal Society, Windsor Castle, Society of Antiquaries of London, National Portrait Gallery, Victoria and Albert National Art Library, and the Wellcome Library, as just a few examples. For a complete list of participating libraries, as well as forthcoming partners, please consult the website.

Books are by far the most commonly represented item in the catalog; however, there are also periodicals, printed and recorded music, videos, and electronic materials dating from the thirteenth century to the present. Approximately one-third of the contents were published after 1980, but, with the efforts of many conversion projects, now about one-quarter of the materials were published before 1900. Foreign-language materials are also well represented. As with *WorldCat*, it is important to understand that *Copac* offers access only to its member libraries' online catalogs, not their entire holdings. To determine what items are covered by each library's online catalog or are still listed only in print catalogs or finding aids, you will need to check each individual library's website.

To search *Copac*, you can either enter directly into the catalog, or you can first sign up for an account; this latter option will enable you to create online bibliographies, save your search history, and possibly search your institutional library catalog simultaneously. The search interface is fairly straightforward, and the "Main Search" provides more specific field and limiting options. Users can search by author/editor, title keywords, publisher, ISBN/ISSN, subject, or keyword, and limit by date and place of publication, material type (e.g., journals and periodicals, sound recordings, visual materials), language, and individual library. Subject searches (as well as keyword searches) will automatically search for both singular and plural forms of your terms (even mouse and mice), and will also search within the title and content notes, since not every record contains an assigned subject heading. Many records employ American terminology and spellings, so it is recommended to search both British and American variants. For example, a subject search with the term *colonization* (12,883 results), limited to the English language, retrieves different results than *colonisation* (3,190 results). If we conduct an author search for *mary pix*, *Copac* finds 317 matching records, which are displayed with brief citations alphabetically by title and then by date. The full records typically give edition, publisher, physical description, notes, subject headings, additional names, and links to holding libraries. Borrowing items found through *Copac* will likely not be as easy as with *WorldCat* titles, but if you find unique titles here, don't hesitate to contact your interlibrary loan office to determine if obtaining a copy is possible. You can also check with your reference librarian to establish whether a digital or microform copy might be available as a surrogate, or contact the holding library directly to inquire what other options might be pursued.

Sporting a title more typical of the early modern period rather than of the twentieth century, the ***National Union Catalog, Pre-1956 Imprints: A Cumulative Author List Representing Library of Congress Printed Cards and Titles Reported by Other American Libraries*** is also, thankfully, referred to as *Mansell* or *NUC*. This iconic reference work is the subject of frequent listserv debates about whether it should be kept in the library or discarded, since some argue that the records it contains are duplicated online. Two studies have documented, however, that approximately 25 percent of the items in the *NUC* are not included in *WorldCat*, thus emphasizing the continued value of this resource to scholars and literary research.[2] The *NUC* is especially useful for identifying editions of older works that may be part of a library's collection but not noted in their online catalog.

If your library has yet to move it to storage, the *NUC's* 754 volumes make an impressive statement on the library's shelves. As the title indicates, the *NUC* reproduces Library of Congress printed catalog cards, in addition to catalog cards for titles from other libraries in the United States and Canada, arranged by author, by title for anonymous works only, and occasionally by editor for anthologies and collections. Canonical authors, in particular, may have entries arranged by categories, rather than listed only alphabetically by title. Henry Fielding, for example, has works organized by 1) Collected works (by language and imprint date), 2) Selected works (alphabetically by title), 3) Selections (also alphabetically), and 4) Individual works and all other entries (alphabetically except for works that have variant titles or that have been translated—these are grouped under a standard title). Further subdivisions are arranged by language and imprint date. Title entries may vary from detailed descriptions to a brief citation and contain the code for libraries that reported holding a copy. The first library listed is typically the one that contributed the catalog information. Because the *NUC* was compiled from the records of many libraries, a title record with any variation is listed as if it were a separate edition. Due to this practice, it is important to be aware that a listed card may not, in fact, represent a distinct work. Any scholar whose research concerns comparisons between editions will want to consult the *NUC* to be certain to identify all potentially relevant works.

Although the **Center for Research Libraries** (**CRL**) is not really a union catalog; this consortium of U.S. and Canadian academic and research libraries acts as a central institution that builds collections that support the research needs of its members. Many unique items and specialized collections, especially runs of older and international periodicals, are part of the CRL holdings. If your library is a member, you will have access to the collections either through interlibrary loan or in digital formats and can identify relevant materials by searching the online catalog or finding CRL items in *WorldCat*. One of the digital collections that might be of interest for eighteenth-century research is the *Digital South Asia Library* of books, journals, maps, and more dating from the colonial period through the present; however, other digital collections, for instance, *African Newspapers* and *Latin American Newspapers*, begin with the early nineteenth century, for those scholars investigating authors and/or topics that cross into that period.

NATIONAL LIBRARY CATALOGS

Catalogue. National Library of Ireland/Leabharlann Náisiúnta na hÉierann. catalogue.nli.ie (accessed 31 July 2012).

Full Catalogue. National Library of Wales/Llyfrgell Genedlaethol Cymru. cat.llgc.org.uk (accessed 31 July 2012).

Library of Congress Online Catalog. catalog.loc.gov (accessed 1 August 2012).

Main Catalogue. British Library. explore.bl.uk/primo_library/libweb/action/search.do?vid=BLVU1 (accessed 1 August 2012).

Main Catalogue. National Library of Scotland/Leabharlann Nàiseanta na h-Alba. main-cat.nls.uk/vwebv/searchBasic?sk=nls_en (accessed 31 July 2012).

Search Our Catalogue, Archives and Manuscripts. British Library. search archives.bl.uk (accessed 1 August 2012).

In addition to searching for items in the union catalogs, you may also want to search directly within a specific national library catalog, especially to identify unique items that may not yet have been included in the collaborative resource. Since a national library receives by legal deposit every title published by its country, and also because it typically collects extensively in all subject areas, a national library catalog will enable you to conduct a broad search for material that matches your research project. Keep in mind, however, that a national library also functions as a library of "last resort"—that is, they will usually not lend their materials if the same title can be borrowed from another library. Be sure to follow up with your reference librarian or interlibrary loan service if you have questions about accessing a particular resource from a national library collection. With the advent of scanning services, however, even national libraries are providing document delivery for selected items.

Literary scholars may think nostalgically about the British Museum and its Department of Printed Books, founded in 1753, which, in many ways, functioned as the national library for years. Central to the museum was the famous domed reading room that, since its opening in 1857, was the working location for many well-known nineteenth- and twentieth-century authors. The British Library, however, wasn't officially established until 1972, when Parliament passed the British Library Act. This legislation originally combined the library departments of the British Museum, the National Central Library, and the National Lending Library for Science and Technology, and then expanded to include the British National Bibliography and the Office for Scientific and Technical Information (1974), the India Office Library and Records (1982), and the British Institute of Recorded Sound (1983).[3]

Still treasured for its impressive collections, the British Library possesses approximately 14 million books; 920,000 journal and newspaper titles; 3 million sound recordings; and significant collections of manuscripts, printed music, and more. The *Main Catalogue* is the primary portal to most of these holdings, but there are also online and printed catalogues for specialized collections, including the *Search Our Catalogue, Archives and Manuscripts*, the *English Short Title Catalogue* (discussed in chapter 4), the *India Office Select Materials* catalog, and the *Sloan Printed Books Catalogue*, as just a few examples. The "Advanced Search" interface permits searching by keyword or phrase anywhere in the record, or in the title or author fields, by publication year, subject, description, place name, map scale, and abstract, with specific limiters for material type and scope. Results will be displayed in relevancy ranking, with facets to refine your search on the left toolbar. You can then select records to view; print; e-mail; send to "My workspace"; or export to RefWorks, EndNote, or Connotea. The "I want it" link will initiate a request to have the item delivered to the Reading Room (for registered readers only) or obtain a document delivery copy for a fee.

In 2009, the British Library began developing a new online catalog, *Search Our Catalogues, Archives and Manuscripts*, which facilitates searching both the archives and manuscripts collections in one catalog for the first time, and which supersedes the *Manuscripts Catalogue*. Completed in the summer of 2012, the catalog's "Advanced Search" interface enables searching anywhere in the record, as well as in the description, name, place, subject, reference code, creation date, and user tags fields. If you are particularly interested in identifying material from the British Library's manuscripts and archives holdings that has been digitized, then search the companion *Digitised Manuscripts* website (www.bl.uk/manuscripts), which features field searching by keyword, date, manuscript number, author/scribe, provenance/acquisition, and bibliography.

Although it can't claim an official designation, the Library of Congress nevertheless functions in every way as the national library of the United States. Established to serve Congress in 1800, the Library of Congress is now one of the largest libraries in the world, holding more than 147 million items, comprised of more than 33 million books and other print material in 470 languages and 63 million manuscripts, in addition to sound recordings, photographs, maps, films, and more. The **Library of Congress Online Catalog** features both "Basic" and "Guided Search" interfaces. In the "Basic" option you can search by ISBN, ISSN, or LCCN; search by keyword in the title, author/creator, subject, and series/uniform title fields; browse by these fields; or browse by call number. The search tips below the interface outline sample searches and note if limits are available. The "Guided Search" is set up for Boolean operators and contains additional field options, including the notes, geographic subject heading, content notes, or holdings fields; this search can be limited by date, language, type (e.g., cartographic material, manuscript material, serial), location, and place of publication. Separate online catalogs search the prints and photographs and audio recordings collections. Scholars will want to utilize the Library of Congress's extensive resources to identify materials not found in other collections.

Even though the majority of their holdings can be discovered through *Copac*, scholars with particular interests in the literatures of Wales and Scotland may want to search those national libraries separately. The National Library of Wales proudly calls itself "one of the great libraries of the world." The library certainly holds an impressive range of materials, including the Welsh Literature Archive and about 25,000 manuscripts, dating from 113 A.D. to 2004. The **Full Catalogue** facilitates searching for most of the library's collections, apart from a few archives and manuscripts that must be searched separately. Users can search by keywords anywhere, or in the author, title, subject, or ISBN or ISSN fields, or use the "Expert" interface for command searching. The "Digital Mirror" section is a gateway to the library's digital projects, namely *Welsh Ballads Online* (cat.llgc.org.uk/cgi-bin/gw/ chameleon?skin=baledi&lng=en), which presents 4,000 ballads from the eighteenth and nineteenth centuries, and *Portread* (www.llgc.org.uk/index .php?id=4064), a collection of more than 65,000 Welsh portraits.

Equally as significant is the National Library of Scotland, which is the focal point for Scottish studies. The **Main Catalogue** has an "Advanced Search" that features searching by keyword anywhere in the record, or in fourteen fields, with limits for year, collection, material type, place, and language. The library's digital resources (digital.nls.uk/gallery.cfm) encompass maps of Scotland from 1560 to 1928, *The Word on the Street* ballad collection (described in chapter 10), Robert Burns materials, and *Early Gaelic Book Collections*, as a few examples.

Scholars of Irish literature will find the National Library of Ireland an important resource. The library's website offers an overview of its collections, comprising books, periodicals, manuscripts, newspapers, photographs, prints, ephemera, music, maps, digital collections, and more, that represent Ireland's history and heritage. The library **Catalogue** provides access to materials cataloged after 1990 (and selected older content), which can be searched by keywords in all fields, title, author, subject, call number, ISBN/ISSN, and publisher, with an option to show only digital items. Separate catalogs cover newspapers, Irish manuscripts, and articles in Irish periodicals.

CONCLUSION

Although it is undergoing significant changes, the library catalog is still the primary means of discovering items in the library's collections. Access by author and title are likely to continue in importance, but subject access is already impacted by the integration of numerous electronic book records without Library of Congress subject headings, the introduction of Google-like interfaces, and simultaneous catalog and database searching. Keyword, rather than subject heading searches, will be the prominent means of finding relevant books, especially as the full text, rather than just the surrogate record, becomes searchable. Until that transition is complete, a savvy researcher will employ traditional field searches, including relevant subject headings, in conjunction with keyword searches, so that the broadest review is conducted. Building upon its traditional gateway role, the library catalog, whether a local, national, or consortial endeavor, truly makes the world's intellectual heritage available as never before.

NOTES

1. Paula R. Backscheider, "Defoe, Daniel (1660?–1731)," in *Oxford Dictionary of National Biography*, online edition ed. Lawrence Goldman (Oxford, UK: Oxford University Press, 2004), www.oxforddnb.com/view/article/7421.

2. Jeffrey Beall and Karen Kafadar, "The Proportion of *NUC Pre-1956* Titles Represented in OCLC WorldCat," *College and Research Libraries* 66, no. 5 (September 2005): 431–35; Christine DeZelar-Tiedman, "The Proportion of *NUC Pre-56* Titles Represented in *RLIN* and OCLC Databases Compared: A Follow-up to the Beall/Kafadar Study," *College and Research Libraries* 69, no. 5 (September 2008): 401–6.

3. British Library, "History of the British Library," *British Library*, www.bl.uk/aboutus/quickinfo/facts/history.

Chapter Four

Print and Electronic Bibliographies, Indexes, and Annual Reviews

The sources described in this chapter will be integral to your research, since bibliographies and indexes are the primary tools (in conjunction with the library catalog) for indentifying literary texts and scholarship. A bibliography is essentially a list of publications, although it may include unpublished sources like manuscripts, compiled under an explicit organizing principle, for example, all works written by a particular author, or a selection of sources about eighteenth-century literary clubs. Indexes, on the other hand, provide a key to the contents of select materials (from one or more books to thousands of journals) arranged by such access points as author, title, or subject. The two major bibliographies for conducting literary research are the *Modern Language Association International Bibliography of Books and Articles on the Modern Languages and Literatures* and the *Annual Bibliography of English Language and Literature*, more commonly known by their acronyms, *MLAIB* (or *MLA International Bibliography*) and *ABELL*. Even though these sources originated as traditional print bibliographies, their current incarnation as electronic, searchable databases, to some extent, blurs their original purpose and function, so that they simultaneously compile relevant material and also supply multiple entry points to their contents.

Bibliographies range from a brief list of sources at the conclusion of an article or book to multivolume monograph endeavors or enormous databases. No matter what size or format, they all present basic publication information about the items that fall within their scope. Bibliographies are typically categorized as either analytic or enumerative. The analytic bibliography, also referred to as critical or descriptive, is concerned with describing the physical characteristics of each item, for instance, the size, paper, binding, and watermarks, and may also include details about its production if it is a published book. For research focused on differences between specific editions, for example, the analytic bibliography will be essential. Enumerative bibliographies are more common; they present the bibliographic rather than physical details of the item, and they may be arranged chronologically or by author, title, or subject. Annotated bibliographies, in turn, feature a summary of each item's contents.

After determining the type of bibliography at hand, the next step is to ascertain its scope and learn whether it attempts to be comprehensive or selective in its coverage. For those bibliographies not listed in this chapter, the introduction, front matter, or "About" section should reveal the compiler or editor's selection guidelines, a strategy that will be useful when a resource is unfamiliar. Comprehensive bibliographies typically, but not exclusively, focus on primary materials, especially in cases where there are a finite number of items that could fall within the boundaries for inclusion. Such a bibliography might list all known works by a deceased author, including manuscripts, letters, editions, and other printed materials, or could have such grand aspirations as the *English Short Title Catalogue*, which attempts to record all books printed in the British Isles and its colonies in any language, in addition to books printed in English anywhere in the world between 1475 and 1800.

Many other bibliographies concentrate on selected items, choosing materials that match a particular subject matter (or other selection criteria), like national literatures, literary periods or movements, genres, or authors. These selective bibliographies can cover either or both primary and secondary sources. *MLAIB*, for example, has a broad but still selective scope—literary criticism on all modern languages and literatures, including books, book chapters, journal articles, and dissertations, whereas *The First Gothics: A Critical Guide to the English Gothic Novel* concentrates more narrowly on 500 novels published between particular dates. Again, it is important to understand the scope and selection criteria of the bibliography you are examining, so that you can find those best suited to your research project.

The annual review is a specific type of bibliography that typically summarizes and evaluates scholarship published within the preceding year. Central to English literature in general, the *Year's Work in English Studies* is valuable for identifying important scholarly contributions to the field and highlighting literary trends overall, as well as gaps in research. The *ECCB: The Eighteenth Century Current Bibliography* provides an overview of recent scholarship concerned with the period. Individual journals often publish annual reviews; *SEL: Studies in English Literature* features "Recent Studies in the Restoration and Eighteenth Century" in its Summer issue, and several period author journals also offer similar scholarly overviews.

As many bibliographies are increasingly presented in online formats, the distinctions between bibliographies and indexes are becoming less obvious. Both *MLAIB* and *ABELL* are bibliographies and indexes simultaneously, as previously mentioned, since they provide bibliographic information about selected items and also offer access to the contents of books and journals by author, title, and assigned subject headings. Although not considered an index in the traditional sense, many full-text journal databases, like *JSTOR, Project Muse,* and *Periodicals Archive Online,* function in the same way, by enabling scholars to discover journal contents by multiple access points. For some, *Google Scholar* may be considered the ultimate discovery tool, even though it isn't particularly strong in humanities sources. Despite its limited field searching and no assigned subject headings, in compensation, it searches the full text of numerous scholarly journal articles and books across disciplines, helping scholars find relevant material buried within their contents.

This chapter introduces the standard bibliographies for general literary study, as well as selected specialized bibliographies for eighteenth-century literature, genres, and authors. We also present strategies for creating and organizing your own author-centered bibliography, using Penelope Aubin as an example. Understanding the general structure and purpose of a bibliography, as well as the types of bibliographies available, will provide a solid framework for your research endeavors.

GENERAL LITERARY BIBLIOGRAPHIES

Annual Bibliography of English Language and Literature. Leeds, West Yorkshire, UK: Maney Publishing for the Modern Humanities Research Association, 1921– . Annual. www.chadwyck.com.

Bateson, F. W., ed. *Cambridge Bibliography of English Literature.* 5 vols. Cambridge, UK: Cambridge University Press, 1940. With a supplement edited by George Watson, 1957.

JSTOR: The Scholarly Journal Archive. JSTOR. www.jstor.org.

MLA International Bibliography of Books and Articles on the Modern Languages and Literatures. New York: Modern Language Association of America, 1922– . Annual. Check www.mla.org/bib_electronic for a list of online vendors.

Periodicals Archive Online. Ann Arbor, MI: ProQuest/Chadwyck-Healey. pao.chadwyck.com.

Periodicals Index Online. Ann Arbor, MI: ProQuest/Chadwyck-Healey. pio .chadwyck.com.

Project Muse. Baltimore, MD: Johns Hopkins University Press. muse.jhu
    .edu.
Shattock, Joanne, ed. *The Cambridge Bibliography of English Literature*, 3rd
    ed. New York: Cambridge University Press, 1999– .
Watson, George, ed. *The New Cambridge Bibliography of English Literature*,
    2nd ed. Cambridge, UK: Cambridge University Press, 1971.
Year's Work in English Studies. Oxford, UK: Oxford University Press, 1921– .
    Annual. www3.oup.co.uk/ywes.

Most academic disciplines have their own subject-oriented bibliography that
was developed in tandem with the field. As previously stated, English literature is distinguished by two principal bibliographies, *MLAIB* and *ABELL*,
both of which originated in the early twentieth century. Although they were
initially designed to serve two separate professional audiences, American and
British, respectively, together these bibliographies meet the current needs of
English literary scholars worldwide.

The **MLA International Bibliography** (**MLAIB**) began in 1921 as an
annual narrative publication in the association's flagship journal, *PMLA:
Publications of the Modern Language Association*. From 1921 until 1955,
it was known as the "American Bibliography," since it focused almost exclusively on scholarship by Americans about English, American, Germanic,
and Romance languages and literatures. In 1956, however, it changed to an
international scope and included work by scholars outside the United States.
The bibliography continued to be published in *PMLA* until 1968. If you are
curious about the early manifestation of *MLAIB*, you can check the reprinted
bibliographies that were published as separate volumes, many of which are
owned by academic libraries, or consult early issues of *PMLA* in *JSTOR*.

After 1968, the bibliography became a freestanding publication, organized
in four volumes, each dedicated to the following subject areas: 1) General,
English, American, Medieval and Neo-Latin, and Celtic literatures; 2) European, Asian, African, and Latin American literatures; 3) linguistics; and
4) pedagogy in foreign languages compiled by the American Council on the
Teaching of Foreign Languages. The volumes contained their own tables of
contents and author/editor/compiler indexes. Folklore was added in 1981, and
the author and subject indexes were compiled for the entire bibliography in
a separate volume.

Published exclusively online since 2008, today *MLAIB* encompasses both
print and electronic books, book chapters, journal articles (print and electronic), dissertations, and selected scholarly websites; however, it does not
include book reviews. The bibliography's scope is extensive, covering all
languages and literatures, linguistics, folklore, and topics related to literature,

including literary theory and criticism, rhetoric and composition, pedagogy, film, printing and publishing, and more. The *MLAIB* website presents a detailed overview of the contents and also notes exceptions, for example, those works that focus only on Classical Greek and Latin literatures, as well as the Bible or Koran, without reference to other literatures or languages. Although the print bibliography started indexing materials published in 1921, the online version initiates coverage in 1926 (with some exceptions for selected titles) through the present, and it is updated ten times a year. According to the website, more than 66,000 books and journal articles are indexed each year, a phenomenal achievement that demonstrates the impressive range and value of this resource. Your library may subscribe to *MLAIB* offered by one of several vendors; the following description is based on the EBSCO version. For an overview and comparison of the different platforms, see www.mla .org/bib_dist_comparison.

In addition to the numerous materials indexed, one of the main strengths of *MLAIB* is the level of indexing for each item and the well-developed thesaurus of subject terms. The bibliography may be searched through a basic or advanced interface and recognizes Boolean operators, truncation, and nesting. Although either interface permits keyword searching (which will look for your terms throughout the entire record), you may want to take advantage of the "Advanced Search" for its numerous field options (more than thirty available depending on the vendor) to conduct more precise searches. The field searches are especially useful when refining inquiries to one or more of the assigned general subject areas, which include "Subject Literature," "Period," "Primary Subject Author," "Primary Subject Work," and "Genre" categories, or by using the thesaurus subject terms. Other field options include dissertation information, folklore topic, linguistics topic, literary technique, literature topic, media, scholarly theory or discipline, and table of contents, in addition to standard fields for author, title, editor(s), language, date, publication information, and so forth. Searches can be constructed with multiple fields and limited by publication type (book, chapter, journal article, website), date, language, genre, and time period, or further limited to retrieve only peer-reviewed journals or electronic publications, or to exclude dissertations from the results.

You will want to consult both the online thesaurus and the "Names as Subjects" index to determine the authoritative descriptors and headings for the topics and authors pertinent to your research. The "MLA Thesaurus" contains more than 50,000 terms to standardize literary, languages, linguistics, and folklore subjects throughout the bibliography and is continually updated to respond to changes in these fields. Descriptors related broadly to eighteenth-century literature are "English Literature," "Irish Literature," "Scottish Literature," "Welsh Literature," "Sentimental Fiction," "English Gothic Novel,"

"Bluestocking," "Scriblerus Club," "Epistolary Novel," "English Enlighten-ment," and "Georgian Period (1714–1830)," as just a few examples.

Aside from "Eighteenth Century Studies," there are no descriptors spe-cifically for eighteenth-century literature. To address this shortcoming, you would instead combine a literary descriptor, like "Scottish Literature" with a "Period" date range, such as 1700–1799. Be aware, however, that the period date ranges can vary from one to several centuries, so that relevant works could be found with period dates beginning before 1700 (e.g., 1600–1799), as well as those starting with that year (e.g., 1700–1850, 1700–1899). The descriptor "Georgian Period (1714–1830)" retrieves only twenty-nine results, so it can't be relied on to find all citations relevant to the eighteenth century. The "Names as Subjects" index provides authoritative names for authors, noting the preferred heading for pseudonyms. For example, if we search the index for Henry Augustus Raymond, we learn that the authoritative heading is "Scott, Sarah," slightly different from the Library of Congress authority heading for her, which includes her birth and death dates, "Scott, Sarah, 1723–1795." Each author entry indicates the official descriptor, any "used for" references, affiliated national literature, and literary period. Although in this example the difference in authoritative headings is slight, it is still impor-tant to understand the preferred form for an author's name in each database that you search, since you will discover variations that could impact your results. *MLAIB* also contains a *Directory of Periodicals*, which is discussed in chapter 5, "Scholarly Journals."

To illustrate how you might search *MLAIB* for a particular topic, for in-stance, antiquarian interests, and limit your results to those about eighteenth-century English literature, we'll use the keyword *antiquar** and combine it with the fields LT Subject Literature "English Literature" and TM Period 1700. This search retrieves the article "Redecorating the Ruin: Women and Antiquarianism in Sarah Scott's *Millenium Hall*," shown in figure 4.1. The record for this article presents a detailed account of the source and gives us additional information for further investigation of the topic. Not only are the search criteria met, with our keyword showing up in the title, subject terms, and abstract, but we now have the name of a period author and specific work, we know the genre of the work (e.g., novel), and we have a relevant descriptor, "relationship to antiquarianism," as well as tangentially related descriptors for architectural imagery and nationalism, and the critical stance employed, feminist approach. This particular record is unusual in that it features a full abstract of the article, since *MLAIB* typically only contains the indexing information. As of April 2008, however, *MLAIB* began adding publisher-provided abstracts, primarily from *PMLA*, *Project Muse*, *JSTOR*, and *German Quarterly*, both to current and retrospective records, so that you can anticipate this feature becoming more prevalent in the future.

Redecorating the Ruin: Women and **Antiquarianism** in Sarah Scott's Millenium Hall

Authors:	Lake, Crystal B.
Source:	ELH 2009 Fall; 76 (3): 661-686.
Notes:	English summary.
Peer Reviewed:	Yes
ISSN:	0013-8304
	1080-6547 (electronic)
General Subject Areas:	*Subject Literature:* English literature
	Period: 1700-1799
	Primary Subject Author: Scott, Sarah (1723-1795)
	Primary Subject Work: A Description of Millenium Hall, and the Country Adjacent (1762)
	Genre: novel
Subject Terms:	by women novelists ; architectural imagery ; relationship to **antiquarianism** ; nationalism ; feminist approach
Document Information:	*Publication Type:* journal article
	Language of Publication: English
	Update Code: 200901
	Sequence Numbers: 2009-1-3545
Electronic Access:	http://0-muse.jhu.edu.bianca.penlib.du.edu/journals/elh/v076/76.3.lake.html
	DOI: 10.1353/elh.0.0055

Abstract: This essay examines **antiquarianism** in Sarah Scott's Millenium Hall (1762). Using a variety of source material, I uncover Scott's personal connections to eminent **antiquaries** and trace previously unknown **antiquarian** antecedents to the novel. I argue that Millenium Hall demonstrates a compelling case study for the ways in which local British history and archaeological interests appealed to eighteenth-century women. Furthermore, I claim that Sarah Scott appropriates **antiquaries'** nationalist sentiments in surprising ways. By overlaying ruined architectural sites with images of ruined women, and by emphasizing women's learning and matrilineal genealogy, Scott shapes **antiquarianism** into a new kind of material history that serves her feminist agenda.

Figure 4.1.   Modified MLAIB record for "Redecorating the Ruin: Women and Antiquarianism in Sarah Scott's *Millenium Hall*." *Source:* MLAIB, via EBSCOhost.

Equally as central to literary research, the ***Annual Bibliography of English Language and Literature*** (***ABELL***) is produced by the Modern Humanities Research Association, a British-based organization with international membership. Like *MLAIB*, *ABELL* began in the early twentieth century. The first volume was published in 1921, and covered material that appeared in print the preceding year. Since that time, some retrospective indexing has incorporated selected material dated back to 1892. *ABELL* indexes books and book chapters, journal articles, critical editions of literary works, essay collections, book reviews, and doctoral dissertations published worldwide in any language that address English language and literature, as well as affiliated subjects, including film, manuscript and textual studies, the history of publishing, and traditional culture of the English-speaking world (e.g., custom, belief, narrative, song, dance, material culture). There are some exceptions to this extensive scope, namely education and pedagogical subjects, as well as the medical application of linguistics.

Although *ABELL* is still issued annually in print format, users tend to prefer the online version offered by Chadwyck-Healey (updated monthly), either as a stand-alone database, or as part of *Literature Online* (*LION*). *LION* also comprises the full text of several hundred journals, as well as reference works. These reference works include the *Encyclopedia of the Novel* and the *New Princeton Encyclopedia of Poetry and Poetics*; biographies for more than 4,000 authors; numerous author bibliographies; the full text of selected poetry, drama, and prose; and websites relevant to English and American literary studies. Depending on your institution's subscription, you might also be able to search *MLAIB* in *LION*, either separately or in a combined search with *ABELL*.

The advanced interface supports searching by keyword or by the following fields: title keyword, subject, author/reviewer(s), publication details, journal, ISBN, ISSN, and publication year, with opportunities to limit to a specific document type (e.g., articles, books, reviews), or to retrieve all records or only those with full text. You can search with Boolean and proximity operators and employ nesting and truncation. To the right of each field search box is a "Select from a List" link that will guide you to the authoritative terminology that can then be pasted to your search. The subject list encompasses individual authors, works, and themes. Some subject terms that are relevant for eighteenth-century British literature include "English Literature: Eighteenth Century" as the main stem, with the following subcategories: "Biography and Autobiography," "Drama and the Theatre," "Fiction," "General," "Literary Theory," "Literature for Children," "Poetry," "Prose," and "Related Studies." Scottish, Welsh, and Irish literature have their own genre headings, but not a subheading for the eighteenth century. There are also headings for "Enlightenment, The"; "Scottish Enlightenment"; and several concerned with the Gothic, namely "Gothic Drama," "Gothic Fiction," "Gothic Horror Fiction," "Gothic Literature," and "Gothic Novel." The "Georgian Culture" heading finds one entry about sport in Georgian England, but "Georgian Poetry" retrieves records concerned with twentieth-century English works and authors.

Figure 4.2 illustrates the *ABELL* record via the Chadwyck-Healey platform for the same journal article, "Redecorating the Ruin: Women and Antiquarianism in Sarah Scott's *Millenium Hall*" that we found in *MLAIB*. You will notice in comparing the two records that the level of indexing is much more detailed in the latter database, although the *ABELL* record provides additional subject terms for the work "Millenium Hall," as well as for "Women Characters" and "Antiquarianism." The one assigned subject heading is straightforward and focused solely on the period and author, "English Literature: Eighteenth Century: Authors: Scott, Sarah."

Although there is some overlap between *MLAIB* and *ABELL*, it is helpful to search both databases to ensure the most comprehensive literature review. Be aware that even the same search terms can produce different results in the databases. This can occur not only because they index unique sources, with *ABELL* providing book reviews and better coverage of books published only

ABELL

Author:	Lake, Crystal B.
Title:	■ Redecorating the ruin: women and antiquarianism in Sarah Scott's *Millenium Hall*.
Publication Details:	ELH (76:3) 2009, 661-86.
Publication Year:	2009
ISSN:	00138304
Subject:	English Literature: Eighteenth Century: Authors: Scott, Sarah
Reference Number:	2009:8092
Full Text:	📄 View Full Text 📷 View Page Image
Additional Search Terms:	Millenium Hall Women Characters Antiquarianism

Figure 4.2.   Modified ABELL record for "Redecorating the Ruin: Women and Antiquarianism in Sarah Scott's *Millenium Hall*." *Source*: ABELL, via Chadwyck Healey's LION.

in Britain and smaller British periodicals and *MLAIB* possessing a greater international scope, but also because they may assign subject headings for even the same source differently.

For example, both databases use the subject term, "Antiquarianism," as we saw in the previous figures. If we conduct a subject search in both databases with this term, however, we would retrieve a citation for "'Poetical Cash': Joseph Addison, Antiquarianism, and Aesthetic Value," by David Alvarez, from *ABELL*, which assigns the subject terms "Antiquarianism," "Numismatics," and "Aesthetics," but not from *MLAIB*, since the latter database appoints the terms "treatment of numismatics," "relationship to aesthetic values," "politeness," "money," and "public sphere" instead. Consequently, when you find a relevant title retrieved in one database, try searching for that same source by title in the other, first, to verify that it truly isn't indexed, and, second, if it is included, to determine which subject terms from the record you should be using to expand your literature review. In short, we recommend searching both *MLAIB* and *ABELL* carefully and regularly, paying attention to your search results, refining search strategies as necessary, and taking advantage of the unique strengths that each database has to offer.

The New Cambridge Bibliography of English Literature (*NCBEL*), covering English literature from the Anglo-Saxon period through 1950, is an important bibliography that still exists only in print. Originally edited by F. W. Bateson and published in its first edition in 1940, as *The Cambridge Bibliography of English Literature*, the second edition, in five volumes and overseen by George Watson, maintains its relevancy for literary research. Of particular value is volume 2, which comprises the years 1660 to 1800. Like the others, this volume serves as the principal guide to identifying primary sources and selected secondary works written by or about authors native to or resident of England, Scotland, Wales, and Ireland. Authors are included in volume 2 if their major works were published during the designated period, inferred in the preface as those authors who were "in some sense established after 1600 and before 1800" (xvi). The bibliography is arranged by a general introductory section and then by genre, in the following manner:

1. Introduction. General works (bibliographies, literary histories, special studies, essay collections), literary theory, literary relations with the Continent, medieval influences, and book production and distribution;
2. Poetry. Histories and surveys, miscellanies, anthologies and collections, Restoration poetry, minor poetry (1660–1700), early eighteenth-century poetry, minor poetry (1700–1750), later eighteenth-century poetry, and minor poetry (1750–1800);
3. Drama. General introduction, theatres and actors, Restoration drama, minor Restoration drama (1660–1700), early eighteenth-century drama, minor drama (1700–1750), later eighteenth-century drama, minor drama (1750–1800), and adaptations and translations;
4. The Novel. General works, principal novelists, minor fiction, children's books;
5. Prose. Essayists and pamphleteers, periodical publications, travel, translations into English, sport, letters, diaries, autobiographies and memoirs, religion, history, literary studies, classical and oriental studies, philosophy, science, law, and education;
6. Scottish Literature. General introduction, poetry and drama, and prose.

This overview illustrates the generous range of material addressed by the bibliography. Although the division into principal and minor categories seems dated (even the font for the individual minor authors' names in the table of contents is smaller), the entries for these less-favored authors can contain valuable information. Depending on the amount of detail provided, an author entry may begin with the location of manuscript collections and a list of bibliographies and collections. Samuel Johnson's entry features additional subsections under "Bibliographies" for manuscripts, exhibition catalogues, special collections, sales and booksellers' catalogues, Johnson's library, and Johnsonian handlists, as an example of the type of treatment accorded some canonical authors.

Following this initial section, the main part of the author entry is devoted first to primary works, indicated by §1, and then selected secondary works, §2, published up until 1969. The primary works section lists titles in chronological order by date of first publication, and it can include contributions to periodicals and collaborative works, translations, letters, diaries and private papers, or other specialized subdivisions. Secondary works consist of criticism generally listed in chronological order, although studies written by an individual scholar are grouped together. Since an author may be associated with more than one genre, it is important to check the index (published as volume 5) so as not to miss any relevant entries.

If your research concerns later Romantic-era authors, you will want to review volume 4 of the third edition, also titled *The Cambridge Bibliography of English Literature*, which is edited by Joanne Shattock. To date, this is the only volume in the new edition to be published. Volume 4 covers the years 1800 to 1900, and, most importantly, includes previously neglected authors, especially poets who published in the later Romantic period, as well as more women authors from all genres; it also eliminates the distinction between principal and minor authors. Bateson's first *Cambridge Bibliography of English Literature* provides sections about social life and political background that have been excluded in the later editions, as well as coverage of Commonwealth literatures from Australia, New Zealand, India, South Africa, and Canada. If your research interests fall within these areas, you may want to consult volume 2 for relevant resources regarding the Restoration and eighteenth-century period, 1660 to 1800. Although it now plays a less important role in guiding scholars to criticism, given the extensive range of *MLAIB* and *ABELL*, *NCBEL* can be particularly useful for identifying early criticism published before the twentieth century, primary works and their subsequent editions, and material related to translations and genres.

In contrast to the bibliographies discussed thus far in this section, the *Year's Work in English Studies* (*YWES*) selectively surveys the important scholarship published within a given year and offers a critical evaluation of these works through narrative essays. This long-standing bibliographic resource, which began in 1921, covers English language and literatures written in English from the Old English period up to present literary endeavors. Although the main emphasis remains British literature, *YWES* also addresses American literature and the literatures of Africa, Australia, Canada, the Caribbean, India, and New Zealand. The bibliography is arranged by chronological and national categories, with separate chapters devoted to the English language and bibliography and textual criticism. In the most recent volume, literary criticism concerned with the British eighteenth century can be found in two chapters, "The Eighteenth Century" and "Literature 1780–1830: The Romantic Period"; earlier volumes approach the period from a Restoration (1660–1770) and eighteenth-century perspective. The current "Eighteenth Century" chapter is divided into sections devoted to general works and prose, the novel, and poetry, whereas previous volumes may also include sections for drama. Each chapter is written by one or several scholars who shape the discussion according to their expertise and point of view, as well as to the availability of work for review. For these reasons, we suggest that you read through the entire chapter to get a sense of the contributors' perspective on the selections and evaluations. At the end of each chapter, you will find a list of the books reviewed, but keep in mind that the authors may also discuss significant book chapters, journal articles, and occasionally reference books published primarily in Great Britain, the United States, and Canada. Two indexes facilitate access to the contents, one for critics, and the other for authors and subjects. You should expect about a three-year time delay between the work discussed and the annual compilation; however, the online *YWES* makes forthcoming chapters available as they are completed.

The *Oxford Journals* website offers institutional and personal subscription access to the full text and abstracts from 1919 to the present, with only the 1999 and 2000 annual reviews missing. This extensive historical coverage makes it possible to trace the critical interest in certain authors and works and to mark trends in literary scholarship throughout time. Although ongoing volumes of *YWES* can be used to identify significant contributions to eighteenth-century literary studies and stay abreast of developments in the field, *MLAIB*, *ABELL*, and appropriate period and author bibliographies should still be consulted so as to not miss works relevant to your specific research project.

Although it cannot replace the major literary indexes, some scholars may wish to supplement their searches of these databases with one or more full-text digital journal collections. **JSTOR**, which stands for "journal storage," was created as a central online archive so that libraries wouldn't have to continue maintaining older print issues at their primary facilities. Currently, *JSTOR* consists of sequentially numbered "Arts and Sciences" collections, as well as "Business and Life Sciences" collections. Depending on your institution's subscriptions, you will have access to certain collections and the titles contained within them. Altogether, *JSTOR* provides more than 1,000 scholarly journals representing multiple disciplines. The "Language and Literature" collection has 249 titles, including many central to eighteenth-century literary studies, including *ELH*, *SEL: Studies in English Literature, 1500–1900*, and *Studies in Romanticism*, as well as important general literature journals like *MLN* and *Publications of the Modern Language Association of America* (discussed in chapter 5).

Fulfilling its role as an archive, *JSTOR* offers coverage back to the first issue of a journal but does not give access to the most current issues. Instead, it maintains a moving wall, typically of one to five years, so that the collection continues to grow. A partnership with *Project Muse*, however, often enables you to link to recent issues. Each journal article is scanned at high resolution and replicates the printed page. *JSTOR* may be browsed by discipline or searched by keyword in the full-text, author, item title, abstract, or caption fields, and limited by item type (e.g., article, review, miscellaneous, pamphlet), date range, language, publication title, and discipline. Since searching for words in the full text sometimes retrieves an overwhelming number of results, often of marginal relevance, we recommend limiting your search terms to the title or abstract field, while keeping in mind that not every article has an abstract. For interdisciplinary projects, you can choose to search the literature titles, in combination with other subject collections. From an article record, *JSTOR* features links to the pages that contain your search terms and to *Google Scholar* for retrieving related articles, citing articles, and finding articles by the author.

Project Muse is similar to *JSTOR* in that it provides full-text access to scholarly journals, but with an emphasis on current rather than back issues. More than 400 journals from the humanities and social sciences are available to be browsed by journal title, discipline, or article-assigned Library of Congress subject headings, or searched by numerous fields, including author, title, author and title reviewed, or all text. Searches may be further limited by content type, journal, discipline, date, and language, and there is an option to incorporate *JSTOR* back issues into the results. Several journals of interest to eighteenth-century literary studies are part of *Project Muse*: *The Eighteenth Century* (2006–present), *Eighteenth-Century Fiction* (1988–present), *Eighteenth-Century Life* (1996–present), *Eighteenth-Century Studies* (1995/1996–present), *ELH* (1993–present), *Journal for Early Modern Cultural Studies* (2004–present), *Romanticism* (2006–2008), *SEL: Studies in English Literature, 1500–1900* (1999–present), and *Studies in Eighteenth Century Culture* (1991), among other general literature titles. Publishers occasionally decide to no longer contribute to *Project Muse*, as with the *Romanticism* example; however, any volumes that were part of *Project Muse* remain in the database, with perpetual access.

Two other databases that deserve mention are **Periodicals Archive Online** (**PAO**) and the companion **Periodicals Index Online** (**PIO**). *PAO* contains hundreds of digitized arts, humanities, and social sciences journals, both in English and foreign languages, many of which span 200 years of publication. *British Periodicals Collection I* and *British Periodicals Collection II* are also included in *PAO*, if your library subscribes to both (see chapter 6 for more details about these journals from the seventeenth, eighteenth, and nineteenth centuries). The journal content may be searched by keyword, author, article title keywords or journal title, language, and broad subject terms, and limited by date range. *PIO* offers the same search interface, but the content is restricted to journal citations rather than the full text. Nevertheless, through *PIO* you can search for articles from thousands of humanities and social-science journals, some dating back to the mid-seventeenth century.

EIGHTEENTH-CENTURY BIBLIOGRAPHIES

Beasley, Jerry C., comp. *A Check List of Prose Fiction Published in England, 1740–1749*. Charlottesville: University Press of Virginia, 1972.

Burling, William J. *A Checklist of New Plays and Entertainments on the London Stage, 1700–1737*. Rutherford, NJ: Fairleigh Dickinson University Press, 1993.

ECCB: The Eighteenth-Century Current Bibliography. New York: AMS Press, 1975– . Previous title, *Philological Quarterly*, with the years 1926–1980 reprinted in *English Literature, 1660–1800: A Bibliography of Modern Studies*. 6 vols. Princeton, NJ: Princeton University Press, 1950–1972.

English Short Title Catalogue, 1473–1800. London: British Library. http://estc.bl.uk (accessed 27 August 2012).

Foxon, D. F. *English Verse, 1701–1750: A Catalogue of Separately Printed Poems with Notes on Contemporary Collected Editions*. 2 vols. New York: Cambridge University Press, 1975.

Frank, Frederick S. *The First Gothics: A Critical Guide to the English Gothic Novel*. New York: Garland, 1987.

———. *Guide to the Gothic: An Annotated Bibliography of Criticism*. Metuchen, NJ: Scarecrow Press, 1984.

———. *Guide to the Gothic II: An Annotated Bibliography of Criticism, 1983–1993*. Lanham, MD: Scarecrow Press, 1995.

———. *Guide to the Gothic III: An Annotated Bibliography of Criticism, 1994–2003*. 2 vols. Lanham, MD: Scarecrow Press, 2005.

Garside, Peter, James Raven, and Rainer Schöwerling, eds. *The English Novel, 1770–1829: A Bibliographical Survey of Prose Fiction Published in the British Isles*. 2 vols. New York: Oxford University Press, 2000.

Horwitz, Barbara Joan. *British Women Writers, 1700–1850: An Annotated Bibliography of Their Works and Works about Them*. Lanham, MD: Scarecrow Press, 1997.

Letellier, Robert I. *The English Novel, 1700–1740: An Annotated Bibliography*. Westport, CT: Greenwood, 2002.

McBurney, William H., comp. *A Check List of English Prose Fiction, 1700–1739*. Cambridge, MA: Harvard University Press, 1960.

Raven, James. *British Fiction, 1750–1770: A Chronological Check-List of Prose Fiction Printed in Britain and Ireland*. Newark: University of Delaware Press, 1987.

"Recent Studies in the Restoration and Eighteenth Century." *SEL: Studies in English Literature, 1500–1900.* Annually in the Summer issue.

Saar, Doreen Alvarez, and Mary Anne Schofield, comps. *Eighteenth-Century Anglo-American Women Novelists: A Critical Reference Guide.* New York: G. K. Hall, 1996.

Spector, Robert D. *The English Gothic: A Bibliographic Guide to Writers from Horace Walpole to Mary Shelley.* Westport, CT: Greenwood, 1984.

———, comp. *Backgrounds to Restoration and Eighteenth-Century English Literature: An Annotated Bibliographical Guide to Modern Scholarship.* Westport, CT: Greenwood, 1989.

Thomson, Douglass H., Jack G. Voller, and Frederick S. Frank, eds. *Gothic Writers: A Critical and Bibliographical Guide.* Westport, CT: Greenwood, 2002.

The bibliographies in this section are primarily concerned with literature of the eighteenth century, although some titles may address the eighteenth century broadly or cover the period from a genre perspective, such as those about Gothic literature. If your work is focused on works and writers of the Romantic period, please see *Literary Research of the British Romantic Period: Strategies and Sources* for bibliographies specific to the later eighteenth century.

Although no longer exclusively devoted to the eighteenth century, the **English Short Title Catalogue, 1473–1800 (ESTC)** is the principal and most extensive bibliography for the period. Originally titled the *Eighteenth Century Short Title Catalogue (ECSTC)*, this first manifestation of the *ESTC* covered books, pamphlets, and ephemera published in English-speaking countries between 1701 and 1800. In its present form, it comprises eighteenth-century material in addition to print bibliographies; Alfred W. Pollard and G. R. Redgrave's *A Short-Title Catalogue of Books Printed in England, Scotland, and Ireland and of English Books Printed Abroad, 1475–1640*; Donald Wing's *Short-Title Catalogue of Books, Printed in England, Scotland, Ireland, Wales, and British America, and of English Books Printed in Other Countries, 1641–1617*; supplemental period publications; newspapers; and serials. Such ephemera as trade and visiting cards, playing cards, theatre programs, and playbills are excluded, as well as some types of engraved material (e.g., music, maps, prints).

At this time, *ESTC* lists more than 460,000 items and represents the holdings of greater than 2,000 libraries, rendering it a union catalog, as well as an impressive bibliography. Hosted by the British Library, the catalog features an advanced interface that permits searching by word or phrase in eighteen field indexes, ranging from words in the author or title field to subject to the copy-specific notes field. Both the indexes and the list of contributing libraries can be browsed. Be aware of a few differences from other databases; the truncation symbol is a ?, and date ranges are indicated by a "->" symbol (e.g., 1700->1800). Searches can be limited by language (although they caution that not all items were assigned a language code or format), date, format, and country. Another point to note about *ESTC* is that not all bibliographic records contain the same level of detail. Even so, the catalog is an outstanding resource for identifying eighteenth-century publications and locating specific editions and copies. Far from being static, *ESTC* continues to add new material as period books and ephemera are discovered, making this bibliography a vital conduit to early modern literary production.

The well-respected ***ECCB: The Eighteenth-Century Current Bibliography*** has been in existence since 1926. Originally published in *Philological Quarterly*, the bibliography focused on Restoration and eighteenth-century English literature criticism until 1970, when it began incorporating other disciplines into its scope. It appeared in the journal under the following titles: "English Literature of the Restoration and Eighteenth Century: A Current Bibliography" (1925–1926), "English Literature, 1660–1800: A Current Bibliography" (1927–1969), and "The Eighteenth Century: A Current Bibliography" (1970–1974). If your institution subscribes to *Philological Quarterly* through *JSTOR* (or another vendor), you will be able to access these earlier bibliographies online. It may also be expedient to consult the compilation *English Literature, 1660–1800: A Bibliography of Modern Studies*, which reprints the *Philological Quarterly* bibliographies from 1926 to 1970.

In 1978, the *ECCB* became a separate monograph published by AMS Press. Although subtitled a "current bibliography," there is, in fact, a significant delay between the time the annual volume is published and the date of the scholarship it addresses. For example, volume 32 was published in 2010, but it covers scholarly works from 2006. As with the *Year's Work in English Studies*, you should anticipate a gap between the scholarship's publication date and its compilation; however, this delay doesn't make the bibliography any less valuable.

The *ECCB* lists books, book chapters, journal articles, and reviews concerned with the long eighteenth century. The bibliography's arrangement has changed throughout the years, and it is currently organized into the following seven thematic sections: "Printing and Bibliographical Studies," "History, Social, and Economic Studies," "Philosophy, Science, and Religion," "Fine Arts," "Foreign Literatures and Languages" (Iberian, French, Italian, German, Scandinavian), "British Literatures," and "New World Literatures and Languages" (Australian, New Zealand). Within each section, the entries are listed alphabetically by author. Some entries offer no more than a bibliographic citation, others receive a longer description about the contents, and some also note where the work was reviewed. Reference works like *A*

Companion to the Eighteenth-Century English Novel and Culture and *The Cambridge History of English Literature, 1660–1780* are also covered. You will find that scholarship about canonical authors appears more frequently, but less-studied authors are not neglected. Selected works are given lengthier, more detailed treatments, typically one to three pages, and written and signed by a scholar in the field. In volume 32, for example, the "British Literatures" section contains eight of these in-depth evaluations.

Although the majority of the scholarship is in English, the *ECCB* also includes foreign-language works about British literary topics and authors. To identify works about a particular author, check the single index for either literary or scholar figures to ensure that you won't miss relevant works in other sections, for instance, in the latest volume, where scholarship about Fielding is addressed in the printing and bibliographical studies and foreign literatures categories, as well as in the expected "British Literatures" section. Previous to volume 25, the *ECCB* dedicated a section to individual authors, but, even for these earlier volumes, it is wise to check the index for additional entries. By compiling the scholarship focused on eighteenth-century literature and other disciplines, the *ECCB* is an excellent tool for staying abreast of developments in the field, drawing connections between disciplinary subjects, and identifying specific works relevant to your own research.

Devoted to a distinct British literary period in each quarterly issue, *SEL: Studies in English Literature, 1500–1900* features the **"Recent Studies in the Restoration and Eighteenth Century"** bibliography in its Summer publication. This bibliography surveys recent books and selected journal issues concerned with literature of the time period, including anthologies and edited works. Presented as a signed, review essay, the bibliography addresses the state of the field and provides comparative evaluations arranged in thematic or genre sections. For example, the Summer 2011 issue covers "History of the Book and History of Reading/Readers," "Colonial/Postcolonial Studies," "Animal Studies," "Considering Enlightenment," "Sexuality, Courtship, and Marriage," "Women's Writing and Gender Studies," "Gothic Studies," "Defoe Studies," "Swift Studies," "Johnson Studies," "Sterne Studies," "Histories of the Novel," "Theater History and Performance Studies," "Poetry of the Long Eighteenth Century," "Cultural Studies," "Literary History," "Journals," and "Scholarly and Classroom Editions." Since these thematic headings vary for each year, they can be used to pinpoint loci of scholarly attention throughout time. The narrative overview is then followed by a listing of books received during the previous year, with full bibliographic citations and price in British and American currency.

The rise of the novel during the eighteenth century is reflected in reference works about the genre. Robert I. Letellier's *The English Novel, 1700–1740:*

An Annotated Bibliography is an extensive compilation of more than 1,700 sources arranged in two parts. The first, "The General Period, 1700–1740: Miscellaneous Works," provides detailed annotations for bibliographies, anthologies (shorter novels, short stories, essays, documentary collections, biographies), and general studies and surveys, including those concerned with historical, social, and cultural approaches, as well as literary subjects and theory. Part II features anonymous and individual authors, as well as specific works of fiction. In this regard, fifty-five anonymous works and ninety-eight authors are represented. Each of the author sections comprises a listing of their works (sometimes with *NCBEL* or *ECSTC* reference numbers), editions, and criticism, with annotations ranging from a sentence or two to more descriptive paragraphs. As can be expected, canonical authors receive more detailed treatments. For example, the Daniel Defoe section is arranged in the following categories: "Collected Works," "Selected Editions of Individual Prose Fiction Titles," "Bibliographies from 1719–1994," "Defoe's Canon," and "Criticism Published between 1995 and 1999," about his works in general or individual titles. On the other hand, the section for Mary Hearne lists only her two works and one modern edition, but no criticism. Other authors have only a few critical studies. For those authors covered by *Eighteenth-Century Anglo-American Women Novelists* (discussed later in this section), the criticism is confined to scholarship published after 1992 (to complement rather than duplicate that of the Saar and Schofield bibliography), and only selected earlier critical works. Letellier also presents limited examples of French works translated into English during the period. Finally, "A Selected Chronological Shortlist of Prose Fiction in English Published Between 1700 and 1740" concludes the bibliography, in addition to scholar and subject indexes.

Several important bibliographies serve as guides for identifying prose fiction, poetry, and drama of the period. We describe a selection of these sources later in this section (please see Harner's *Literary Research Guide* for additional resources). Surveys of primary works can also be supplemented with the *ESTC*. Covering the first part of the century, William H. McBurney's *A Check List of English Prose Fiction, 1700–1739* lists 391 fictional works written by "native authors or translators" (ix) that were originally published in England during the specified dates. Some shorter fiction is excluded, including character sketches, jest books, pamphlets, chapbooks, and fiction contained in periodicals. Arranged chronologically, the entries present the complete title (with original spelling and punctuation), the names of printers and booksellers listed on the title page, pagination, format, price, and library call number of an extant copy. Translation entries note the author, original title, date of original publication, and the translator's name. Subsequent editions through 1739 are also described. A concluding section is entitled "Dubious or Unauthenticated Titles, 1700–1739," in addition to a bibliography and single index.

Jerry C. Beasley's *A Check List of Prose Fiction Published in England, 1740–1749* continues with a chronological survey of novels, reprinted works, and translations published during one decade. Like the previous checklist, this one omits chapbooks, jest books, character sketches, and dialogues. The arrangement is also similar. Entries provide the short title; imprint; names of booksellers; pagination; format; price; location of one extant copy, with preference for an American library; and subsequent editions through 1749. Descriptive annotations enhance the value of this work, since they offer readers an initial summary of the contents, for example, "Routine narrative of the escapades of a notorious forger and robber, including his apprehension, trial, and execution" (41) and "satirical romance includes conversations between the author and the banished demon Astaroth, and incorporates secret histories of French Court life, as well as scandalous stories of monks and nuns" (40). Unverified editions of authentic works and unauthenticated titles are treated in two appendixes.

James Raven's *British Fiction, 1750–1770: A Chronological Check-List of Prose Fiction Printed in Britain and Ireland* was designed to assist researchers with tracing the development of the early novel during the middle years of the century. The introduction surveys the literature, authors, readers, and booksellers that comprise the checklist and features several tables that illustrate the printing of novels by place of publication, the most popular novelists by editions printed during certain years, publication of novels by women authors, and publication of translated fiction. The checklist proper covers prose fiction for the most part identified as a novel, including reprints and translations, in addition to representative fictional biographies, narratives of imaginary voyages, and miscellanies. Excluded works are similar to the other checklists described in this section, namely jest books, chapbooks, children's books, serial and magazine fiction, as well as works printed in English but published outside of Britain and Ireland. Arranged alphabetically by title of anonymous works first, and then by either known or attributed author for each year, the 1,363 entries list the author or translator, title, imprint, number of pages or volumes, format, price (either from advertised binding or contemporary advertisements), references to reviews in the *Critical Review* and the *Monthly Review*, references to other bibliographies, information about attributed authorship, former and/or subsequent editions with cross-references to their own entries where applicable, and the location of extant copies held by major libraries in Britain and the United States. Entries for representative fictional biographies, imaginary voyages, and miscellanies are grouped together under the "Miscellanies" category. The work concludes with an index of authors and translators and another of titles.

Addressing the later eighteenth century, *The English Novel, 1770–1829: A Bibliographical Survey of Prose Fiction Published in the British Isles*, edited by Peter Garside, James Raven, and Rainer Schöwerling, is also concerned with fictional works of the period, rather than secondary critical works about them. Aiming to be comprehensive, the introduction to this two-volume set states that the bibliography "seeks to list all novels of the period whether or not surviving in extant copies, their publication and pricing details, and contemporary review information" (1–2). Indeed, the bibliography covers first editions of English-language novels published in the British Isles, first English translations of novels originally published in Europe, and first British editions of novels published in North America during the specified dates. The titles described in the bibliography were examined where extant, and, if not, their existence was verified from printing and publishing records, contemporary reviews, or advertisements and circulating library catalogs. Acknowledging the ambiguity of defining what constitutes a novel, the editors selected works for inclusion based on contemporary identification of novels from periodical reviews and circulating library catalogs; however, religious tracts, chapbooks, children's literature, and short, separately issued tales are excluded.

Volume I covers the years 1770 to 1799, and begins with a substantial (more than 100-page) historical introduction entitled "The Novel Comes of Age," in which Raven addresses the development of the genre; individual authors; translations and translators; the English novel abroad; bookseller-publishers and printers; production and marketing; design; and reception, readers, and reviews. This essay is illustrated with several tables and figures related to authorship and book production during the period. The bibliography proper is arranged chronologically by year of imprint and then alphabetically by anonymous title or by author's or translator's name, or by pseudonym. Each entry features detailed bibliographic information, including the author's name; full title from the title page; place of publication and imprint; pagination; format; price; references to contemporary reviews and selected extracts; location and shelfmark of the copy consulted; selected additional holding libraries; and notes that cover dedications, subscription lists, advertisements, past incorrect attributions of authorship, and subsequent editions through 1850. The review extracts from the *Monthly Review* and the *Critical Review* make this bibliography particularly central to research about contemporary reception. An appendix listing novels for children and another outlining selected nonfiction associated with novels, as well as four indexes (authors and translators, titles, booksellers and printers, and notes) round out the second volume of this impressive bibliography.

Referring to his work as a "short-title catalogue with frills," (xi) rather than a descriptive bibliography, D. F. Foxon's *English Verse, 1701–1750:*

A Catalogue of Separately Printed Poems with Notes on Contemporary Collected Editions covers approximately 10,000 entries for separately published verse written in English, verse written in other languages but printed in the British Isles, and collections of verse by a single author. Exceptions include works published in miscellanies and periodicals, broadside ballads, slip songs, chapbooks, engraved sheets or half-sheets, and oratorios and opera libretti, as well as works consisting of prose and verse that begin with prose. Arranged alphabetically by author or the first word of the title, with translated works listed under the translator rather than the original author, the entries for individual works contain the short title; imprint; collation; a bibliographical note with information about specific editions, impressions, and copies; first line, notes on authorship and subject matter; and library locations in Great Britain and the United States.

As with many of these bibliographies, consulting the introduction will give you a more thorough explanation of the scope and arrangement, if needed. Entries for collected works are first listed in chronological order under an author's name, followed by the single poems. Daniel Defoe, for example, is represented with one collection and approximately nineteen individual works. The second volume comprises six indexes of first lines, imprints, bibliographical notes, descriptive epithets, subjects, and first editions in chronological order so that contemporary works can be identified. Any scholar studying poets and poetry of the period, especially those conducting textual investigations, will want to review this important resource.

Concerned with a broad range of theatrical performances, William J. Burling's *A Checklist of New Plays and Entertainments on the London Stage, 1700–1737* outlines plays, pantomimes, ballad-operas, operas, afterpieces, and other genres arranged chronologically by theatrical season. Entries contain the date of premier, venue, title, author(s) or attribution, genre, publisher or printer, publication date, and notes that may address attribution or performance history. Many of these notes, as well as the entries themselves, draw upon information from contemporary newspaper advertisements. Since the checklist was designed to complement *The London Stage, 1660–1800*, users will want to consult that source for specific page references. Two appendixes are entitled, "New Plays at Minor London Venues, 1700–1737" and "Unperformed Plays."

The impact of early feminist scholarship is seen in several reference books published during the 1990s, which examine women's literary output during the eighteenth century. *Eighteenth-Century Anglo-American Women Novelists: A Critical Reference Guide* provides an overview of twentieth-century literary criticism about thirty-five authors from the period, so that the range and development of critical attention can be assessed. Compiled by Doreen

Saar and Mary Anne Schofield, the bibliography addresses both canonical and lesser-known authors, and covers figures whose publications span the century. Arranged alphabetically, each author section begins with a listing of her novels, followed by citations for scholarship (including reference works and dissertations, but not unpublished manuscripts). The critical works are listed by year, and each one receives a succinct, one- to three-sentence descriptive annotation. The Penelope Aubin section, for example, begins with an annotation on *The Rise of the Novel of Manners: A Study of Prose Fiction between 1600 and 1740* (1911), in which Aubin is characterized as "highly didactic, pro-Roman Catholic, and an imitator of Defoe," and traces the critical reception of her works through the twentieth century, when the tone changes to such examples as *Seductive Fictions. Women's Amatory Fiction from 1684 to 1740* (1992), in which the author states that Aubin "seeks 'to revive moral vigor in feminocentric representations of love' because her roots lie in didactic prose" (8). This bibliography is not only useful for identifying twentieth-century criticism about eighteenth-century women novelists, but the annotations and arrangement of criticism by year enable the scholar to trace the patterns of critical trends as well.

Adopting a broader generic approach, Barbara Joan Horwitz's ***British Women Writers, 1700–1850: An Annotated Bibliography of Their Works and Works about Them*** examines novelists, poets, and dramatists from eighteenth-century and early nineteenth-century Great Britain. The first of two introductory chapters, "England, 1700–1850," describes political and literary events and provides annotations for selected political, social, intellectual, and literary histories, and a brief chronology of major events. In the second chapter, "Literature Written by Women, 1700–1850," the focus is turned to women authors' experience, in particular, and the annotations cover anthologies of writing by women, bibliographies, guides, history, and criticism, including specific studies of the novel, poetry, and drama. The main part of the bibliography is devoted to forty-six individual authors, ranging from Jane Austen to Ann Yearsley. Each of these entries presents brief biographical information, lists their works, and describes selected criticism that was recent at the time the volume was published (from the 1960s through the early 1990s). The annotations themselves are typically a solid paragraph and contain ample quotes from the source being described. The bibliography concludes with subject and author indexes.

The enduring fascination with Gothic literature is reflected in several bibliographies about the genre. Robert D. Spector's ***The English Gothic: A Bibliographic Guide to Writers from Horace Walpole to Mary Shelley*** stands out for its narrative rather than its enumerative structure. Five chapters offer evaluative assessments of selected important English-language secondary works about the genre and some of the principal authors from the eighteenth and nineteenth centuries. Following an introduction that traces the development of the genre, chapter 1, "Gothic, Gothicism, and Gothicists," discusses definitions, general works, influence on literature and art, critical reception, and minor authors. The additional four chapters cover pairs of related authors: "The Beginnings: Horace Walpole and Clara Reeve," "Sentimental Gothicism: Charlotte Smith and Ann Radcliffe," "Schauer-Romantik: Matthew Gregory Lewis and William Beckford," and "The Inheritors: Charles Robert Maturin and Mary Shelley." Each essay begins with a biographical profile of the author and provides an overview of critical and scholarly biographies, early reviews, and secondary criticism, including journal articles, book chapters, books, and "miscellaneous comments on the authors' writing and lives" (x) from the eighteenth or nineteenth century until approximately 1980. Works discussed in the essays are then listed in the bibliographical references at the conclusion of each chapter. One index facilitates access to authors, titles, and subjects.

Frederick S. Frank has published four bibliographies concerned with Gothic literature. *The First Gothics: A Critical Guide to the English Gothic Novel* focuses on the novels themselves by giving publication information and critical plot synopses for 500 English Gothic titles chosen to be representative of the genre's range in that country. Frank selected the titles based on the following criteria: contemporary availability of the novel; artistic merit, historical importance, and popularity with their original audience and with scholars; and the novel's role in the development of the Gothic movement. Arranged alphabetically by author, each entry contains information about the first edition and modern editions, a "Gothic Type" classification (e.g., doppelganger, monastic shocker), and secondary sources about the author and individual work. The plot synopses range from as brief as one paragraph to up to two pages, and they frequently address the novel's influence within the genre. This bibliography is further enhanced by a "Glossary of Gothic Terms," including definitions of Gothic-type terms assigned to each title; a bibliography of selected twentieth-century criticism; and a chronology of the titles listed by year of publication. The work concludes with three indexes to Gothic authors, titles, and critics.

With a broader scope, yet complementing *The First Gothics*, Frank's other bibliographies comprise brief annotations to criticism about Gothic literature spanning the twentieth century and into the twenty-first. *Guide to the Gothic: An Annotated Bibliography of Criticism* is divided into several broad categories: previous guides to the Gothic; English, Canadian, American, French, and German Gothic literature; other national Gothic literatures; and special subject areas. The "English Gothic" section covers general histories, definitions, and theories, as well as fifty-six individual authors from Horace Walpole to Mervyn Peake. The themed section highlights criticism on such topics as "Pre-Gothicism, Graveyard Verse, and Supernatural Poetry," "Catholicism, Revolution, Religion, and the Gothic Novel," and "Demono-logical Roots of the Gothic," and it also outlines special collections of Gothic literature and criticism on Gothic films. The annotations themselves are brief, ranging from one or two sentences to a paragraph, and they address criticism published between 1900 and 1982. This volume has a list of journals and two indexes, "Index of Critics" and "Index of Authors, Artists, and Actors."

Guide to the Gothic II: An Annotated Bibliography of Criticism, 1983–1993 has a similar arrangement and provides annotations for nearly 800 works of criticism published during the noted years for the "English Gothic" section. The "Special Subject Areas" section is much condensed in this vol-ume but discusses recent anthologies of Gothic fiction and miscellaneous and fugitive Gothic sources. Two indexes give access to critics, editors, illustra-tors, and translators, and authors, titles, artists, and actors.

Testament to the explosion in critical attention, *Guide to the Gothic III: An Annotated Bibliography of Criticism, 1994–2003* encompasses annotated entries for 1,651 new critical works, in addition to unannotated references from the previous volumes (*Guide to the Gothic I* and *Guide to the Gothic II*), for a total comprising 5,706 sources. Published in two volumes, the arrange-ment is similar to the preceding bibliographies, although the English section has become "British Gothic Fiction." This version has information about modern editions and new sections, including "Gothic Chapbooks, Bluebooks, Shilling Shockers, and Short Tales of Terror" and "Classical English Authors and the Gothic." *Guide to the Gothic III* has two indexes to critics and editors and to titles and authors for each volume.

Frank is coeditor, along with Douglass H. Thomson and Jack G. Voller, of *Gothic Writers: A Critical and Bibliographical Guide*. More than an an-notated bibliography, *Gothic Writers* provides signed, critical discussions of approximately fifty authors, ranging from two to ten pages, that address their literary careers and place within the Gothic tradition. For each of these figures, there is also a list of the author's Gothic works, modern reprints and editions, and an annotated selection of twentieth-century criticism. Since the bibliography adopts an alphabetical rather than chronological arrangement, you may need to check the timeline of Gothic authors and works from 1762 to 1999 to identify eighteenth-century authors. Three additional entries cover "Gothic Chapbooks, Bluebooks, and Short Stories in Magazines from 1790 to 1820," "Gothic Drama," and "Jane Austen and the Northanger Novelists." An introduction surveys critical reception to the Gothic, and the "General Bibliography of Critical Sources and Resources" lists primary and secondary bibliographies of the Gothic, works that examine the Gothic in history and literature, reference works, general histories and studies in definition and theory, journals and special journal issues, and Web resources. One index compiles critics, editors, and translators.

To support interdisciplinary investigations of eighteenth-century authors, works, and themes, Robert D. Spector compiled *Backgrounds to Restoration and Eighteenth-Century English Literature: An Annotated Bibliographical Guide to Modern Scholarship*. While not aiming to be comprehensive, this bibliography offers a wide selection of English-language books and journal articles published during the twentieth century that address eighteenth-century life, institutions, and social and cultural contexts. Twelve chapters cover general sources, for example, bibliographies, but most focus on subjects, including publishing, printing, and journalism; history and politics; religion; philosophy; science, medicine, and technology; economics; crime and the law; society, manners, customs, and attitudes (such as family, women, sex, race); education and scholarship; language and rhetoric; and literature and the arts (e.g., criticism, satire, music, painting, engraving, sculpture, architecture, gardening, decorative arts, the "Sister Arts"). Each entry summarizes the contents and occasionally features evaluative remarks. Although Harner cautions that some important works are not part of Spector's compilation, while some superseded works are, the bibliography can be used as a preliminary tool for eighteenth-century interdisciplinary research.

EIGHTEENTH-CENTURY AUTHOR BIBLIOGRAPHIES

Brown, Anthony E. *Boswellian Studies: A Bibliography*, 3rd. ed. Edinburgh, Scotland: Edinburgh University Press, 1991.

Fleeman, J. D., comp. *A Bibliography of the Works of Samuel Johnson: Treating His Published Works from the Beginnings to 1984*. 2 vols. New York: Oxford University Press, 2000.

Hannaford, Richard Gordon. *Samuel Richardson: An Annotated Bibliography of Critical Studies*. New York: Garland Publishing, 1980.

Rogers, Deborah D. *Ann Radcliffe: A Bio-Bibliography*. Westport, CT: Greenwood, 1996.

Spedding, Patrick. *A Bibliography of Eliza Haywood*. Brookfield, VT: Pickering and Chatto, 2004.

Windle, John. *Mary Wollstonecraft Godwin, 1759–1797: A Bibliography of the First and Early Editions, with Briefer Notes on Later Editions and Translations*, 2nd ed. New Castle, DE: Oak Knoll Press, 2000.

In addition to the general and period-specific bibliographies discussed so far in this chapter, scholars will also want to determine if there are any bibliographies dedicated to the author or authors central to their research. *NCBEL* is one place to start in identifying recommended author bibliographies; you can also search your local catalog, a union catalog, or *WorldCat*, employing the strategies outlined in chapter 3 for finding author reference sources. Be aware that author bibliographies can be published as a separate monograph, as part of a book chapter, in a journal, or on the Web, so you may also want to check chapter 5, "Scholarly Journals," and chapter 9, "Web Resources," for other ideas. Not all eighteenth-century authors will have monograph bibliographies devoted to their work, so you may need to search for this information creatively, especially for women and nontraditionally canonical authors. You may also encounter author bibliographies that were published several or many years ago. Don't necessarily disregard these sources. Many older bibliographies remain valid scholarly works, especially in regard to early critical reception, and they can be updated by searching *MLAIB* and *ABELL*. The bibliographies described in this section are representative examples of eighteenth-century British author-monograph bibliographies.

At nearly 850 pages, Patrick Spedding's *A Bibliography of Eliza Haywood* is an impressive and formidable work. Scholars will find the introduction enlightening for its discussion about the development and current state of Haywood's canon, as well as the process of compiling the bibliography. They will also be well served by reading the overview to using the bibliography, with particulars about its arrangement and entry components. Spedding has aimed to be as comprehensive and thorough as possible by listing and describing "every edition of all the works known to be by Eliza Haywood. For works published in the eighteenth and nineteenth centuries this includes every issue of every work and every state and variant of every issue" (15). Twentieth- and twenty-first-century editions are listed in print, microform, and electronic formats. This monumental effort is reflected in the details provided for each entry, for example, the history of the attribution and the evidence and reasons for its inclusion, publishing and printing history, and related biographical or literary information. In addition, Spedding addresses Haywood's career as a publisher and bookseller and her relationship with William Hatchett.

The bibliography is organized into the following sections: "A. Works by Haywood Published before 1850," which covers collections, individual works, reprints in monographs, and reprints in periodicals; "B. Works by Haywood Published after 1850," which includes reprints, facsimiles, microform collections, CD-ROM collections, and online electronic texts; "C. Works Attributed to Haywood," which lists rejected attributions and ghosts; and "D. Miscellanea," which features works published and sold by Haywood and collections, individual works, and attributed works for William Hatchett. Finally, a series of thirteen appendixes present important information about

Haywood's career and popularity, ranging from "The Trade in the Copyright of Ab.16 *La Belle Assemblée*" to "Haywood's Annual Output, Measured in Sheets Printed," and from "Evidence for Haywood's Arrest for Publishing Ab.66 *A Letter from H[enry] G[orin]g*" to "Haywood's Most, and Least, Popular Works." The "Bibliography of Works Consulted" acts in its own right as an initial guide to secondary sources about Haywood and her time. Three indexes conclude the volume: first editions listed chronologically, printers and publishers, and a general index. *A Bibliography of Eliza Haywood* is a significant contribution to Haywood scholarship and is essential in researching her work.

J. D. Fleeman's *A Bibliography of the Works of Samuel Johnson: Treating His Published Works from the Beginnings to 1984* is an equally impressive endeavor. Representing thirty years of effort, this bibliography presents every work written by Johnson, including his translations, contributions (prefaces or dedications), revisions, and selected attributed works, throughout his entire literary career. Arranged in chronological order by publication date, entries provide details about the title page, format, collational formula, statement of signing, contents, pagination, press figures, catchwords, explicit, paper, type, plates, references, notes, and copies. The introduction explains the arrangement and each of these categories. Volume I covers works published from 1731 to 1759, and volume II spans the years 1760 to 1816; however, as the title indicates, subsequent editions are noted through 1984. Altogether, the bibliography encompasses more than 1,700 pages. Supplementary material, equally as valuable to the Johnson scholar, includes a list of manuscript and documentary sources about Johnson and the book trade, an extensive bibliography of printed works (42 pages long) consulted to compile the bibliography, and a chronological list of publications from 1731 to 1984. An index of items and an index of people and places conclude the last volume.

Also focused exclusively on primary sources, *Mary Wollstonecraft Godwin, 1759–1797: A Bibliography of the First and Early Editions, with Briefer Notes on Later Editions and Translations*, by John Windle, provides entries for Wollstonecraft's published writings, excluding her periodical contributions, compiled mainly from the Huntington Library and the William Andrews Clark Library, UCLA, collections and the Carl H. Pforzheimer Shelley and His Circle Collection, New York Public Library, and checked against the *ESTC*. The bibliography is arranged in three sections: "Part A. Primary Titles," "Part B. Contributions and Translations," and "Part C. False Attributions." Each main entry comprises the full title, imprint, physical description, sometimes individual copy notes, and library holdings (according to the *ESTC*), followed by entries for subsequent editions. This slim and attractive volume is illustrated throughout with portraits of Wollstonecraft and title-page reproductions from many of the enumerated works. A brief bibliography of secondary sources about Wollstonecraft's life and times, drawn from Claire Tomalin's *The Life and Death of Mary Wollstonecraft* (1992), and a chronology of events, 1759 to 1797, round out the volume, as well as a brief index of works.

Deborah D. Rogers's *Ann Radcliffe: A Bio-Bibiography* begins with an overview of Radcliffe's life, rich with excerpts from many of the titles described in the bibliography proper. This volume covers both primary and secondary sources, arranged in the following order: "Primary Bibliography: Editions and Translations," "Early Reviews and Notices, 1789–1826," "Criticism, 1827–1899," "Twentieth-Century Criticism, Part I: 1900–1949," "Twentieth-Century Criticism, Part II: 1950–Present," "Full-Length Works," "Dissertations," and "Bibliographies." As illustrated by this list, the bibliography represents an extensive effort to catalog and describe Radcliffe's literary output and scholarship about Radcliffe through 1994. Each entry gives bibliographic information, is assigned a unique number by section, and includes a one- to two-sentence to full-paragraph annotation. The bibliography concludes with appendixes regarding adaptations and abridgments, parodies and imitations, and spurious attributions.

The purpose and arrangement of *Samuel Richardson: An Annotated Bibliography of Critical Studies* is similar to that of the Radcliffe bibliography. Richard Hannaford presents an introductory survey of Richardson criticism from the earliest assessments through the 1970s, followed by the complete bibliography of primary and secondary sources. Aiming to be comprehensive in scope, the bibliography covers 1,460 sources, arranged in six parts, with subdivisions for individual sections. The initial section lists novels and miscellaneous works, selected editions (including collected works, individual novels, and miscellaneous works), correspondence, and bibliographies. The section on eighteenth-century criticism organizes the entries chronologically from 1740 to 1800, so that reception can be traced throughout time, and then provides an alphabetical arrangement by author of criticism, remarks, and tributes contained in letters, diaries, memoirs, biographies, and poems. Nineteenth- and twentieth-century criticism is listed alphabetically by author. Twentieth-century criticism spans through 1978, and is further divided into the following: primary works about Richardson and his period; literary histories and collections about the development of the novel; literary and biographical criticism in periodicals, festschrifts, and literary studies; and the individual novels *Pamela*, *Clarissa*, and *Sir Charles Grandison*. The final part of the bibliography addresses Richardson's influence and foreign critical reception, as well as doctoral dissertations and theses. Although the annotations for the sources are brief, they summarize major arguments or contents and cross-reference other entries. A subject index facilitates access to epistolary technique, morality, and Richardson's influence, among many other topics, and an author index is also available. Although it was published in 1980, this bibliography is still valuable for identifying primary works and early criticism, and it can be updated by searching *MLAIB* and *ABELL*.

The third edition of ***Boswellian Studies: A Bibliography***, compiled by Anthony E. Brown, serves as an extensive guide to editions of Boswell's primary works, and also to scholarly and nonscholarly works published through 1989. In addition, Brown provides citations to extraneous material, including advertisements, notices, reviews, extracts, commentaries, obituaries, memoirs, and eighteenth-century newspaper and magazine paragraphs, which help construct a richer portrait of Boswell and his milieu. The bibliography is arranged in three main sections: "Editions, 1760–1989," "Memorabilia," and "General Studies," followed by sections for the eighteenth-century periodical sources, theses and dissertations, bibliographies, and addenda, and a subject index. The section on editions is further divided into the following: "Boswell's Works, with Advertisements, Notices, Reviews, Extracts, and Commentaries, 1760–1793, with Subsequent Editions through 1989," "Unpublished Works, with Notices, etc., from 1857–1989," "Discovery and Publication of 'The Boswell Papers,'" "Trade Editions of Boswell's Journal, 1950–1989," "Research Editions of Boswell's Papers and Letters, 1966–1988," and translations of his works. The "Memorabilia" section features obituaries and memoirs of Boswell from 1795 to 1803, and biographies from 1891 to 1984. "General Studies" covers scholarship, but also "whimsical sketch and parody" (xiii), organized alphabetically by author (or title, if no author is given).

Readers will need to consult the "Abbreviations" list to decipher some bibliographic citations. Annotations for secondary sources are typically brief, consisting of one or two sentences. Although scholars will need to supplement the "General Studies" section with more recent criticism, this bibliography remains a viable source for literary investigations of Boswell.

COMPILING YOUR OWN
AUTHOR-CENTERED BIBLIOGRAPHY

As previously mentioned, it may not be possible to find a separately published bibliography for every author. Online access to the major literary databases and to *WorldCat* and the *ESTC* make it feasible to compile your own author bibliography, which you can supplement by consulting *NCBEL* or other relevant print bibliographies, and possibly bibliographies on the Web.

The primary and secondary sources that you identify can then be exported or entered manually into a management tool, like RefWorks or Endnote, and duplicates removed, to create a working bibliography for your research.

The eighteenth-century novelist, playwright, poet, and translator Penelope Aubin serves well as an example of an author who has yet to have her own monograph bibliography. Since we know that she has an entry in *Eighteenth-Century Anglo-American Women Novelists*, we can start by looking there for a list of Aubin's novels, as well as twentieth-century criticism published to the 1990s. To begin identifying additional books, book chapters, scholarly journal articles, and dissertations about Aubin, we searched in *MLAIB* with the primary subject author heading "Aubin, Penelope (ca. 1685–1731)," which found fifteen works, followed by the keyword search *aubin penelope*, which retrieved five additional items. The earliest works of criticism in this database date from the 1950s, with renewed attention seen in the 1980s, which continued to build into the twenty-first century. Scanning the subject headings revealed that this author has two primary subject author headings, one that includes Mrs., and the other without (e.g., "Aubin, Mrs. Penelope [ca. 1685–1731]"), so both should be employed. A search in *ABELL* with the subject heading "Aubin Penelope" achieves fifteen results, and a keyword search with her name obtains three more sources, including a full-text search of the journals. The first source in *ABELL* dates to the early 1980s. To take advantage of full-text searching, you can also search "*penelope aubin*" or "*mrs. aubin*" in *Google Scholar* to find additional sources, although they may vary in relevancy.

Using the Library of Congress author heading "Aubin Penelope, 1679–1731" in *WorldCat* results in 275 records, representing print, microform, and electronic versions of her authored or translated works. Searching for Penelope Aubin as a subject with the official heading retrieves only six items, four of which are dissertations or theses. A keyword search of *mrs n1 aubin* recalls 212 items, including the 1944 book *Women Writers, Their Contribution to the English Novel, 1621–1744*, which discusses Aubin's work in a chapter, along with eight other authors. Most of these records are actually electronic versions of Aubin's own or translated works, rather than works of criticism. The *ESTC* can be used to identify thirty-one primary sources, if you conduct a search with *aubin penelope* as a word from the author field. A keyword search for *aubin penelope* retrieves a few more unique records, including one work with the dedication signed Penelope Aubin.

To identify additional primary and secondary sources, we consulted the *Oxford Dictionary of National Biography*, which provides books, book chapters, journal articles, and related documents, including parish registers.

The *Dictionary of Literary Biography* volume *British Novelists, 1660–1800*, edited by Martin C. Battestin, contains a list of Aubin's books, with selected later editions from the 1970s, works edited and translated by her, and a few critical articles. Likewise, the subscription database *Orlando: Women's Writing in the British Isles from the Beginning to the Present* features a link to the *A Celebration of Women Writers* website and presents a list of her novels, along with information about individual poems, a play, translations, and collected fiction. Unfortunately, *NCBEL* doesn't treat Aubin with an individual author entry; however, two of her works, *The Life of Madam de Beaumont, a French Lady* and *The Life and Adventures of the Lady Lucy*, are listed in the "Minor Fiction" section, with dates for selected later editions. Since Aubin wasn't in the volume 2, 1660–1800, index, her example reinforces the importance of always checking the *NCBEL* complete index in volume 5.

From these preliminary results, it is evident that, thus far, minimal scholarly work has been written about Penelope Aubin, although interest in her during the twenty-first century is growing. There will certainly be duplication among the results gathered from these multiple sources, but once citations have been exported into RefWorks, EndNote, or another bibliographic management program, extraneous records can be identified and removed. If desired, the records can also be organized by primary and secondary sources, with perhaps additional categories for criticism treating individual works or other subject arrangement. With systematic and comprehensive searching of the major resources, it is possible to compile a workable, useful bibliography that can be checked against and added to as new sources are discovered.

CONCLUSION

As a scholar of eighteenth-century British literature, your research will be intimately connected to and built upon earlier criticism. Bibliographies will play a central role in enabling you to identify the critical tradition concerned with your particular literary investigation, whether it focuses on a specific work, author, genre, or other thematic approach. Fortunately, there is a wealth of general literary, period, and author-centered bibliographies to aid you in your endeavors. Period print bibliographies with targeted scopes can guide scholars to important primary and secondary sources, including early reviews, and such online bibliographies as *MLAIB* and *ABELL* feature the additional bonus of speed, multiple access points, ongoing updates ensuring access to recently published criticism, and, often, links to full-text resources.

Annual reviews and journal bibliographies, with their surveys of recent scholarship, enable you to understand current critical trends and issues, thereby placing your own work in the context of the field. With such resources in hand and careful, thorough surveying of the critical landscape, you can enrich your research and be better prepared to make your own contribution to eighteenth-century British literary studies.

Chapter Five

Scholarly Journals

So far we have focused on describing reference resources and discovery tools for literary research. In contrast, this chapter examines one of the main forums for scholarly communication—the academic journal. Although books are an essential component of scholarly research, especially in the humanities and for English literature in particular, journals also play a crucial role in disseminating ideas. In fact, since the review and publication process for journal articles is much quicker than that for monographs, journals tend to be the first to reflect new critical concerns and approaches in the field. For that reason, you may want to make it a practice to review the table of contents for those journals central to your research, to be aware of emerging discoveries. Many of the journals listed here may already be familiar to you if eighteenth-century British literature has been an ongoing interest, and, if not, you are sure to encounter these titles frequently as you pursue your research in *MLA International Bibliography* (*MLAIB*) and *Annual Bibliography of English Language and Literature* (*ABELL*), in addition to other bibliographies.

As a scholar, you will also want to identify journals suitable for publishing your own work on eighteenth-century literary figures and topics. Although many general English literature journals also address period authors and texts (and we provide descriptions for a selection of these in this chapter), the journals that form the main basis for this chapter specifically concentrate on British eighteenth-century literature and/or culture. Our list primarily focuses on English-language journals; however, you can consult the International Society for Eighteenth-Century Studies website for eighteenth-century journals in German, French, Russian, Spanish, Italian, Polish, and Greek (www.isecs .org/isecs_sieds/pages_english/18thC_journals.php).

The scholarly journals described here share several common features. In addition to their concern with British eighteenth-century literature and culture, they are most often peer-reviewed and published by a university press or professional association, they contain book reviews or list recently published books received, and they may post calls for papers, especially for thematic issues. They also offer an overview of scholarship within the past year and announce relevant conference events. Most of these journals have a Web presence, where you can find tables of contents and occasionally abstracts or full-text postings of past issues. To assist you with staying current, you can often register to receive table of contents alerts, either through e-mail or RSS feeds. Many of the journals are indexed in *MLAIB* and *ABELL*, and several are available in full text through *Project Muse*, *JSTOR*, or *Periodicals Archives Online* databases. You should be aware, however, that not every title will be indexed in the main databases comprehensively, and that you may encounter uneven coverage for individual titles. To conduct the most comprehensive review, it will still be important to search through literature journals broadly with large databases like *MLAIB* and *ABELL*, and also to consult relevant print bibliographies, annual reviews, and other reference sources; however, knowing the main eighteenth-century British literature journals will enable you to place your work in context with the current concerns and issues in the field and, ideally, prepare you to make your own contribution to the ongoing scholarly conversation.

PERIODICAL RESEARCH RESOURCES

Magazines for Libraries. Bowker, 1969– . www.ulrichsweb.com.
MLA Directory of Periodicals. New York: Modern Language Association of America. Available online through subscription to *MLAIB* and freely available to MLA members at www.mla.org.
Ulrich's Periodicals Directory. Bowker, 1932– . www.ulrichsweb.com.

If you need details about a specific journal, the quickest way to obtain that information is often by consulting the journal's website. Most journals will list their scope, typical contents (e.g., number of essays and book reviews), editorial board and policy, ISSN, frequency of publication, submission guidelines, and contact information. There are also several reference tools that can assist with acquiring journal information.

For literary journals, the **MLA Directory of Periodicals** is the main resource, since it provides entries for all of the titles indexed in *MLAIB*. Available both in print and online, the online version can be accessed through the database and offers the advantage of being searched by multiple fields (e.g., editorial names, scope, sponsoring organization, title abbreviation). Each journal entry features a detailed profile, including the journal acronym, scope, subject headings, language, publication details (e.g., start date, frequency, circulation, alternate media, URL), whether it is peer reviewed, journal status (e.g., actively indexed), editorial contact information, and subscription notes, as well as submission details and requirements, which address questions about suggested article length, time between submission and publication decision, and preferred editorial style. The *MLA Directory of Periodicals* can also be browsed by nine indexes; journals for eighteenth-century literary research can be identified through the subject index and browsed by using the terms *eighteenth* or *enlightenment*, for example.

Although the *MLA Directory* offers extensive information about literary journals, it does not evaluate those titles. *Magazines for Libraries* (*MFL*), however, was developed to guide librarians in identifying and selecting the core journals for a particular field. To that end, the entries are arranged by subject category, and they list such standard details as title, frequency, ISSN, editors, contact information, whether the resource is peer-reviewed, and intended audience. They also give an evaluative description that covers the journal's main focus, methodological approaches, the types of articles it publishes, its reputation, and whether subscription is recommended for a particular library (e.g., academic, public). You may want to consider browsing the entries for the "Literature" and "Theater" categories, or, if your research spans several disciplines, you can review the corresponding subject categories to identify additional disciplinary journals of interest.

Finally, *Ulrich's Periodicals Directory*, known online as *Ulrichsweb*, offers a comprehensive listing of periodicals worldwide, with brief profiles that include title, publisher, ISSN, country of origin, start year, frequency, content type (e.g., academic/scholarly), notes on whether a resource is refereed, language, price, special features, indexing information, website, and a brief description. Both *Magazines for Libraries* and *Ulrich's Periodicals Directory* are available online through *Ulrichsweb*, so that if a journal title also features a review in *MFL*, a "Review" tab will appear in the periodical entry, making the online version particularly useful for obtaining both basic information and an evaluative overview.

EIGHTEENTH-CENTURY LITERATURE

Age of Johnson: A Scholarly Annual. New York: AMS Press, 1987–. Annual. ISSN: 0884-5816. www.amspressinc.com/aj.html.

Digital Defoe: Studies in Defoe and His Contemporaries. Normal: Illinois
State University, 2009–. Annual. ISSN: 1948-1802. english.illinoisstate
.edu/digitaldefoe/index.shtml.

Eighteenth-Century Fiction. Toronto, Ontario, Canada: University of Toronto
Press, 1988– . Quarterly. ISSN: 0840-6286. www.humanities.mcmaster
.ca/~ecf.

The Eighteenth-Century Novel. New York: AMS Press, 2001– . Annual.
ISSN: 1528-3631. www.amspressinc.com/ecn.html.

Johnsonian News Letter. New York: Modern Language Association of America,
1940– . 2/yr. Formally 5/yr and irregular. ISSN: 0021-728. projects.vassar
.edu/jnl/.

Literature Compass. Hoboken, NJ: Blackwell, 2004– . Monthly. ISSN: 1741-
4113. literature-compass.com.

New Rambler: Journal of the Johnson Society of London. London: Johnson
Society of London, 1941–. Annual. ISSN: 0028-6540. www.johnsonsociety
oflondon.org/newrambler.html.

Restoration and Eighteenth-Century Theatre Research. Denver, CO: University of Denver, 1963– . 2/yr. ISSN: 0034-5822. Former title: *17th and 18th
Century Theatre Research* (1962). www.du.edu/centersinstitutes/rectr.

Scriblerian and the Kit-Cats. Waterloo, IA: Pro Image, 1968– . 2/yr. ISSN:
0036-9640. www.scriblerian.net.

SEL: Studies in English Literature, 1500–1900. Houston, TX: Rice University, 1961– . Quarterly. ISSN: 0039-3657; Electronic ISSN: 1522-9270.
www.sel.rice.edu.

Swift Studies. Paderborn, Germany: Wilhelm Fink Verlag, 1986– . Annual.
ISSN: 0938-8036. www.online-swift.de.

This section describes journals that focus on eighteenth-century British and
American literature, including many that view the period from the Restoration through the beginning of the nineteenth century. Although some essays
in these journals adopt an interdisciplinary perspective, for the most part, the
journals listed here are primarily concerned with period authors, literature,
genres, and literary topics. If your interest is in traditional figures of the
Romantic period, please consult chapter 5, "Romantic Literature: Scholarly
Journals" in *Literary Research and the British Romantic Era: Strategies and
Sources* for recommended journals. In particular, you will want to review
European Romantic Review; *Prism(s): Essays in Romanticism*; *Romanticism:
The Journal of Romantic Culture and Criticism*; *Romanticism on the Net: An
Electronic Journal Devoted to Romantic Studies* (now titled *Romanticism
and Victorianism on the Net*); *Studies in Romanticism*; and *The Wordsworth*

Circle. It will also be helpful to consult titles devoted to individual Romantic authors.

The well-regarded *SEL: Studies in English Literature, 1500–1900* dedicates a separate quarterly issue to each time period, with the Summer issue covering literature of the Restoration though the eighteenth century. Other issues address the "English Renaissance" (Winter), "Tudor and Stuart Drama" (Spring), and the "Nineteenth Century" (Fall). Scholars will typically find eight to ten essays that range in length from fifteen to thirty pages, as well as a narrative overview of recent studies in the field for the specified literary period. Recent Summer issues have treated Pope's "Windsor Forest," Catherine Trotter and the humane libertine, "Property, History, and Identity in Defoe's Captain Singleton," and "Mary Wollstonecraft, Jonathan Swift, and the Passion in Reading." Although the tables of contents are posted on the journal's website at Rice University (1961–present), the full text of recent years is available to subscribers of *Project Muse.*

Published exclusively online, *Literature Compass* is similar in organization to that of *SEL*, in that it focuses on different literary time periods, treating them in separate sections within each of its monthly issues (from volume 7, 2010, onward, and previously bimonthly and annually). In addition to an "Eighteenth Century" section, each volume also publishes "Medieval," "Renaissance" "Shakespeare," "17th Century," "Romanticism," "Victorian," "20th Century and Contemporary," and "American" sections. The "Eighteenth Century" section examines the literary output on both sides of the Atlantic from various critical perspectives, with frequent assessments of the field in such articles as "The Contemporary Study of Eighteenth-Century Poetry," "Gender Studies and Eighteenth-Century British Literature," "Restoration and Eighteenth-Century Drama: New Directions in the Field," and "New Directions in Eighteenth-Century Periodical Studies." Approximately four to twelve essays are presented on the eighteenth century each year; those centered on individual authors have covered Jonathan Swift, Celia Fiennes, Samuel Johnson, Eliza Haywood, Daniel Defoe, and Sir William Jones. Other articles explore topics like Indians' travel narratives, ecocriticism, theories of metaphor, the Anglo-Indian canon, uses of antiquity in literature, garden literature, and transatlantic critical race theory. The website enables readers to browse by issue or section, search within the journal, and set up contents alerts and RSS feeds.

A little more than a decade old, *The Eighteenth-Century Novel* examines prose fiction throughout the eighteenth century, from the Restoration in 1660 to 1830. Peer-reviewed essays investigate canonical and less-familiar authors, from Daniel Defoe, Henry Fielding, Laurence Sterne, Eliza Haywood, and Samuel Richardson, to Penelope Aubin, Mary Davys, Henry Brooke, and

John Cleland. Each volume typically contains ten to fifteen articles, about fifteen to forty-five pages in length; three to fifteen book reviews; and an index. Striking a balance between authors and works at the beginning and end of the century, a recent issue offers such diverse topics as "Penelope Aubin's Novels Reconsidered: The Barbary Captivity Narrative and Christian Ecumenism in Early Eighteenth-Century Britain," "Specters of Romance: *The Female Quixote* and Domestic Fiction," and "Charlotte Smith's *Celestina* and the Rousseauvian Moral Self." Past issues have considered British Orientalist romances, Radcliffe and eighteenth-century legal practices, and the "deserving object of charity" in eighteenth-century novels.

Published for McMaster University by the University of Toronto Press, ***Eighteenth-Century Fiction*** presents essays about literature and culture during the period from 1660 to 1832. Published in English and French, the essays address a mix of authors, including Samuel Richardson, Daniel Defoe, Laurence Sterne, Eliza Haywood, Mary Wollstonecraft, Tobias Smollett, Sarah Fielding, Samuel Pratt, Frances Burney, Eliza Fenwick, Jane Barker, Sarah Scott, and Robert Bage. Featuring approximately six essays in each issue, twenty to thirty pages in length, the articles cover such topics as "Utopian Voyeurism: Androgyny and the Language of the Eyes in Haywood's *Love in Excess*," "'Seeing Something That Was Doing in the World': The Form of History in *Colonel Jack*," and "Gentlemen and Gentle Women: The Landscape Ethos in *Millenium Hall*." Several issues have a special thematic focus, for example, "Form and Formalism and the British Eighteenth-Century Novel" and "Exoticism and Cosmopolitanism," and five to twenty book reviews typically round out the content.

Restoration and Eighteenth-Century Theatre Research focuses on British and European drama and staging of the late seventeenth and eighteenth centuries. Each issue offers three to seven articles, ranging in length from ten to thirty-five pages, and also features several theatre and book reviews, as well as occasional interviews. A sample of recent articles illustrates the journal's content: "Balloon and Seraglio: Burkean Anti-Imperialism in Elizabeth Inchbald's *The Mogul Tale*," "Abject, Delude, Create: The Aesthetic Self-Consciousness of Early Eighteenth-Century Farce," and "'The Shame of This Pacific Reign': Engagement with the Past and Domestic Tragedy during the 1730s." It should be noted that the publication schedule is usually delayed, so that the most recent issue available may date from a few years ago.

Strictly a review journal, ***The Scriblerian and the Kit-Cats*** features one- to two-page reviews of literary scholarship concerned with British authors of the eighteenth century, including reviews of books, book chapters, and journal articles. This biennial publication presents approximately eighty or more unsigned reviews in each issue, organized on the website by format (articles, books), and also by literary author addressed. A "Miscellaneous" category catches cultural and historical studies, for example, eighteenth-century attitudes toward business, "Sympathy Machines: Men of Feeling and the Automaton," "Darby and Joan and the *Athenian Mercury*," and "The Poetry of Friendship: Connecting the Histories of Women and Lesbian Sexuality in the Undergraduate Classroom." A recent issue offers reviews of scholarship about Addison, Defoe, Henry Fielding, Sarah Fielding, Haywood, Inchbald, Mandeville, Manley, Parnell, Pope, Richardson, Sterne, Swift, Thomson, and Young, as well as Restoration-era authors. The author list reflects the nature of the content reviewed, but the previously mentioned names are fairly representative. In addition to the longer reviews, the journal also provides a selection of "Books Briefly Noted." *Scriblerian* is a good forum, not only for identifying recent scholarship in the field, but also for obtaining critical assessments of these publications.

A few journals are devoted to individual eighteenth-century authors. Although the main emphasis is on the particular author, the journal will also likely accept work concerned with other period authors, their contemporaries, and contextual historical studies. Published by the Friends of the Ehrenpreis Centre for Swift Studies at the Westfälische Wilhelms-Universität, Münster, since 1986, *Swift Studies* offers an annual selection of six to ten essays about Jonathan Swift and his works, life, and contemporaries, such as the Earl of Shaftesbury, Lawrence Sterne, James Arbuckle, Thomas Tickell, and Edward Young. Recent volumes have featured articles that include "Swift and Religion: From Myth to Reality," "Jonathan Swift's Historical Novel: *The Memoirs of Capt. John Creichton* (1731)," and "A Most Unlikely Friendship? Jonathan Swift, George Berkeley and the Bonds of Philosophy with, Perhaps, An Answer to an Age-Old Problem." Many of the essays are substantial in length, ranging from twenty to fifty pages. Each issue also contains an editorial, a list of recent books and articles received, and sometimes a "Notes" section. The centre's website has a complete table of contents from volume 1 to the present. Scholars might also be interested in *Online.Swift*, a project that provides an online critical edition of prose works of Jonathan Swift, with introductions and commentaries, in addition to the *Swift Criticism Database*, which is described in chapter 9, "Web Resources."

Johnson scholars are well-served by several publications. Aptly titled, *The Age of Johnson: A Scholarly Annual* is concerned with Samuel Johnson and his literary contemporaries, with articles that emphasize the "historical and political contexts of the works and authors studied." Typically featuring ten to twenty essays in each volume, the journal regularly presents a few essays specifically about Johnson and then rounds out the selection with some focusing on other authors, including Sarah Fielding, George Ballard, James

Boswell, Daniel Defoe, Frances Burney, Jane Collier, Elizabeth Inchbald, Joseph Addison, Thomas Gray, and Eliza Haywood, among many others. Recent essays have examined "The Haphazard Journey of a Mind: Experience and Reflection in Samuel Johnson's *Journey to the Western Islands of Scotland*," "Johnson, the Moral Essay, and the Moral Life of Women: The *Spectator*, the *Female Spectator*, and the *Rambler*," and "'Through the Spectacles of Books': Shakespeare, Milton, Dryden, and a Johnsonian Intertextual Topos." Volume 21 (January 2012) will be of particular interest to scholars for its special forum on electronic resources, with essays on the *English Short Title Catalog*, *18thConnect*, and electronic resources for studying eighteenth-century British periodicals. *The Age of Johnson* is also distinguished by its detailed review essays, in addition to shorter book reviews. Volume 10 published Jack Lynch's "A Bibliography of Johnsonian Studies, 1986–1997."

The ***Johnsonian News Letter*** began in 1940, with the goal of connecting the "many and disparate people who take an interest in the life and works of Samuel Johnson" (from website). The journal continues to focus on Johnson in contemporary and historical contexts, and it also publishes columns with news about his circle, such as James Boswell and Fanny Burney. A typical issue includes several feature articles, reports from Johnson societies and related activities, notes and queries, and book reviews. Only the most recent issue's contents are available on the website (currently 2009), and the journal is indexed only minimally in *ABELL* and *MLAIB*, mainly from the 1940s and 1950s.

Also concerned with Samuel Johnson's life, works, and contemporary times, the ***New Rambler: Journal of the Johnson Society of London*** publishes papers delivered to the organization, in addition to book reviews and articles. Actively indexed in *MLAIB*, the journal has been contributing to Johnson scholarship since 1941. Approximately six to eight articles each year examine such topics as Johnson and public monuments, Johnson's relationships with John Nichols and John Wesley, the abolition of slavery, and Bluestocking feminism.

Digital Defoe: Studies in Defoe and His Contemporaries represents an innovative approach to scholarly communication and defines itself as a "hybrid mediator," or rather a supplement to traditional journals, that takes advantage of new technologies to study the works of Defoe and other eighteenth-century writers. Based at Illinois State University, this peer-reviewed, online-only journal features academic articles, but also personal reflective essays and digital and multimodal projects. In keeping with this theme, the inaugural issue in 2009 was entitled "Defoe 2.0" and presented five articles, a pedagogical essay, one book review, a list of recent dissertations, and conference abstracts. This format has remained fairly consistent, and the journal's website is organized into features, exclusives (poster presentations), pedagogies, reviews, and dissertation abstracts categories, with the "Archive" displaying contents for the first two issues. Sample articles include "Building the Wall: Crusoe and the Other," "'A Thousand Little Things': Seriality and the Dangers of Suspense in *The Spectator* and *Moll Flanders*," and "Robinson Crusoe, Home School Hero." Although published only once each year, this journal makes an interesting contribution to Defoe studies.

EIGHTEENTH-CENTURY CULTURE

1650–1850: Ideas, Aesthetics, and Inquiries in the Early Modern Era. New York: AMS Press, 1994– . Annual. ISSN: 1065-3112. www.amspressinc .com/16501850.html.
Bulletin de la Société d'Etudes Anglo-Américaines des XVIIe et XVIIIe Siècles. Lille, France: Les Presses de l'Université Charles de Gaulle. 1975– . 2/yr. ISSN: 0291-3798. web.univ-pau.fr/saes/pb/guestsit/SiteSEAA/ SEAAcadresBulletin.htm.
Eighteenth-Century Ireland/Iris an dá chultúr. Dublin, Ireland: Eighteenth-Century Ireland Society, 1986– . Annual. ISSN: 0790-7915. www.ecis.ie/ journal/.
Eighteenth-Century Life. Durham, NC: Duke University Press, 1974– . 3/yr. ISSN: 0098-2601; Electronic ISSN: 1086-3192. www.dukepress.edu/ecl.
Eighteenth-Century Studies. Baltimore, MD: Johns Hopkins University Press, 1967– . Quarterly. ISSN: 0013-2586. Available online at www .press.jhu.edu/journals/eighteenth-century_studies.
Eighteenth-Century: Theory and Interpretation. University of Pennsylvania Press, 1979– . Quarterly (as of 2010). Formally 3/yr. ISSN: 0193-5380; Electronic ISSN: 1935-020. Former titles: *Burke Newsletter* (1959–1967) and *Studies in Burke and His Time* (1967–1978). ecti.pennpress.org.
Eighteenth-Century Thought. New York: AMS Press, 2003– . Annual. ISSN: 1545-0449. www.amspressinc.com/ect.html.
Eighteenth-Century Women: Studies in Their Lives, Work, and Culture. New York: AMS Press, 2001– . Annual. ISSN: 1529-5966. www.amspressinc .com/ecw.html.
Gothic Studies. Manchester, UK: Manchester University Press, 1999– . 2/ yr. ISSN: 1362-7937. www.manchesteruniversitypress.co.uk/journals/ download.asp?id=2.
Huntington Library Quarterly: Studies in English and American History and Literature. Berkeley: University of California Press, 1937– . Quarterly.

ISSN: 0018-7895; Electronic ISSN: 1544-399X. ucpressjournals.com/
journal.php?j=hlq.

Journal for Early Modern Cultural Studies (JEMCS). Bloomington: Indiana
University Press, 2000– . 2/yr. ISSN: 1531-0485. jemcs.pennpress.org.

Journal for Eighteenth-Century Studies. Hoboken, NJ: Blackwell, 2008– .
Quarterly. ISSN: 1754-0208. Former titles: *Newsletter—British Society
for Eighteenth-Century Studies* (1972–1977) and *British Journal for Eighteenth-Century Studies* (1978–2007). www.wiley.com/bw/journal.asp?
ref=1754-0194.

*Lumen: Selected Proceedings from the Canadian Society for Eighteenth-Cen-
tury Studies/Travaux de la Société Canadienne d'Etude du Dix-Huitième
Siècle*. Kelowna, British Columbia: Academic Printing and Publishing,
1982– . Annual. ISSN: 0824-3298. csecs.ca/lumen.

Studies in Eighteenth-Century Culture. Baltimore, MD: Johns Hopkins University Press, 1971– . Annual. ISSN: 0360-2370; Electronic ISSN: 1938-
6133. asecs.press.jhu.edu/secc.html.

This section describes journals that address eighteenth-century British authors and literature, but typically in concert with studies of eighteenth-century
history and culture. The individual articles may themselves be interdisciplinary investigations, or they may have a single, disciplinary focus, including
art history, music, popular culture, politics, or economics. In addition to
eighteenth-century cultural studies journals, we have also included those that
cover the century from a broader historical or genre perspective, ranging from
the early modern period to studies of the Gothic. Early modern journals that
end coverage before the eighteenth century are excluded.

Founded in 1978, as the *British Journal for Eighteenth-Century Studies*,
the ***Journal for Eighteenth-Century Studies (JECS)*** reflects the journal's
broader focus on the eighteenth century, as it was experienced in Britain, Europe, North America, and the rest of the world. Celebrating multidisciplinary
and interdisciplinary work, the journal covers literature, history, art, music,
science, economics, religion, geography, and popular culture, from theoretical to empirical studies. Each issue features three to fifteen essays and twenty
or more book reviews. Articles from a recent issue with a literary emphasis
range from "Addisonian Afterlives: Joseph Addison in Eighteenth-Century
Culture" and "Iniquity, Terror and Survival: Welsh Gothic, 1789–1804," to
"James Arbuckle's *Glotta* (1721) and the Poetry of Allusion" and "'A Closet
or a Secret Field': Horace, Protestant Devotion, and British Retirement
Poetry." The December 2011 special issue assesses the state of eighteenth-
century studies in fifteen disciplines and areas, including English literature,

British history, and art, as well as the Muslim world, Sub-Saharan Africa, South Asia, and China, among others. Previous special issues explore "Contesting Creativity," "Mutual Perceptions of Britain and Italy in the Eighteenth Century," animals, and theatre in France during the period. *JECS* is published for the British Society for Eighteenth-Century Studies.

Calling itself the "most wide-ranging journal of eighteenth-century studies," ***Eighteenth-Century Life*** offers interdisciplinary scholarship on European and world cultures of the period from a variety of critical and methodological perspectives. The eighteenth century is defined here as spanning from 1660 to 1815. Each issue features three to ten essays, of approximately fifteen to thirty pages, and one or several review essays. Although dedicated to cultural investigations, the journal usually highlights British period authors, and recent issues address Jonathan Swift, Samuel Richardson, Eliza Haywood, Sarah Scott, Alexander Pope, and Lawrence Sterne, in addition to such topics as "Selling Celebrity: Actors' Portraits in *Bell's Shakespeare* and *Bell's British Theatre*," " Negotiating Marriage and Professional Autonomy in the Careers of Eighteenth-Century Actresses," and "Satiric Strategy in Ned Ward's London Writings."

Also concerned with interdisciplinary explorations of eighteenth-century culture, ***Eighteenth-Century Studies (ECS)*** covers literary figures and topics but employs a wider lens across Britain, Europe, and North America. Five to seven articles in each issue examine such diverse subjects as popular culture and sporting life, the culture of war and civil society, the spectator and the public sphere, and early ballooning. Recent essays with a literary emphasis include "Gray's Ode and Walpole's China Tub: The Order of the Book and The Paper Lives of an Object," "How a Pie Fight Satirizes Whig-Tory Conflict in Delarivier Manley's *The New Atalantis*," and "Reason and Religious Tolerance: Mary Astell's Critique of Shaftesbury." The journal also provides review articles; single-title reviews; a list of books received; and occasionally film, exhibition, theatre, and opera reviews. Some issues are devoted to a special theme, for example, "The Disorder of Things" (Fall 2011), "China and the Making of Global Modernity" (Spring 2010), and "Dangerous Liaisons in the South Pacific" (Winter 2008). *ECS* is the official journal of the American Society for Eighteenth-Century Studies (ASECS).

Studies in Eighteenth-Century Culture is an annual publication of ASECS that presents revised versions of papers given at the society's national and regional conferences. With an emphasis on highlighting new research in the field, each volume offers ten to fifteen essays, ranging from ten to thirty pages in length, that traverse disciplines and geographies. The journal addresses British literature, but also other national literatures, the arts, and history. The most recent volume's content spans from the Bavarian Rococo to early eighteenth-century French literature, and from print and oral culture in Irish ballads to the play *Polly Honeycombe*. Readers will find essays on such British literary figures as Sarah Fielding, Henry Fielding, Anne Finch, Charlotte Lennox, and Ann Yearsley. Notes on contributors, editorial readers, and ASECS executive board members and patrons, as well as an index, are also provided.

The Eighteenth Century: Theory and Interpretation covers literature, history, science, fine arts, and popular culture of the period, from 1660 to 1800, underscoring theoretical and interpretive research. Each issue typically features three to five essays, twenty to thirty pages in length, and several signed book review essays. Recent articles have examined such topics as "Shaftesbury Takes an Ethiopian to the Carnival: Foreignness, Subjectivity, and Intersubjectivity in 'Sensus Communis,'" "The Spouters' Revenge: Apprentice Actors and the Imitation of London's Theatrical Celebrities," and "Disjecta Membra: Smollett and the Novel in Pieces," and works by Defoe, Fielding, Burney, Swift, Blake, Wollstonecraft, Richardson, and Dunton are investigated. Some issues have a special thematic focus, including "Animal, All Too Animal" (Spring 2011) and "The Drift of Fiction: Reconsidering the Eighteenth-Century Novel" (Winter 2011). Issues conclude with a note on the contributors. The journal was formally known as *Studies in Burke and His Time*, before it became *The Eighteenth Century: Theory and Interpretation* in 1979.

Also employing a multidisciplinary perspective, *Eighteenth-Century Women: Studies in Their Lives, Work, and Culture* is concerned with women's writing and cultural roles during the long eighteenth century until the death of Jane Austen in 1817. Although there is a marked emphasis on literary women from Great Britain, contributions from women in the Americas and Europe are explored as well. The journal features approximately twelve essays in each volume, ranging from ten to forty pages or so in length. Although described as an annual, there have been gaps in publication between volumes, with only six published between 2001 and 2011. Despite this delay, literary scholars of the British eighteenth century will find intriguing work on period novelists, poets, and playwrights, including such recent contributions as "Magdalen House Narratives in Frances Sheridan's Life and *Memoirs of Sidney Bidulph*," "Notorious Celebrity: Mary Wells, Theatricality, and Madness," and "Through Others' Eyes: Representations of Actresses in Eighteenth-Century Drama." Book reviews and an index are part of each volume.

Eighteenth-Century Thought may be of interest to those scholars whose research investigates the intersections between literature and philosophy, medicine, law, political theory, religion, human sciences, or economics, since all of these various subjects are treated. This annual journal publishes approximately nine to twelve essays in each volume, in addition to several review essays and book reviews. Recent essays explore miracles in the eighteenth-century public sphere, innateness in British philosophy, and animal ascension during the period; volume 3 (2007) is devoted to John Locke's legacy, from 1704 to 2004. Like some of the other AMS Press annuals, volumes aren't produced each year; five have been published from 2003 to 2012.

A refereed journal of the Eighteenth-Century Ireland Society, *Eighteenth-Century Ireland/Iris an dá chultúr* publishes one volume each year that addresses Irish history, literature, music, and the Irish abroad. Each volume offers approximately ten essays, about ten to fifteen pages in length, in addition to occasional notes, a longer review article, and one- to two-page reviews of recent books. Recent literary articles discuss Protestant rhetoric in Swift's *Drapier's Letters*, loneliness and delight in the eighteenth-century *Aisling*, and migration and maternal absence in Georgian children's fiction. Other essays examine the Apothecaries Act of 1791, sermons and the charity school movement, and Berkeley and the idea of a national bank. Although the website does not present current tables of contents, an archive features contents for volumes 1 through 13 (1986–1998).

The Canadian Society for Eighteenth-Century Studies publishes *Lumen: Selected Proceedings from the Canadian Society for Eighteenth-Century Studies/Travaux de la Société Canadienne d'Etude du Dix-Huitième Siècle* to highlight selected papers from its annual conference. This refereed collection offers articles in French or English about such topics as Eliza Haywood and the literary marketplace, Suzanne Curchod Necker and divorce, and Johann Gottfried Herder's concept of intellectual biography. Although the focus is certainly European, British authors are represented, including Daniel Defoe, Sarah Scott, Tobias Smollett, Lady Mary Wortley Montagu, Anna Barbauld, and Henry Fielding. Each volume contains approximately twelve to twenty essays, with contents for volumes I through XXIV (1982–2005) posted on the society's website.

Covering the long eighteenth century, *1650–1850: Ideas, Aesthetics, and Inquiries in the Early Modern Era* provides a forum for multidisciplinary investigations of the period, including literature, philosophy, theology, art, music, architecture, and notable people. Each volume contains approximately twelve to twenty essays, and many have a special thematic section edited by a guest editor, such as "Metaphor in the Poetry and Criticism of the Restoration and Early Eighteenth Century" and "Critical Voices: Humor, Irony, and Passion in the Literary Critics of the Long Eighteenth Century." Recent articles look at Alexander Pope's imitation of satire, Eliza Haywood's publishing activities, and Jonathan Swift's rhetorical style. Although authors and literature are perennial concerns, the journal's broader focus offers such interesting contributions as "British Portraits of Women Reading," "Thinking Outside the Box: The Non-English Speaking World in the First Decade of 1650–1850," and "Steering Towards Sanity: The Compass Points of Madness in Eighteenth-Century Britain." Volume 18 (2011) also has a research methods update about the digital humanities. Tables of contents are available on the website from 1994 to the present.

Spanning two centuries, the *Bulletin de la Société d'Études Anglo-Américaines des XVIIe et XVIIIe Siècles* publishes on a wide range of period authors, including Addison, Blake, Boswell, Cibber, Godwin, Haywood, Johnson, Pope, Richardson, Smollett, Sterne, Swift, Woodward, and Young. The majority of articles are in French and average about ten pages. They investigate such topics as Mary Delany's correspondence, republican sentiment in Royall Tyler's *The Contrast*, and religious controversies in Scotland during the eighteenth century, among other literary and cultural topics. Articles are occasionally presented in English. Each issue also contains short, signed book reviews.

Journal for Early Modern Cultural Studies (*JEMCS*) employs common theoretical approaches (e.g., cultural studies, gender studies, postmodernism, colonial and postcolonial studies) to explore cultural history across a wide range of disciplines, from literary criticism to anthropology, art history to sociology, and political science to economics, as well as African, European, American, and Asian studies. The early modern period is interpreted broadly, from the late fifteenth through the late nineteenth centuries. This extensive time frame is roughly divided into early and late periods, so that one issue concentrates on the fifteenth, sixteenth, and early seventeenth centuries, and the other covers the late seventeenth, eighteenth, and nineteenth centuries. Each issue typically offers four to six essays, ranging from twenty to thirty-five pages in length, and one to three review essays. Recent eighteenth-century-focused articles investigate print technology and the pastoral body in John Gay's *The What D'Ye Call It*, European selfhood in Lady Mary Wortley Montagu's *Letters from the Levant*, and pantomimic poetics and the rhetoric of Augustan wit. A few issues are organized around a special theme, including the plague (Fall/Winter 2010), "The Spanish Connection: Literary and Historical Perspectives on Anglo-Iberian Relations" (Spring/Summer 2010), and "Climate and Crisis" (Fall/Winter 2008). The journal is the official publication of the Group of Early Modern Cultural Studies.

Published for the Huntington Library by the University of California Press, the *Huntington Library Quarterly: Studies in English and American History and Literature* reflects the library's collecting interests in the literature, art, and history of the early modern period during the sixteenth, seventeenth, and eighteenth centuries. Within these subject areas, the journal is particularly concerned with textual and bibliographical studies; the history of printing and publishing; social and political contexts; interactions between literature, politics, and religion; the performance history of music and drama; and American studies. Each issue features three to five substantial essays that range anywhere from twenty-five to forty-five pages in length, as well as a selection of book review essays, ranging from five to ten pages in length, and shorter reviews. Scholars of eighteenth-century British literature will find recently explored topics the likes of "The Socio-Politics of London Comedy from Jonson to Steele," "Writings of the Left Hand: William Blake Forges a New Political Aesthetic," "'In Wit Superior, as in Fighting': Kitty Clive and the Conquest of a Rival Queen," and "A True Account of the Design and Advantages of the South-Sea Trade: Profits, Propaganda, and the Peace Preliminaries of 1711." An "Intramuralia" section notes the Huntington's recent acquisitions of rare books, manuscripts, and ephemera. The journal also publishes special issues, including those on prison writings, religion and cultural transformation, and early modern London.

Centered on manifestations of the Gothic from the eighteenth century through the modern era, **Gothic Studies** explores this genre primarily in literature, but also in film, popular culture, and interdisciplinary endeavors. Often beginning with an introduction, more recent issues then present five to seven articles that range from ten to twenty pages in length; review essays and shorter reviews may also be included. Not every issue addresses the eighteenth century, but sample articles that cover the period are "Gothic Gothicism: Norse Terror in the Late Eighteenth to Early Nineteenth Centuries," "Sublime Patriarchs and the Problems of the New Middle Class in Ann Radcliffe's *The Mysteries of Udolpho* and *The Italian*," "Gothic Threats: The Role of Danger in the Critical Evaluation of *The Monk* and *The Mysteries of Udolpho*," and "'Myself Creating What I Saw': The Morality of the Spectator in Eighteenth-Century Gothic." Some issues are organized around a theme, for instance, "Italy and the Gothic," "Contemporary Scottish Gothic," "Exploring Gothic Sexuality," and "Postfeminist Gothic." Although the journal is available in full text through a subscription database, one issue (May 2004) is currently offered as an open-access gesture on the Manchester University Press website.

GENERAL

Éire-Ireland: A Journal of Irish Studies. Morristown, NJ: Irish American Cultural Institute, 1966– . 2/yr. ISSN: 0013-2683; Electronic ISSN: 1550-5162. www.iaci-usa.org.

ELH: English Literary History. Baltimore, MD: Johns Hopkins University Press, 1934– . Quarterly. ISSN: 0013-8304; Electronic ISSN: 1080-6547. www.press.jhu.edu/journals/english_literary_history.

English Language Notes. Boulder: University of Colorado at Boulder, 1963– . 2/yr. ISSN: 0013-8282. www.colorado.edu/journals/eln.

Essays in Criticism: A Quarterly Journal of Literary Criticism. Oxford, UK: Oxford University Press, 1951– . Quarterly. ISSN: 0014-0856; Electronic ISSN: 1471-6852. eic.oxfordjournals.org.

Modern Language Quarterly: A Journal of Literary History. Durham, NC: Duke University Press, 1940– . Quarterly. ISSN: 0026-7929; Electronic ISSN: 1527-1943. depts.washington.edu/mlq.

Modern Language Review. London: Maney Publishing for the Modern Humanities Research Association, 1905– . Quarterly. ISSN: 0026-7937. www.mhra.org.uk/Publications/Journals/mlr.html.

New Literary History: A Journal of Theory and Interpretation. Baltimore, MD; Johns Hopkins University Press, 1969– . Quarterly. ISSN: 0028-6087; Electronic ISSN: 1080-661X. www.newliteraryhistory.org.

Philological Quarterly. Olwa City: University of Iowa, 1922– . Quarterly. ISSN: 0031-7977. english.uiowa.edu/pq.

PMLA: Publications of the Modern Language Association of America. New York: Modern Language Association of America, 1884– . 6/yr. ISSN: 0030-8129. www.mla.org/pmla.

Review of English Studies. Oxford, UK: Oxford University Press, 1925– . 5/yr. ISSN: 0034-6551. res.oxfordjournals.org.

Scottish Literary Review. Glasgow, Scotland: Association for Scottish Literary Studies, 2009– . 2/yr. ISSN: 1756-5634. Former titles: *Scottish Literary Journal* (1974–2000) and *Scottish Studies Review* (2000–2008). www.asls .org.uk.

Studies in the Novel. Denton: University of North Texas, 1969– . Quarterly. ISSN: 0039-3827; Electronic ISSN: 1934-1512. www.engl.unt.edu/sitn.

Women's Writing. New York: Taylor & Francis, 1994– . 3/yr. ISSN: 0969-9082; Electronic ISSN: 1747-5848. www.tandf.co.uk/journals/titles/ 09699082.asp.

Yearbook of English Studies. London: Maney Publishing for the Modern Humanities Research Association, 1970– . Annual. ISSN: 0306-2473. www .mhra.org.uk.

This final section addresses a selection of core journals for the study of British literature in general, with titles that cover multiple literary periods, in addition to, in some instances, the literatures of America and Europe. Although their focus is not on any one particular time period, these principal publications often feature articles about authors and literary subjects of the eighteenth century. Keep in mind that this list is not exhaustive. Rather, the intent is to introduce the main journals recognized in the field of literary studies. Perusing the tables of contents of these journals is one way to keep abreast of new scholarship and literary trends; however, searching *MLAIB* and *ABELL* will be the most expedient way to identify articles of relevance for your particular research project.

As the Modern Language Association of America's flagship journal, ***PMLA: Publications of the Modern Language Association of America*** plays a preeminent role in literary scholarship. In existence since 1884, the journal is concerned with language and literature broadly and thus publishes a variety of literary topics and theoretical perspectives. Issues contain five to eight articles that range from fifteen to twenty pages in length, and a selection of shorter articles in sections titled "The Changing Profession," "Theories and Methodologies," "Little-Known Documents," and "Criticism in Translation." The November issue is devoted to the annual conference. In a recent special topic issue, "Celebrity, Fame, and Notoriety," Colley Cibber's adaptation of Shakespeare's *Richard III* is examined in relationship to celebrity and surveillance in eighteenth-century England. Other articles about eighteenth-century literature include "'Stock the Parish with Beauties': Henry Fielding's Parochial Vision," "From Idiot Beast to Idiot Sublime: Mental Disability in John Cleland's *Fanny Hill*," and "Devouring Posterity: *A Modest Proposal*, Empire, and Ireland's 'Debt of the Nation.'"

The Modern Humanities Research Association (MHRA), the British equivalent of the Modern Language Association, has been publishing ***Modern Language Review*** since 1905. This long-standing journal presents scholarship on medieval and modern European languages, literatures, and cultures, including English, American, French, German, Spanish, Latin American, and Italian literatures; comparative literature; critical theory; and linguistics. Each issue usually offers approximately ten articles of fifteen to twenty pages in length and numerous book reviews, with a total of about 500 reviews for the year. Given this wide subject matter, articles relevant to eighteenth-century British literature appear just a few times per volume, but this is an excellent source if your interests lie in comparing British authors and literature to other eighteenth-century European authors and literatures. For example, recent issues examine "The Value of Money in *Robinson Crusoe, Moll Flanders*, and *Roxana*," "Frances Burney as Satirist," "William Hymers and the Editing of William Collins's Poems, 1765–1797," "'A Man's a Man for A' That' and 'trotz alledem': Robert Burns, Ferdinand Freiligrath, and Their Reception in the German Folksong Movement," and "The Concept of Irritability and the Critique of Sensibility in Eighteenth-Century Germany."

The MHRA also publishes *The Yearbook of English Studies* as a forum for additional, specialized articles that specifically concern English-language literatures. Many of the articles in this annual are commissioned to meet a particular theme or topic for the volume, which consists of approximately sixteen to twenty articles, ranging from ten to twenty pages each, and eighty book reviews. Some examples of eighteenth-century focused content are "Cultural Possession, Imperial Control, and Comparative Religion: The Calcutta Perspectives of Sir William Jones and Nathaniel Brassey Halhed," "Consuming Time: Narrative and Disease in *Tristram Shandy*," and "Time and Tense in Eighteenth-Century Narratives of Madness."

Literary history is the principal concern of several journals. *ELH: English Literary History* has been addressing English and American literature through critical, historical, and theoretical studies since 1934. This respected journal features nine or ten articles in each quarterly issue, twenty to forty pages in length, but it does not publish book reviews. Authors and themes of the eighteenth century are covered on a regular basis, the likes of Richardson, Shaftesbury, and Finch, as well as convict transportation and penitence in *Moll Flanders*, gentleness and irony in *Gulliver's Travels*, and "Parting Shots: Eighteenth-Century Displacements of the Male Body at War" in the works of Defoe, Swift, Manley, Sterne, Pope, and Smollett. If your work centers on Romantic figures, volumes 4 through 16 (1937–1949) contain "The Romantic Movement: A Selective and Critical Bibliography" for the years 1936 to 1948.

Modern Language Quarterly: A Journal of Literary History (*MLQ*) has been investigating historical origins since its foundation in 1940. Proclaiming an emphasis on literary change throughout time, from the medieval period to the present, *MLQ* publishes essays that explore different theoretical and cultural analyses of literary texts as "vehicles of change." Each issue contains three to six essays, ranging from fifteen to thirty pages, and eight signed book reviews of two to four pages. The most recent issue features an essay by Gayatri Chakravorty Spivak entitled "Why Study the Past?" The journal covers British, American, and European literatures and occasionally offers thematic issues devoted to such topics as "Literary Value," "Romancing Scotland," "Performance and History: What History?" and "Defining Influences." Since the journal's scope is so broad, articles about eighteenth-century British authors appear infrequently; however, issues in the past few years have included studies of "Henry Fielding and the 'Scriblerians,'" "Alternative Antiquarianisms of Scotland and the North," and "The Female Penseroso: Anna Seward, Sociable Poetry, and the Handelian Consensus." The *MLQ* website lets you view titles of forthcoming articles about six months in advance.

The recipient of six awards from the Council of Editors of Learned Journals, *New Literary History: A Journal of Theory and Interpretation* examines the relationship between literary and cultural texts from a wide theoretical lens. The essays in this journal are typically concerned with theoretical topics rather than individual authors, as represented by the article "Readers' Temperaments and Fictional Character," and illustrated by the special themes "Comparison," "New Sociologies of Literature," "What Is an Avant-Garde?," "Character," and "Context?" Some exceptions include "Dialogues with/and Great Books: With Some Serious Reflections on *Robinson Crusoe*" and "Henry Mackenzie's Ruined Feelings: Romance, Race, and the Afterlife of Sentimental Exchange." Issues frequently feature an introduction and seven to ten essays, ranging from fifteen to twenty-five pages, but no book reviews.

Women's Writing looks at women's literary endeavors from the Elizabethan era through the long nineteenth century, encompassing both theoretical and historical perspectives. With a goal of providing a "forum for dialogue, discussion, and debate," the journal encourages a range of critical studies about women's writing during this period. Many issues are devoted to special topics, whether centered on individual authors, genres, national literatures, or literary themes, including Mary Robinson, Mary Wollstonecraft, "Augustan Women," "Female Gothic Writing," "Women Dramatists of the Early Modern Period," "Scottish Women's Writing," "Women's Letter Writing," "Transgressive Women," "Women and Science," and "Sex, Gender, and the Female Body." General, rather than thematic, issues have recently published such eighteenth-century content as "Recognizing Women's Dramas as Political Writing: The Plays of 1701 by Wiseman, Pix, and Trotter," "Susanna Blamire's Ecological Imagination: *Stoklewath; or, the Cumbrian Village*," and "Life Lessons: Self-Defence and Social Didactism in Elizabeth Gooch's Life-Writing and *The Contrast*." Approximately six or seven scholarly articles, ranging from fifteen to twenty pages, comprise each issue, in addition to three or four two-page signed book reviews. The journal's website offers an index to issues from volumes 1 through 16, listed chronologically, and by women writers, theme and literary periods, and country.

Given the rise of the genre during the eighteenth century, *Studies in the Novel* will be of particular interest to scholars working with novelists of the period. Although the journal examines this literary form in any era, scholarly articles treat such authors as Burney, Wollstonecraft, Richardson, Fielding, Radcliffe, Sterne, Smollett, Hearne, Defoe, and Haywood. A typical issue contains five or six essays, ranging from twenty to thirty pages; one or two review essays of about five pages; and approximately ten shorter book reviews. Recent articles primarily cover late eighteenth-century authors and themes, for example, "The Economics of Plot in Burney's *Camilla*" and "Mocking the Mothers of the Novel: Mary Wollstonecraft, Maternal Metaphor, and the Reproduction of Sympathy." Special topical issues are published on occasion. Forthcoming issues will address David Foster Wallace, science fiction, and Willa Cather.

Two interdisciplinary journals provide nationally focused investigations of literature and culture. Considered one of the leading journals for Irish Studies, *Éire-Ireland: A Journal of Irish Studies* has been published since 1966, by the Irish American Cultural Institute. The humanities, arts, and social sciences all fall within its wide scope. Scholarly articles range from twenty to thirty pages, usually about ten to fifteen in each issue, although shorter notes are also accepted. Literary topics appear on a regular basis, and recent articles about the eighteenth century include "The Famine of 1740–1741: Representations in Gaelic Poetry," "Jonathan Swift's Childhoods," and "'Evanescent Impressions': Public Lectures and the Popularization of Science in Ireland, 1770–1860." Some issues are centered on a specific theme, for example. urban Ireland, "Children, Childhood, and Irish Society," and Ireland and imperialism. The Irish American Cultural Institute website features a comprehensive index to volumes 1 through 34 (1966–1999), with access by subject, author, and title.

The *Scottish Literary Review* is primarily concerned with Scottish literature, but the journal also examines historical, cultural, social, and philosophical contexts and the relationship between literature, film, and theatre. A typical issue presents eight or ten essays, often ten to twenty-five pages in length. The Autumn/Winter issue offers approximately twenty or more signed book reviews of two to five pages, and the Spring/Summer issue has a list of selected publications for the year. Recent examples of eighteenth-century topics range from "Three New James Boswell Articles from *The Public Advertiser*, 1763" to "Mungo Park, Man of Letters," and from "'This Changeableness in Character': Exploring Masculinity and Nationhood on James Boswell's Grand Tour" to "'In Costume Scotch o'er Bog and Park, My Hame-Bred Muse Delighted Plays': Samuel Thomson's Poetic Fashioning of the Ulster Landscape." Formerly known as the *Scottish Literary Journal* (1974–2000) and *Scottish Studies Review* (2000–2008), the journal continues to be published by the Association for Scottish Literary Studies.

Two Oxford University Press journals play an influential role in literary studies. Published since 1925, *The Review of English Studies* is more conservative in its focus on historical scholarship, rather than "interpretative criticism." In this case, English literature means British, American, and postcolonial literatures in English. The four to six essays in a typical issue, which range from five to thirty pages in length, regularly address canonical figures and texts, from Old English riddles to twentieth-century authors, although lesser-known authors are also covered. Articles concerned with the eighteenth century appear frequently, for instance, "'Happy Copiousness'? *OED*'s Recording of Female Authors of the Eighteenth Century," "Lord Hervey, Poetic Voice and Gender," "The Difficulties of Swift's *Journal to Stella*," and "'It Ought not to be Lost to the World': The Transmission and Consumption of Eighteenth-Century Lyric Verse." Each issue also contains approximately twenty to twenty-five reviews. Every year, one essay is designated *The Review of English Studies* prize essay, currently featured in the June issue.

Essays in Criticism: A Quarterly Journal of Literary Criticism (EIC), also published by Oxford University Press, complements *The Review of English Studies* with its emphasis on theoretical interpretations of literature from Chaucer to contemporary works. Founded in 1951, by distinguished scholar F. W. Bateson, *EIC* features a selection of two to five essays (fifteen to twenty-five pages in length); a "Critical Opinion" section that poses such questions as the "Fate of Beauty" and the "Fate of Stupidity," or explores topics like "Shakespeare's Williams"; and approximately five book reviews. The April issue usually highlights the F. W. Bateson Memorial Lecture, which, in 2011, was given by Adrian Poole on Henry James and charm. The journal's website makes a recording of the lecture available to subscribers (2010–present). Examples of articles of relevance for earlier eighteenth-century studies are limited and include "Sterne's Patriotic Shandeism" and "Accumulation in Johnson's *Dictionary*," although Wordsworth and the Romantics are well represented.

Philological Quarterly (PQ) is another journal of long-standing importance in the field that covers European medieval to modern languages and literatures. One issue each year is typically devoted to a special theme; in 2009 this emphasis was "Unexpected Encounters: Rewriting Women in the Eighteenth and Nineteenth Centuries." Other special themes have addressed modernist studies, the transnational picaresque, the Middle Ages, and new formalism. Each issue provides five to ten articles, ten to forty pages in length, and a list of books received. Several essays from 2010 investigate Defoe and questions of authorship, including "Did Defoe Write *Moll Flanders* and *Roxana?*" "On the Attribution of Novels to Daniel Defoe," and "Did Defoe Write *Roxana?* Does It Matter?" in addition to an article about Henry Fielding's antisocial affectation. Scholars will also find essays about other eighteenth-century authors examined on a regular basis throughout this journal's career. *PQ* published "The Romantic Movement: A Selective and Critical Bibliography for the Year" from 1949 to 1963, represented in volumes 29 through 43 (1950–1964).

Based at the University of Colorado at Boulder, ***English Language Notes (ELN)*** is an interdisciplinary journal "devoted exclusively to special topics in all fields of literary and cultural studies." In the past few years, those top-ics have concerned "The Shape of the I," "Transnational Exchange," "Juris-Dictions," and "Genre and Affect." *ELN* is published twice a year, presenting approximately twenty articles in each issue that range from six to fifteen pages. A few examples of eighteenth-century content include "Hyper-Reality and the Gothic Affect: The Sublimation of Fear from Burke and Walpole to *The Ring*," "Courtship and Private Character in Johnson's *Rambler* Essays on Marriage," "The Crusonian Alphabet: Thomas Spence's *Grand Repository of the English Language*," and "'Sweetness' in the Poetry of William Collins." Carrying on the responsibility for "The Romantic Movement: A Selective and Critical Bibliography for the Year," *ELN* published this bibliography as a supplement to volumes 3 through 17 (1965–1979).

CONCLUSION

Understanding the current scholarly conversation in your field is crucial for building the platform upon which to situate your own research, with the ulti-mate goal of contributing to the dialogue. The journals described in this chap-ter are one of the principal ways to identify new scholarship in eighteenth-century literary studies. The articles featured in these journals reflect recent trends in the field and ongoing areas of inquiry and will help you to become familiar with the work of future colleagues. Book reviews, lists of books received, and annual or thematic overviews of current scholarship included in many of these titles will provide an additional means of staying informed. Be sure to take advantage of electronic alerting services through e-mail or RSS feeds to survey the contents of journals particularly suited to your work. Although it is still essential to consult the main bibliographies to ensure more comprehensive reviews of the literature, following eighteenth-century liter-ary journals places you at the center of new scholarly work and will be key to enriching your research, as well as your knowledge of eighteenth-century literary studies.

Chapter Six

Eighteenth-Century Books, Periodicals, and Newspapers

At the end of the seventeenth century, the Licensing Act expired and the Stationers' Company lost its royal charter and, therefore, lost its monopoly on printing.[1] By the turn of the century, with these two barriers gone, the publishing industry began to evolve, and printing spread beyond the confines of London, Cambridge, and Oxford to the provinces.[2] Throughout the century, such genres as the novel, daily newspaper, weekly and monthly periodical, dictionary, and encyclopedia developed and began to assume recognizable and distinct traits. Literacy rates grew, and, since books, newspapers, and periodicals were expensive, reading matter was shared through coffee houses, circulating libraries, subscription libraries, and book clubs.[3] The former habits of intensive reading in selected, primarily religious, texts transitioned into extensive, broader tastes in reading matter.[4]

In the opening decade of the century, the first regional newspaper (*Norwich Post*, 1701) and the first London daily newspaper (*Daily Courant*, 1702) were founded,[5] and the essay periodical was born. Although the implementation of the Stamp Act, in 1712, made serial publishing more precarious because of high taxes, these early efforts were the seeds of the robust and vital magazine and newspaper industry to come. By 1808, there were more than 100 provincial newspapers, in addition to the large number of dailies, triweeklies, and biweeklies in London.[6] At the beginning of the century, there were no clear demarcations between various types of serial publications, for they shared similar traits. Even so, today scholars group the emerging periodical genre into three general categories: essay, monthly magazines, and review periodicals.[7]

The essay periodical, the most successful being Addison and Steele's *Tatler* (1709) and *Spectator* (1711), was the prevalent form, but, in 1731, when Edward Cave's *Gentleman's Magazine* was founded, the periodical began to shift to an edited monthly that covered a broad range of topics, with original articles and articles reprinted from other sources.[8] The *Oxford English Dictionary* cites Cave's publication title as the source for the definition of the word *magazine* as a "periodical publication containing articles by various writers; esp. one with stories, articles on general subjects, etc., and illustrated with pictures, or a similar publication prepared for a special-interest readership."[9] *Museum,* another term frequently seen in eighteenth-century periodical titles, had a similar definition at the time, but that meaning did not survive,[10] and scholars frequently refer to these monthlies as miscellanies.

In 1749, Ralph Griffiths introduced the third type of periodical, the review, to provide guidance for readers to the abundance and varieties of books being printed and sold (discussed in-depth in chapter 7). Suarez summarizes these statistics for fiction publishing, writing that there were approximately 45 works in the first decade of the century, 210 in the 1740s, 292 in the 1760s, 405 in the 1780s, and 701 in the 1790s, and he also notes that, "Another 10 percent of the known output of fiction has probably vanished without a trace."[11] This represents a small portion of the subject matter published, which included agriculture, biography, business, education, leisure and travel, history, science, music, politics, and religion, to name a few.[12]

For the eighteenth-century literary researcher, the ongoing growth and changes in the print culture as it moved from the bookseller into a commercial industry, and the rapid comings and goings of serial publications, offer challenges in terms of gaining a complete picture of and access to primary source materials. But through modern editions and print facsimiles, as well as microform and digital collections, today's scholar does have a wealth of reproduced material available that provides the widest possible access to the print culture of the eighteenth century. This chapter, divided into three broad categories of books and other printed matter, periodicals, and newspapers, begins with an overview of the types of materials a researcher will encounter and strategies for finding relevant resources.

PRINT, MICROFORM, AND DIGITAL FORMATS

Unless conducting research in a geographic area with rich eighteenth-century rare book collections, many researchers will depend upon modern editions and print, microform, and digital facsimiles of eighteenth-century books, journals, and newspapers. In chapter 3, we identify techniques for finding reprints and scholarly editions using library catalogs. When working on a canonical figure, where various editions of a work exist, the editor attempts to create the best text possible, while at the same time providing the textual variations for the reader.

As digital facsimiles of texts become more readily available via commercial and open-access venues, is there a need for edited versions?

Discussing the possible demise of the scholarly editions, or indeed any edited editions, in the digital age, J. Stephen Murphy advocates the need for editors to select the "form of a text that is most worthy of preservation in a complete and clear reading text, but also preserves the textual variants not included there," a practice that some scholars see as invasive, as coming between the reader and the text.[13] But as university press budgets shrink, will any scholarly edition, even in digital form, continue to exist when electronic versions of the original printed text are available online? Murphy points out the problems he sees with such an outcome, using a Google search for William Blake's "The Tyger" as an example:

> To begin with, if a student misspells the poem "The Tiger," she will get to the poem, but it will be a reproduction from a 1919 anthology. Unfortunately, misspelling the poem in the Blake Archive search engine will provide no results, which ensures that a visitor to the site will not read the poem there. . . . Worse yet, a search for "The Tyger" on 11 April 2008 provided 888 results, not one of which was the Blake Archive.[14]

The differing punctuation in the three sample results Murphy chose changes the tone of the poem. He declares that even going to the Blake Archive with no guidance, the "novice Blake reader is unlikely to know where to start" or how to choose the variation of the poem that her classmates and scholars will read and discuss.[15] We are, however, in a period where digital collections, in particular, offer facsimile copies for editions of eighteenth-century publications. Scholars can peruse not only multiple editions of *Robinson Crusoe*, the *Spectator*, and *Pamela*, but he or she can also discover forgotten works not available in modern print. "Of the 2,500 or so fiction titles published during the century, fewer than twenty-five are read for pleasure by nonspecialists today."[16] Facsimiles permit unprecedented opportunities for access, but scholarly editions supply more than an edited text, for editors identify obscure references, give background information, and compile detailed indexes to access the text. The scholarly edition provides the reader with a foundation from which to work, so that each person interested in that literary figure doesn't have to continually reidentify all the obscure details of a text to understand it. Anyone who has tried to search for specific references in the many editions of the *Spectator* in *Eighteenth Century Collections Online* (*ECCO*) comes to appreciate the detailed index found in Donald F. Bond's edition of the *Spectator* (see the following discussion).

Microforms, once a staple of twentieth-century libraries, are rapidly being replaced by digital Web-based versions of the content. Several of the older collections discussed in the upcoming sections are available in both formats, while newer content is largely available online. Commercial projects were initially focused on digitizing the large microform collections, while smaller, online subject collections on narrow topics were not seen as financially viable; more recently, however, such commercial publishers as Gale and Adam Matthew have begun creating niche collections, which used to be available only as small microform collections, for example, *Aristocratic Women: The Social, Political, and Cultural History of Rich and Powerful Women*. We are in a transition period between these two formats, and, while digital may never replace print completely, it will almost certainly eventually replace microforms.

There are several reasons why microforms were, and still are, attractive formats: A great deal of data can be stored in a compact format; they are easy to preserve; and, for certain types of microforms, the technology is basic and affordable. The most common types of microform are microfilm (generally 35 mm film on a reel) or microfiche (3″ x 5″ film cards). Other early formats, including microopaque (white cards with text, requiring technology that bounces light off the card onto a screen) and ultramicrofiche (extremely reduced images packed into a card even smaller than microfiche), fell out of favor, although relevant eighteenth-century texts are found in both formats, for instance, *Three Centuries of English and American Plays: England 1500–1800* and *The Microbook Library of English Literature*. Newspapers were early microfilm candidates for libraries because long runs of dailies could be stored in small boxes as opposed to keeping unwieldy stacks of print copies. UMI, now ProQuest, began microfilming rare books in the 1930s for the *Early English Books* project, thus providing wider access for scholars without easy access to these books and preserving the originals from overuse and deterioration.[17] For titles only available in microform, many libraries have microform scanners that allow film or fiche to be digitized by the patron.

Digital content varies in terms of type, quality, and access. The quality of the image is generally dependent upon the purpose of the project and procedures used. Google Books, HathiTrust Digital Library (HathiTrust), and Internet Archive all have scans of pre-1923 books and make them freely available on the Web. Google's initial intent was to scan for access, not for preservation; therefore, the quality can be poor. Materials were scanned rapidly in black and white, and sometimes the fingers of the person doing the work were copied as well; such reproduction is intended for online consumption, not digital preservation. Commercially available digital facsimile collections (*ECCO* and the *17th and 18th Century Burney Collection Newspapers*) were scanned from microfilm. With other projects, the facsimile is intended to provide as close an approximation to the original as possible, so that the color and even the texture of the paper is captured. Collections of literary texts, such *Eighteenth-Century Fiction*, do not contain facsimiles but are transcriptions and allow scholars to search easily across various literary genres from different eras.

Eighteenth-century literary scholars will encounter all alternative formats serving in place of the original, possibly even in archives and special collections. As discussed in chapter 1, keyword searches in digital collection databases using OCR and fuzzy searching can be problematic. While print or electronic scholarly editions of texts may have annotations to explain the context of words and works, this is not necessarily true for facsimile collections, whether online or in microform; therefore, developing excellent search skills is vital to successfully using the abundance of digital content available to the eighteenth-century literary scholar.

Those without access to the digital collections may need the microform. When a digital collection is also available in microform, that information is noted. The *WorldCat* discussion that appears in this chapter provides strategies for locating microforms to borrow via interlibrary loan. For further information about manuscript and archival materials, see chapter 8, "Archives and Manuscripts Collections."

FINDING REPRINTS, MICROFORM, AND DIGITAL COLLECTIONS

Adam Matthew Publications. Available online at www.ampltd.co.uk.

Bibliographies and Guides. Library of Congress Microform Reading Room. www.loc.gov/rr/microform/guide (accessed 25 July 2012).

Dodson, Suzanne Cates. *Microform Research Collections: A Guide*, 2nd ed. Westport, CT: Meckler Publishing, 1984.

Eighteenth-Century English Microform Holdings. Michigan State University Libraries. libguides.lib.msu.edu/content.php?pid=90457 (accessed 27 July 2012).

Gale Cengage Learning. www.gale.cengage.com/product_sites/index.htm (accessed 25 July 2012).

Pickering & Chatto. www.pickeringchatto.com/categories/eighteenth_century (accessed 25 July 2012).

Topic Guide: Great Britain. Center for Research Libraries. www.crl.edu/collections/topics/great-britain (accessed 25 July 2012).

WorldCat. OCLC. Available online at www.oclc.org/firstsearch.

WorldCat.org. www.worldcat.org (accessed 24 July 2012).

For specific authors, titles, and subjects, whether facsimiles, reprints, or modern or scholarly editions, consult chapter 3 for effective search strategies. For digital and microform collections, the best place to discover relevant collections available for eighteenth-century literary research is by consulting the reference librarians at your institution. Librarians also frequently create subject guides to collections, made available via the library website, that identify nonprint resources, and may also include records of microforms and commercial and freely available digital sources in the library's catalog. With the advent of the Web, directories to microform collections in print have fallen out of use, and, because of the rapidly changing digital environment, no single source for online resources exists. Determining whether the resources required for a project are available in either of the two formats can be as easy as searching the library catalog, the *English Short Title Catalogue* (*ESTC*), or *WorldCat*, or it may require consulting finding aids to a collection to determine if the item desired is available.

Although dated and no longer as vital because many of the records for materials in major collections are now available in library catalogs or *WorldCat*, Suzanne Cates Dodson's **Microform Research Collections: A Guide** was long valued as a tool for understanding the background and contents of major microform collections. Entries are arranged by title and typically include the publisher, format, arrangement and source of collection, finding aid and/or other bibliographic sources, and the scope and content of the collection. Several collections contain eighteenth-century content, including the previously mentioned *Three Centuries of English and American Plays: England 1500–1800* and *The Microbook Library of English Literature*, and although collections like *The Eighteenth Century* and *Early English Newspapers* have been digitized, there are subject specific collections to be discovered, for example, The Newberry Library's *Early English Courtesy Books, 1571–1773*, now part of ProQuest's Newberry Library microfilm collections, which also has the *Covent Garden Prompt Books, 1710–1824*. Other microform collections are comprised of English cartoons, sessional papers from the House of Commons (part of ProQuest's digital collection *Eighteenth-Century Parliamentary Papers*), radical periodicals (1794–1881), sources on radical politics and the working man, and the seventeenth- and eighteenth-century manuscripts from Winchester College. To identify specific items within the collections, consult the bibliographies Dodson lists in the entry; if unavailable locally, order via interlibrary loan or search the Web to see if the finding aid has been made available. For example, the checklist for the Newberry courtesy books collection is available online via HathiTrust (hdl.handle.net/2027/mdp.39015027623399).

Other useful Web-based guides to microform collections may be library specific, but they can help in discovering relevant resources. The **Eighteenth-**

Century English Microform Holdings guide from Michigan State University's libraries lists approximately thirty-five collections covering various aspects of British life, politics, arts, and economy. Entries, listed alphabetically by author or title, comprise the name of the collection, format and number of units, brief descriptions, and guides to the contents. Again, several of these are also available digitally, but not all, so it is worth browsing through the list for potential sources. Both *Bibliographies and Guides* from the Library of Congress and the *Topic Guide: Great Britain* from the Center for Research Libraries are broader in scope, but they still focus on the holdings within their own institutions.

Bibliographies and Guides is a Web-based guide to the extensive microform collections held by the Library of Congress. Access to the list is either alphabetical or through the A–J and K–Z indexes. Entries for Great Britain are scattered throughout the index, so use the "Find" command to scan for the terms *Britain, British, England, Scotland, Wales,* or *Ireland* in the A–Z list. Of potential interest to eighteenth-century literary scholars are *Hanoverian State Papers, Domestic, 1714–1782* and *Home Office Papers and Records: Order and Authority in England: Series One, Home Office Class HO 42 (George III, Correspondence, 1782–1820)* (both discussed in chapter 8); *British Biographical Archive, 17th–19th centuries*; *British Sessional Papers, 1731–1900*; *Radical Periodicals of Great Britain, 1794–1950*; *Anti-Slavery Collection, 18th–19th Centuries*; and *Ladies of Llangollen: Letters and Journals of Lady Eleanor Butler (1739–1829) and Sarah Ponsonby (1755–1831) from the National Library of Wales.*

The *Topic Guide: Great Britain*, from the Center for Research Libraries, lists microform sets, newspaper runs, dissertations, and, where available, links to digital versions or finding aids. Subjects cover church archives, government publications and documents, manuscripts, personal papers, political parties and movements, and sections on Northern Ireland and Scotland. Eighteenth-century collections include *Records of the Court of Arches at Lambeth Palace Library* (the ecclesiastical court of appeals for southern England and Wales from 1660 to modern times); *The Papers of William Pitt the Younger (Prime Minister, 1783–1801 and 1804–1806)*; *Great Britain Colonial Office, 1600–1950*; the Hanoverian domestic state papers discussed in chapter 8; the personal papers of Barron Jeffrey Amherst, 1740–1783, soldier and statesman; *Blenheim Papers from the British Library* (personal papers, 1650–1722, of John Churchill, Duke of Marlborough); and the Thynne family papers from the archives of Longleat House (1542–1780).

Websites for commercial publishers of microform and digital collections are another means to keep abreast of the production of eighteenth-century content. **Gale Cengage Learning** has traditionally published large, comprehensive collections available both digitally and in microform, for example, the *Eighteenth Century Collections Online, British Literary Manuscripts, State Papers Online,* and the *17th and 18th Century Burney Collection Newspapers.* More recently, they have launched a new series of digital content, *Archives Unbound,* which offer small, focused collections on specific topics (*Witchcraft in Europe and America, 1500 to 1930* and *The Dublin Castle Records, 1798–1926*). Primary Source Media, part of Gale, continues to maintain the microform collections, with online guides to the contents for such relevant collections as *English Stage after the Restoration: 1733–1822* and *Madden Ballads.*

The "Subject" tab for **Adam Matthew Publications** has a link to "Britain," which presents an alphabetical list of relevant publications, including microform and digital collections, and, when available, links to online finding aids. For example, the site offers a description and a link to the online guide to the reels for the Elizabeth Inchbald microfilm collection discussed in chapter 8, and the Web page for the *Eighteenth Century Journals* portal provides overviews for each part of the collection and lists of journals in each part.

In its ongoing eighteenth-century collections, **Pickering & Chatto** publishes print facsimiles of literary, theatrical, political, economic, social, and cultural works, many with no other modern editions. Volumes may be dedicated to an author, a genre, or a theme. Some titles related to women include *Bluestocking Feminism: Writings of the Bluestocking Circle, 1738–1790; Chawton House Library: Women's Novels; The Complete Plays of Frances Burney; Conduct Literature for Women; The Diaries of Elizabeth Inchbald; Female Education in the Age of Enlightenment; Memoirs of Scandalous Women; Nonconformist Women Writers, 1720–1840;* and *Women's Travel Writings* (Iberia, North Africa and the Middle East, revolutionary France, Italy). Volumes generally have an introduction, with brief editorial notes to give context. The first four volumes of *Women's Travel Writings in Italy* contain the writings of Lady Anna Riggs Miller (1777) and Hester Piozzi (1789), and they also include general introductions, selected bibliographies, and editorial explanatory notes. Although texts in the Pickering & Chatto collections may be available in digital form via some of the sources discussed in this chapter, the contextual information adds value for the reader.

WorldCat and *WorldCat.org* can be used to locate specific digital or microform collections and, if cataloged, individual titles within the collection. In addition, these can be used to discover if there are digital or microfilm collections related to the topic of interest. For example, while browsing the Adam Matthew website, we found the microfilm collection *Aristocratic Women: The Social, Political, and Cultural History of Rich and Powerful Women* with the online guide to the contents of each reel. A search in *WorldCat* and *WorldCat.org* found several libraries that own the collection and may lend it via interlibrary loan.

To search the Online Computer Library Center's *WorldCat* for collections related to a topic, either limit the search beforehand to "microform" or "Internet," or after the search by clicking on the tab for "Internet." An author search on *mrs mary delany* limited to "Internet Resources" retrieves records with links to freely available resources from Google Books and HathiTrust, and records for digital content from the commercial publishers Alexander Street Press and *Electronic Enlightenment*. If using *WorldCat.org*, execute the same author search, but limit to either e-books or microforms using the facets to the left.

BOOKS AND OTHER PRINTED MATTER

Eighteenth Century Collections Online, Part I and Part II. Detroit, MI: Gale, 2003– . www.gale.cengage.com. Part I also available in the *Eighteenth Century* microfilm collection.

Eighteenth-Century Fiction. Ann Arbor, MI: ProQuest/Chadwyck-Healy, 1996– . collections.chadwyck.co.uk.

English Drama. Ann Arbor, MI: ProQuest/Chadwyck-Healy, 1996– . collec tions.chadwyck.co.uk (accessed 26 July 2012).

Google Books. books.google.com (accessed 26 July 2012).

HathiTrust Digital Library. www.hathitrust.org.

Internet Archive. archive.org (accessed 26 July 2012).

***Eighteenth Century Collections Online, Part I and Part II* (*ECCO*)**, which originated as the *Eighteenth Century* microfilm collection, is a core resource for eighteenth-century studies. The more than 180,000 titles, representing more than half of the nearly 348,000 eighteenth-century items listed in the *ESTC*, primarily include English-language books, pamphlets, broadsides, and literary periodical publications sold as bound volumes (the *Spectator* and the *Tatler*), published in Britain and its colonies and covering all subjects. The third edition of Daniel Defoe's *Robinson Crusoe*, published in 1719, discussed in chapter 3, can be found in *ECCO*.

For those without access to the digital collection, search *ESTC* to identify the microfilm number for titles or for other surrogates that may be available. The database can be browsed by author or works. The advanced option offers Boolean operators, full-text, field (e.g., title, author, subject, keyword, *ESTC* number), and fuzzy searching, as well as limiting by broad categories ("Literature and Language," "History and Geography," "Social Sciences," "Religion and Philosophy," "General Reference," "Fine Arts," "Law," "Medicine, Science, and Technology"), language, illustrated works, and publication dates. Entries typically present the full citation, libraries that hold the print version, an electronic table of contents, a list of illustrations, and the digital facsimile of the publication. The full text of the document is further searchable from within the record or the document, with links to the relevant page and image numbers and terms searched highlighted. Entire documents can be downloaded as PDFs to computers and e-readers.

Although *ECCO* is a rich resource of eighteenth-century printed works, it can also be used to illustrate challenges related to searches for multiple editions of the same work. Several editions of Alexander Pope's *The Rape of the Lock* are present, including the 1712 two-canto version printed as part of Bernand Lintott's *Miscellaneous Poems and Translations by Several Hands*, and subsequent editions containing the expanded five-canto poem published from 1714 onward. To illustrate the difficulty of searching in what would seem a logical fashion, a combined author/title field search in *ECCO* does not retrieve the 1712 printing because the poem title is not the title of the book. Also, "Lock" is spelled "Locke" in this first copy. This early printing can be found by other methods: a combined author (*pope*) and publication date (*1712*) search, by an author (*alexander pope*) and "entire document" (*rape of the lock**) search, and by a low fuzzy full-text search on *rape of the lock* limited to 1712. Examining the bibliographic record, Pope is not listed in the author field for this item, but, oddly enough, he can be searched as the author. This is because *ECCO* uses the metadata from *ESTC* for the bibliographic information but does not display all the fields. *ECCO* searches but doesn't display the 700 MARC field (see the MARC discussion in chapter 1), which is an added personal name tag; therefore, it is possible to search for Pope as author even though he doesn't appear in the full citation (see figure 6.1).

Similarly, an author search on *anna letitia barbauld* (not spelled *laetitia*) limited to *1773* will retrieve the *Miscellaneous Pieces, in Prose*, which she wrote with her brother John under her maiden name Aikin, but browsing *barbauld* as author does not retrieve this first printing, although this method does find subsequent corrected editions of the volume. Because Barbauld is identified in the *ESTC* record in the 700 field as an author, the first edition can be found by an author search, but it cannot be found in *ECCO* by author browse, which doesn't have that information. Nor can the item be found by searching *anna letitia aikin*, because she only used her initials on the publication. Other databases may list Barbauld's maiden name instead for this early edition, so if you know the first edition date of an item, but can't find it, try different strategies to locate it. In the case of *ECCO*, the *ESTC* number can also be searched, which would allow you to find the exact copy you require, so the two resources can be used in tandem.

ProQuest/Chadwyck-Healy offers transcriptions of eighteenth-century fiction and drama via *Literature Online* (*LION*). **Eighteenth-Century Fiction**

Title:	Miscellaneous poems and translations. By several hands.
Imprint:	London : printed for Bernard Lintott, 1712.
Language:	English
Pages:	356
***ESTC* Number:**	T005777
Microfilm Reel#:	Eighteenth Century Collections Online: Range 5005
Physical Description:	[8],320,[3],356-376,[8]p.,plate ; 8°
Notes:	Contains a number of poems by Alexander Pope, including the first printing of 'The rape of the locke' in two cantos. The whole probably edited by Pope. With a half-title and final four advertisement leaves. Text is continuous despite pagination.
Source Library:	British Library
Subject Headings:	English poetry--18th century
Module Subjects:	Literature and Language
ECCO Release Date:	06/01/2004
Holding Libraries	

Figure 6.1.   Record for the 1712 edition of Alexander Pope's *The Rape of the Lock.* Source: *Eighteenth Century Collections Online,* via Gale.

comprises ninety-six works of prose from thirty-one authors associated with the rise of the novel and published between 1700 and 1780. Categories cover epistolary (Samuel Richardson's *Pamela* and *Clarissa*, Tobias Smollett's *Humphrey Brinker*, Frances Burney's *Evelina*), sentimental (works by Laurence Sterne, Frances Brooke, Charlotte Lenox, Frances Sheridan), documentary (Daniel Defoe's *Robinson Crusoe*), allegorical and satirical (Jonathan Swift's *Gulliver's Travels*, Samuel Johnson's *Rasselas*), and gothic (Clara Reeve's *The Old English Baron*, Horace Walpole's *The Castle of Otranto*) novels. Editions used to create the transcriptions are noted in the bibliographic details. Texts can be searched by keywords, title, author, publication dates, genre, and author details (life dates, gender, nationality). Keyword searches in the full text will display the results with the keywords in context.

English Drama has more than 3,900 plays from the Middle Ages to the end of the nineteenth century, 1,137 published between 1700 and 1799, or 861 performed during that time frame. Representative playwrights include Susanna Centlivre, George Farquhar, Henry Fielding, David Garrick, John Gay, Oliver Goldsmith, John Hawkesworth, Eliza Haywood, Elizabeth Inchbald, Robert Jephson, Charlotte Lennox, Hannah More, Mary Pix, Richard Sheridan, and Catherine Trotter. Entries typically contain bibliographic details for the source text, genre, date first published, date first performed, front matter with list of characters, and main text. The database can be searched by keywords in play, author, title, speaker, first performed, publication date, genre, gender, and literary period fields. For both *English Drama* and *Eighteenth-Century Fiction*, the transcribed text permits more precise searches than OCR'd text in other digital databases, and it may be easier to use keywords to find themes explored through the literary works. *English Poetry* (from the eighth through the early twentieth century), is another potentially useful collection in *LION*.

Google Books, HathiTrust, and Internet Archive are different, yet intertwined, initiatives for digitizing and making freely available via the Web public-domain books and periodicals. Both HathiTrust and Google Books also contain scanned copyrighted materials. Although controversial because publishers believe this doesn't constitute fair use, these works can be keyword searched to find page numbers within the items where the keyword occurs, without displaying the content, and thus serving as an index to the text.

In 2004, Google partnered with libraries to scan the millions of books in their collections and make them available via **Google Books**. Books in the public domain are viewable and often downloadable, while those still under copyright either allow previews, snippets, or no views, depending upon the agreement with the publisher. Because there is no authority control (discussed in chapter 3), variant author names must be searched.

HathiTrust Digital Library (**HathiTrust**), formed in 2008, is a collaborative project, involving more than sixty libraries and library consortia, with the goal of preserving and providing access to public domain and copyrighted digital books and journals, scanned by participating institutions, by Google, or for the Internet Archive. The public domain works can be fully viewed and downloaded. On the date accessed, the site had 10,424,950 total volumes, with 5,525,754 book titles and 272,203 serial titles, 30 percent of these (or 3,120,505 volumes) in the public domain. The site can be searched using the "Catalog Search" or "Full-Text Search" options, or browsed by "Public Collections," the latter compiled by partners or individuals, for example, the eighteenth-century cookbook collection.

Internet Archive, a nonprofit organization founded in 1996, seeks to preserve and offer access, not only to born-digital content, but to digitized content in various formats (text, audio, video, software), and to archived Web pages. Its partners for content include the Library of Congress and Smithsonian. Eighteenth-century as well as later editions of books (e.g., Barbauld's *Miscellaneous Pieces, in Prose*, Pope's *Rape of the Lock*) and periodicals (e.g., *Monthly Review, The Craftsman, The True Briton*) can be found in all three of these digital collections, although runs of periodicals may be incomplete. Libraries and institutions that scan pre-1923 books may contribute the content to one, two, or all three of these initiatives, so there is some overlap.

The public domain content can be searched full text and viewed and browsed online, and it is often downloadable to computers and mobile devices. All three allow individuals to create their own collections within the system.

It is disappointing that Google did not start its project with preservation in mind, for the black-and-white, and sometimes clumsily scanned, works detract from the beauty and character of the printed works. Compare the Google scan of Barbauld's 1773 *Miscellaneous Pieces, in Prose*, from the University of Michigan (tinyurl.com/barbauld1), with the high-quality Internet Archive copy from Duke University (tinyurl.com/barbauld2), for, scanned in color, it reveals the richness of the aged paper and more closely preserves the look and feel of the original than the stark black-and-white scan found in Google Books.

NEWSPAPERS

17th and 18th Century Burney Collection Newspapers. Farmington Hills, MI: Gale, 2007– . gdc.gale.com/products/17th-and-18th-century-burney-collection-newspapers.

Concise History of the British Newspaper in the Eighteenth Century. British Library. www.bl.uk/reshelp/findhelprestype/news/concisehistbritnews/britnews18th/index.html (accessed 3 July 2012).

Early English Newspapers. New Haven, CT: Research Publications, 1978–?.

Eighteenth Century English Provincial Newspapers. Brighton, England: Harvester Press Microform Publications, 1985–1991.

English Short Title Catalogue, 1473–1800. British Library. estc.bl.uk (accessed 5 July 2012). A list of microfilm sets noted in *ESTC* records are located at http://estc.ucr.edu/estcfilm.html.

The Guardian (1821–2003) and The Observer (1791–2003). ProQuest Historical Newspapers. Ann Arbor, MI: ProQuest. www.proquest.com/assets/literature/products/databases/guardian_observer.pdf.

Irish Newspaper Archives. www.irishnewsarchive.com.

Irish Newspapers in Dublin Libraries, 1685–1754. Ann Arbor, MI: University Microfilms.

Main Catalogue. British Library. catalogue.bl.uk (accessed 3 July 2012).

Palmer's Index to the Times Newspaper. 1790–June 1941. 100 vols. Vadux: Kraus Reprint, 1965–1966. ProQuest/Chadwyck-Healy, 1790–1905, www.proquest.com/en-US/catalogs/databases/detail/palmers_index.shtml.

Times Digital Archive, 1785–2006. Farmington Hills, MI: Gale, 2002– . www.gale.cengage.com/servlet/ItemDetailServlet?region=9&imprint=000&titleCode=DABF&cf=n&type=3&id=195856.

Watson, George, ed. *The New Cambridge Bibliography of English Literature: Volume 2, 1660–1800*, 2nd ed. Cambridge, UK: Cambridge University Press, 1971.
WorldCat. OCLC. www.oclc.org/firstsearch.
WorldCat.org. www.worldcat.org (accessed 24 July 2012).

Although digital versions of newspapers from the era are discussed in this section, the resources are not comprehensive, and finding aids to identify other possible titles will be necessary. On the *Concise History of the British Newspaper in the Eighteenth Century* website, experts from the British Library offer a brief, chronological survey of newspaper titles published in Britain, from the first provincial newspaper, the *Norwich Post* (1701), and the first daily paper, the *Daily Courant* (1702), to the first Sunday London newspaper, *E. Johnson's British Gazette and Sunday Monitor* (1779), to the founding of *Bell's Weekly Messenger* (1796). Significant events, for example, the first Copyright Act (1709), the Stamp Act (1712), suppression of parliamentary reporting (1738), and first open reporting of Parliament since 1738 (1763), are included. As newspapers were not as distinctly identified separately during this time, the *Tatler*, the *Spectator*, and *Gentleman's Magazine* are also noted.

George Watson's volume 2 of *The New Cambridge Bibliography of English Literature* (*NCBEL*) is a good, standard research tool to consult for titles of newspapers. The "Periodical Publications" section lists, in chronological order, brief entries for London newspapers with the editor, if known, and dates of publication (pages 1,313–40). Newspapers published in English provinces (pages 1,353–70) are arranged alphabetically by town (Aylesbury, Bath, Birmingham, Blackburn, Bristol, and so forth), and then chronologically. Newspapers published in Scotland (pages 1,373–78) and Ireland (pages 1,381–90) are listed as well. Secondary sources about specific regions or newspapers are interwoven with these lists.

The *English Short Title Catalogue, 1473–1800* (*ESTC*), discussed in chapter 4, is another good source for identifying relevant titles, locating copies, and discovering if surrogate (facsimile) copies, for instance, microforms, exist. The database can be searched in both the "Subject" or "Genre (Subject)" fields for *newspapers* and limited by location (England, Scotland, Ireland; no results were retrieved for Wales) and publication years (*1700–>1800*) to generate lists of titles. Using both fields is recommended because some titles have one subject heading or the other heading. As seen in figure 6.2, the genre heading retrieves 809 records, while the subject field retrieves 568, with an overlap of 419 newspaper titles from England between the years of 1700 and 1800. Records include publisher and publishing history, dates,

Advanced Search of ESTC

Quick tips - for this page

Search by		Type word or phrase	Exact phrase?	No. of records
Subject	⌄	newspapers	⦿ No ○ Yes	**568**
Genre (subject)	⌄	newspapers	⦿ No ○ Yes	**809**
Word(s) anywhere	⌄		⦿ No ○ Yes	
Click Total number of docs to view records.			**Total: 419**	
Go	Clear			

Limit search to:

Language:	All	⌄
Year:	1700->1800	yyyy (Use -> to limit to a range of years, e.g. 1790->1799)
Item Format:		(e.g. obl.120 for obl.12mo or 1/40 for 1/4mo)
Country:	England (enk)	⌄

Figure 6.2. Sample genre search in the English Short Title Catalogue "Advanced Search." Source: English Short Title Catalogue.

title changes, frequency, references to citations in standard research tools like *NCBEL*, surrogates, locations of copies, and notes providing additional facts about the publication. For example, *The Bath Advertiser* by Steven Martin, a weekly published from 1755 to 1760, was the second newspaper to be published in Bath, and it reported European and North American news, news on wars, and a "series of purported letters on the history of Bath addressed to 'Julian Alberti, at Florence.'" It was cited in *NCBEL* and others, is held in four British libraries and one North American library, and is available in the microfilm collection *Eighteenth Century English Provincial Newspapers*. A "Word(s) Anywhere" search on the phrase *eighteenth century english provincial newspapers* retrieves the entries for all forty-two titles in the microform collection.

To discover the titles in the microform collection *Early English Newspapers*, which comprises the Burney Collection of English newspapers at the British Library and the John Nichols Collection at the Bodleian Library, from the 1640s to the early nineteenth century, search the phrase *early english newspapers* and limit to dates *1700->1800*. Note that the surrogate field also indicates when a publication that was bound into volumes and resold in the eighteenth century is available digitally in *ECCO*, as in the case of *The Adventurer* (1752–1754). On the date *ESTC* was accessed, the surrogate field did not indicate availability in other digital collections, for instance, *17th and*

18th Century Burney Collection Newspapers, which also contains *The Adventurer*. *WorldCat* can also be searched for specific newspaper titles, newspapers by geographic location and time frame, and newspapers within specific microform collections. For example, to find the titles in the microform collection, do a keyword search on *"early english newspapers"* and limit by date *1700-1800* and to format "Microform." Titles in the **Irish Newspapers in Dublin Libraries, 1685–1754** microfilm collections are discoverable in both *ESTC* and *WorldCat* using similar strategies.

Individual library catalogs can also be searched for newspapers by subject and specific title to discover holdings within the collection. For example, the British Library's newspaper collection can be searched in the **Main Catalogue**. Using facets, a search on the keyword *bristol* can be limited to the material-type newspapers to generate a list of records containing the word and then limited by dates. These results can then be sorted by oldest date and scanned for relevancy. The oldest available in the newspaper collection is the *The Oracle; or, Bristol Weekly Miscellany*, from 1742. The "Details" tab provides more information, including location and holdings.

Few indexes to eighteenth-century newspapers exist, which makes digital access all the more valuable for finding relevant articles. That being said, human-created indexes utilizing standard vocabulary are still useful for researchers. Jayn Pearson and Keith Soothill's study on the printed *Times Index*, with its controlled vocabulary, provides a level of quality control to the research process that keyword searching in an online database may not.[18] Using the index from 1977 to 1999 to track articles listed under the heading "Murder, manslaughter and related charges," the authors found that, when compared to the newspaper itself, there were few omissions in this category, and those omissions were due to the fact that the death wasn't recognized as murder, that it had happened as part of another event (e.g., a riot), that the individual had not yet died, or that no charges had been filed. The index, arranged in alphabetical order by victims and containing short descriptions, allowed the researchers to grasp the essence of the article at the index level. Cross-references within the index permitted other potentially relevant reports to be located. When searching the CD-ROM index, a comparison revealed that it was much more difficult to be specific about the crime, and that false positives, where the word is present but not in the right context (football teams that murder the opposition or getting away with murder as a youth), or false negatives, where the report isn't found because the word isn't used (stories with the word killers instead of murder) often occur. The authors remind researchers that modern technology may not always be the most exhaustive, and that older research tools still have their strengths, such as **Palmer's Index to the Times Newspaper**, which offers indexing to the newspaper at the end of the eighteenth century.

David Deacon, who studied *LexisNexis* to determine how easy it is to find articles on his topic, Quangos (quasi-autonomous nongovernmental organizations), to analyze results and track trends in the media, also cautions that care must be taken when searching digital newspaper collections.[19] He discovered that journalists often do not use the term *Quangos* in articles, so he had to discover and search by the vocabulary they used to describe these types of organizations to find relevant pieces. He discusses the difficulties of capturing complex thematic issues via keywords, a concern most relevant to eighteenth-century researchers. Fortunately, other issues of concern to Deacon, such as the context of news and loss of visual dimensions, are irrelevant because the eighteenth-century digital collections of newspapers are full-page facsimile views of the pages.

Simon Tanner, Trevor Muñoz, and Pich Hemy Ros examined the British Library's *19th Century Online Newspaper Archive* collection, which uses OCR, to assess accuracy of results. They found that significant words, for instance, proper nouns, names, and place names, are more difficult for OCR engines to interpret, so that the lower the significant word accuracy, the lower the accuracy of results returned. "Thus, the BL's Burney Collection loses a lot of search capacity because the long 's' character reduces word accuracy to such a low point that searching can become very difficult."[20] The authors recommend that vendors improve the dictionary of names to improve OCR performance and compare different OCR engines to select the right technology.

These studies point to the need for eighteenth-century literary researchers to be flexible when searching and in building a vocabulary of terms that will retrieve relevant sources. Effective fuzzy searching will be crucial, but fuzzy searches are not always successful, either. It may be that, in some cases, a newspaper will need to be viewed page by page to determine if relevant articles are present.

The *17th and 18th Century Burney Collection Newspapers* (*Burney*) contains digital facsimiles of the newspapers, newsbooks, broadsides, and pamphlets collected by Charles Burney, the brother of Fanny Burney, during his lifetime. Burney's library, which contained books, manuscripts, materials related to the English stage, and newspapers, was sold to the British Library after his death in 1817. As a youth, Burney was expelled from Cambridge for selling books he took from the university library to London booksellers. He was able to complete his education at Kings College, Aberdeen, in classics, and he then became a schoolmaster and, ultimately, successfully redeemed his reputation. Upon his return to London from Aberdeen in 1781, he began his collection of newspapers, starting with the old newspapers he gathered from the coffee house his aunts managed.[21]

Use of the fragile originals is restricted at the British Library, but researchers do have access either via the *Early English Newspapers* microform collection, previously described, or the digital version discussed here; *Burney*, however, does not include the *John Nichols Collection* found in the microfilm version. *Burney* covers approximately 1,270 titles, mainly from London, representing a significant collection of news media publications from the seventeenth to the early nineteenth centuries. The advanced option offers Boolean and fuzzy searching, as well as full-text and field (document title, publication title, publication date, issue, day of the week, document number) searching. Limiting can be by date range, publication title, place of publication, publication section (advertising, arts and sports, business news, news), language, and documents with images. Results can be viewed by article and full page, issues can be browsed, and pages can be enlarged for easier reading. There are also options to browse by publication title, with entries containing brief histories, and by geographic locations. The title list contains details about title format (newspaper, broadside, pamphlet, etc.), start and end dates, city, and country (England, Ireland, Scotland, United States, Jamaica, etc.).

To find articles and advertisements in *Burney* related to Robert Jephson's play, *The Count of Narbonne*, begin with a nonfuzzy, full-text search combining *"count of narbonne"* and *jephson*. Four results, all advertisements, are retrieved. Changing to "low" fuzzy retrieves fifty-three articles and advertisements published between February 1781 and June 1795, which mention both the playwright and the play. Changing to "medium" fuzzy unearths sixty-one items, while "high" finds too many results and the search reverts back to "low." A researcher may be satisfied with these results, but, as already discussed, full-text searches in newspapers can be challenging, and in newspapers using fuzzy searching, even more so. A graduate student working on this topic found a lengthy article reviewing Jephson's play, which opened on November 19, 1781, at Covent Garden Theatre. Unfortunately, even though she downloaded the article, the database does not include the citation as part of the downloading or printing process, and she could not find it again even though she had the text before her and knew that references had been made to Walpole's *The Castle of Otranto* and the crusades (see figure 6.3). The combination of so many proper names, italics, the long "s," and the poor quality of the typeface were probably partly responsible. The play's title in the first paragraph is in uppercase, and the "B" in "Narbonne" looks like a "D." In the list of characters and cast members, "Narbonne" is hyphenated "Nar-bonne" (see figure 6.4).

Further into the article we noticed that Narbonne was clearer and decided, even though it was a proper noun, to try searching that word, "medium" fuzzy, limited to the date range November 15, 1781 and January 1, 1782, with success. The article was in *Lloyd's Evening Post*, November 19, 1781–November 21, 1781, issue 3810. In addition to the actual article, we found a total of 222 advertisements and articles with this search. Although we saw

THE FABLE on which this Tragedy is built, is taken from the celebrated Novel of *The Caſtle of Otranto*, and the Scene of it is laid in Languedoc, a maritime Town in France. The period of time at which it is ſuppoſed to have had its birth, is to be traced to that memorable æra of hiſtory; when the Chriſtian Princes united together in their cruſades, for the recovery of Paleſtine.

Figure 6.3. Excerpt from review of Robert Jephson's *The Count of Narbonne* in *Lloyd's Evening Post*, November 19, 1781–November 21, 1781, Issue 3810. *Source: 17th & 18th Century Burney Collection Newspapers, Gale.*

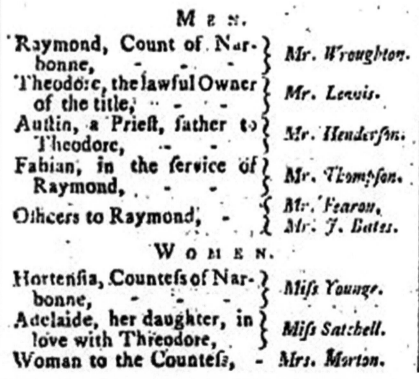

M E N.

Raymond, Count of Narbonne,	Mr. Wroughton.
Theodore, the lawful Owner of the title,	Mr. Lewis.
Auſtin, a Prieſt, father to Theodore,	Mr. Henderſon.
Fabian, in the ſervice of Raymond,	Mr. Thompſon.
Officers to Raymond,	Mr. Fearon, Mr. J. Bates.

W O M E N.

Hortenſia, Counteſs of Narbonne,	Miſs Younge.
Adelaide, her daughter, in love with Theodore,	Miſs Satchell.
Woman to the Counteſs,	Mrs. Morton.

Figure 6.4. Cast and characters from review of Robert Jephson's *The Count of Narbonne* in *Lloyd's Evening Post*, November 19, 1781–November 21, 1781, Issue 3810. *Source: 17th & 18th Century Burney Collection Newspapers, Gale.*

in these results that Narbonne was discoverable in other articles, even when it had been hyphenated and broken into two lines or was in all uppercase, the term, which occurred a few times in our three-column article, was only highlighted once; something about the OCR in our article made the word unfindable. Searching *covent garden* or *theatr** and limiting to the date range in which the play was performed is another possible strategy, although the latter is too broad and will return false drops. If articles are desired over advertisements, the latter search could be limited to "News" and "Arts and Sports" sections. Although this example is very specific, the strategies will be helpful for developing search techniques in this and other OCR'd digital collections.

Also available on microfilm, the ***Times Digital Archive, 1785–2006***, from Gale, is devoted to this single newspaper. The advanced option provides Boolean and fuzzy searching of the full text and by field (article title, author, day of the week, page number, issue, keyword, document number), as well as limits by publication dates, advertising (classified, display, property), news (news, news in brief, law, politics and parliament, court and social), business, people (births, deaths, marriages, obituaries, official appointments and notices), editorial and commentary, and features (arts and entertainment, reviews, sports).

The Observer, the oldest surviving Sunday newspaper, launched on December 4, 1791, is available on microform (*Early English Newspapers*), in *Burney*, and as part of the digital *ProQuest Historical Newspapers **The Guardian (1821–2003) and The Observer (1791–2003)***, where the advance option offers Boolean, full text, and field (author, document title, publication title, page, section) searches, and limiting by date range and document type. The ***Irish Newspaper Archives***, which has as its goal to digitize all of Ireland's historical newspapers, at present contains two eighteenth-century Irish newspapers: *Freeman's Journal* (1763–1924) and *Finn's Leinster Journal* (1792–1828).

PERIODICALS

Addison, Joseph, and Richard Steele. *The Spectator*. 5 vols. Edited by Donald F. Bond. Oxford, UK: Clarendon Press, 1965.

Balay, Robert. *Early Periodical Indexes: Bibliographies and Indexes of Literature Published in Periodicals before 1900*. Lanham, MD: Scarecrow Press, 2000.

British Periodicals. Ann Arbor, MI: ProQuest, 2006– . britishperiodicals .chadwyck.com.

Early British Periodicals. Ann Arbor, MI: University Microfilms International, 1970–1979.

Eighteenth Century Journals: A Portal to Newspapers and Periodicals, c. 1685–1815. Marlborough, England: Adam Matthew Publications, 2007– . www.18thcjournals.amdigital.co.uk.

English Literary Periodicals. Ann Arbor, MI: University Microfilms, 1951–1977.

English Short Title Catalogue, 1473–1800. British Library. estc.bl.uk. List of microfilm sets noted in *ESTC* records located at estc.ucr.edu/estcfilm.html.

Gentleman's Magazine. 16 vols. Brookfield, VT: Pickering & Chatto, 1998.

Mayo, Robert D. "A Catalogue of Magazine Novels and Novelettes, 1740–1815." In *The English Novel in the Magazines: 1740–1815.* Edited by Robert D. Mayo, 431–620. Evanston: Northwestern University Press, 1962.

Periodicals Archive Online. Ann Arbor, MI: ProQuest, 2001– . pao.chadwyck.com.

Periodicals Index Online. Ann Arbor, MI: ProQuest, 1997– . pio.chadwyck.com.

Sullivan, Alvin, ed. *British Literary Magazines: The Augustan Age and the Age of Johnson, 1698–1788.* Westport, CT: Greenwood, 1983.

Watson, George, ed. *The New Cambridge Bibliography of English Literature: Volume 2, 1660–1880,* 2nd ed. Cambridge, UK: Cambridge University Press, 1971.

WorldCat. OCLC. www.oclc.org/firstsearch.

The first installment in a four-volume reference set, Alvin Sullivan's **British Literary Magazines: The Augustan Age and the Age of Johnson, 1698–1788** (**AAAJ**) contains invaluable short historical essays on eighty-seven periodicals, from the *London Spy* to the *Aberdeen Magazine*, that began during and reflect this era of the eighteenth century. The concept of "literary" periodical shifts throughout the century. Early on, this type of publication was part of the constant, frequently divisive, political debates between the Whigs (Steele's *Englishman*) and Tories (Defoe's *Review* and Swift's *Examiner*), and between the Jacobites and patriots. Often intertwining social, political, and literary concerns, Sullivan selected titles that represent the range and types of magazines with literary content.

Figures we consider almost purely for their literary works today were involved with magazines, as writers and as editors, giving even periodicals primarily political in scope literary significance. Pope contributed to the "calculatedly offensive" *Grub-Street Journal*; Fielding began the *Champion, True Patriot, Jacobite's Journal*, and *Covent Garden Journal*; Johnson edited the *Gentleman's Magazine* and started the *Rambler*; Smollett established the *Critical Review* and *British Magazine*; Boswell contributed to the *Scots Magazine*; and Goldsmith contributed to the *Busy Body* and founded the *Bee*.

In the "Introduction," Morris Golden provides a helpful overview of periodical publishing throughout the era, which gives context for the entries that follow. Arranged in alphabetical order by title, the signed entries written by forty-one contributors are generally two to five pages in length. Each begins with a short history of the publication, describing format, dates, editors, editorial policies, contributors, audience, biases, tone, and reputation, followed by a bibliography, indexes to content (e.g., "each volume indexed," "none," "indexes in some reprint editions"), reprinted editions (print or microform), British and American libraries holding print copies, and publication history (title changes, volume and issue data, frequency, publishers, editors). The volume concludes with five appendixes (title lists included in *AAAJ* and, because they overlap during the century, *The Romantic Age, 1789–1836*; a chronology; an essay on the successors, imitators, and contemporaries of the *Tatler*; and a selective list of predominately political journals with literary contents, many profiled in *AAAJ*), an index, and a list of contributors.

As stated in the "Newspapers" section, the "Periodical Publications" section of *NCBEL*, Watson's volume 2 is a helpful, standard starting point for identifying serial titles. Titles of publications are arranged chronologically, with brief publication information and selected secondary sources for each entry. The section is organized by the following categories: "Periodical Essays Published in London by Themselves, in Newspapers, or in Magazines and Miscellanies," "Magazines, Miscellanies, Learned Journals and Reviews Published in London, 1660–1800," "Annuals," "Periodical Publications: English Provinces," "Scotland," and "Ireland."

Identifying periodical titles in the **English Short Title Catalogue, 1473–1800 (ESTC)** can be tricky. As has been stated, there were no clear differences between periodicals and newspapers early in the century; titles considered by some scholars to be periodicals, for instance, the *Grub-Street Journal*, are identified as newspapers in the *ESTC*. Some literary periodicals were reprinted and bound into volumes and sold after their demise, so that there are records for both the magazines and volumes. Generally, a "Genre (Subject)" or "Subject" search for *periodicals* limited to *1700->1800* and *England* will produce a list of titles that could potentially be relevant, but it is best to try to narrow the search to a particular time frame or by additional subject or keywords (e.g., theatre, poetry, book reviews). Records indicate when surrogates for the originals are available. In **WorldCat**, a search on the subject terms *periodicals* and *Britain*, limited to the years *1700-1800*, is somewhat more successful as a means of identifying relevant periodicals, since the *Grub-Street Journal*, and others described in *AAAJ*, have the word *periodicals* as a subject heading. This difficulty of creating lists of titles from various catalogs reflects the fact that newspapers, magazines, annuals, and almanacs did not yet have set features and rules, so that classification can be fluid.

As discussed in chapter 4, indexes do not exist for periodicals from the eighteenth century, although there are some methods for finding articles. Chapter 7 details book review sources, and those with access to the available eighteenth-century journal digital collections are able to search by keyword. *AAAJ* should be consulted, since entries indicate if indexes for individual titles exist. When reprinting periodicals as bound volumes in the eighteenth century, some publishers indexed the contents at that time, and scholarly or other modern editions of periodicals may have indexes.

In *Early Periodical Indexes: Bibliographies and Indexes of Literature Published in Periodicals before 1900*, Robert Balay identifies approximately 400 printed and electronic pre-1900 titles arranged into categories (general, humanities, history and area studies, social and behavioral sciences, science and technology, library and information sciences) and then subcategories (the humanities subcategory "Britain," with a further subcategory of "Book Reviews" will be of most interest). Subjects with the best pre-1900 coverage include medicine, geology, and classics. Four indexes (author, title, subject, chronological dates of coverage) conclude the volume, with the chronology being most helpful for quick discovery of possible relevant titles. Balay points out that prior to the twentieth century, indexing was not a commercial venture, and most indexes were done on specific topics of interest to scholars or librarians. As most of the literary indexes from the eighteenth century are discussed in our volume, Balay is useful for finding sources in other disciplines and languages covering the time period.

Robert D. Mayo offers a list of 1,375 magazine novels and novelettes in **"A Catalogue of Magazine Novels and Novelettes, 1740–1815,"** part of his study on this genre. His goal is to identify works of fiction printed in magazines, excluding newspapers, that are longer than 5,000 words. Plays and opera are excluded, but book reviews in miscellanies, with substantive portions of a novel quoted in the review, are included. Mayo found 238 periodicals containing novels and novelettes that met his criteria, and he provides a register of these in an appendix. The catalog is in alphabetical order by title, followed by an index to the contents and a chronological index. Stories by Eliza Haywood published in the *Female Spectator*; reprints of stories by Daniel Defoe, Sarah Fielding, and Henry Fielding; and extracts from Ann Radcliffe's novels are cited.

ProQuest and Adam Matthew have both developed digital collections of eighteenth-century magazines that reflect the range of subjects of interest to the culture, covering literature, theatre, music, politics, social issues, conduct, social affairs, science, the Empire, and more. ProQuest's **British Periodicals** Collection I and Collection II, which incorporates the microfilm collections **Early British Periodicals** (Collection I) and **English Literary Periodicals** (Collection II), contains approximately 470 titles, roughly 130 of these published during the eighteenth century, largely English, but with some Scottish and Irish publications as well. The digital collections are sold separately, thus libraries may only hold part of the contents. Titles include *London Spy, Busy Body, Bee, Critical Review, Female Spectator, Gentleman's Magazine, Grub-Street Journal, Lady's Magazine, Monthly Review, New Lady's Magazine, Rambler, Spectator, Tatler* (here called *The Lucubrations of Isaac Bickerstaff, esq.*), and more.

For those without access to the online version, both *ESTC* and *WorldCat* can be searched, using the techniques described in the "Newspapers" section in this chapter, to find titles in the microform collections. The online database offers full-text and field (author, title, publication title, subject, editor) searching, and limiting by date range, document type (advertisement, article, drama, fiction/narrative, poem, review), place of publication, and frequency (annually, daily, monthly, irregularly). Although the database provides helpful searchable transliterated extracts of articles, ProQuest does not offer a fuzzy search option, so care must be taken when searching the full text. Searching *jephson and "count of narbonne"* limited to *1781-1782* retrieved four articles. The *"count of Narbonne"* retrieved sixty, but this search still missed relevant items because of the challenges with eighteenth-century fonts. The play is listed in the table of contents for the February 1782 *Gentleman's Magazine*, but the search did not retrieve the reference in the magazine on page fifty-eight, so additional strategies will need to be tried to be as exhaustive as possible. Signed items, for example, a poem by Pope in the *Grub-Street Journal*, can be found by author, but, as most items were published anonymously, this type of search is not effective. At present, both Samuel Johnson and Henry Fielding can be found as editors, but not Richard Steele, because his name was not in the document scanned.

Although this database is a rich source for the content of the magazines, further research using secondary resources to locate references, or browsing through the issues to find articles of relevance, may be required. For those libraries that have all three, the *British Periodicals* collection can be searched in ProQuest/Chadwyck-Healy's **Periodicals Index Online** (**PIO**) and **Periodicals Archive Online** (**PAO**), with links to the full text from *PIO* to *PAO* if searching in those platforms. These latter two databases cover periodical literature published internationally in the arts, humanities, and social sciences between 1665 and 1995. Keyword, article title, author, journal title, journal subject, and date ranges are searchable in both *PIO* and *PAO*, with limits by language and dates. The full text is searchable in *PAO*.

Adam Matthew's *Eighteenth Century Journals: A Portal to Newspapers and Periodicals, c. 1685–1815*, published in four sections and covering the long eighteenth century, offers digital facsimiles of approximately 200 titles from the following institutions: journals from the Hope Collection at the Bodleian Library (Section I, also available on microfilm from the same company);[22] newspapers and journals from the Harry Ransom Humanities Research Center (Section II); newspapers from the British Newspaper Library at Colindale and Cambridge University Library from outside London and from the British Empire (Section III); and newspapers and journals from Chetham's Library in Manchester, reflecting the growing industrial interests of that community (Section IV). As with *British Periodicals*, libraries may purchase individual sections, so, if your library owns it, check with your reference librarian to see which parts your library holds. Although there is some overlap with *ECCO*, *British Periodicals*, and *Burney*, *Eighteenth Century Journals* does not have the depth of coverage, sometimes including only an article, an issue, a volume, or a year of a title. In the case of *The Adventurer*, mentioned earlier, the database contains a single essay from the periodical that is from a reprint in George Colman's *Prose Works on Several Occasions* (1787). *Eighteenth Century Journals* does contain searchable transcriptions, which alleviates the problems encountered when searching OCR texts.

There are scholarly and modern reprints of a select number of serial titles. The *Spectator* has been reprinted many times since the early eighteenth century, and copies are freely available in Google Books, HathiTrust, and Internet Archive. Eighteenth-century bound reprints may include short notes and indexes. In the case of George Etherege, the Restoration playwright who wrote *The Man of Mode* and *She Would If She Could*, the indexes in the later bound versions helpfully indicate that the name is spelled "Etheridge" in the publication, and full-text searches in several of the databases do retrieve the latter spelling, but do not find all references to the playwright.

Donald F. Bond's five-volume scholarly edition *The Spectator*, published by Clarendon Press, contains informative footnotes that indicate textual differences, explain literary and cultural references, provide references to contemporary commentary on culture found in other publications, and give translations for the Latin mottos. The detailed index to the text supplies access, not just to the words of the text, but also to the context. There are sixteen references to Etherege listed in the index, but two issues, number 65 (Tuesday, May 15, 1711) and number 75 (Saturday, May 26, 1711), which discuss Etherege's play *Man of Mode*, do not contain Etherege's name or the title *Man of Mode*. Instead, the play is referred to as *Sir Foplin Flutter* in the former issue, and the play of *Sir Fopling* in the latter. Bond's footnote in number 65 helpfully informs the reader that the play is Etherege's comedy from 1676, which had been performed on April 20, 1711, at Drury Lane, and he lists the cast and characters. In comparison, *Burney* retrieved three references to Etherege using the medium fuzzy search option, but did not find all references to him, for instance, "Sir Roger was what you call a fine Gentleman, had often supped with my Lord Rochester and Sir George Etherege" in number 2 (March 2, 1711) and the "Polite Sir George Etherege" in number 51 (April 28, 1711). Bond's work offers a rich, detailed framework for *The Spectator* that doesn't exist in the digital versions available, and the comparison illustrates the challenges of searching for specific information and understanding obscure references from past cultures, without such guidance. If we didn't have Bond's scholarly edition, individuals studying *The Spectator* would have to do this groundwork themselves.

Pickering & Chatto has reprinted facsimiles for *Defoe's Review, Gentleman's Magazine*, and *Grub-Street Journal, 1730–1733*. The sixteen-volume ***Gentleman's Magazine*** reproduces the first fifteen volumes of the publication, from 1731 to 1745, what the publisher's website calls the "Age of Samuel Johnson." The sixteenth volume contains the *Miscellaneous Correspondence: Containing Essays, Dissertations, Ec. on Various Subjects, Sent to the Author of the Gentleman's Magazine, Ec. (1742–1748)* and an index. An introduction by Thomas Keymer provides a history and context for the magazine, which Samuel Johnson credited with giving "new meaning to a word that had previously been used only in its primary sense of treasury or arsenal" (volume I, p. vii). The index is a transcription of "An Index to the Essays, Dissertations, and Historical Passages," in volume 1 of the *General Index to Fifty-Six Volumes of the Gentleman's Magazine, from Its Commencement in the Year 1731 to the End of 1786*, compiled by Samuel Ayscough, in 1818. Pickering & Chatto's facsimile editions do not have the depth of information seen in Bond's *Spectator*, because the company has a different philosophy about editing texts: They offer the image of the texts, with brief notes, and frequently do not include indexes.

CONCLUSION

Although much of the surviving monographic and periodical publications from the eighteenth century are available as reprints or facsimiles, there are challenges for the literary researcher. Scholarly and modern edited editions variously include notes to explain context and indexes to provide access, whereas digital and microform facsimiles do not. Full-text searching is an invaluable asset for exploring digital versions of texts, but, because of the nonstandard fonts used at the time, even with fuzzy searching, the researcher will have to try a variety of searches and may need to browse through the publications to look for additional relevant items. If no modern or scholarly editions exist for a text, and if multiple editions from the eighteenth century are available, then the scholar will want to compare texts to select the best resource for the purposes of the study. For individual literary magazine titles, check Sullivan's *British Literary Magazines: The Augustan Age and the Age of Johnson, 1698–1788* to discover if an index exists, or check the digital collections to see if the serial was reprinted and bound into volumes with an index. The eighteenth-century literary scholar is fortunate to have the monographic and ephemeral publications of the time in digital facsimile, but effective search strategies and techniques are essential to benefit from this wealth of access.

NOTES

1. Iona Italia, *The Rise of Literary Journalism in the Eighteenth Century: Anxious Employment* (New York: Routledge, 2005), 8.

2. Jeremy Gregory and John Stevenson, *The Longman Companion to Britain in the Eighteenth Century, 1688–1820* (New York: Longman, 2000), 301.

3. Ian Jackson, "Approaches to the History of Readers and Reading in Eighteenth-Century Britain," *Historical Journal* 47, no. 4 (2004): 1,051; Bob Harris, "Print Culture," in *A Companion to Eighteenth-Century Britain*, ed. H. T. Dickinson (Malden, MA: Blackwell, 2002), 291.

4. Jackson, "Approaches to the History of Readers and Reading in Eighteenth-Century Britain," 1,050, 1,053; Italia, *The Rise of Literary Journalism in the Eighteenth Century*, 7.

5. Uriel Heyd, *Reading Newspapers: Press and Public in Eighteenth-Century Britain and America* (Oxford, UK: Voltaire Foundation, 2012), 15–16.

6. Harris, "Print Culture," 286–87.

7. Harris, "Print Culture," 287–88.

8. Italia, *The Rise of Literary Journalism in the Eighteenth Century*, 20.

9. "magazine, n.," *OED Online*. New York: Oxford University Press, www.oed .com/view/Entry/112144?rskey=3hArDJ&result=1&isAdvanced=false (accessed 8 July 2012).

10. Italia, *The Rise of Literary Journalism in the Eighteenth Century*, 18.

11. Michael F. Suarez, "Publishing Contemporary English Literature, 1695–1774," in *The Cambridge History of the Book in Britain*, vol. 5, 1695–1830, ed. Michael F. Suarez and Michael L. Turner (New York: Cambridge University Press, 2009), 663.

12. Suarez, "Towards a Bibliometric Analysis of the Surviving Record, 1701–1800," in *The Cambridge History of the Book in Britain*, vol. 5, 1695–1830, ed. Michael L. Turner (New York: Cambridge University Press, 2009), 48.

13. J. Stephen Murphy, "The Death of the Editor," *Essays in Criticism: A Quarterly Journal Founded by F. W. Bateson* 58, no. 4 (October 2008): 289–90, 304.

14. Murphy, "The Death of the Editor," 302.

15. Murphy, "The Death of the Editor," 302–3.

16. Suarez, "Publishing Contemporary English Literature, 1695–1774," 663.

17. *Early English Books Online*, "The Early Chronology of UMI and the *Early English Books* Microfilm Collections" (Ann Arbor, MI: ProQuest/Chadwyck-Healey), eebo.chadwyck.com/about/about.htm#chron.

18. Jayn Pearson and Keith Soothill, "Using an Old Search Engine: The Value of the *Times Index*," *Sociology* 37, no. 4 (November 2003): 781–90.

19. David Deacon, "Yesterday's Papers and Today's Technology: Digital Newspaper Archives and 'Push Button' Content Analysis," *European Journal of Communication* 22, no. 5 (2007): 22.

20. Simon Tanner, Trevor Muñoz, and Pich Hemy Ros, "Measuring Mass Text Digitization Quality and Usefulness: Lessons Learned from Assessing the OCR Accuracy of the British Library's *19th Century Online Newspaper Archive*," *D-Lib Magazine* 15, no. 7/8 (July/August 2009), www.dlib.org/dlib/july09/munoz/07munoz .html.

21. Lars Troide, "Burney, Charles (1757–1817)," in *Oxford Dictionary of National Biography*, ed. H. C. G. Matthew and Brian Harrison, online edition ed. Lawrence Goldman (Oxford, UK: Oxford University Press, 2004), www.oxforddnb.com/ view/article/4079?docPos=2.

22. Online guide to the *Eighteenth Century Journals from the Hope Collection at the Bodleian Library, Oxford* microfilm collection, available online at tinyurl.com/ hopecollectionjournals.

Chapter Seven

Contemporary Reviews

As the publishing industry grew throughout the first half of the eighteenth century, and a wider selection of books became available to a broader audience, a new type of publication emerged: the Review periodical. (To differentiate between the type of publication and the evaluative article, the former will be capitalized as Review.) Ralph Griffiths's *Monthly Review*, the first to be launched in 1749, did not initially intend to depart radically from earlier formats of abstract journals, for example, *Memoirs of Literature* and *History of the Works of the Learned*, which summarize a highly selective list of titles to keep "serious readers informed about the progress of knowledge in all fields."[1] Griffiths's goal was to expand this format to identify all new books and pamphlets on a regular basis, including literary works, and provide brief judgments about each title to indicate whether it was worth notice. Antonia Forester summarizes how Griffiths had explained the "role of the reviewer in simple, practical terms to a reading public unused to the phenomenon of purchasing literary judgments or descriptions of books that might preempt any necessity of reading the books themselves" to offer "recommendations to ensure against intellectual fraud and theft . . . placing the new Review in a mediating position between the booksellers and the reading public."[2]

With this value-added feature, the business of criticism began. The *Monthly Review* was followed by other review periodicals, which copied its format and inclusive philosophy, for example, the *Critical Review* (1756), the *London Review* (1775), the *English Review* (1783), the *Analytical Review* (1788), the *British Critic* (1793), and the *Anti-Jacobin Review* (1798). The Reviews generally used a two-tier approach to organizing new publications: one section with roughly ten to fifteen main articles and a second section with a long list of brief catalog entries, some only a few words long and others a page of small type.[3] While copying the groundbreaking *Monthly*, subsequent review journals each proclaimed why a new Review was necessary, because each accused the others of using biased, corrupt, ignorant, malicious hack writers to do the evaluating, and each was, in turn, accused of the same behavior by other Reviews, publishers, and authors. "The innumerable complaints, pleadings, and attacks at reviewers in prose and verse and in newspapers, magazines, pamphlets, and books soon made it clear that whether or not reviewers' opinions really influence readers, there was widespread fear that they did."[4]

This printed clamor was partly responsible for the negative perception of the eighteenth-century Reviews during much of the nineteenth and the twentieth centuries, but there are varying perspectives about the veracity of some of the accusations laid against the Reviews. Derek Roper argues in his study *Reviewing before the Edinburgh, 1788–1802* that these charges were largely untrue, because the audience would not have been fooled by reviews that blatantly favored a specific publisher, and that the publications were fairly esteemed, collected, and kept by individuals, subscription libraries, literary societies, and book clubs.[5] These publications were rather profitable. Roper refutes the "hack" label because literary figures we study today were reviewers themselves: Tobias Smollett founded the *Critical Review*, with Samuel Johnson, David Hume, and Oliver Goldsmith acting as early contributors and, in later years, Samuel Taylor Coleridge. The *English Review*, largely written by Scots, had William Godwin as a critic. The *Analytical Review*, with a reputation for radical political and religious opinions, published reviews by Alexander Geddes and Mary Wollstonecraft. Roper points out that we know a great deal about the *Monthly Review* and its policies and practices, and we even know the names of almost all the critics, between 1749 and 1815, thanks to the two indexes compiled by Benjamin Nangle, *The Monthly Review: Indexes of Contributors and Articles*, first series 1749 to 1789, and second series 1789 to 1815 (1934 and 1955, respectively). Roper refers to these individuals as "men of learning or talent."[6]

Frank Donoghue doesn't deny the value of knowing who the reviewers were, but he cautions that "much of the influence wielded by the Reviews derives from their policy of anonymity, from the fact that their judgments did not issue from individuals, but rather came directly and impersonally from the journals themselves . . . the practice of anonymous reviews cannot be underestimated and is a prominent complaint in many attacks on the journals."[7] Our intent here is not to address whether the charges are true, but rather to point out, if intending to make judgments about literary reputation based upon articles in these publications, the need to understand the culture.

In the end, the eighteenth-century approach to reviews became outmoded. The *Edinburgh Review*, founded at the dawn of the nineteenth century, returned to the early eighteenth-century selective practice and chose to review only what the editors considered worthy. On the one hand, the *Edinburgh Review* approach was intended to ensure that only quality writing was considered, and to exclude, for example, the plethora of mediocre books that overwhelmed Coleridge as a reviewer. The emerging Romantic poets and authors, however, were overlooked by these new publications, but they were covered by the Reviews that still existed because of their inclusive policy.[8]

The eighteenth century was a transition period from the traditional patronage support, whether aristocratic or subscription, to an industry where authors worked with publishers to make their works available to the public, and authors could get caught in the confusion of the transition. The influx of Reviews added a new twist to the literary marketplace. In his chapter on Laurence Sterne, "'I wrote not to be fed but to be famous,'" Donoghue examines the impact this transition period had on the author. Sterne understood fame as coming through the patronage system, but, with the publication of *Tristram Shandy*, he was instantly confronted by a different reality as other forces were determining fame: the Reviews, on the one hand, with their anonymous evaluations of literary works, and, on the other, by the responses to and imitators of his work found in pamphlets.[9]

Sterne courted Lord Bathurst and David Garrick as benefactors and supporters of his book, even while he was beguiled by the sometimes cultish responses in the pamphlets; the amazing responses found in pamphlets in the 1760s have been republished by Garland Press, in a multivolume set *Sterneiana*. Sterne wrote the remaining installments of the book while trying to comprehend and court these two new publishing audiences. He initially chose to engage with the pamphlets and attacked the *Monthly Review* but later revised which audiences he would address. He entered the mid-century literary market naively, "unaware that the famous author now bore no resemblance to his heroic classical or even Renaissance predecessors, but was rather the site of an assortment of institutional forces that combined to legitimize him."[10]

Donoghue assesses Sterne's experience as a professional writer at the time of transition, when, because he didn't understand the nature of his audience, he began to respond and write to the pamphlets and Reviews as his audience, much as he would for a patron. This chapter on the far more visible, contradictory, and confusing review environment is an intriguing case study about the evolving relationships between authors and audience. For our purposes here, it also illustrates the types of publications that can be mined to discover contemporary responses to a literary work and some of the pitfalls of relying on the Reviews and pamphlets as evidence.

For literary researchers working on authors who published before the Reviews, contemporary opinions are more difficult to determine systematically and require various approaches to uncover. In his introduction to *Defoe: The*

Critical Heritage, Pat Rogers notes that Defoe died the year the *Gentleman's Magazine* was founded, and years before the Reviews came to be, so that his work was never seriously assessed as literature during his lifetime, or even during the eighteenth century. Known as a controversialist, a "scribbler with more talent that most perhaps—as Pope allowed," and distinguished "by his fecundity and his talent for making enemies . . . Defoe is notable rather for the quantity of hostile material directed against him in his lifetime . . . a popular target of newswriters and pamphleteers for thirty years."[11]

Discussed in more detail later in the chapter, such series as *The Critical Heritage* and author-centered bibliographies identify these early contemporary judgments found in printed publications and ephemera. We will describe digital collections containing eighteenth-century newspapers and periodicals to search for additional relevant sources, including advertisements and reviews. Scholarly articles and monographs surveying criticism of an author may have references to eighteenth-century commentary or information about literary status, while scholarly biographies frequently assess reputation. The *Oxford Dictionary of National Biography* (*ODNB*) and *Dictionary of Literary Biography* (*DLB*), both discussed in chapter 2, frequently summarize an author's contemporary reception. Although more difficult to find, opinions might be found in eighteenth-century letters and diaries, and in the marginalia found in books.

Other possibilities are obituaries, elegies, or death notices published to mark an author's death. The obituary was another genre that was finding its way in the eighteenth century. According to Bridget Fowler, the "first *modern* obituaries in newspapers or periodicals or death announcements accompanied by brief biographies appeared in 1731, in the London-based *The Gentleman's Magazine* . . . the precursors for these magazine obits were earlier books of short biographies" (italics Fowler's).[12] Defoe died before this new procedure for announcing deaths on a regular basis was in place. If cited in the *ODNB* biographical essay, the *Gentleman's Magazine* death notices can be identified, although this is truer for lesser-known figures, for whom little information survives. The death notice for William Taverner is cited in the *ODNB* biography on the poet, but the *Gentleman's Magazine* death notice for John Gay, who died the same year, is not. Otherwise, the magazine can be searched in *British Periodicals* (see the "Contemporary Reviews in Eighteenth-Century Periodicals and Newspapers" section) or browsed in the month of the figure's death to see if a notice is present. Searching *17th and 18th Century Burney Collection Newspapers*, several newspapers published virtually the same article about the death of Horace Walpole in 1797, although the *Times Digital Archive, 1785–2006* did not seem to carry book reviews or publish obituaries at the end of the eighteenth century. As another measure, the popularity of an author could be determined by the number of reprints of a literary work or the amount of money paid to publish a piece. This chapter covers resources and strategies for finding contemporary opinions using modern indexes and reference works and digital collections of eighteenth-century publications.

MODERN INDEXES TO EIGHTEENTH-CENTURY REVIEWS

Forster, Antonia. *Index to Book Reviews in England, 1749–1774*. Carbondale: Southern Illinois University Press, 1990.

———. *Index to Book Reviews in England, 1775–1800*. London: British Library, 1997.

Ward, William S., comp. *Literary Reviews in British Periodicals, 1789–1797: A Bibliography with a Supplementary List of General (Non-Review) Articles on Literary Subjects*. New York: Garland, 1979.

———. *Literary Reviews in British Periodicals, 1798–1820: A Bibliography with a Supplementary List of General (Non-Review) Articles on Literary Subjects*. 2 vols. New York: Garland, 1972.

Watson, George, ed. *The New Cambridge Bibliography of English Literature: Volume 2, 1660–1800*, 2nd ed. Cambridge, UK: Cambridge University Press, 1971.

Antonia Forster's two volumes are invaluable indexes to book reviews in England that were published in selected major and minor magazines and review journals during the time. ***Index to Book Reviews in England, 1749–1774*** encompasses sixteen periodicals, including *British Magazine, Critical Review, Gentleman's Magazine, London Magazine, Monthly Review*, and *Universal Museum and Complete Magazine of Knowledge and Pleasure*, while ***Index to Book Reviews in England, 1775–1800*** has twenty-seven, adding in the new publications *Analytical Review, Annual Register, British Critic, Anti-Jacobin Review, Lady's Monthly Museum, New Lady's Magazine, Monthly Magazine*, and *Edinburgh Magazine and Review*. Published works of fiction, poetry, and drama, including translated works, are indexed, while reviews to theatrical productions are not.

The 3,023 entries in *1749–1774* and 4,981 entries in *1775–1800* are arranged alphabetically by author or, if the author is unknown, by title. In the later volume, Forster used Janet Todd's *Dictionary of British and American Women Writers, 1660–1800* (discussed in chapter 2) and Virginia Blain, Patricia Clements, and Isobel Grundy's *Feminist Companion to Literature in English* to identify women authors of anonymous pieces, with cross-references from the title to the author. Entries typically offer the author's name (in brackets if published anonymously at the time); a complete transcription of the title; the number of volumes; the place of publication; the publication date; the format; the price; the bookseller's name; and, if viewed, the library where Forster examined the book.

For those she couldn't examine, Forster took the information found in the Reviews. The bibliographic information is followed by citations to the reviews themselves. Frances Burney's *Evelina* (1778) was reviewed by the *Monthly Review, Critical Review, Gentleman's Magazine*, and *London Review*; *Cecilia* (1782) was assessed by those four, plus the *English Review, Town & Country Magazine, New Annual Register, European Magazine*, and *British Magazine & Review*; and *Camilla* (1796) by the *Monthly, Critical, English*, and by the *Analytical Review, British Critic, Monthly Magazine*, and *Monthly Mirror*. The 1778 reviews run anywhere from one to two pages, while the 1782 and 1796 reviews are five pages or more in length. Although Forster does not intend for these indexes to be comprehensive, she does attempt to identify reviews of all major and most minor literary works during the time periods. Forster's scholarly introduction gives insights into the culture and practices of reviewing during the eighteenth century, with a key to the abbreviations and symbols used in the entries.

Although there are eleven years of overlap with Forster's second index and William S. Ward's *Literary Reviews in British Periodicals, 1789–1797: A Bibliography with a Supplementary List of General (Non-Review) Articles on Literary Subjects* and *Literary Reviews in British Periodicals, 1798–1820: A Bibliography with a Supplementary List of General (Non-Review) Articles on Literary Subjects*, it is important to consult both resources because the editors have different criteria for inclusion (Ward indexes theatrical performances and nonfiction prose) and index somewhat different periodicals. Ward's volumes are arranged by author, or under "Anonymous" if unknown, and entries are listed alphabetically by brief title (or full title where necessary), publication date, abbreviation for genre (P = poetry, D = drama, F = fiction, Pr = nonfiction prose) if noted in the review, and the list of citations where reviewed. Francis Burney's works listed are *Brief Reflections Relative to the French Clergy* (Pr), with one review in the *European Magazine*; *Camilla* (F), with six of the reviews found in Forster, plus two more from *Freemason's Magazine* and *Scots Magazine*; and *Edwy and Elgiva, A Tragedy* (D), a performance of her play, with three 1795 reviews. In the appendixes, Ward indexes articles related to literature, arranged by "General (Non-Review) Articles on Authors and Their Works," "General and Genre Criticism" (volumes of criticism covered in the index and articles on general criticism, poetry, fiction, and drama and theatre), and "Reviews of Operas and Musical Dramas." These appendixes are helpful for finding articles that generally discuss an author and his or her works, which may speak to reputation (such as the three pieces about Burney in the *1789–1797* appendix on general, nonreview articles), and for discovering contemporary views of genres. Additional appendixes are "Reviews of Volumes Dealing with Contemporary Authors and Their Works" (Thomas Paine and others) and "Reviews of Books and Articles Dealing with Selected Authors before 1789" (Shakespeare, Milton, Pope, Johnson).

As we have seen in several chapters in this volume, the foundational bibliographic compilations found in George Watson's volume 2 of *The New Cambridge Bibliography of English Literature* (*NCBEL*) continue to contribute to our knowledge of eighteenth-century English literature and authors and, in this case, for locating opinions outside the Reviews and before the Reviews. Arranged in chronological order by author, the bibliographies and brief entries for secondary sources, at times, begin with references to contemporary opinions. These lists are not exhaustive and do not have the depth of Forster and Ward's indexes, but they may lead to nonperiodical perceptions. The entry for Defoe contains a short list of some of the attacks on him.

Contemporary opinions, especially those in found letters, diaries, poems, elegies, and biographies, may not truly reflect how the author was valued at the time, but instead may either be intended as laudatory or derisive. A researcher must try to look behind the commentary to discover who the author of the piece is, and what the context is, to determine its intent. For example, the earliest secondary source listed for John Gay in *NCBEL* is a biographical pamphlet, printed by the notorious Edmund Curll, the year after his death. Curll pirated three poems by Pope, Gay, and Montagu (Pope was so enraged that he slipped an emetic into Curll's drink, causing Curll to become very ill). This may or may not be relevant in terms of the biographical sketch, for short biographies of the recently deceased were growing in popularity, so Curll's intent may have been purely financial. Still, it is worth examining the text in light of his relationship with Gay and his reputation as a publisher.

Many of the major periodicals in these modern indexes are available full text in the digital collections discussed later in the chapter. The citations can be used to find the articles in the publications, thus avoiding the potential problems with fuzzy searching, discussed in chapters 1 and 6.

AUTHOR-SPECIFIC RESOURCES

Hannaford, Richard Gordon. *Samuel Richardson: An Annotated Bibliography of Critical Studies*. New York: Garland, 1980.

Rogers, Pat. *Defoe: The Critical Heritage.* Boston: Routledge and Kegan Paul, 1972.

Smith, Sarah W. R. *Samuel Richardson: A Reference Guide.* Boston: G. K. Hall, 1984.

Spedding, Patrick. *A Bibliography of Eliza Haywood.* Brookfield, VT: Pickering & Chatto, 2004.

Bibliographies and collections of critical assessments focused on an author or literary movement are good starting points for locating contemporary opinions. These types of reference tools are compiled by scholars intimately acquainted with the subject matter, because they have conducted in-depth investigations to identify the most obscure references. *NCBEL* (discussed in the previous section) and the *Dictionary of Literary Biography* (discussed later in the chapter) list potentially useful bibliographies. Searching the subject field in the library catalog for both the author's name and *bibliography* will retrieve useful results, if an author-centered bibliography has been compiled. For example, the Library of Congress subject heading for Eliza Haywood is *Haywood, Eliza Fowler, 1693?-1756 – Bibliography.* To find whether the author is included in the "Critical Heritage" series, search the author's name and *critical heritage* by keyword; *defoe and critical heritage* will retrieve *Defoe: The Critical Heritage. MLA International Bibliography* can be searched by such subjects as *reputation, literary reputation, reception study,* or *reception,* combined with the author's name or time period (*eighteenth century* or *18th century* or *1700–1799*), to find scholarly discussions on an author's reputation.

Pat Rogers's **Defoe: The Critical Heritage** is part of the Routledge "Critical Heritage" series, which are handy compilations of criticism edited by experts primarily on the traditional canonical literary figures. Volumes typically offer an introduction by the editor, followed by extracts of opinions and reviews in chronological order, starting with contemporary reports and moving forward through the centuries. In the introduction, Rogers describes Defoe's reputation while he was alive, throughout the rest of the eighteenth century, and into the nineteenth century, when an appreciation for his literary work began. The volume is arranged into thirty-four sections, each headed by a short overview. The first section is comprised of a group of eight representative opinions written between 1703 and 1718; comments from Pope, Swift, and the Scriblerians (1709–1731); a satire on *Robinson Crusoe* (1719); a biographic entry (1723); the mid-century view (1753); and other extracts from the rest of the eighteenth century to 1879. The volume concludes with a longer, but still selective, list of comments made during Defoe's lifetime, spanning the years 1701 to 1729; a list of his books and pamphlets mentioned in the text, with the reference numbers to John Robert Moore's annotated *A*

Checklist of the Writings of Daniel Defoe; and an index arranged alphabetically by category (books and pamphlets by Defoe, reviewers and critics, journals, names). Other *Critical Heritage* volumes focus on Addison and Steele, Swift, Pope, Johnson, Fielding, Goldsmith, Smollett, Sterne, Walpole, Burns, Blake, Wordsworth, and Coleridge.

Patrick Spedding's *A Bibliography of Eliza Haywood* is a descriptive bibliography of all editions of works known to be by Eliza Haywood. Although not specifically intended for research on contemporary opinions, Spedding's detailed bibliographical analysis of various editions reveals information about Haywood, her relationships, her strategies for promoting her works, and her reputation, with footnotes that lead to contemporary opinions. The hefty bibliography is arranged as follows: works by Haywood published before 1850 (collections, individual works); works by Haywood published after 1850 (reprints, facsimiles, microforms, CD-ROM, online e-texts); works attributed to Haywood (rejected attributions, ghosts); miscellanea (works published and sold by Haywood, collections, individual works, works attributed to William Hatchett); appendixes; a bibliography of works consulted; and indexes (chronological index of first editions, index printers and publishers, general index).

Each entry is headed by an overview of the publication, followed by a detailed description of the volume, with a transcription of the title, collation, contents, dates of publication, notes, references to major bibliographic works that list the title (e.g., *English Short Title Catalogue*, *WorldCat*), reviews (when published), and reproductions (e.g., EBF = Early British Fiction, EBP = Early British Periodicals, EC = Eighteenth Century; see later in this chapter and chapter 6 for more about digital versions of these collections). Although there are few entries with reviews listed, Spedding's accompanying analysis provides insights about Haywood's life and offers known contemporary opinions, with footnotes to source materials. In Ab.1, "Love in Excess," Richard Savage wrote a tribute to Haywood for part two of the title. In entry Ab.17, "Memoirs of a Certain Island Adjacent to the Kingdom of Utopia," 1724 to 1725, Spedding reveals that Savage, possibly Haywood's lover and father of her eldest child, wrote this and a second poem of tribute in *The Rash Resolve*, but also two attacks on her in 1725, in *The Authors of the Town*, and, in 1729, in *An Author to be Lett*. Spedding informs us that Savage is suspected of being Pope's informant for *The Dunciad*, in which Pope attacks Haywood and identifies her in a footnote as the author of *Memoirs*. Spedding's citations can be traced back to the original sources in order to build a critical heritage focused on Haywood. While this resource was not intended to be used the way we are proposing here, our purpose is to show how a bibliography of an author can be mined for references to contemporary reception.

Two bibliographies from the early 1980s devoted to Samuel Richardson are useful for understanding some of the challenges of researching contemporary opinions of the author: Richard Gordon Hannaford's ***Samuel Richardson: An Annotated Bibliography of Critical Studies*** (discussed in chapter 4) and Sarah Smith's *Samuel Richardson: A Reference Guide*. Although both serve as bibliographies to criticism well into the twentieth century, the focus here is on the contemporary reception in the eighteenth century. In their introductions, each author explains why it is important to go beyond traditional sources of contemporary responses, like reviews, to examine the powerful positive and negative influences Richardson had on the people around him. Reactions are found in correspondence, memoirs, pamphlets, imitations, and parodies, and in French and German criticism. In terms of the foreign response, as Smith points out, "What, for instance, did Diderot read, an English or a French *Clarissa*?" It matters because "Prévost's *Lettres angloises*, ostensibly a translation of *Clarissa*, was actually a drastic revision of the book, abridged by half and much prettified" (xviii).

The first section of Hannaford's "Eighteenth-Century Criticism" includes a chronology of criticism from 1740 to 1800, followed by the reception of and allusions to Richardson found in letters, diaries, memoirs, biographies, and poems. In more than 150 helpful annotated entries, the chronology tracks Richardson's reception from a review article of his role as editor of *The Negotiations of Sir Thomas Roe* in 1740, to Charlotte Smith's assessment of his strengths and weaknesses in her *The Letters of a Solitary Wanderer* in 1800. In between are references to parodies and imitations, and critiques in review periodicals and books. The next section, "Criticism of, Remarks About, and Tributes to Richardson in Letters, Diaries, Memoirs, Biographies, and Poems," offers nearly 120 annotated entries. Arranged alphabetically by author, or by title when anonymous, the section begins with a 1758 poem praising Richardson in *American Magazine, Monthly Chronicle for the British Colonies* and concludes with Zachariä's recommendation in the 1757 *Die vier Stufen des weiblichen Alters* that the ideal young woman would read Richardson's novels almost exclusively. There are other references to comments by Fanny Burney, Robert Burns, David Garrick, Thomas Gray, Lady Mary Wortley Montagu, Catherine Talbot, Voltaire, and Horace Walpole.

Smith arranges ***Samuel Richardson: A Reference Guide*** chronologically, combining writings by and about Richardson from 1723 to 1978. Her volume is a bit more cumbersome to consult. Whereas Hannaford provides separate entries, Smith, at times, briefly lists the reviews and responses beneath the main entry for the novel and, at other times, has separate entries. The English and Continental critical assessments of *Pamela* from 1740 to 1749 are contained in the annotation under "1740," with brief comments ("hostile," "praises naturalness") following the references. The responses to *Sir Charles Grandison* are listed separately. In addition to the parodies and imitations in the body of the bibliography, Smith concludes the volume with four appendixes: "Richardsonian" novels (e.g., Eliza Haywood, *History of Miss Betsy Thoughtless*, 1751; Sarah Fielding, *The Adventures of David Simple*, 1752) and "Richardsonian" dramas, juvenilia, and minor poetry addressed to Richardson or about his works.

In terms of the contemporary reception of Richardson's work, there is a great deal of overlap in Smith and Hannaford's bibliographies. Although Forster is an excellent resource, she doesn't include references to Richardson's works that are not purely reviews; the citation she lists for *Grandison* is not in either Hannaford or Smith, while none of their references are in Forster. As a best practice, consult all bibliographies devoted to your author, as well as Forster, Ward, and *NCBEL* to be as comprehensive as possible; refer to chapters 3 and 4 for additional types of potentially useful author-specific reference sources. After you have exhausted these, if you have access, we recommend that you search in *British Periodicals*, *Eighteenth Century Journals*, and *17th and 18th Century Burney Collection Newspapers* for additional references in the press, and in *Eighteenth Century Collections Online* (*ECCO*) for published responses in books and pamphlets.

CONTEMPORARY REVIEWS IN EIGHTEENTH-CENTURY PERIODICALS AND NEWSPAPERS

17th and 18th Century Burney Collection Newspapers. Farmington Hills, MI: Gale, 2007– . gdc.gale.com/products/17th-and-18th-century-burney-collection-newspapers.

British Periodicals. Ann Arbor, MI: ProQuest, 2006– . britishperiodicals.chadwyck.com.

Eighteenth Century Collections Online, Part I and Part II. Detroit, MI: Gale, 2003– . www.gale.cengage.com. Part I also available in the *Eighteenth Century* microfilm collection.

For overviews of the resources in this section, and for information on their microform equivalents, consult chapter 6. If you don't have access to the digital collections and your library doesn't have the microform versions, you can request the articles via interlibrary loan. If interested in browsing the journal, request the microfilm reels.

Many of the Reviews indexed by Forster and Ward are available on microform or digitally in the collections discussed in this section. In addition, the pamphlets, poems, and biographies cited and extracted in the author-centered bibliographies may be available in *ECCO*, or through Google Books, HathiTrust, or Internet Archive (see chapter 6). Searching digital collections can be both rewarding and frustrating: It can be rewarding when authors have been identified and titles transcribed, but frustrating when they haven't been; rewarding when the search retrieves new materials and not only the known items found in indexes and bibliographies, but frustrating because of the shortcomings of OCR'd text. As discussed in chapters 1 and 6, eighteenth-century literary scholars must understand the challenges of searching digital versions of primary source materials and be flexible and patient by trying various keywords and approaches.

The most straightforward strategy for locating contemporary opinions is to look for known items identified in secondary sources, for example, indexes or bibliographies. For reviews found in Forster and Ward, you should determine whether the database contains that publication; if searching directly by author name or title is unsuccessful, you can browse the volume or search by publication title and date. It is best to search the full text in the databases discussed in this section for the author or title. If the author published anonymously at that time and was identified as "by the author of," search the title of the book by which the individual is generally known. First names of authors may not always be used, for instance, a *European Magazine* review of *Cecilia*, in which the author is referred to as "Miss Burney" (September 1782) and, later, in the same publication, as "Mrs. D'Arblay, formerly Miss Burney" in the review of *Edwy and Elgiva* (April 1795). Because many publications of the time italicized author names and titles, which can make it difficult for OCR to recognize, searching by unique names of characters or unique phrases from the text may retrieve relevant references. Death notices, elegies, or obituaries published at the time may speak of the individual's literary reputation. Examples of these types of search strategies are described later in this chapter.

British Periodicals contains the major Review journals (*Analytical Review, Anti-Jacobin Review, British Critic, Critical Review, English Review, London Review, Monthly Review*), magazines (*Gentleman's Magazine, London Magazine, Literary Magazine and British Review*), and periodicals from throughout the century that may include references to authors or literary works. The advanced option allows limiting by document type "review," and by dates. Authoritative work has not been done for the bibliographic records, so writers who published anonymously should be searched by the title of the piece. Limiting by "review" may not retrieve titles evaluated in the second-tier sections of Reviews, described earlier, which largely consist of lists with brief, sometimes one-word, critiques ("for this silly story" see figure 7.1) or reviews of theatrical productions. A keyword search on Sarah

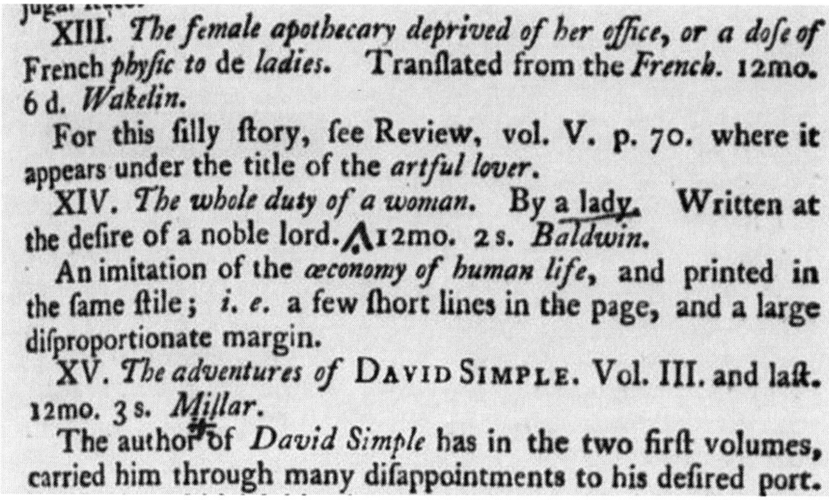

XIII. *The female apothecary deprived of her office, or a dofe of* French *phyfic to* de *ladies.* Tranflated from the *French.* 12mo. 6 d. *Wakelin.*

For this filly ftory, fee Review, vol. V. p. 70. where it appears under the title of the *artful lover.*

XIV. *The whole duty of a woman.* By a lady. Written at the defire of a noble lord. 12mo. 2 s. *Baldwin.*

An imitation of the *œconomy of human life,* and printed in the fame ftile; *i. e.* a few fhort lines in the page, and a large difproportionate margin.

XV. *The adventures of* DAVID SIMPLE. Vol. III. and laft. 12mo. 3 s. *Millar.*

The author of *David Simple* has in the two firft volumes, carried him through many difappointments to his defired port.

Figure 7.1. Section of a page from the *Critical Review* illustrating brief reviews. Source: *British Periodicals,* via ProQuest.

Fielding limited by "review" did not find items before the *Critical Review's* 1762 article on her translation of *Xenophon's Memoirs of Socrates.* Searching by keywords from the title, without limiting to "review," found a second-tier review in the February 1753 *Monthly* for the third volume of *The Adventures of David Simple* (see figure 7.1).

To discover the brief death notices in *Gentleman's Magazine,* search the author's name and limit by publication title, by the year of death, and by document type "obituary." The death notice in January 1731 for William Taverner, a playwright, reads "8 [January 8]. Mr. William Taverner, Proctor, at his House in Doctor's Commons. He was son to Mr Jer. Taverner, Face-painter, remarkably honest in his business, and Author of the 5 following Plays, viz. The faithful Bride of Canada; The Maid, the Mistress; The Female Advocates, or the Fanatick Stock-jobbers; The Artful Husband; The Artful Wife." John Gay's death notice, in December 4, 1732, was even briefer, reading as follows: "John Gay, at the D. of Queensberry's, Author of the Beggar's Opera, and many other poetical Pieces." Both obituaries provide clues to the literary works that would be known to the magazine's audience.

The *17th and 18th Century Burney Collection Newspapers,* which also include publications that can be identified as periodicals, allows limiting by advertising, arts and sports, and news, but not by review. Because of the font and difficulty with OCR'd text, patience will be required to find relevant references. As an example, although the review in the *London Chronicle,* from April 7, 1759 to April 10, 1759, for Sarah Fielding's *The History of the Countess of Dellwyn* can be found in the table of contents, with the author listed as "By the Author of David Simple," the review itself was not, even using the fuzzy option; it could, however, be found using the words *david simple*. Fielding's characters' names have the long "s" (Bilson, Lemster), perhaps making those unreadable as well. Patience and creative searching are required to find such reviews that are not in Forster and may not be in other bibliographies.

Eighteenth Century Collections Online (*ECCO*) can be searched directly for contemporary responses to literary works or those that speak to an individual's reputation, or, most straightforwardly, searched to find known items discovered in author-specific bibliographies, *NCBEL*, indexes, or other secondary sources. In addition, the database contains periodicals that were resold as bound volumes, for example, the *The Annual Register, or a View of the History, Politicks, and Literature*. Early eighteenth-century pamphlets attacking Defoe and the pamphlets imitating and responding to *Tristram Shandy* are present, as well as the entire critical pamphlet about Fielding's *Tom Jones*, by the anonymous Orbilius, *An Examen of the History of Tom Jones*. ECCO also holds the Curll biography on John Gay discussed earlier, and it is a good source for locating this type of biographical publication for other individuals. As seen with other digital collections, thoughtful and flexible strategies must be taken to ensure success. It is more difficult to search the database directly to find publications that speak to reputation and opinions. Strategies include searching the author's name by keyword, and *not*-ing out the name in the author field in an attempt to eliminate books by the person but keep those that are about him; however, if the author's name is part of the long title of the work, this strategy won't be as effective. For popular literary works and characters, a keyword search on the title or character's name, again *not*-ing out the author's name in the author field, may prove fruitful, or, if an author has become known by a particular work, searching for subsequent reviews that refer to "by the author of."

LETTERS, DIARIES, VERSE, AND MORE

Electronic Enlightenment. Oxford, UK: Humanities Division, University of Oxford, 2008– . Distributed by Oxford University Press at www .e-enlightenment.com.

Nelson, Carolyn. *Union First Line Index of English Verse, 13th–19th Century (Bulk 1500–1800)*. Washington, DC: Folger Shakespeare Library. firstlines .folger.edu (accessed 24 July 2012).

UK RED: The Experience of Reading in Britain, from 1450 to 1945. Milton Keynes, Buckinghamshire, UK: Open University. www.open.ac.uk/Arts/ reading/UK (accessed 24 July 2012).

Finding references to authors and literary works through letters, diaries, poetry, and marginalia is challenging, and, while author-centered bibliographies may refer to such documents, there isn't a systematic way to search across such documents. *Electronic Enlightenment*, discussed in chapter 8, contains digital versions of letters from scholarly editions, primarily from eighteenth-century figures. Although the database is still growing, it is currently limited in terms of the numbers of correspondents, so that a complete picture of a literary figure's contemporary reputation cannot be judged by this resource. It is still worth searching the contents, however, to discover if any of the writers refer to your author and in what context the comments are made.

UK RED: The Experience of Reading in Britain, from 1450 to 1945, a freely available website, provides a peek into these types of comments, presenting remarks made by readers that have been found in letters, diaries, commonplace books, marginalia, sociological surveys, and criminal court and prison records. Housed at The Open University, the database contains more than 30,000 records. The goal is to offer as much detail as possible about the reading experience found in the documents, including what was read, the title and genre, the gender of the reader, age, location, profession, and means of access, so that the data can be extracted in a variety of ways and patterns of reading examined. The database can be browsed by author and reader, so that if one wishes to find contemporary comments on Anne Radcliffe's novels, browsing the "R" section of the alphabetical author list will do the trick, or to see what Horace Walpole read, clicking on the "W" section of the alphabetical reader list will locate the newspapers articles, novels, poetry, and nonfiction he wrote about.

The advanced option allows keyword searching, limiting by "Century of Experience," "Reader/Listener/Reading Group" (name as reader, listener, or reading group; gender; age; socioeconomic group, for instance, servant, gentry, professional, aristocracy; occupation; religion), "Text Being Read" (author; title; genre/subject, including fiction, poetry, drama, conduct books, classics, history, science, and so forth), "Form of Text Print" (serial/periodical; book; newspaper; broadsheet; pamphlet), "Form of Text Manuscript" (codex; pamphlet; letter), "Provenance" (borrowed; owned; reading group; subscription library), "Time of Experience" (morning; afternoon; evening), and "Place of Experience." A search on author *radcliffe* limited to the eighteenth century found nineteen quotations by or references to what is known of their views of her works by Jane Austen, Edmund Burke, Frances Burney, Elizabeth Carter, Charles Maturin, Richard Sheridan, Mary Wollstonecraft, and William Wordsworth.

Carolyn Nelson's *Union First Line Index of English Verse, 13th–19th Century (Bulk 1500–1800)*, discussed in chapter 8, can be searched for references to authors found in manuscript poems. A keyword search on *samuel richardson* retrieves five records, four related to the eighteenth-century author, listed in a table by first line, author, title, last line, library, shelfmark, and folio; the results can be further sorted by any of these fields by clicking on the heading. Three of the poems (William Cowper, John Lockman, and anonymous) are comments on Richardson or his work, while one is an epitaph upon his death by John Hawkesworth.

CONCLUSION

Publishing developed into a robust industry during the course of the eighteenth century, and with it the idea of critically evaluating the merit of individual publications. The literary researcher will need to adapt strategies and expectations about finding contemporary commentary, depending upon when in the era the author lived and wrote. If the individual published in the latter half of the century, it is best to start with Forster and Ward. Traditionally canonical figures will have scholarly apparatus such as bibliographies and biographies, which may identify useful sources. It is important to determine whether an author-specific bibliography has been compiled that might include relevant references. For lesser-known authors, the *ODNB* and *DLB* may provide clues about an author's reputation at the time. For all known items, it is best to search the relevant subscription and freely available resources, as well as library catalogs, for electronic, microform, or reprinted versions. It is also useful to explore the subscription digital book, periodical, and newspapers collections, as well as Google Books, HathiTrust, and Internet Archive, limiting the searches to the eighteenth century. In addition, searching for obituaries, eighteenth-century and scholarly biographies, letters, and diaries is a key step. As always, if the research becomes too challenging and frustrating, consult a reference librarian for help.

NOTES

1. Derek Roper, *Reviewing before the Edinburgh, 1788–1802* (Newark: University of Delaware Press, 1978), 19.
2. Antonia Forster, "Book Reviewing," in *The Cambridge History of the Book in Britain*, vol. 5, 1695–1830, ed. Michael F. Suarez and Michael L. Turner (New York: Cambridge University Press, 2009), 632–33.
3. Forster, "Book Reviewing," 634.

4. Forster, "Book Reviewing," 642.

5. Roper, *Reviewing before the Edinburgh*, 19–36.

6. Roper, *Reviewing before the Edinburgh*, 30.

7. Frank Donoghue, *The Fame Machine: Book Reviewing and Eighteenth-Century Literary Careers* (Stanford, CA: Stanford University Press, 1996), 19.

8. Roper, *Reviewing before the Edinburgh*, 40–41.

9. Donoghue, *The Fame Machine*, 73.

10. Donoghue, *The Fame Machine*, 85.

11. Pat Rogers, *Defoe: The Critical Heritage* (Boston: Routledge and Kegan Paul, 1972), 4.

12. Bridget Fowler, *The Obituary as Collective Memory* (New York: Routledge, 2007), 4.

Chapter Eight

Archives and Manuscripts Collections

In the first part of this chapter, we will focus on using manuscript and archival collections, while in the second part we will introduce print, microform, and digital representations of eighteenth-century printed matter. Although facsimiles of selected literary manuscripts may be available in monograph, microform, or digital formats, some research projects will require a trip to a library or archive to examine the original primary materials. In this chapter we will discuss how to discover if manuscripts and documents related to an author or topic exist and, if so, where they are located and whether they are accessible to the public or scholars. We will also outline best practices for visiting institutions and using collections.

You may be able to locate the documents you need for your research in manuscript repositories or archival collections. According to the Society of American Archivists glossary of terms, the term *archives* (commonly used in the United States) or *archive* (common in other English-speaking countries) is defined variously as the records created by an individual, family, or organization, as the department or division within an organization responsible for collecting and maintaining the records, or the building that houses the collections, while the term *manuscript repository* is sometimes employed instead to refer to a collection of records that are brought together from sources other than the original individual, family, or organization.[1] The departments within institutions that house manuscripts may also be referred to as manuscript repositories or special collections.

As described by Frank G. Burke, the forms of materials found in archives are largely unique, "noncommercial" materials (that is, not produced in quantities for distribution or for sale) that fall into two categories, corporate and private. Corporate bodies are defined as "those [that] produce materials in pursuit of their corporate aim, and not the private aims of the individual members,"[2] for example, the records for the bookseller and publisher Longman at the University of Reading (www.reading.ac.uk/special-collections/collections/sc-longman.aspx). The Longman archives is another example of an archives no longer with its original organization; the archives for institutions that find that they cannot make such historic documents accessible for researchers, or where the organization no longer exists, might be found in collecting repositories such as the University of Reading. Other examples of corporate records are letters written to governmental officials by private citizens; files associated with lawsuits; or trial documentation involving authors, publishers, or booksellers found in national or governmental archives.

"Personal materials are those created by individuals that have not attained a commercial state, or were never intended to be either commercial or public."[3] Burke categorizes personal materials as household accounts, family correspondence, diaries, letters, photographs, and the working papers of an author. Collections of personal papers found in manuscript repositories or special collections are typically referred to as "'artificial collections,' so called because they have been consciously put together, usually around a subject area or a type of material, and have not accumulated naturally over the course of time."[4] Most papers of literary figures are found in artificial collections.

Because of the differences between archives and library organizational practices and access policies, different strategies are required for research and use. Archival collections of unique, irreplaceable types of materials are organized by their own sets of rules. The documents may or may not be cataloged, that is, individually described and organized for retrieval. If cataloged, the archive might have an online catalog or only a print version; if in print, the library might have published it to make it available to libraries worldwide, or it may only be available on-site. If not cataloged, a collection could have an online or print finding aid that describes the collection generally, for instance, the types of papers held (letters, diaries, commonplace books), without providing specifics about each piece.

In terms of access, opening hours to such collections are often limited to weekdays. All items are paged from closed stacks, so that it can be several hours or more before the items are available; typically, only a few items are permitted to be examined at a time, and sometimes only a limited number of items may be requested per day. Certain personal papers may be restricted, requiring letters of introduction before permission to view is granted, and, if frail, might only be available in microform format. More and more special collections and archives allow laptops and offer mediated scanning and photocopying services. Although no longer widely required, gloves may be provided for handling the manuscripts. These rare materials are kept in secured areas, necessitate special handling, and must be studied on-site in protected reading rooms that not only forbid food and drink, but may also prohibit items that can damage manuscripts (pens, glue, highlighters, chewing gum) and items that can be used to conceal and steal manuscript pages (coats, notepads, briefcases, laptop cases). Fortunately, most institutions with manuscript and archive collections have websites with information about rules and restrictions or e-mail addresses for making inquiries.

It isn't essential to understand why a manuscript is physically located where it is to do effective research, but the provenance of papers may prove illuminating. Introductions to standard editions, author-centered bibliographies, or printed guides or catalogs may describe the formation of particular literary collections or how the papers became dispersed. Literary papers that survive from the eighteenth century were preserved for a variety of reasons by the author, publisher, bookseller, or descendants or friends of an individual, but the fame of the author does not ensure the existence of manuscripts: For instance, none of the manuscripts of major works by Daniel Defoe or Henry Fielding are extant.

When documents do survive, they can be scattered around the globe; held in libraries, archives, or private hands; or possibly be unavailable to researchers. Literary papers still largely intact may have been sold together at auction or have remained in the family; Lady Mary Wortley Montagu's papers, still held by her descendants at Sandon Hall, are an example of the latter. In other cases, the documents may have been sold in pieces, like Richard Sheridan's literary works, which were auctioned off in parts by his twentieth-century descendents. Papers could have been destroyed by fire (it is conjectured that Fielding's manuscripts were burned in a fire at his half-brother's house during the Gordon Riots of 1780)[5] or by relatives who did not want information in the documents made public (Mary Wortley Montagu's daughter, Lady Bute, burned the diary her mother had kept from 1712 until her death).[6] Others may have vanished for some period of time, as was the case with Fanny Burney: Her papers were sold as part of the d'Arblay collections and thought lost to fire until the New York Public Library acquired them in 1941 from a private collector, cataloged them, and made them available to scholars in 1945.[7] The history of an individual's literary papers may prove helpful in understanding why documents are located where they are, and why they may no longer exist. In the following discussions, we will introduce resources that point to locations of specific types of manuscripts, as well as significant collections.

BEST PRACTICES

Before traveling to conduct research in archives, it is best to plan your visit carefully so that you maximize the amount of time you have. It is important to determine exactly what you need to examine and why. Consult the resources in this chapter to identify papers of interest and the institutions that hold them and determine if the manuscripts have already been filmed or digitized. Explore the Web to see if the institution has an online presence; if it does, look for links to "Archives," "Special Collections," or "Research," and then search for the papers you wish to consult to see if they are cataloged or if there is a finding aid. If the items you want are listed in one of the directories mentioned in this chapter or in the catalog of the institution you wish to visit, examine the record closely to see if it is an autograph or holograph (a document written in the author's hand), a copy, or on microfilm; depending upon your project, microfilm might be adequate. (For unfamiliar archival vocabulary, consult a specialized dictionary, for example, the Society of American Archivists' *A Glossary of Archival and Records Terminology*.) Once you are in the right area of the site, look for such links as "Planning a Visit," "Admission to the Research Library," or "Using the Collections" to read about the rules and regulations for researching in the collections. If the Web page doesn't have information about the archives, as is the case with Lady Mary Wortley Montagu's papers at Sandon Hall, look for an e-mail address, phone number, or mailing address to make inquiries; you can consult the *Index of English Literary Manuscripts*, *Location Register of English Literary Manuscripts and Letters*, and other directories discussed in this chapter to identify the documents at Sandon Hall.

At larger manuscript repositories and archives, you will be required to register, and some institutions allow preregistration online. Don't travel thousands of miles to a different continent without the documents you need. Whichever institution you visit, pay close attention to the types of identification necessary for registration, because if, for example, an official document with your home address is required and you fail to bring it with you, you could be denied access or permitted only limited access. As institutions may ask for written recommendations to work with manuscripts, have letters of introduction on letterhead from someone who can speak to the importance of your project. Contact the institution you wish to visit to ensure that the specific collection or documents you need to consult will be available on the specific dates you will be there and that they have not, for instance, been lent to a traveling exhibit.

Websites for libraries and archives generally provide details about use of the collections. Look for information about the rules of the library. What types of writing implements and paper are permitted? Are laptops permitted? Personal books? Digital cameras or hand-held scanners? Are scanning or photocopy services offered, and, if so, what are the costs? How many items may be requested per day, and what is the typical turnaround time for a request? Are the documents on-site or in remote storage, and, if the latter, how long is the retrieval time? Can requests be submitted prior to the visit, so that materials are immediately available upon arrival? What are the hours of the reading room, and how long before closing can last requests be submitted? The answers to questions like these can help you plan which tools to employ to transcribe or record the documents and how much time should be allotted for using the documents once you reach your destination. When permitted, digital cameras are incredibly valuable, since a great deal of material can be captured quickly and the resulting images can be transferred to a computer and examined at leisure in detail. Flash photography is generally not allowed, so test the camera in low-light conditions with no flash prior to your visit.

Handwriting, spelling, standard abbreviations, paper, and writing implements changed throughout the eighteenth century. Before traveling to look at original manuscripts, familiarize yourself with the handwriting of the times. If examining the papers of a single individual, try to find print, digital, or microform facsimiles of his or her handwriting. If studying the papers of more than one person across the century, look for a variety of samples. The *Index of English Literary Manuscripts*, discussed later in the chapter, provides facsimile samples of handwriting for each of the fifty-five authors included, while *British Literary Manuscripts Online* contains digital facsimiles of a variety of authors throughout the centuries. The National Archives created *Palaeography: Reading Old Handwriting, 1500–1800: A Practical Online Tutorial* (www.nationalarchives.gov.uk/palaeography) to help researchers work through samples of handwriting, from the easiest to the most difficult, with tips and strategies for effective transcription of older scripts. As you may need to examine unfamiliar words letter by letter, a magnifying glass is a useful tool to have on hand.

THE BRITISH LIBRARY MANUSCRIPTS READING ROOM

To illustrate the specific rules and regulations of a major collection of manuscripts, let's discuss the Manuscripts Reading Room of the British Library (www.bl.uk/reshelp/findhelprestype/manuscripts/msscollect/manuscripts collections.html). Located at the central London St. Pancras site, the department holds vast numbers of personal papers collected throughout the centuries, including literary manuscripts, letters, diaries, commonplace books, and more. To register for a reader's pass to the library as a whole, visitors must be eighteen years of age or older, although there are exceptions. First-time readers can register online, but, upon arrival, everyone must bring two forms of identification, at least one showing a home address and one showing a signature. According to the British Library website, valid forms of proof of address include driving licenses, recent utility bills, credit card statements, and other types of commercial or official documents that contain the home address. The website also lists acceptable items (laptops, PDAs, pencils), restricted items (mobile phone cameras may not be used, although they can be brought into the area; only one personal bag, although the library supplies clear plastic bags to carry papers and laptops), and forbidden items (cameras, scanners, coats, pens, highlighters, scanner pens, umbrellas, and more). The library provides lockers and a cloakroom to store personal belongings that are not allowed in the reading rooms.

You will need your reader's pass to enter the Manuscripts Reading Room, and, upon departure, your papers and laptop will be searched by a security guard. Even with a reader's card, additional permissions to see particular materials in the Manuscripts Reading Room may be required. It is important to bring a signed letter of introduction from an academic colleague, professor, chair, dean, or director, or from your editor, that explains your expertise, project, and need for access. This letter will be useful in case a curator needs to approve additional permissions for access to manuscripts. A reader can request up to ten items per day, four items at a time. For items stored on-site, the normal delivery time is seventy minutes, while items stored off-site may require at least forty-eight hours to retrieve. When requesting items, you will be asked to indicate your seat number. Laptops are restricted to particular areas in the room, and free wireless is available. Gloves are only required in particular instances; it is recommended that readers wash their hands frequently and keep them free of lotions. Although you may be able to borrow a magnifying glass at the Reference Enquiry Desk, bring your own to examine the text closely. In cases where manuscripts are too fragile or have been sold, you might be given microform or photocopies instead; at present, microform readers do not have printing or scanning capabilities. In addition to the Reference Enquiry Desk, where you can ask for help with your research questions, there are computers with access to the library's catalogs and databases subscribed to by the British Library and print reference books, including the collections catalogs and the multivolume *Index of Manuscripts in the British Library*.

The British Library is just one example of an institution with archives and manuscript collections. As stated in the "Best Practices" section, it is vital to plan ahead for any visit by learning about the rules specific to the library or archives with collections you need to consult.

LOCATING ARCHIVES OR MANUSCRIPTS

Access to Archives. Surrey, England: National Archives. www.national archives.gov.uk/a2a (accessed 24 July 2012).

Archive Finder. Ann Arbor, MI: ProQuest, 1997– . archives.chadwyck.com (accessed 27 July 2012).

Archives Wales/Archifau Cymru. www.archiveswales.org.uk (accessed 27 July 2012).

ARCHON Directory. Surrey, England: National Archives Historical Manuscripts Commission. www.nationalarchives.gov.uk/archon (accessed 27 July 2012).

Ash, Lee, and William G. Miller, comps. *Subject Collections: A Guide to Special Book Collections and Subject Emphases as Reported by University, College, Public, and Special Libraries and Museums in the United States and Canada,* 7th ed., revised and enlarged. 2 vols. New Providence, NJ: R. R. Bowker, 1993.

Dictionary of Literary Biography. Detroit, MI: Gale, 1978– . Also available online as the *Dictionary of Literary Biography Complete Online* and as part of the *Gale Literary Databases.* www.gale.cengage.com.

Foster, Janet, and Julia Sheppard, eds. *British Archives: A Guide to Archive Resources in the United Kingdom,* 4th ed. New York: Palgrave, 2002.

Matthew, Henry C. G., and Brian Harrison, eds. *Oxford Dictionary of National Biography,* rev. ed. (in association with the British Academy). 61 vols. New York: Oxford University Press, 2004. www.oxforddnb.com.

National Register of Archives. Surrey, England: National Archives Historical Manuscripts Commission. www.nationalarchives.gov.uk/nra (accessed 24 July 2012).

National Union Catalog of Manuscript Collections. Washington, DC: Library of Congress. www.loc.gov/coll/nucmc (accessed 24 July 2012).

Nelson, Carolyn. *Union First Line Index of English Verse, 13th–19th Century (Bulk 1500–1800).* Washington, DC: Folger Shakespeare Library. firstlines.folger.edu (accessed 24 July 2012).

Scottish Archive Network. Edinburgh, Scotland: Scottish Archive Network Ltd. www.scan.org.uk (accessed 24 July 2012).

Smith, Margaret M., and Alexander Lindsay, comps. *Index of English Literary Manuscripts: Volume III, 1700–1800.* London: Mansell, 1986–1997.

Sutton, David C., ed. *Location Register of English Literary Manuscripts and Letters: Eighteenth and Nineteenth Centuries.* 2 vols. London: British Library, 1995.

WorldCat. OCLC. www.oclc.org/firstsearch.

WorldCat.org. www.worldcat.org (accessed 24 July 2012).

The two best resources for locating particular eighteenth-century literary manuscripts by author are the *Index of English Literary Manuscripts*, for traditionally canonical figures, and the *Location Register of English Literary Manuscripts and Letters: Eighteenth and Nineteenth Centuries*, for more comprehensive coverage. The *Oxford Dictionary of National Biography* (*ODNB*) can be useful for locating specific manuscript numbers in institutions such as the British Library, but generally only the names of archives and types of holdings are listed. The *Dictionary of Literary Biography* offers brief overviews of archives and manuscripts locations, while the *National Register of Archives Directory* allows searching by personal name to locate collections in Britain and beyond. *WorldCat* contains records for archives located in the United States and records provided by the *National Union Catalog of Manuscript Collections*. You will need to consult a combination of the sources in this section to locate the archives and manuscripts you are seeking, if they are extant.

The four-part set of the ***Index of English Literary Manuscripts: Volume III, 1700–1800*** offers background information and locations of papers for fifty-six British, Scottish, and Irish authors. Each part contains a brief preface describing how it differs from others in the series, and, as previously mentioned, with facsimiles of handwriting for each author in that part. Chapters are arranged in alphabetical order by surname, from Joseph Addison to Edward Young. Each chapter opens with an introduction to the history of the author's papers, which typically explains which manuscripts are extant and theorizes why others don't exist, indicates the papers' known provenance, and describes the larger holdings in specific collections; these informative introductions are valuable, even for researchers whose authors are not included, because reading through the histories of the papers reveals the various reasons why documents do or do not survive. Introductions are followed by lists of known locations for individual papers, arranged into sections; in the case of James Boswell, the sections include verse, prose, dramatic works, diaries and notebooks, and marginalia in printed books and manuscripts. William Blake is the exception, since the authors of this set believe that Blake is well served by other compilations, so, in this case, they provide a literature review of sources to consult. Letters are excluded, although the introductions do give information about these types of documents. Literary works are then listed alphabetically by title within each section, followed by first known publication (if traced), cross-references, and the individual manuscripts related to that title. In the following sample entry, Hester Lynch Thrale's (later Piozzi) *Anecdotes of the Late Samuel Johnson, LL.D.* was initially published in 1786, with cross-references to other relevant items.

Anecdotes of the Late Samuel Johnson, LL.D.
First pub. 1786; see also conjectural '[Journal of Johnsonian Anecdotes]', 'Thaliana', and Introduction.
ThH 908 Autograph fair copy, 211 pages.

Discussed and quoted in James L. Clifford 'The Printing of Mrs. Piozzi's Anecdotes of Dr. Johnson', BJRL, 20 (1936) 157-72; facsimile in *British Literary Manuscripts*, I, 118.
Pierpont Morgan, MA 322.

"ThH 908," the first of the five manuscripts listed beneath the title, refers to an autograph fair copy of 211 pages, with a citation to a discussion of the manuscript, a reference to a facsimile of a page, and the document's location at the Pierpont Morgan, call number MA 322. "ThH" refers to Thrale Hester and 908 to the number assigned to this manuscript in this list. The length of each chapter depends upon the number of papers that have survived: Henry Fielding's chapter contains a two-page introduction and one page of manuscripts because so few exist, whereas William Cowper's seven-page introduction is followed by a fifty-one-page list. Three of the four parts conclude with first-line indexes. An index to titles and names would have been useful, to help the researcher to find connections between authors and their literary papers; Google Books provides a preview to parts 2 (Gay-Philips) and 4 (Sterne-Young), which does allow some full-text searching of the content and could operate as a makeshift index to the text. Although limited in the number of authors covered, this set serves as an excellent overview for tracing the history of manuscripts and brief descriptions of and locations for particular items.

Another invaluable resource, David Sutton's *Location Register of English Literary Manuscripts and Letters: Eighteenth and Nineteenth Centuries*, is more comprehensive. This two-volume set lists locations of specific manuscripts or copies of manuscripts in British institutions, with general headnotes pointing to other major collections, or lack of collections, abroad. Arranged in alphabetical order by author surname and then by title, entries may contain as little as one item to several pages of items, depending upon the number of manuscripts that have survived and are in British institutions; authors with no extant papers, for example, the novelist and translator Penelope Aubin, are omitted. Literary papers include handwritten essays, novels, plays, poems, letters, commonplace books, diaries, journals, memoirs, and even receipts. The major canonical figures are listed, including Blake, but there are omissions of authors who might be considered more political or philosophical than literary, although John Dennis, a literary critic from early in the century, who has a few papers in the British Library, is also omitted. Title entries generally include the title of the piece, its genre, the date of creation, information about the document (autograph, copy, facsimile, owned, on deposit), location, shelf number (if applicable), and access restrictions (by appointment only; approved researchers by written appointment only). Volume 2 concludes with the addresses of the English, Scottish, Irish, and Welsh institutions referenced in the set.

James Woolley calls Carolyn Nelson's *Union First Line Index of English Verse, 13th–19th Century (Bulk 1500–1800)* the "obvious first-resort first-line index for the period 1650–1800. *Users should bear in mind that in most cases the original individual indexes provide fuller information and therefore remain useful.* The union index may indeed be considered a finding aid to the index on which it is based" (italics Woolley's).[8] Sponsored by the Folger Shakespeare Library, this freely available online index brings together into one database the first lines of manuscript verse that had previously been compiled in various indexes. Institutions contributing to the project and sources used to build this database (listed on the website) include the British Library, Oxford University's Bodleian Library (compiled by Margaret Crum), the Huntington Library, the Osborn Collection in Yale University's Beinecke Library (compiled by Carolyn Nelson), Leeds University Library's Brotherton Collection (compiled by Oliver Pinkering), and Harvard University's Houghton Library (compiled by Peter Seng), plus nonmanuscript first lines from Wing.

Basic and advanced search options, with limiting by institution and women, are offered, and results may be sorted by first line, author, gender, or library. The ability to retrieve first lines that are limited to women is a useful feature, because many women, discouraged from publishing except anonymously or pseudonymously, "confined their writings to manuscript, and there too their works often bore no ascription."[9] The advanced screen allows Boolean searches by keyword, first line, author, title, last line, shelfmark, reference number, names, translations, and musical settings, but unfortunately not by date. A sample advanced search for first lines that contain the word *eyes*, excluding "Wing" and the "STC (1603–1640 only)," retrieves 1,271 entries. Further limiting by women brings back thirty-nine poems, including references to eighteenth-century poems by Anna Laetitia Barbauld, Catharine Trotter, Hannah More, and Catherine Talbot. Results can be further sorted by first line, author, title, last line, library, shelfmark, and folio, but not by year, so that items must be scanned for eighteenth-century dates. An author search on *pope, alexander*, combined with the keyword *montagu*, retrieves three manuscript poems in which Pope references Lady Mary Wortley Montagu, two in the British Library and one at Yale. The site offers helpful searching advice, especially because there are inconsistencies in the content due to different practices by contributing libraries and individuals.

The *Dictionary of Literary Biography* (*DLB*) is another useful source, although it is limited in the number of eighteenth-century figures covered. Discussed in detail in chapter 2, this multivolume source, also available online, provides biographical sketches of authors that often contain brief but descriptive summaries about locations of manuscripts. A typical entry with this feature notes where significant manuscripts and substantive collections are located. The *DLB* tells us, for instance, that Richard Sheridan's materials are "scattered throughout England and the United States, both at research libraries and in private hands. Yale, Georgetown, Harvard, and Princeton University libraries house particularly rich collections,"[10] or that Oliver Goldsmith's *The Haunch of Venison*, in the New York Public Library, is one of the few literary manuscripts written in his handwriting.[11]

For literary figures with multiple representations in the series, such as Defoe, who is in several volumes devoted to specific genres, the descriptions of manuscript and papers summaries may vary; therefore, it is worth looking at all entries. Lack of summaries does not necessarily mean that there are no manuscripts; check several resources discussed in this chapter, and any biographies on the author, before concluding that nothing exists. In the Defoe entry in this same volume, the author states that only a few manuscripts have survived, along with letters and other documents, while in *Eighteenth-Century British Historians, Vol. 336*, the locations for *The Compleat English Gentleman* and *Of Royal Education* are listed, and in *British Novelists, 1660–1800, Vol. 39*, the correspondence between Defoe and Harley is included. Robert Dodsley's entry in this volume doesn't have a section on manuscripts, but he does have surviving letters, legal papers, and a play listed in the *Location Register of English Literary Manuscripts and Letters*, as well as other papers noted in *ODNB*; perhaps because no manuscripts of poems are extant, the author of Dodsley's biographical sketch does not include a summary. *DLB* is worth exploring as a resource for leads, but this resource should not be used as definitive in terms of surviving papers.

Other sources are not specifically focused on literary figures, but they do cover them. Also discussed in-depth in chapter 2, the biographical entries in the **Oxford Dictionary of National Biography (ODNB)** conclude with references to known locations for and types of archival materials concerning various historical figures. Among many repositories that hold his papers, Richard Sheridan's correspondence, literary manuscripts, and papers related to Drury Lane are in the British Library, a copy of the manuscript for *School for Scandal* is in the Bodleian, notes and memoranda are in the Victoria and Albert National Art Library, and so forth. The "People" search option features searching by "Fields of Interest," "Sex," "Life Dates," "Religious Affiliation," and "Text Search." The last option allows the "Archive" field to be searched. Someone interested in examining papers of eighteenth-century literary women in a specific archive, such as the British Library, can search by date (active 1700–1800), sex (Female), field of interest (literature, journalism, and publishing), and specific archive to generate a list of entries that meet those criteria.

WorldCat and *WorldCat.org* searches can be limited to archival materials. In *WorldCat*, a search on the Library of Congress subject heading "English literature—18th century," limited to archives, retrieves records to a variety of literary collections and individual manuscripts, largely in U.S. libraries, including Catherine Talbot's papers at Yale University. A subject search on Talbot's name, limited to archives, finds references to the Yale collections, plus an eighteenth-century commonplace book with a copy of a work by her.

The Library of Congress's *National Union Catalog of Manuscript Collections* (*NUCMC*) began as an annual print resource listing records to archive and manuscript collections in U.S. repositories. Published in twenty-nine volumes from 1959 to 1993, the set contains records for materials available in archives and special collections; each volume has an index, with cumulative indexes every five years. The cumulative publications *Index to Personal Names in the National Union Catalog of Manuscript Collections, 1959–1984* and *Index to Subjects and Corporate Names in the National Union Catalog of Manuscript Collections, 1959–1984* make accessing the set much easier. Since 1993, the Library of Congress has produced online records on behalf of eligible institutions; all online *NUCMC* records from 1986 to the present are available free of charge via the *NUCMC* gateway to *WorldCat* (www. loc.gov/coll/nucmc/oclcsearch.html), while records prior to that are only available in the printed volumes or through the subscription database *Archive Finder*. There is some overlap with the *NUCMC* gateway to *WorldCat* and the subscription-based *WorldCat*, but, as there are unique records in both versions, it is best to search both.

The *National Register of Archives*, a freely available website maintained by the National Archives Historical Manuscripts Commission, is an online directory of business (32,000), individual (52,000), family (9,000), and organization (108,000) manuscripts related to British history in collections worldwide. The information about the manuscripts is collected from print and online repository catalogs, surveys, printed publications (for instance, the previously mentioned *Location Register of English Literary Manuscripts and Letters* and *Index of English Literary Manuscripts*), and staff contributions for collections not publicly accessible. As is noted in the FAQs, the quality of the entries depends upon the original source, but entries generally contain dates and a description of the main parts of the collection, including correspondence, letters, notebooks, literary MSS, and literary papers. The contents can either be browsed or searched by corporate name (business and organizations combined), personal name (either by name or description, for example, woman, writer, poet, critic), family name, or place name (town and county). The personal name option, which searches both the personal index and the diaries and papers index, will be the most useful to literary scholars.

A search on *burns, robert* points to manuscripts in the National Library of Scotland (correspondence, verses, miscellaneous family papers), the British Library (letters, songs), the Burns House Museum (letters, verses, literary MSS), the Huntington Library (letters, literary MSS), Edinburgh University Library (letters, MSS poems), the Mitchell Library (poems, letters, miscellaneous papers), the Pierpont Morgan Library (correspondence with Frances Dunlop), the Writer's Museum (letters, MSS), and Strathclyde University Archives (miscellaneous MSS). The names of the institutions are linked to Web pages with hours, contact information, URL, and street map. When included, links to the catalog record for the materials are provided, for instance, the National Library of Scotland catalog record for Burns's "Glenriddell Manuscripts of Poetry of Robert Burns" encompassing "volumes with copies of poems, letters, etc. of Robert Burns, compiled by the poet, 1791–1793, for presentation to Robert Riddell of Glenriddell." The advanced search has limiting by gender and year, but not by range of years, so that the researcher must scroll through the alphabetical list and scan the dates to find relevant individuals. *Access to Archives*, another directory from the National Archives, offers searching across detailed catalogs from approximately 400 record repositories in England and Wales for documents from the eighth century to the present.

Although the *Location Register of English Literary Manuscripts and Letters* and *National Register of Archives* are both good places to start for eighteenth-century literary authors from England, Scotland, Wales, and Ireland, websites that allow searching across archives within a country, such as *Archives Wales* and *The Scottish Archive Network*, are also recommended. *Archives Wales/Archifau Cymru* hosts an online catalog that was created from existing finding aids from twenty-one archives in Wales. The browse by personal name index is the most effective means for finding documents related to an individual, especially when searching for a common name, such as Evan Evans, the minister, poet, and scholar who lived from 1731 to 1788. The website includes advice on planning visits and using archives and links to other useful archival pages, for example, the national archives for England, Scotland, and Ireland, as well as paleography sites.

The *SCAN* online catalog, available through the *Scottish Archive Network* (*SCAN*), permits browsing or searching across 20,000 Scottish collections. An "All Words" search on *Alexander MacDonald*, the eighteenth-century Gaelic poet, retrieves 111 catalog records and 20 matching name authorities; to locate relevant collections in *SCAN*, browse through the results looking for the name in bold and with his dates (1700–1780), or with the date *18th century*. Website links lead to information about digitization projects, to other archives, and to a practical guide to Scottish handwriting.

Archive Finder, integrating records from *ArchivesUSA* and the *National Inventory of Documentary Sources in the UK and Ireland* (*NIDS UK/Ireland*), provides information on primary source materials in repositories throughout the United States, Britain, and Ireland. Although the strength of this research tool is as a directory to archival records, it also contains the records from *NUCMC* from 1959 to the present. The *NIDS* number in the record points to the finding aid on microfilm for that collection.

Although somewhat dated, Janet Foster and Julia Sheppard's one-volume ***British Archives: A Guide to Archive Resources in the United Kingdom***, now in its fourth edition, remains relevant because of the brief summaries about an institution's history and collections, and because of its geographic organization. The 1,231 entries, which range from small museums devoted to a literary figure to large government organizations and university libraries to local government and history collections, include both archives containing documents originating from a single source and "artificial" collections "consciously put together [during] the course of time" (ix). Arranged alphabetically by town and then by institution, entries typically comprise the name of the repository, contact information, e-mail address, website, hours, access restrictions/instruction, the historical background of the institution, a brief description of the organization's archives, major collections, nonmanuscript material, finding aids, facilities (e.g. photocopying, photography, microform readers), methods of conservation (e.g. in-house, contracted out), and publications about the collections. Many of these elements may no longer be correct, but the background history and short descriptions of collections provide a snapshot that may not be available online or in other print directories. The geographic arrangement by town allows the researcher to browse for other relevant collections in the area that may be of value: For those traveling to the Burns House and Museum, it would be beneficial to investigate the entries for the other organizations in Ayr with potentially useful eighteenth-century collections, including the Ayrshire Archives and the Carnegie Library. The volume concludes with alphabetical and subject indexes.

The literature section in the "Guide to Key Subjects" has subcategories for general, plays, poetry, popular, and writers, but, because all time periods are covered, it will be necessary to go to each entry to determine if eighteenth-century collections are present. The more valuable "Alphabetical Listing" of names, organizations, institutions, and so forth indexes the information in the entries, so that the listing for Frances Burney leads to her correspondence with Mary Delany located in the Newport Central Library, while the listing for Samuel Johnson leads to the University of Manchester's John Rylands

University Library, containing Hester Piozzi papers related to the circle of Samuel Johnson. Oddly enough, Piozzi is not in the alphabetical listing, but Johnson is there. Most information in this volume can be found elsewhere, but as an early guide to British archives, it is worth consulting for the condensed, informative descriptions.

The *ARCHON Directory*, maintained by the National Archives Historical Manuscripts Commission, is an online directory to about 2,500 records repositories in Britain and Ireland, with a list of additional collections abroad. Entries generally list contact information (address, telephone, e-mail address, website, curator), links to online maps, links to *National Register of Archives* entries about the repository, and online finding aids. Repositories are alphabetically arranged in broad geographical areas (England: North East, South West, Yorkshire and the Humber, London; Wales; Scotland; Northern Ireland; Republic of Ireland; Channel Islands; Isle of Man; list of overseas repositories). The directory can be browsed or searched by keyword in the repository name or by type, town, county, or country. A repository search on Johnson retrieves *Dr. Johnson's House* and *Samuel Johnson Birthplace Museum*, while searches on Lichfield, where the Johnson museum is located, or on the county Staffordshire, where Lichfield is located, reveal other repositories in the area. As is noted in reference to the *British Archives* volume, this source can be useful for discovering other archives in the vicinity to determine if additional research opportunities exist. To learn about archives and manuscripts related to specific individuals, however, the *National Register of Archives* is still the recommended starting point.

Although also dated, Lee Ash and William G. Miller's *Subject Collections: A Guide to Special Book Collections and Subject Emphases as Reported by University, College, Public, and Special Libraries and Museums in the United States and Canada* may still be valuable for identifying institutions in the United States and Canada that have strong book and manuscript collections for canonical eighteenth-century British authors. Arranged alphabetically by author or topic, and then by geographic location, brief entries include the name of the institution and contact information, holdings, and a notes section describing the collections. The entry for Horace Walpole contains nine entries for institutions in California; Connecticut; Delaware; Massachusetts; Washington, DC; Illinois; and North Carolina. The entry for the Lewis Walpole Library in Connecticut states that there are 29,000 volumes, that the collection is cataloged, and that the library holds rare books and manuscripts, while the notes field describes this library, a department of Yale University, as a research center for English eighteenth-century studies and as a principal resource for Walpole studies.

ARCHIVE AND MANUSCRIPT
REPOSITORIES AND COLLECTIONS

DocumentsOnline. Surrey, England: National Archives. www.nationalarchives .gov.uk/documentsonline (accessed 24 July 2012).

Index of Manuscripts in the British Library. 10 vols. British Library, Department of Manuscripts. Teaneck, NJ: Chadwyck-Healey, 1984–1986.

The Lewis Walpole Library. www.library.yale.edu/walpole/index.html (accessed 24 July 2012).

The National Archives. www.nationalarchives.gov.uk (accessed 24 July 2012).

The National Archives of Ireland/Chartlann Náisiúnta na hÉierann. www. nationalarchives.ie (accessed 24 July 2012).

National Library of Ireland/Leabharlann Náisiúnta na hÉierann. www.nli.ie/ en/homepage.aspx (accessed 24 July 2012).

National Library of Scotland/Leabharlann Nàiseanta na h-Alba. www.nls.uk (accessed 24 July 2012).

National Library of Wales/Llyfrgell Genedlaethol Cymru. www.llgc.org.uk (accessed 24 July 2012).

National Records of Scotland. www.nas.gov.uk (accessed 24 July 2012).

Search Our Catalogue Archives and Manuscripts. London: British Library. searcharchives.bl.uk (accessed 24 July 2012).

The British Library has collected manuscripts since it was established in 1753, with Cotton, Harley, and Sloane as the foundational collections. The largest collection, the Additional MSS series, comprises all the manuscripts, other than those from closed or named collections, acquired since 1756 by gift, purchase, or bequest. The Department of Manuscripts is divided into three curatorial areas, although the manuscripts themselves are not arranged thematically: "Medieval and Earlier Manuscripts" (c. 300 B.C.–1603), "Modern Historical Collections" (1603–present), and "Literary and Theatrical Collections" (4th century B.C.–present).

The **Search Our Catalogue Archives and Manuscripts** interface has both simple and advanced searching, with the advanced search offering keyword ("anywhere") and field (description, name, place, reference code, creation date) options. A simple search on *letter** retrieves more than 120,000 results. Facets on the left allow limiting by creation date, person, institution, collection, and language. Results can be sorted by relevance, date-newest, date-oldest, title, or reference. Each record has a link to details, reviews and tags, and "I want this." Typical details include title, collection area (Western Manuscripts, India Office Records), creation date, extent and access (how large the collection is and restrictions), language, creator, and contents and scope.

A name search on Catharine Trotter retrieves thirteen results, which can be refined to "Cockburn, Catharine" (her married name) using the facets and the results browsed for relevant documents. If the correspondent for a particular letter is desired, that name can be added to the search in the "anywhere" field. The "Links" area on the right side of the detailed record provides context by noting the collection it is connected to and names of individuals associated with the documents.

The ten-volume *Index of Manuscripts in the British Library* is an amalgamation of entries in catalogs to collections within the British Library manuscripts division. The content is in the British Library's manuscript and archives catalog, but this source remains valuable for browsing. Twenty years in the making, the A to Z index, with entries by place name or by person, offers entries copied and pasted from the various catalogs to collections and charters from the Western Manuscripts Division (e.g. Additional MSS, Arundel, Ashley, Burney, Egerton, Hargrave, Harley, Landsdown, Sloane, Stowe). Place and personal names have been standardized. Entries are brief, with fuller descriptions in the separate catalogs. There is a cross-reference from Trotter to Cockburn for entries related to Catharine Trotter. She is briefly described as a dramatist and philosophical writer who died in 1749, with her works and correspondence from 1693 to 1749 published in 1751. This heading is followed by the list of manuscripts, dates, and manuscript numbers, with specifics for the manuscript (autogr., partly copies, drafts) noted when relevant.

The National Archives (**TNA**), the official archive for the United Kingdom, holds more than 1,000 years of government documents related to its history, including cabinet papers; foreign and domestic correspondence with government officials; birth, marriage, and death records; wills; military records; transport records; and so forth. The catalog allows basic and advanced searching, but the current interface requires specialized knowledge about the organization of the document in the archive. At the time this volume was written, TNA offered both their traditional catalog interface and the beta catalog, *Discovery*, which will eventually replace *The Catalogue*. *Discovery*, which is a discovery-type catalog, as discussed in chapters 1 and 3, is searchable by keywords, and results may be limited using the facets (subject, date, collection). TNA is also making the most requested content available digitally for a fee through *DocumentsOnline*, including text and images related to war and military records, famous wills, early Irish maps, Victorian prisoners, looted art, ancient petitions, UFO reports, and the RMS *Titanic*. Using the quick keyword search on *bookseller* with dates limited to *1750-1799* will lead to wills and death duty registers of booksellers from around Britain. At present, this resource is not strong on documents from the eighteenth century, but it has the potential to grow and become more robust.

Although eighteenth-century records from these countries may be held in TNA, Scotland, Ireland, and Wales have their own national libraries and archives, with their own catalogs, finding aids, and digitization projects. Once the resources discussed in the "Locating Archives or Manuscripts" section have been exhausted, it may be fruitful to explore the national library and archives websites for relevant literary manuscripts and papers. Look for information concerning manuscripts and archives related to literature, as well as for catalogs and finding aids related to manuscripts and archives, especially literary documents. The Department of Manuscripts at the **National Library of Ireland/Leabharlann Náisiúnta na hÉierann (NLI)** contains a literature collection with correspondence, diaries, notes, drafts, and working copies of published and unpublished manuscripts. *Sources: A National Library of Ireland Database for Irish Research* allows searching for manuscripts in the library cataloged to the 1980s, plus Irish manuscripts held in other libraries listed between the 1940s and 1970s, as well as articles from Irish periodicals to 1969. A search on Seán Ó Neachtain, the poet and writer of stories in Irish, retrieves twenty-one results for manuscripts held by NLI and other British institutions. Due to fire and an explosion at the beginning of the Civil War, most records before 1922 in **The National Archives of Ireland/Chartlann Náisiúnta na hÉierann** were destroyed, although there are a few court and exchequer rolls dating to the fourteenth century, plus archives, some from the eighteenth century, acquired since 1922.

The **National Library of Scotland/Leabharlann Nàiseanta na h-Alba** holds manuscripts related to all aspects of Scottish life, including Gaelic manuscripts and manuscripts and correspondence of Sir Walter Scott, Robert Burns, and Allan Ramsay. **The National Records of Scotland** was formed in 2011, by the merger of the General Register Office of Scotland and the National Archives of Scotland. The National Archives contains Scottish government records from the twelfth century to the present, as well as private records from businesses, estates, families, courts, churches, and other corporate bodies, while the General Register Office has family history records (birth, death, marriage, census).

The **National Library of Wales/Llyfrgell Genedlaethol Cymru** maintains both manuscripts and the country's archives not kept at TNA in England. For example, they hold papers of Evan Evans and the only known item in handwriting of the hymn writer Ann Griffiths, a letter from about 1800, which has been made available in the "Digital Mirror" online collection, one of the library's digital projects (www.llgc.org.uk/index .php?id=anngriffithsnlwms694d).

The Lewis Walpole Library, a department of Yale University since 1980, located in Farmington, Connecticut, is a research library for eighteenth-century studies (books, manuscripts, prints, drawings, paintings, decorative arts), with an essential collection related to Horace Walpole and Strawberry Hill, including half of Walpole's library from Strawberry Hill and letters and manuscripts written by him. The original collection belonged to Wilmarth Sheldon Lewis, who was fascinated by Walpole, his contemporaries, and the eighteenth-century world Walpole described. Lewis began collecting in 1923, and he continued to acquire books, manuscripts, and prints throughout his life. He left his collection, house, and grounds, which now form The Lewis Walpole Library, to Yale University. Subjects encompass art, music, literature, drama, politics, history, diplomacy, and travel, with a substantial collection of prints and drawings of visual satire. Freely available digital collections contain all forty-eight volumes of Lewis's *The Yale Edition of Horace Walpole's Correspondence* and the *Digital Image Collection* (caricatures, satires, prints, drawings, watercolors, trade cards, advertisements, ballads, broadsides, and more). Physical access to the library is restricted to scholars and researchers, by appointment only. The institution has fellowship and travel grants, as well as internship opportunities.

DIGITAL AND MICROFORM COLLECTIONS

The Boswell Collection. New Haven, CT: Yale University Beinecke Rare Book and Manuscript Library. beinecke.library.yale.edu/digitallibrary/boswell.html (accessed 24 July 2012).

British Literary Manuscripts Online, c. 1660–1900. Farmington Hills, MI: Gale. infotrac.galegroup.com.

Complete Hanoverian State Papers Domestic, 1714–1782. 164 reels. Hassocks, England: Harvester Press, 1978–1982. Online finding aid in the Center for Research Library catalog records for the collection available at http://images.crl.edu/044.pdf.

Diaries and Papers of Elizabeth Inchbald, from the Folger Shakespeare Library and the London Library. 4 reels. Marlborough, Wiltshire, England: Adam Matthew Publications, 2005. Online guide to contents available at www.ampltd.co.uk/digital_guides/elizabeth_inchbald/Contents-of-Reels.aspx.

Electronic Enlightenment. Oxford, UK: University of Oxford, Humanities Division, 2008– . Distributed by Oxford University Press at www.e-enlightenment.com.

Home Office Papers and Records: Order and Authority in England: Series One, Home Office Class HO 42 (George III, Correspondence, 1782–1820). 172 reels. Brighton, Sussex, England: Harvester Press, 1981– . The Domestic Letters are freely available online via the Digital Microfilm project

in The National Archives *DocumentsOnline* at discovery.nationalarchives
.gov.uk/SearchUI/browse/C1905620 (accessed 24 July 2012).

The John Johnson Collection: An Archive of Printed Ephemera. Oxford, UK:
Bodleian Library. Available online via ProQuest.

*Literary Manuscripts: 17th and 18th Century Poetry from the Brotherton
Library, University of Leeds.* Marlborough, Wiltshire, England: Adam
Matthew Publications, 2006.

Mapping the Republic of Letters. Stanford, CA: Stanford University. republic
ofletters.stanford.edu.

State Papers Online: The Government of Britain, 1509–1714. Detroit,
MI: Gale/Cengage Learning. gale.cengage.co.uk/state-papers-online
-15091714.aspx.

In addition to the digital initiatives by British national libraries and archives,
there are commercial and noncommercial ventures to create digital collections, and there are still microform collections available. The following
include examples of such projects, which somewhat mimic the two different types of physical manuscript and archival collections: One model brings
together documents from various locations to create an artificial digital collection (e.g., *British Literary Manuscripts Online* and the microfilm collection for Inchbald), and the other model focuses on documents from a single
repository (e.g., State Papers and Boswell). Other types of digital ventures,
Electronic Enlightenment and *Mapping the Republic of Letters*, illustrate
ways that primary source materials are being transformed so that scholars can
explore the eighteenth-century network and interconnectedness through the
letters written at the time. For more about digital and microform collections
in general, consult chapter 6.

Gale's **British Literary Manuscripts Online, c. 1660–1900** contains facsimile images of literary manuscripts; drafts of poems, plays, and novels;
letters; diaries; translations; and other types of literary works. Approximately 250 eighteenth-century documents, scanned from microfilm collections (*British Library Series II: 1700–1800*; *Foster and Dyce Collections,
c. 1500–1800*; *National Library of Scotland, c. 1700–1800*; and *William
Cowper and Others*), represent roughly 100 eighteenth-century authors.
Swift, Cowper, Pope, and Johnson each have ten or more manuscripts
available, while Wordsworth, Seward, Crabbe, and Garrick have at least
one document. Manuscripts from the British Library, Huntington Library,
the National Library of Scotland, the National Art Gallery at the Victoria
and Albert Museum, and Princeton University Library can be browsed by
author or title, and the advanced option allows keyword searching of the
full citations, but not the full text. Images may be viewed full screen and

zoomed, adjusted for brightness and contrast, and printed or downloaded. Links to related sources, for instance, paleography courses, images, digital scholarship, catalogs, and maps, are listed on the home page. For those without access to the digital collection, *WorldCat* can be searched to locate holdings for the eighteenth-century microform collections from which the digital collection are drawn.

Adam Matthew's *Literary Manuscripts: 17th and 18th Century Poetry from the Brotherton Library, University of Leeds* offers digital facsimiles, with transcriptions, of 190 verse manuscripts containing more than 6,600 original, copied, and translated compositions, songs, and riddles held in the Brotherton Library. Representative authors include Anna Letitia Barbauld, Sneyd Davies, Ann Finch, David Garrick, John Gay, Alexander Pope, and Anna Seward. Contents can be browsed or searched by author, title, first line, and verse form, or by subject, keywords in the first and last lines, and verse length. Additional features include essays on the Brotherton collections and samples of seventeenth-century (but not eighteenth-century) handwriting, with transcriptions of texts.

The Beinecke Rare Book and Manuscript Library at Yale University began scanning *The Boswell Collection* as part of the tercentenary celebration of Samuel Johnson in 2009, and as a means of supporting scholarship on the two men. This project has its roots in the first digital project the library undertook in the 1990s: To reduce the amount of travel for the editors of the Boswell scholarly editions, the library began scanning the manuscripts needed.[12] The initial focus was on scholarly communication rather than on access to collections, but the project has since grown to allow broader access to Boswell's correspondence, diaries, and manuscripts. The core collection of Boswell family papers was purchased by Yale University in 1949 from Lieutenant Colonel Ralph H. Isham, and, although the collection spans the years 1428 to 1936, the majority of the papers are from the eighteenth century. The digital collection can be browsed from *The Boswell Collection* Web page, and it includes the *Life of Johnson* manuscript, London journal, journal of the tour to the Hebrides, correspondence, and other miscellaneous papers. Entries generally offer the full catalog record for the item and the ability to enlarge or zoom in for closer inspection of the images.

As the title makes plain, the four reels of *Diaries and Papers of Elizabeth Inchbald, from the Folger Shakespeare Library and the London Library* bring together papers from this writer and actress. Reel 1 contains manuscripts (14), diaries (11), letters (13), and account books, while the other three contain printed works of rare volumes and original editions of plays. The finding aid is available online at the Adam Matthew website.

Once the Licensing Act, which required that all printed materials be examined and approved prior to publication, lapsed in 1695, Britain moved from a precensor to a postcensor model, passing laws to prohibit works seen as blasphemous, profane, obscene, or seditious libel. Documents related to these types of cases can be found in the state papers. Britain's foreign and domestic state papers from the early eighteenth century are available online from Gale in *State Papers Online: The Government of Britain, 1509–1714*. Covering the last of the Stuarts, William and Mary (1689–1702), and Anne (1702–1714), the digital collection of documents from the National Archives (TNA) covers printing violations and individuals of concern to the government. An advanced search on *daniel defoe*, limited to the reign of Anne, retrieves eight calendar entries and manuscripts related to the author, including *3 Jan 1703. Royal and Secretaries' Warrants: Secretaries' Warrants: To search for and arrest Daniel Fooe [Defoe], and his papers. High crimes and misdemeanours*; a list of his visitors, including a man who squints but whose name is unknown; and a manuscript petition from Defoe to Queen Anne, *Assuring the queen that certain pamphlets he has published [And what if the Pretender should come; Reasons against the succession of the house of Hanover; An answer to a question nobody thinks of, viz But what if the queen should die] contain nothing but 'ironical discourse' and praying for a free pardon 1713 [?Nov]*. A search on *pamphlets*, limited to Anne's reign, retrieves documents related to investigations concerned with this type of publication in the years after the Licensing Act expired.

The *Complete Hanoverian State Papers Domestic, 1714–1782*, on microfilm, continues the domestic state papers for the greater part of the eighteenth century, including the domestic documents of George I (1714–1727), George II (1727–1760), and George III (1760–1782) from TNA. Its successor, *Home Office Papers and Records: Order and Authority in England: Series One, Home Office Class HO 42 (George III, Correspondence, 1782–1820)*, is also on microfilm, although the "Domestic Correspondence" section is freely available on digital microfilm via *DocumentsOnline*. The finding aid for the *Complete Hanoverian State Papers Domestic* is available online via the Center for Research Libraries.

Microfilm and digital collections of ephemera provide access to very rare materials. *The John Johnson Collection: An Archive of Printed Ephemera*, a digital collection from the Bodleian Library at Oxford University, brings together more than 65,000 items documenting everyday British life from the eighteenth through the early twentieth century. John de Monins Johnson (1882–1956), printer to the University, was responsible for assembling and preserving this printed heritage, which he called "everything [that] would ordinarily go into the waste paper basket after use, everything printed [that] is not actually a book. Another way of describing it is to say that we gather everything [that] a museum or library would not ordinarily accept if it were offered as a gift" ("Introduction," paragraph 14). Document types include clippings, advertisements, auction catalogs, lottery tickets, lottery bills, humorous pictures, warrants (law), portrait prints, broadsides, periodical prospectuses, gallows speeches, handbills, trial proceedings, playbills, sermons, keepsakes, jury summonses, and dozens of other categories.

The digital archive, scanned from the original documents, can be browsed broadly by topic (advertising, book trade, crime, entertainment, prints), or searched by keywords, name, title/first line, subject, illustration subject, place, document type, printing process, printer/publisher, engraver/lithographer, date, physical form, and special features (various printing and typeface options). One of the earliest eighteenth-century documents is a crime broadside, *The last words of William Parry a lawyer, who suffered for endeavouring to depose the Queen's Highness, and bring in Q. Mary and her young son James*, and one of the last, a panorama of a *Short Account of Lord Nelson's Defeat of the French at the Nile*. Periodical prospectuses of the *Analytical Review*, *Anti-Jacobin*, *British Critic*, and *Family Magazine* are a few of the forty available.

Although not archival or manuscript resources themselves, the following digital collections make interesting use of primary resources to forge new connections. Researchers should pay attention to newly developed digital resources because they may offer unexpected insights into the culture of the time, as in the following cases, where connections are made through correspondence. These two examples illustrate new ways of thinking about and organizing primary sources, which may lead to new directions in archival and manuscript research.

Electronic Enlightenment is a digital collection of letters written by individuals throughout Europe, the Americas, and Asia from the early seventeenth to the mid-nineteenth century. As of 2011, the collection offered more than 59,000 letters and documents of more than 7,200 correspondents representing 45 nationalities and 707 occupations. The letters are not facsimiles, but they are from scholarly editions of collected correspondence published by university and academic presses, including Cambridge, Oxford, and Edinburgh, as well as the Voltaire Foundation. Transcriptions are accompanied by notes, references, and biographical information. At present, the editions of Addison, Boswell, Cowper, Defoe, Dodsley, Gay, Gray, Pope, Richardson, Sheridan, Steele, Sterne, and Swift have been added, with more forthcoming.

The goal of the project is to bring together the correspondence that encompasses both the well-known and the unknown, to explore a "network of interconnected documents, allowing you to see the complex web of personal relationships" ("About EE"). Topics discussed in the letters cover art, literature, medicine and health, social activities, education, science and mathematics, philosophy and religion, travel, and war. Researchers can search by correspondents (writer and recipient), in contents (words included or to exclude), language, date (specific or range), and location (written from and written to). Letters can be browsed by decade as well. A search for documents in English limited for the date range 1700–1799 retrieves 16,052 items. Unfortunately, at the time of this writing, the results can't be limited to nationalities or occupations.

Developed by three teams from Stanford University, the University of Oklahoma and its Center for Spatial Analysis, and the Electronic Enlightenment Project at Oxford University, *Mapping the Republic of Letters* uses digital technology to visually map eighteenth-century correspondents. The "Republic of Letters" was a phrase used in the early modern era to the nineteenth century to describe intellectual communities and networks.[13] The goal of the project is to create visual interconnections between individuals via maps of the world, to see the network of who was writing to whom and the location of each person. The correspondence stretches around the world. By using the acknowledged network of letters, in combination with twenty-first-century digital technology, the creators hope that this type of digital humanities resource will enable scholars to study patterns generated by historical data sets to generate new knowledge about the eighteenth century.

CONCLUSION

Research in archives and special collections has its own challenges and rewards. The process may be intimidating, but thorough preparation for a research excursion will ensure that you make the most of the time with the papers and artifacts necessary to the project. The information available via the Web about specific archives and special collections, including contact information, hours, online catalogs, finding aids, and regulations, can make the preparation and organization of research trips much easier and, for those institutions that allow digital cameras, much more comprehensive. As the last section of this chapter reveals, ongoing digital projects are enabling scholars to conduct research with digital or microform facsimiles, enabling research using primary materials available to a wider audience of scholars.

NOTES

1. Richard Pearce-Moses, "Archives," *A Glossary of Archival and Records Terminology* (Chicago: Society of American Archivists, 2005), www.archivists.org/glossary/term_details.asp?DefinitionKey=156 (accessed 23 July 2012).

2. Frank G. Burke, *Research and the Manuscript Tradition* (Lanham, MD: Scarecrow Press, 1997), 9–10.

3. Burke, *Research and the Manuscript Tradition*, 9–10.

4. Janet Foster and Julia Sheppard, eds., *British Archives: A Guide to Archive Resources in the United Kingdom*, 4th ed. (New York: Palgrave, 2002), ix.

5. Margaret M. Smith and Alexander Lindsay, comps, *Index of English Literary Manuscripts: Volume III, 1700–1800, Pt. 1* (London: Mansell, 1986–1997), 355.

6. Margaret M. Smith and Alexander Lindsay, comps, *Index of English Literary Manuscripts: Volume III, 1700–1800, Pt. 2* (London: Mansell, 1986–1997), 187.

7. Joyce Hemlow, *A Catalogue of the Burney Family Correspondence, 1749–1878* (New York: New York Public Library, 1971), xiii–xiv.

8. James Woolley, *Finding English Verse, 1650–1800: First-Line Indexes and Searchable Electronic Texts* (New York: Bibliographical Society of America), www.bibsocamer.org/bibsite/woolley/index.pdf (accessed 23 July 2012).

9. Michael Londry, "On the Use of First-Line Indices for Researching English Poetry of the Long Eighteenth Century, c. 1660–1830, with Special Reference to Women Poets," *Library* 5, no. 1 (2004): 12.

10. Mark S. Auburn, "Sheridan, Richard Brinsley (1751–7 July 1816)," in *Restoration and Eighteenth-Century Dramatists, Third Series*, ed. Paula R. Backscheider, *Dictionary of Literary Biography*, vol. 89 (Detroit, MI: Gale Research, 1989), 321.

11. Richard Bevis, "Goldsmith, Oliver (10 November 1730?–4 April 1774)," in *Restoration and Eighteenth-Century Dramatists, Third Series*, ed. Paula R. Backscheider. *Dictionary of Literary Biography*, vol. 89 (Detroit, MI: Gale Research, 1989), 171.

12. Nicole Bouché, *Digitization for Scholarly Use: The Boswell Papers Project at the Beinecke Rare Book and Manuscript Library* (Washington, DC: Council on Library and Information Resources, 1999), www.clir.org/pubs/reports/pub81-bouche/pub81.pdf (accessed 28 July 2012).

13. "Digging into the Enlightenment: The Project." Stanford, CA: Stanford University, Stanford Humanities Center, enlightenment.humanitiesnetwork.org (accessed 28 July 2012).

Chapter Nine

Web Resources

As is illustrated by previous chapters in this book, a good portion of literary research is mediated through a Web interface. Even though the transformation from a print-based to a completely electronic environment is far from complete, there is no doubt that electronic resources play an increasingly central role in academic, as well as daily, life. We identify relevant books and journal articles through online library catalogs, databases, and Web searches and often read digital versions of these sources; we verify facts and obtain background information from *Wikipedia*, as well as from university, institutional, government, and other websites; we stay abreast of recent trends in the field via RSS feeds and e-mail alerts; and we correspond with colleagues through listservs, blogs, and virtual conferences. Although some of these practices are free, access to many journals, electronic books (under copyright), digital archival materials, and core databases, like *MLA International Bibliography* (*MLAIB*), are proprietary and only available by institutional or sometimes individual subscriptions. If you are a currently enrolled student or faculty at a college or university and prefer searching open sources like *Google Scholar*, you might not even realize the extent to which your library provides access to scholarly journals you find by that means. In most cases, your research will involve a combination of subscription and open-access Web resources.

This chapter introduces freely available, scholarly Web resources pertaining to the study of eighteenth-century British literature to complement your research endeavors. We describe many of the core sites, including scholarly gateways, text archives, author sites, reference tools, and current awareness sources and associations, in addition to a selection of historical and cultural sources. Since some resources serve multiple roles and can be classified in several categories, it is wise to read through each section so as not to miss a relevant resource. Far from comprehensive, this list will give you an idea of the types of sources available and establish a base from which to discover other literary sites. You might also want to review the freely available Web resources described in previous chapters, especially the national and union catalog websites, open-access journals, and manuscript and archival indexes presented in chapters 3, 5, and 8, respectively. As with other chapters in this book, our scope is the eighteenth century; however, if your work is specifically concerned with Romantic-era authors and subjects, consult the "Web Resources" chapter in *Literary Research and the British Romantic Era: Strategies and Sources* or the corresponding chapter in *Literary Research and the British Renaissance and Early Modern Period: Strategies and Sources* if your work focuses on the long eighteenth century. The series website also presents updates to resources at libguides.du.edu/literaryresearchseries.

Freely available resources concerned with British literature are prolific on the Web—the trick lies in finding those with substantial content that will contribute to the goals of your research project. The selections provided here will give you a solid start in identifying Web projects. You will also want to search for additional sites or pursue links to other resources that sound promising. Be sure to review the search tips in chapter 1 for suggestions about searching Google and the differences between searching a database versus the Web. Since the Web is an open environment, you will need to be cautious in your assessment of unfamiliar resources and follow the evaluation criteria outlined in this chapter. It is important to not only determine if the site's content matches that of your project, but also to ascertain its purpose and the creator's credentials. When you search in *MLAIB* or another subscription database, you can usually rely on the scholarly nature of the sources you identify, but the Web can feature any type of content, from commercial interests to student projects. When evaluating Web resources, it is important to ask yourself the following questions:

Authority: Is the site based at an academic or government institution? Is it authored or edited by someone with expertise in the field? What does the domain tell you about the site (e.g., .edu, .gov, .org, .com)? Is there an "About" section, so that you can determine the author's or publisher's credentials and the website's purpose?

Currency: When was the site last updated, and how frequently is it maintained? Does the site state when it was last updated? Is the information time sensitive? Are links to outside sources still active or are they broken?

Scope: What is the subject matter and range of coverage? Who is the intended audience for the website?

Objectivity: What, if any, particular bias does the author (or contributors) possess? How does that affect the website's content?

Accuracy: How accurate is the material presented? Can the information be verified in other sources?

Context: What other websites are linked to the site, and what do they indicate about the authority or place of this website within a particular community?

In addition to this general overview, you can look for guides to evaluating Web resources for even more suggestions, many of which have been created by professors or librarians and are featured on academic websites. Search with the phrase, *"evaluating web resources"* and limit your results to an .edu domain. One final word of advice: The Web is a fluid environment where change is natural and expected. Even reliable, scholarly projects may disappear or languish without updates or attention. Rather than getting discouraged, remember that for every terrific site that vanishes, several new exciting resources are there to take its place.

SCHOLARLY GATEWAYS

Fraistat, Neil, and Steven E. Jones, eds. *Romantic Circles*. College Park: University of Maryland. www.rc.umd.edu (accessed 28 August 2012).

Howard, Sharon. *Early Modern Resources*. www.earlymodernweb.org (accessed 28 August 2012).

Liu, Alan. "Restoration and 18th Century." *Voice of the Shuttle*. Santa Barbara: University of California, Santa Barbara. http://vos.ucsb.edu/browse .asp?id=2738 (accessed 28 August 2012).

Lynch, Jack. *Eighteenth-Century Resources*. http://andromeda.rutgers.edu/ ~jlynch/18th (accessed 28 August 2012).

Ockerbloom, Mary Mark, ed. *A Celebration of Women Writers*. Philadelphia: University of Pennsylvania. digital.library.upenn.edu/women (accessed 28 August 2012).

Sauer, Geoffrey. *Eighteenth-Century Studies*. Pittsburgh, PA: Carnegie Melon University. 18th.eserver.org (accessed 28 August 2012).

The Web can be overwhelming when a single Google search potentially retrieves hundreds of thousands of results. In contrast, the best Web gateways guide you to a selection of the most pertinent resources for the given scope, describe their content, provide structure through browse or search features, and make sure that broken links are fixed and dead resources removed. Unfortunately, it is difficult for individual scholars, who often sponsor portals to academic resources, to always maintain these standards. The two primary gateways for literary studies generally are Alan Liu's *Voice of the Shuttle* and Jack Lynch's *Literary Resources*, but both of these sites suffer from broken links and varying degrees of neglect. Although it isn't focused specifically on literature, Sharon Howard's *Early Modern Resources* is more effective at representing current and viable Web projects for eighteenth-century studies. In addition to the portals described in this section, *18thConnect: Eighteenth-Century Scholarship Online* directs scholars to many freely available primary and secondary resources, and most of the eighteenth-century association sites also offer lists of related Web resources.

Although it hasn't been updated since January 2006, Jack Lynch's **Eighteenth-Century Resources** is still one of the primary entry points to period resources on the Web. Defining the long eighteenth century as spanning from Milton to Keats, Lynch's collection is arranged in eleven categories: "Art, Architecture, Landscape Gardening," "History," "Literature," "Electronic Texts," "Music," "Philosophy," "Religion and Theology," "Science and Mathematics," "Other Fields," "Professional Resources and Journals," and "Home Pages of People Working in the Eighteenth Century." The "Literature" category consists of general resources, bibliographies, links related to specific genres (e.g., the novel, poetry, theatre and drama, periodicals, satire, Gothic, Romanticism), and national literatures other than British (e.g., French, German, Italian), as well as resources for individual authors.

Each source receives a brief annotation to describe its contents, and the author/editor and sponsoring institution are often noted. The "Electronic Texts" section features electronic editions of long eighteenth-century works, many available from large projects, including *Project Gutenberg*, *Representative Poetry Online*, *Poetry Archives*, and the *Electronic Text Archive* at the University of Virginia, but smaller university and some commercial sites are also represented. The texts are accessed by author, with an additional category for anonymous and various authors, and are listed alphabetically by title or sometimes in chronological order by publication date. The other subject categories follow a similar format of general resources and then specific thematic resources. Be aware that you will find broken links on the site, since it hasn't been updated in several years, but you can try searching for the current location, if it exists, by typing the title in Google.

Alan Liu's *Voice of the Shuttle* (*VOS*) has been serving as a portal to literary and other humanities Web resources since 1994. Although you may find relevant links in multiple categories, the main one of interest for eighteenth-century literary research is **"Restoration and 18th Century,"** which is part of the "Literature (in English)" section. The authors represented here are primarily canonical (Addison, Barbauld, Cowper, Defoe, Fielding, Goldsmith, Gray, Haywood, Johnson, Pope, Richardson, Sterne, and Swift), but there are also a few links for less-studied authors. Some of the choices are to biographical sources, society pages, chronologies, bibliographies, or individual poems or texts. In addition to the standard selection of general resources and those for specific authors and works, the site also offers a few options for cultural and historical contexts, including sources like one about the South Sea Bubble financial crisis, Captain James Cook's *The Endeavor Journal, 1767–1771*, and the philosophers David Hume and John Locke. Other categories include course syllabi, literary criticism, eighteenth-century British literature journals, listservs and newsgroups, and conferences. *VOS* can be searched by keyword, and results are displayed both for categories and individual links. Like its counterpart, *Eighteenth-Century Resources* (described in the previous two paragraphs), *VOS* contains many outdated or broken links, which can be frustrating. The same advice applies in this case: Search for the title in Google to either find the current location or verify that it no longer exists.

With ***Early Modern Resources***, Sharon Howard has compiled a valuable collection of freely available sources that are primarily concerned with early modern history from 1500 to 1800. This easily navigated and well-presented site can be searched by keyword or browsed by five main categories, which include "Making History" (popular histories, historians, blogs), "Reference" (reviews, bibliographies, e-journals, associations), "Regions" (Africa, Americas, Asia, Australasia, Europe), "Themes" (arts, culture, gender, law and order, learning, material worlds, new worlds, politics), and "Primary Sources" (images, maps, editions). Within the "Arts" category, the "Writing" subsection offers nearly eighty resources, each one featuring a description of contents and assigned thematic headings. Some of these resources highlight individual authors, while others focus on author or generic groups, for example, the Bluestockings, British women's novels, or poetic miscellanies; you will also find portals, bibliographies, blogs, digital texts, and audio recordings. The "Britain" category presents a wide range of interesting sources, from *Capital Punishment in Eighteenth-Century England* to *The First Asians in Britain*. A rotating display of specific resources is showcased on the main page, and new additions to the site are also introduced. Scholars will enjoy exploring the wide array of resources here and also appreciate the currently maintained content.

Aiming to "promote awareness of the breadth and variety of women's writing," ***A Celebration of Women Writers*** is a portal to resources about published women authors worldwide who lived from 3000 B.C. to the twentieth century. Links to both biographical and bibliographical resources are included in the site, in addition to full-text works, when available. The type of writing represented is broad in scope and ranges from novels, poetry, plays, and travel writing to letters, biographies, histories, and scientific works. The site may be searched to find individual authors by name, dates within which they lived or specific years of birth and/or death, country (Albania to Zimbabwe), and ethnicity (e.g., African American, First Nations, Jewish, Muslim,

Romani). Browsing is also encouraged, and opportunities to review the collection are offered by author's name, century, country, and ethnicity. The "Writers Living between 1701 and 1800" category features hundreds of authors, most with links to outside sources or to *A Celebration of Women Writers* electronic editions, but there are some authors for whom only a name and dates are provided. Clicking on the name will typically lead to a biographical source; links to texts are listed below the author, and hosting sites are often noted (e.g., *Project Gutenberg*, HathiTrust Digital Library). Although most sources are in English, foreign-language resources are also incorporated.

In addition to serving as a portal to outside resources, *A Celebration of Women Writers* also publishes electronic editions of older, out-of-copyright works called "Local Editions." These texts may be accessed separately by author, genre category (e.g., utopias, diaries, fairy tales, spiritual life, gardening), Library of Congress subject headings, or copyright status, but they are also incorporated into the main list of resources. The latest text to be added to the "Local Editions" is Mary Astell's *Some Reflections upon Marriage, Occasioned by the Duke and Dutchess of Mazarine's Case; Which Is Also Considered*, first published in 1700, and the collection now represents more than 360 titles. Some of these texts are presented as thematic groupings, for instance, "Pre-1923 Utopias and Science Fiction by Women: A Reading List of Online Editions" and "Diplomatic Difficulties." The "Utopias" list leads to six texts by eighteenth-century authors Mary de la Riviere Manley, Eliza Fowler Haywood, Charlotte Lennox, Sarah Scott, Lady Mary Hamilton, and Ellis Cornelia Knight. *A Celebration of Women Writers* is edited by Mary Mark Ockerbloom and hosted on the University of Pennsylvania server. If your work concerns women authors of the period, you will have much to discover at this site.

In addition to the gateways already described in this section, you might also pick up some unique sources from Geoffrey Sauer's **Eighteenth-Century Studies** collection. This alphabetical list presents both primary texts and criticism related to eighteenth-century literature and culture, including links to plays, novels, poems, memoirs, and treatises. The period is defined as 1700 to 1800; however, selected earlier and later sources are also represented. Individual examples range from poems by Anne Finch to Hogarth prints to mathematicians of the seventeenth and eighteenth centuries to Thomas Rutherforth's *The Credibility of Miracles Defended*, and more. This portal is maintained by the eighteenth-century studies group at Carnegie Mellon University.

Although not necessarily a portal, since it hosts many of its own resources, **Romantic Circles** deserves mention, as it offers the scholar of the late eighteenth century a substantial collection of material for studying Romantic-era literature and culture. This refereed website features seven main sections: a blog for posting news and announcements; an archive of hypertext editions of Romantic-era works; the *Praxis* series of theoretical and critical essays; a collection of scholarly resources, including chronologies, indexes, and bibliographies; reviews of related print and electronic resources; a selection of audio recordings of Romantic poetry read by current poets; and "Pedagogies," which presents online materials for teaching.

The primary emphasis of the site is on canonical figures of the Romantic movement, but you will also find resources broader in scope, including an electronic text collection of twenty-one British authors, entitled *Norse Romanticism: Themes in British Literature, 1760–1830*, and an electronic edition of William Dodd's 1777 poem *Thoughts in Prison*, while the *Praxis* series examines such themes as the sublime and education or constructions of sexuality in the Romantic period. Likewise, the "Reviews" section addresses works about Romanticism or individual authors, but also such titles as *Women, Literature, and the Domesticated Landscape: England's Disciples of Flora, 1780–1870* and *The Orders of Gothic: Foucault, Lacan, and the Subject of Gothic Writing, 1764–1820*. *Romantic Circles* is an essential tool for scholars studying Romantic authors specifically, but it will also be of interest to anyone whose work focuses on authors and themes of the later eighteenth century.

PERIOD AND GENERAL ELECTRONIC TEXT ARCHIVES

18thConnect: Eighteenth-Century Scholarship Online. www.18thconnect .org (accessed 28 August 2012).

Bear, Risa, ed. *Renascence Editions*. www.luminarium.org/renascence editions (accessed 28 August 2012).

British Women Romantic Poets, 1789–1832. Oakland: University of California, Davis General Library. digital.lib.ucdavis.edu/projects/bwrp (accessed 28 August 2012).

Crochunis, Thomas C., and Michael Eberle-Sinatra, eds. *British Women Playwrights around 1800*. Montreal, Quebec, Canada: University of Montreal. www.etang.umontreal.ca/bwp1800 (accessed 1 August 2012).

Google Books. books.google.com (accessed 28 August 2012).

HathiTrust Digital Library. www.hathitrust.org (accessed 28 August 2012).

Jokinen, Anniina. *Luminarium: Anthology of English Literature*. www .luminarium.org (accessed 28 August 2012).

Lancashire, Ian, ed. *Representative Poetry Online*. Toronto, Ontario, Canada: University of Toronto Libraries. rpo.library.utoronto.ca (accessed 28 August 2012).

Lynch, Jack. *Eighteenth-Century E-Texts*. Newark, NJ: Rutgers University. andromeda.rutgers.edu/~jlynch/18th/etext.html (accessed 28 August 2012).

Modern English Collection. Charlottesville: University of Virginia Library Electronic Text Center. etext.virginia.edu/modeng (accessed 28 August 2012).

Novels-On-Line. Hampshire, England: Chawton House Library. www.chawton house.org/?page_id=55488 (accessed 1 August 2012).

Pauley, Benjamin. *Eighteenth-Century Book Tracker*. www.easternct.edu/~pauleyb/c18booktracker (accessed 28 August 2012).

Project Gutenberg. www.gutenberg.org (accessed 28 August 2012).

University of Oxford Text Archive. Oxford, UK: University of Oxford. ota.ahds.ac.uk (accessed 28 August 2012).

Digital text archives are richly represented and have a fairly stable presence on the Web. Many of these projects are based at well-known universities, including Oxford, Toronto, and Virginia, or important cultural institutions, like the British Library; others are collaborative digital projects sponsored by several contributors or labor-of-love projects begun or maintained by individual scholars. We are fortunate to have so many freely available options providing digital facsimiles or transcript versions of eighteenth-century books, poems, miscellanies, journals, newspapers, manuscripts, and other textual material.

Although it may seem easy enough to find precopyright texts on the Web, texts can vary in reliability and quality. In fact, some projects don't always present complete bibliographical information about the texts or state which specific edition they are basing the digital version on. Other problems range from excessively dark scans to errors in transcriptions. Be sure to match the online text to your specific research need. Reading for pleasure or casual background will require less stringent attention to the online copy than for close textual analysis. And although it seems like all precopyright material should be scanned and freely available, it isn't. You will still need to consider print facsimiles, modern print or electronic editions, subscription collections, and archives. The resources described in this and the following section, "Specialized Electronic Text Archives," specifically focus on texts from the eighteenth century, or they cover them as part of a larger scope, for example, the early modern period, British literature in general, such genres as poetry or broadsides, or in the case of Google Books, HathiTrust Digital Library, and *Project Gutenberg*, as many books as possible.

Calling itself a finding aid, *18thConnect: Eighteenth-Century Scholarship Online* serves as a portal to 674,308 peer-reviewed digital objects from both open-access and subscription sources relevant for eighteenth-century literary and historical studies. These digital objects range from eighteenth-century texts and other primary sources to current scholarship and are drawn from seventeen federated sites, including the *English Short Title Catalogue* (*ESTC*), *Eighteenth Century Collections Online* (*ECCO*), *Eighteenth Century Journals*, *Irish Women Poets of the Romantic Period*, and the *Old Bailey Online*, among others. An advanced search interface permits searching by keyword, title, author, editor, publisher, and year across the metadata records and, in some cases, across the full text. Once your results are displayed, you can limit by resource type (e.g., peer-reviewed projects, other digital collections), genre, and access (e.g., free culture only, full text only, TypeWright enabled only). The "Genre" limit comprises more than thirty categories and represents the range of material aggregated here, from subjects like architecture, family life, religion, science, and travel, to such genres as bibliography, criticism, ephemera, fiction, letters, manuscripts, and review, as well as citations, photographs, and reference works.

Although you will not be able to access the full text for proprietary content if your institution doesn't have a subscription to the resource (such as to *ECCO*, *Eighteenth Century Journals*, or *JSTOR* and *Project Muse* journals), you can choose to limit your results to "free culture only" to retrieve freely available objects. A search for *mary davys* finds forty-three matches, of which twenty-eight are to works written by Mary Davys, either citations to works cataloged in the *ESTC* or to full-text versions that are part of *ECCO*. After creating a free account, you can save selected items by using the "Collect" button. Other features include an "Exhibits" section for scholars to gather and highlight digital content, a classroom space used by universities, a news section, and a discussion forum to foster collaboration among the *18thConnect* community.

Benjamin Pauley's *Eighteenth-Century Book Tracker* provides an important service to the academic community by acting as a portal to eighteenth-century digital facsimile texts available for free on the Web (many from Google Books) and offering a searchable database of bibliographic records associated with those texts, thereby bringing "bibliographical order to the sometimes haphazard world of mass digitization." In effect, the *Eighteenth-Century Book Tracker* serves as an alternative resource for those who don't have access to *ECCO* and *Eighteenth Century Journals* subscription databases. Pauley emphasizes that the portal links not just to texts, but specifically to page-image reproductions of printed books that were published before 1800, to support the study of eighteenth-century print culture and book history. There are also links to some eighteenth-century books that were published after 1800, as well as selected later editions of eighteenth-century works (he gives Sir Walter Scott's editions of Daniel Defoe's works as an example).

The database currently features records for 1,171 texts and 21 periodicals. In keeping with its academic mission, distinct editions have their own record, each one linking to the relevant online text. The "Find Texts" section on the left navigation bar presents an alphabetical index of authors that lists the number of texts associated with each author; a search interface with name, title, edition, place of publication, imprint, publication year, bibliographical authority (e.g., *ESTC*, OCLC), citation number, and language fields, as well as the ability to limit to only pre-1800 editions; and a separate list of eighteenth-century periodicals, including *Gentleman's Magazine, Monthly Review, Scots Magazine, Lady's Magazine, Political Register,* and others, that can be filtered by decade from 1660 to 1849. For example, the author Robert Dodsley is represented by eleven texts, including the third and fourth editions of *Cleone, Theatrical Records: or, An Account of English Dramatic Authors, and Their Works* by anonymous but attributed to Dodsley, and the miscellany *Collection of Poems by Several Hands.* The initial results display the author, title, imprint, year, and bibliographical reference; clicking on the title will retrieve the full record, links to electronic copies and/or volumes with holding library copy indicated, and links to related works. Since many digital projects don't always state the bibliographic details of their source texts, *Eighteenth-Century Book Tracker* is an essential tool for finding specific editions on the Web that can be relied on for scholarly research.

Renascence Editions is a smaller, more narrowly focused collection of 222 English-language, electronic literary texts that were originally printed between 1477 and 1799. Now hosted by multiple mirror sites (HTML versions at *Luminarium* and *Early Modern Literary Studies* websites; PDF versions at the University of Oregon's *Scholars' Bank*) but no longer enhanced with additional sources, these works can be browsed by author, or the site can be searched by keyword. Although the transcribed texts are not peer-reviewed scholarly editions, Risa Bear, the original creator of *Renascence Editions*, recommends that they be used for teaching editions, reading, and casual references. Each text contains a head note that describes the editor responsible for the transcription, source text, and copyright information. Consisting of primarily sixteenth- and seventeenth-century authors, a few eighteenth-century British authors are also represented, among them Defoe, Fielding, Goldsmith, Hume, Johnson, Wortley Montagu, Smith, Sterne, Swift, Thomson, and Wollstonecraft.

Created and edited by Anniina Jokinen, **Luminarium: Anthology of English Literature** features literary texts from the medieval, Renaissance, and seventeenth- and eighteenth-century periods, with thematic collections of religious writers, Renaissance drama, metaphysical poets, and Cavalier poets. The "English Literature: Restoration and 18th Century (1660–1785)" section highlights the work of twenty-six authors, such as Addison, Collins, Cowper, Defoe, Gay, Goldsmith, Gray, Johnson, Wortley Montagu, Pope, Prior, Smart, Steele, Swift, and Thomson, although there isn't yet any information for George Crabbe or James Boswell. For each of these authors, subsections lead to a biographical profile; a select list of published works, including collected works, with links to full-text versions either on the *Luminarium* website or on an outside source (e.g., Google Books); essays about the author (some to Digital Commons articles from journals like *Eighteenth-Century Fiction*, but also many of which appear to be broken links); quotes; related books to purchase from Amazon; and a catchall category of links to biographical, image, and miscellaneous Web resources. These subcategories vary slightly between authors, with some figures naturally represented by more extensive resources. Since this is a commercial site, you will need to ignore the sidebar ads. Despite this distraction, *Luminarium* offers a good selection of canonical, eighteenth-century texts with some interesting contextual links.

Jack Lynch maintains **Eighteenth-Century E-Texts**, a subset of his *Eighteenth-Century Resources* page. Interpreting the eighteenth century broadly, Lynch provides links to full-text electronic works for authors ranging from Milton to Byron. Twelve major collections form the basis from which most of these texts are drawn, including some sources described in this chapter, like *Representative Poetry Online*, *Luminarium*, and the *Modern English Collection*, but also *The Poetry Archives*, *British Women Romantic Poets*, *Scholarly Electronic Text and Image Service*, and Christian Classics Ethereal Library. The authors are listed alphabetically, with a separate category for "Anonymous or Various Authors." At least one text for each author is given, although some authors are represented by several texts, and the electronic collection is noted, along with a date, viewing requirements, format, or brief annotation. Reflecting Lynch's interest in French literature, there are several links for French authors and collections, such as the Parisian Fairground Theatre and *French Revolutionary Pamphlet*. Although Lynch's *Eighteenth-Century Resources* site hasn't been updated since 2006, many of the sources in this collection are still viable, especially those to the larger, stable Web collections.

Novels-On-Line is a project of the Chawton House Library, which specializes in women's writing in English during the long eighteenth century, from 1600 to 1830. Some of the rarest works in this collection have been transcribed from the originals and made available to scholars and the interested public. Faithfulness to the original has been of paramount importance, so that even obvious printers' errors are reproduced. *Novels-On-Line* currently

includes sixteen titles by anonymous authors and twenty-three known au-
thored texts, some of which were published in the eighteenth century by
Penelope Aubin, Anna Maria Bennett, Mary Charlton, Anne Hughes, Mrs.
Johnson, Marie-Madeleine Pioche de la Verne La Fayette, Alethea Lewis,
Anna Maria Mackenzie, Mrs. Mathews, Elizabeth Purbeck, Jane Purbeck,
Elizabeth Sophia Tomlins, and others. For each text, the author, title, place
and date of publication, publisher, edition, and number of volumes are noted,
if known, and many also present a brief introduction and sometimes link to
other related texts in the collection, or to articles in the Chawton House Library's quarterly, the *Female Spectator.*

The library's website also features a selection of biographies for many of
the women authors in the print collection that address their life, work, and
ongoing critical reception from their contemporaries to the present day. They
conclude with a bibliography of books and journal articles for further read-
ing. Scholars will find signed biographies of Penelope Aubin, Jeanne Marie
Le Prince de Beaumont, Susanna Blamire, Frances Brooke, Frances Burney,
Maria Edgeworth, Sarah Fielding, Mary Hays, Eliza Haywood, Elizabeth
Inchbald, Harriet Lee, Sophia Lee, Charlotte Lennox, Delarivier Manley,
Lady Mary Wortley Montagu, Laetitia Pilkington, Ann Radcliffe, Mary
Darby Robinson, Maria Regina Roche, Anna Seward, Charlotte Smith, and
Mary Wollstonecraft.

An additional project, "Fiction in the *Hampshire Chronicle*, 1772–1829,"
gives scholars an opportunity to investigate the presentation of fiction in a
provincial newspaper by listing the authors, titles, and publishers/booksellers
who appeared in the newspaper during that time. For research concerned with
women's writing of the eighteenth century, the *Novels-On-Line* electronic
text collection and the other contextual material at the Chawton House Library will be of great value. Scholars may also want to consider visiting the
library, since the physical collection contains more than 9,000 texts, including novels, poetry, drama, published letters, memoirs, autobiographical writings, educational works, advice manuals, children's literature, travel writing,
and other nonfiction, that present a rich resource for studying the writing and
lives of women during the period.

Focusing on poetry of the later eighteenth and early nineteenth centuries,
British Women Romantic Poets, 1789–1832 offers transcribed, electronic
texts for more than 100 British and Irish writers from the Kohler collection
at the University of California, Davis General Library. The texts can be
browsed alphabetically by author, from anonymous to Helen Maria Williams,
or searched through several digital collection interfaces, including *Online
Archive of California*, *NINES*, and *Michigan Digital Library*. As an example,
the California interface permits searching by header keyword, title, author/

poet, and creation date of the original. The collection features a handful of texts published at the end of the eighteenth century, from Elizabeth Bentley, Mary Matilda Betham, Hannah Brand, Eliza Day, Esther Milnes Day, Helen Leigh, Janet Little, Maria Logan, Mary Robinson, Anna Seward, and Margaret Turner. Each text is available in SGML or XML and HTML versions, with notes on the creator of the electronic text and copyright information.

British Women Playwrights around 1800 provides the full text of seventeen plays published between 1776 and 1835, with the goal of supporting the work of theatre historians and scholars of British literature and culture. Although it doesn't appear that the site has been updated since 2008, the plays and contextual information presented here remain useful. The earliest play featured is Hannah Cowley's *The Runaway*, and playwrights Burney, Craven, Inchbald, Harriet and Sophia Lee, Plumptre, Stark, and Wallace are also represented. Edited by scholars in the field, many of the plays are also accompanied by a signed introductory essay. Additional scholarly essays and "e-mail conversations" are available that address women playwrights of the period, as well as theatrical and cultural contexts. A chronology outlines plays and performances, including closet and unacted works between the dates 1770 and 1854, with links to full-text plays in the collection noted in bold.

Now released as edition 6.0, ***Representative Poetry Online*** (***RPO***) continues to be a vital contributor to the literary webscape, despite the often transient nature of the medium. This online anthology comprises 4,700 poems in English and French, beginning with Caedmon and spanning into the twenty-first century and currently includes the work of more than 700 poets. Originally based on the print collection *Representative Poetry*, published in 1912, the online version debuted in 1994, under the general editorship of Ian Lancashire, Department of English at the University of Toronto, who still oversees the project. The entire collection can be searched by keyword or browsed by poets or poems. Within these categories subsections provide browsing access to poets by name; date; period (e.g., Age of Johnson, Augustan, Romantic); movement (e.g., Graveyard poets); nationality; or honors and to poems by title, date, form (e.g., heroic couplets), rhyme, or collection. The "Age of Johnson" list, for example, features nineteen poets, from such well-known figures as Cowper, Goldsmith, Gray, Johnson, and Sheridan, to those less familiar, like Grose, Madan, and Whitefield.

Each poem is annotated with general and line-specific notes; additional information covers the original source text, editors, *RPO* edition number, and rhyme scheme. Individual poets are treated with a biographical profile that presents a list of their poems, a likeness, a recommended biography or biographical source, and notes about their life and works that vary greatly in detail. For example, the William Collins profile lists birth and death dates, nationality, literary period, illness, and education, whereas the Alexander Pope profile offers a biographical summary, in addition to notes about education, illnesses, and religion. Like any good anthology, *RPO* is enriched with contextual information. A "Timeline of Poetry in English" outlines significant historical and poetry-related events, for instance, birth and death dates of poets, important poems, poetry awards, and poems about poems from 449 to almost the present day. Other components include a glossary of poetic terms; a selection of poetry criticism (in prose and verse), for example, John Dennis's *The Grounds of Criticism in Poetry* (1704), Alexander Pope's *Preface to His Translation of Homer's Iliad* (1715), and Edward Young's *Conjectures on Original Composition* (1759); maps that indicate poet birth and death places, major residences, and places mentioned in poems; and an extensive bibliography of poetry anthologies, as well as biographies, criticism, histories, verse forms, and Internet poetry collections.

The *University of Oxford Text Archive* (*OTA*) maintains a collection of more than 2,000 digital literary and linguistic texts with the intent of fostering "research, teaching, and learning." Searching the *OTA* is straightforward, with only a single search box for keywords available. Consequently, searching for known items or authors is easier than trying to identify texts from a particular time period, especially since the collection covers material from ancient Greece to the twentieth century. You can browse and sort results by author, title, language, and date. To browse eighteenth-century works, select the "Catalogue" link (which is the complete listing of texts) and then reorder the list by clicking on "Date" and scroll down the chronological list to find texts published in the eighteenth century. There are works listed by most of the eighteenth-century canonical authors and some unusual texts as well, including *The report of the physicians and surgeons, commanded to assist at the dissecting the body of His late Majesty at Kensington, March the tenth MDCCI/II. From the original delivered to the Right Honourable the Privy Council* (1702), by an unknown author, and *The black art detected and expos'd: or, a demonstration of the hellish impiety, of being, or desiring to be a wizzard, conjurer, or witch. . . . In a letter to a country gentleman* (1707).

In March 2012, *OTA* announced the addition of 179 public-domain texts from *ECCO*, strengthening its holdings of eighteenth-century sources. Most of the collection is freely available; however, due to licensing restrictions, some titles require permission to use from the depositor. In that case, you will need to submit a request form and anticipate a delay of a few days or several weeks before the text can be accessed. This barrier isn't applicable for the majority of the collection.

Also general in nature, the *Modern English Collection* at the University of Virginia covers a wide range of literary texts from the sixteenth century to the present, from fiction, poetry, drama, and manuscripts to nonfiction, letters, newspapers, and illustrations. The primary form of access is to browse the collection either by author's last name (or anonymous) or by topical categories, such as "Texts by Women Writers," "Texts by and about Native Americans," and "Texts by and about Thomas Jefferson." Many of the texts are freely available to the public; however, some are restricted to University of Virginia affiliates. A simple search interface permits a keyword search within all or specific fields of the publicly available texts, which can be limited by date range. The collection is strong in colonial and later American authors and texts, but it also incorporates British eighteenth-century authors, including William Blake, Frances Brooke, Colley Cibber, John Cleland, Ann Batten Cristall, Daniel Defoe, Henry Fielding, John Gay, William Godwin, Oliver Goldsmith, David Hume, Samuel Johnson, Matthew Gregory Lewis, Lady Mary Wortley Montagu, John Oldmixon, Alexander Pope, Mary Robinson, Frances Sheridan, Adam Smith, and Jonathan Swift. You can typically choose to download the entire rekeyed text or select specific sections, and notes about both the electronic and print version are stated.

Three additional, wide-scale electronic book projects provide access to numerous sources published in the eighteenth century or reprinted in later nineteenth- and early twentieth-century editions or anthologies. The first of these, *Project Gutenberg*, has been in existence since 1971, when Michael Hart founded the project. *Project Gutenberg* has grown to more than 39,000 freely available electronic books that can be searched by keyword. They can also be browsed by author; title; language; most recently added; or thematic bookshelves, includng "Women Writers," "Gothic Fiction," or "Poetry." The collection is much broader than just literature, encompassing many subject areas from agriculture to technology. Although you will probably have the most luck retrieving texts for canonical British authors, you will find minor authors represented as well. The texts are retyped rather than digitized versions, often available in multiple formats, and each record has information about the author, title, language, e-book number, release date, copyright status, and occasionally transcribers' notes. Keep in mind that these are not authoritative versions, and, since publisher, edition, or date information is not given, these texts are best used for casual reading, rather than to be cited in your research.

Google Books features millions of digitized public-domain books and journals from library collections in the United States and Britain, as well as selected books under copyright from individual publishers. You can search the full text of these resources and either download the complete version as a PDF in a pre-1923 text or obtain a preview of copyrighted material. After conducting your initial keyword search, you can limit your results to "Free Google eBooks"; books or magazines; and nineteenth, twentieth, or twenty-first centuries, or a custom date range. You can also sort by date rather than relevance. If we search *"eliza haywood"* and limit to public-domain books, Google currently finds 30,300 texts, ranging from an early twentieth-century biography, *The Life and Romances of Eliza Haywood*, to a published edition of the *Female Spectator*, to the text of her play *A Wife to Be Lett: A Comedy*, and references to her in collected works of other eighteenth-century authors, as a few examples. The advanced search interface offers more control, since you can search in title, author, publisher, subject, ISBN, and ISSN fields, as well as limit to specific publication dates.

HathiTrust Digital Library is the collaboration between research institutions and libraries, not only to digitize texts, but to actively work to "ensure that the cultural record is preserved and accessible long into the future." The library currently contains more than ten million volumes, including more than three million public-domain books and periodicals. Select the advanced catalog search to access author, title, subject, publisher, series title, year of publication, and ISBN/ISSN fields, as well as to limit to language, original format, and full view only. You can also choose to search the full text, which allows limiting by full view, year of publication, language, and original format. The "Collections" section enables members of affiliated institutions to log in and create personal collections that can either be private or viewable by the public. There are currently more than 900 public collections; samples reflect individual interests, and some are relevant to eighteenth-century studies, for example, "18th C. Cookbooks," "British Book Trades," "Gothic Literature," "Great Britain," and "Letter Writing, History, and Lit."

If you are interested in finding full-text period journals, start at the advanced search and limit to full-view sources, original format—journal, language—English, and year, between 1700 and 1799. You can further limit the results to place of publication (e.g, Great Britain, England, Scotland, Ireland). There are twelve serial titles available that were published in Scotland, *The Bee: or, Literary Weekly Intelligencer*, *Edinburgh Magazine: or Literary Miscellany*, *Edinburgh Magazine and Review by a Society of Gentlemen*, *The Mirror: A Periodical Paper Published in Edinburgh in the Years 1779 and 1780*, and *Scots Magazine: or, General Repository of Literature, History, and Politics* among them. HathiTrust Digital Library will continue to add public-domain texts as they become available. The control provided by the library catalog-type search interface and the wealth of texts make this a valuable collection for identifying primary eighteenth-century literary sources.

SPECIALIZED ELECTRONIC TEXT ARCHIVES

Bodleian Library Broadside Ballads. Oxford, UK: Oxford University. www.bodley.ox.ac.uk/ballads (accessed 28 August 2012).

The Proceedings of the Old Bailey, 1674–1913. Old Bailey Proceedings Online. www.oldbaileyonline.org (accessed 28 August 2012).
Voller, Jack G. *The Literary Gothic.* www.litgothic.com/index_fl.html (accessed 28 August 2012).
The Word on the Street. Edinburgh: National Library of Scotland. www.nls
.uk/broadsides/index.html (accessed 28 August 2012).

Broadside ballads offer literary scholars, as well as those of music, art, and
history, insight into the popular themes and concerns of the period. Originally
created to be sung, rather than read, this form of popular literature combines
both text and illustrations. Ubiquitous but ephemeral in nature, we are fortunate to have several major collections of broadside ballads available in digital
format on the Web.

The **Bodleian Library Broadside Ballads** project at the University of Oxford brings together more than 30,000 ballads and broadsheets (where more
than one ballad was printed on a single sheet), primarily from its Ashmole,
Wood, Rawlinson, Douce, Curzon, Johnson, Harding, and Firth collections.
The ballads cover the sixteenth through the twentieth centuries, including
many political ballads from the eighteenth century. Each individual ballad
has been scanned and cataloged to facilitate access through the project's
searchable database. Keywords may be entered for eight different indexes:
title, first lines, tunes; tune keywords; subjects; authors, performers (if noted),
or venues; publishers or printers (when known); shelfmark; date (it is important to note that most ballads do not have a date); and Iconclass. This last
index permits searching of the illustrations and provides subject codes for
the themes, people (e.g., female street trader, soldier, social classes), places,
and items portrayed in the woodcuts. The ballads and broadsheets can also
be browsed; perusing the subject index, for example, shows the fascinating
range of topics addressed, from the visit of the American Indians to England
in 1710 (6 items) to seduction and abandonment (242 items). Some ballads
possess musical notation, and, in these cases, a sound file has been attached.
The "Help" section contains an introduction to the ballads, a chronological
guide to the contents, and search tips.

The National Library of Scotland hosts its own collection of digitized
broadside ballads called **The Word on the Street.** Featuring approximately
1,800 Scottish broadsides created between 1650 and 1910, the collection is
particularly strong in ballads from the eighteenth and nineteenth centuries.
Although the search interface is less robust than that of the Bodleian project,
you can use Boolean operators, truncation, and phrases to search the full
text by keyword or exact year, or browse the collection by title or subject.
Forty-nine subject categories reveal not only the most common subjects (e.g.,
courtship, murder, humor, executions and executioners, politics), but also a

Catholic interest from apparitions to Jacobites and robbery to transvestites. Each ballad is introduced with a brief commentary, and readers have the option of consulting an original digital facsimile and a modern transcription. *The Word on the Street* also offers concise overviews about the development of the genre, ballad illustrations, and distribution. Finally, the "Resources" category presents a bibliography of books for further reading and related broadside and street literature Web pages.

In keeping with some of the broadside ballad themes, ***The Proceedings of the Old Bailey, 1674–1913*** provides an account of 197,000 trials that occurred at London's central criminal court during this period. While it started out just summarizing selected trials, the publication evolved over time to record all the trials, and, around 1712, it began to incorporate verbatim testimonies, "especially in trials [that] were thought to be salacious, amusing, or otherwise entertaining." Before diving in to the actual *Proceedings*, scholars may want to read the fascinating introductory material, which covers the publishing history but also gives background overviews about crime, justice, punishment, London and its environs, specific communities (e.g., Chinese, gypsies, homosexuals, Jewish, Huguenot, Irish), gender roles and tips for researching gender in the *Proceedings*, and the architecture of the Old Bailey. Research and study guides also address how to read a trial, search techniques, and statistical research. The *Proceedings* and the *Ordinary's Accounts* (1679–1772) may be searched by keyword in the full text or by surname, given name, alias, offence, verdict, punishment, and reference number, and limited by time period or to specific parts of the *Proceedings*, for instance, advertisements, front matter, punishment summaries, supplementary material, and trial accounts. The "Custom Search" features additional fields, including gender, age range, occupation, person or crime location, crime date, and offense or punishment descriptions.

After conducting a search, results are presented with associated records and transcripts, and you can also view a page image of the original text. A "Place and Map Search 1674–1834" enables you to locate place names that occur in the trials on three eighteenth- and nineteenth-century maps of London. Reviewing the list of crimes, from theft to vagabonding, to bankruptcy and murder, as well as punishments, and from the pillory to branding, to transportation and execution, brings the eighteenth century to life.

Created by one of the coeditors of *Gothic Writers: A Critical and Bibliographical Guide*, ***The Literary Gothic*** reflects Jack G. Voller's ongoing interest in and passion for the genre. Voller defines the term *literary Gothic*, for the purposes of this website, as ghost stories, classic Gothic novels, and Gothic fiction published between 1764 and 1820, but he includes both earlier and post-Gothic and supernatural texts published before 1950. The site has two main components, a collection of electronic texts and an extensive list of related Web resources. Although there isn't a search function, the texts can be browsed by either author or title, and they comprise works by Addison, Akenside, Collins, Cowper, Defoe, Godwin, Gray, Lee, Lewis, Macpherson, Parsons, Radcliffe, Reeve, Robinson, Roche, Shenstone, Sleath, Smith, Smollett, Thomson, Walpole, Warton, Wollstonecraft, and Young.

The profile for each author presents their birth and death dates, if known; a headnote about their literary career and relationship to the Gothic tradition; a list of websites for the author; links to electronic versions of their texts, sometimes with a brief annotation; availability of print versions of the texts; and discussion lists. The Web resources section is arranged in six categories: "Overviews, Directories, and Collections"; "Essays"; "The Gothic Community," which covers associations and discussion lists; "Book Reviews"; "Publishers/Journals/'Zines"; and "Timelines and Chronologies." Author-specific Web resources are listed on the individual author pages. An additional "Gothic Research" section is intended to help students new to the genre begin their academic investigation by recommending print and electronic sources, as well as offering general research advice. With *The Literary Gothic*, Voller has created a useful portal to the Gothic on the Web.

AUTHOR SITES

Bullard, Paddy, ed. *Journal to Stella*. www.swiftiana.com/stella (accessed 28 August 2012).

Huber, Alexander, ed. *Thomas Gray Archive*. Oxford, UK: University of Oxford. www.thomasgray.org (accessed 28 August 2012).

Landow, George P., ed. "Jonathan Swift, 1667–1745." *Victorian Web*. www .victorianweb.org/previctorian/swift/swiftov.html (accessed 28 August 2012).

Lynch, Jack. *Samuel Johnson*. Newark, NJ: Rutgers University. andromeda .rutgers.edu/~jlynch/Johnson (accessed 28 August 2012).

Ockerbloom, Mary Mark, ed. "Anna Laetitia Aikin Barbauld (1743–1825)." *A Celebration of Women Writers*. Philadelphia: University of Pennsylvania. digital.library.upenn.edu/women/barbauld/biography.html (accessed 28 August 2012).

Uchida, Masaru. *Laurence Sterne in Cyberspace*. www1.gifu-u.ac.jp/~masaru/ Sterne_on_the_Net.html (accessed 28 August 2012).

This section provides some examples of websites devoted to a specific eighteenth-century British author. These kinds of sites typically feature one or more of the following: biographical information; transcriptions or digital works by the author or links to these resources; bibliographies of primary or secondary sources with some access to full text; a chronology; images; and related links. More often than not, you will find an author site incorporated into a larger project, like the Chawton House Library Women Writers biographies (see the information on *Novels-On-Line* in the "Period and General Electronic Text Archives" section), *Luminarium*, or *The Literary Gothic*. If you want to determine if there is a site for a particular author, check one of the scholarly portals described earlier in this chapter, for example, Lynch's *Eighteenth-Century Resources*, *Voice of the Shuttle*, or *A Celebration of Women Writers*. Although these sources primarily link to full-text works by the author, they also occasionally direct you to a page for an individual author.

Sponsored by the Bodleian Library at the University of Oxford, the **Thomas Gray Archive** is a model site that best demonstrates how the Web can support scholarly research. The archive features two main sections, "Primary Texts," with an emphasis on electronic editions of Gray's works and resources to support textual investigations, and "Materials," which offers secondary critical essays and reference tools. Within "Primary Texts," there are six subsections: "Poems," "Prose Work," "Letters," "Concordance," "Digital Library," and "Finding Aid." Gray's complete poetic output is here, including his poems in English and Latin, and the Greek poem "Inscription for a Wood in a Park." The English poems are arranged by date (anthumous and posthumous poems), title, and genre (e.g., lyric and dramatic poems, humorous and satirical poems, imitations and translations, poems of doubtful authenticity), and they can be accessed alphabetically by title and first line. A box to the right highlights the most frequently read poems, with "Elegy Written in a Country Churchyard" at the top of the list.

Scholars can contribute to an ongoing, collaborative commentary that currently contains 3,496 variants, notes, and queries. The "Prose Works" section, arranged by title and topic, presents Gray's critical essays, many of which concern the history and theory of lyric poetry, as well as close readings of individual texts. Although the prose collection is small, you will find essays about such diverse subjects as Norman architecture, verse and rhyme, philosophy, and travel writing.

Rather than featuring digital copies, the "Letters" section is a calendar and description of Gray's known correspondence, which can be retrieved by the following categories: letters written by Gray, letters addressed to Gray, correspondence between Gray and forty-five individuals, date or place of composition, and holding library. Clicking on the identification number for an individual letter from the results list will display information about the writer's name, age, date, place of composition, incipit, and language, but also surrogates (if available), library or holding institution, availability, and a bibliography. The online concordance represents every word in the archive's collection of Gray's complete poems, both in English and Latin, and the words can be generated alphabetically or by corpus word occurrence. After selecting a word, the concordance will retrieve the list of poems in word occurrence order. The word *sorrow*, for example, appears ten times in eight poems, and it is displayed each time within the contextual line. The corpus word occurrence list illustrates the importance of the words eyes (30), hand (25), day (23), heart (22), light (21), know (21), and love (21) to Gray's poetic imagination.

The "Digital Library" provides editions of Gray's poems; translations; imitations and parodies; prose works; letters; and audiovisual material, which consists of readings of select poems (through RealAudio). Serving as a guide to Gray's manuscripts, the finding aid lists autograph poetry manuscripts and transcripts by his contemporaries and early editors, with 288 manuscripts in total. Prepared by the site editor, Alexander Huber, the finding aid is described as a "work in progress" and will eventually include Gray's prose works, personal papers, and marginalia as well.

The "Materials" section of secondary sources enhances the study of Gray's work by offering digital versions of both contemporary and current criticism and teaching materials; an introductory biography; a chronology of Gray's life and works; a glossary of personal names, place names, and literary terms; a bibliography of important printed primary and secondary materials, currently consisting of 532 sources listed by type of publication; and a gallery of eighty-one images pertaining to Gray, his friends, acquaintances, correspondents, and places of interest, with maps. Finally, a list of seventy-seven freely available Web resources specifically about Thomas Gray, but also for general eighteenth-century studies, rounds out this exceptional author site.

Representing an author resource that is part of a larger project, the **"Anna Laetitia Aikin Barbauld (1743–1825)"** page at *A Celebration of Women Writers* (*CWW*) website offers a straightforward, no-frills introduction to Barbauld's life and works. Beginning with a brief biography that traces Barbauld's literary career, hyperlinks within the text lead to online transcriptions of specific works at *CWW*, including *Poems* (1773) and *Hymns in Prose for Children* (1781). Many of these texts, as well as additional poems, are listed by genre in the "Selections" section, and the page concludes with a bibliography of Barbauld's works in editions spanning from 1773 to 1994. Although it would benefit from more content and pales in comparison to the *Thomas Gray Archive*, this page gathers together online versions of Barbauld's works and makes them accessible to a general audience.

Scholars of Jonathan Swift are well-served by the ***Journal to Stella*** website. Although the main focus of this site is an electronic edition of Swift's series of "letter-diaries" (now called *Journal to Stella*), which he wrote from London between 1710 and 1713, to his friend, Esther Johnson, the journal is enriched with background and other reference material. The electronic edition was rereleased in 2010, so that the entries would correspond with dates as they unfold 300 years later, from 2010 to 2013. Offering a fascinating window into Swift's life and a particular relationship, the letters are not self-conscious literary creations, but rather are described as "gentle, curious, flirtatious, oblique, and often spectacularly silly." Many of the letters contain embedded hypertext links, so that if Swift mentions a specific person, such as the Lord Treasurer or Goody Stoyte, the reader can click to obtain a brief biographical profile or link to a previous letter or other text as referenced. The biographical profiles can also be browsed separately. Additional features include a bibliography of recommended modern editions of Swift's works, as well as bibliographies, biographies, and research guides; two chronologies, one of Swift's life and another focused on literary and historical events (1664–1745); related Web resources; and commentary by Virginia Woolf about the journal. Edited by Paddy Bullard at the University of Oxford, this dual-purpose electronic text and author site is a fine example of a high-quality resource for eighteenth-century literary research.

Hidden away in the "Before Victoria: Selected Authors from the Eighteenth and Nineteenth Centuries" part of the *Victorian Web*, the **"Jonathan Swift, 1667–1745"** overview is actually a respectable collection of biographical, critical, and contextual material that also presents links to selected online texts. Arranged in several thematic sections, the entry covers Swift's life, works, political and social history, religion, literary relations, literary style, literary mode, literary genre, science, visual arts, and related Web resources. Within each of these sections you will find either a signed essay (many by David Cody, associate professor of English at Hartwick College, or George P. Landow, editor in chief of the *Victorian Web*), for instance, those about Swift's political beliefs, Swift's satire on Calvin in *Tale of a Tub*, and Neoclassical wit, or such resources as a chronology of Swift's life and a timeline of British history from 1642 to 1945, as well as illustrations from *Gulliver's Travels*. The "Related WWW Resources" section is no longer viable, since the pre-Victorian authors section hasn't been updated in many years, but the essays still offer foundational information. In addition to the Swift entry, you will also find similar overviews for Samuel Johnson, Alexander Pope, and Ann Radcliffe; however, the Laurence Sterne entry contains only dead links.

The ***Samuel Johnson*** page is another example of an author site that hasn't been updated in several years, but that still presents useful content. Created by Jack Lynch, who not only maintains the *Eighteenth-Century Resources* portal, but who also edits the journal *The Age of Johnson: A Scholarly An-*

nual (see chapter 5), the site was originally designed to serve as a central hub for Internet resources about Johnson and his circle. Lynch recommends that students new to Johnson begin with his "A Guide to Samuel Johnson," which introduces the author and his works and covers standard editions, anthologies and selections, biographies, bibliographies, introductions, general works of criticism, and specific editions and criticism for Johnson's poetry, *Irene*, political writings, periodical essays, the *Dictionary*, Rasselas, sermons, prayers, meditations, the Shakespeare Edition, *Journey to the Western Islands of Scotland*, and the *Lives of the Poets*. In addition to this detailed reference guide, there are sections dedicated to electronic texts, an extensive and searchable "Bibliography of Johnsonian Studies" representing scholarship published from 1986 to the early 2000s, quotations from Johnson and his contemporaries, a preset search for Johnson within the "Eighteenth-Century Chronology," links to Johnson societies, and a resource about Burns and Boswell.

Available in English or Japanese, **Laurence Sterne in Cyberspace** is the product of Masaru Uchida, professor of English literature at Gifu University. Although the format and presentation make the site look dated, this gateway to Sterne resources is updated and well maintained, with no detectable dead links, and it provides a wide array of material for Sterne research. Featured on a single page, you will find an extensive list of resources listed in the following categories: electronic versions/editions of *Tristram Shandy*, *A Sentimental Journey*, *A Political Romance*, and *Letters from Yorick to Eliza* from different digital archives and universities; books and journals about Sterne; adaptations, including radio and movie adaptations and presentations; study guides; blogs and Twitter; bibliographies; essays and online books; and a miscellaneous category that contains links to biographical sources, Shandy Hall, the Reynolds portrait of Sterne from the National Portrait Gallery, book marbling, and literary York, among many others. The last two sections present a selection of resources about hypertext and the eighteenth century in general. This site will help scholars launch their investigations into Sterne on the Web.

REFERENCE TOOLS

BibSite. New York: Bibliographical Society of America. www.bibsocamer.org/bibsite/bibsite.htm (accessed 28 August 2012).

Brady, Corey, Virginia Cope, Mike Millner, Ana Mitric, Kent Puckett, and Danny Siegel. *Dictionary of Sensibility.* graduate.engl.virginia.edu/enec981/dictionary (accessed 28 August 2012).

British Book Trade Index. Birmingham, England: University of Birmingham. www.bbti.bham.ac.uk (accessed 28 August 2012).

de Montluzin, Emily Lorraine. *Attributions of Authorship in the European Magazine, 1782–1826*. etext.virginia.edu/bsuva/euromag (accessed 28 August 2012).

———. *Attributions of Authorship in the Gentleman's Magazine*. etext.virginia .edu/bsuva/gm (accessed 28 August 2012).

Digital Miscellanies Index. Oxford, UK: University of Oxford, Faculty of English and Literature. digitalmiscellaniesindex.org (accessed 28 August 2012).

Franklin, Ian. *18th Century Bibliography*. www.c18th.com/index.aspx (accessed 28 August 2012).

A Gothic Chronology. Marlborough, Wiltshire, England: Adam Matthew Publications. www.ampltd.co.uk/digital_guides/gothic_fiction/chronology .aspx (accessed 28 August 2012).

Leeds Verse Database (BCMSV). Leeds, West Yorkshire, England: University of Leeds. www.leeds.ac.uk/library/spcoll/bcmsv/intro.htm (accessed 28 August 2012).

Lynch, Jack, ed. *c18 Bibliographies On-Line*. Newark, NJ: Rutgers University. andromeda.rutgers.edu/~jlynch/C18/biblio/index.html (accessed 28 August 2012).

Mandell, Laura, and Alan Liu, eds. *Romantic Chronology*. english.ucsb .edu:591/rchrono (accessed 28 August 2012).

Norton Topics Online. Part of *Norton Anthology of English Literature*. New York: W. W. Norton and Company, 2012. www.wwnorton.com/college/ english/nael/18century/welcome.htm (accessed 28 August 2012).

Scottish Book Trade Index. Edinburgh: National Library of Scotland. www .nls.uk/catalogues/scottish-book-trade-index (accessed 28 August 2012).

Swift Criticism Database. Münster, Germany: University of Münster, Ehrenpreis Centre for Swift Studies. www.anglistik.uni-muenster.de/Swift/ Database/index.html (accessed 28 August 2012).

Toubiana, Guy, and Kevin D. Dodson, eds. *18th Century Online Encyclopedia: Enlightenment and Revolution*. www.enlightenment-revolution.org/ index.php/Main_Page (accessed 28 August 2012).

Yadav, Alok. *Historical Outline of Restoration and 18th Century British Literature*. mason.gmu.edu/~ayadav/historical%20outline/overview.htm (accessed 28 August 2012).

The Web is often our first choice for answering a simple question or verifying a fact. Sometimes it can seem like a boundless reference tool, with an answer to everything. Although this perception isn't always true, you can often use the Web the same way you might use a traditional print encyclopedia, dictionary, or other reference source, as long as you are careful to follow the evaluation criteria discussed at the beginning of this chapter. Bibliographies and indexes are central to literary research, in particular, and the Web presents these tools in electronic formats, enhancing their general usefulness with improved search capabilities. The following section describes a selection of reference tools for studying eighteenth-century British literature.

Several general and thematic chronologies provide scholars with quick reference to key historical and cultural events of the period. Covering the long eighteenth century, ***Historical Outline of Restoration and 18th Century British Literature*** focuses on historical and literary events, listed by year from the civil wars in 1642 through George III's reign in 1820, with additional events from the beginning of the seventeenth century until the death of authors Hunt, de Quincey, and Macaulay in 1859. Each year lists historical events, followed by important English-language literary publications, with some indication of genre (e.g., poetry, drama, fiction, anthology, periodical), as well as some European-language works. Alok Yadav, a professor at George Mason University who created the chronology, uses the Gregorian calendar dates so that the new year begins on January 1 and adjusts dates accordingly.

A nice feature of this resource is that many of the entries are one or more paragraphs in length, as is the case as for the Act of Settlement, the Union of England and Scotland, the Copyright Act of 1709, the death of Sir Isaac Newton, the Jacobite Rebellion, the adoption of the Gregorian calendar, the establishment of the British Museum, the repeal of the Jewish Naturalization Act, the Seven Years' War, the Chatham ministry, the Gordon riots, the Age of Steam, the War of American Independence, and the French Revolution, as just a few examples. In addition to the expected major events, you will also find interesting facts noted, for instance, the prevalence of cattle disease in southern England during 1715, Lady Huntingdon's house being open for preaching in 1748, the discovery of Uranus in 1781, and George III's first recovery from madness in 1789. Literary publications are listed alphabetically by author and sometimes include notes about edition or composition rather than publication date. The chronology can either be browsed in its entirety as one long document or by specific period (e.g., ruling monarch, the Revolution of 1688–1989). Although there isn't a separate search function, you can use your browser's "Find" command to search with keywords for individuals, specific events, or years. A "Sources" section on the left toolbar leads to the bibliography of works used to compile the chronology; references to these sources are integrated into and linked from the chronology.

Beginning with selected events from the seventeenth century, the ***Romantic Chronology*** covers much more than the traditional Romantic period; it addresses the entire eighteenth century, but much of the nineteenth century as well. The chronology can be accessed by selecting a preset date range from the main page (e.g., "18th-Century to 1784," "1785–1791"), by choosing a topic, or by searching for a specific event. The "18th-Century to 1784" category currently lists 440 events, from the publication of Congreve's *The Way of the World* in 1700, to Samuel Johnson's death on December 13, 1784. Many of the entries are literary in nature and concern authors and publications; however, other cultural and historical events are also addressed. For each entry, a "Details" link to the left offers further information, sometimes including sources and related links.

The "Topics Catalogue" enables you to trace related events for forty-five subjects that reflect common themes for the era, for instance, abolition, Anglo-Jewish history, the Bluestockings, colonialism, economics, industrial revolution, the Jacobites, Parliamentary reform, Scotland, and sensibility. To find a specific person, publication, or event, or to select a specialized date range, use the advanced search interface, which offers fields for these categories. A separate archive of Web links that are embedded into the chronology may be browsed alphabetically or searched by keyword, URL, or archive topic. For example, a search for Johnson retrieves links to several electronic transcriptions of Johnson's works, a copy of his last will and testament, a critical essay, and the journal *The Age of Johnson: A Scholarly Annual*. The *Romantic Chronology* is edited by Laura Mandell and Alan Liu at the University of California, Santa Barbara.

Adam Matthews has produced *A Gothic Chronology* to enhance the digital finding aid to the *Gothic Fiction: Rare Printed Works from the Sadleir-Black Collection of Gothic Fiction at the Alderman Library, University of Virginia* microfilm collection. Beginning in 1717, with the births of Horace Walpole, Richard West, and David Garrick, and the publication of Pope's *Poems* and *Elegy to the Memory of an Unfortunate Lady*, this chronology offers brief paragraphs for each year that mark significant historical, literary, and cultural events to help place the development of Gothic literature in context, and it continues to trace these events through 1854, by closing with John Martin's painting "The Great Day of His Wrath." The chronology contains birth and death dates for authors; publications, both Gothic and otherwise; and related notes, including official reports of Vampirism circulating in Europe in 1729 and Henry Mayo's publication describing the disinterment of a vampire in 1732. In addition to the chronology, scholars may also want to consult the finding aid's historical overview of the genre, written by Peter Otto at the University of Melbourne, and an introduction to Gothic satires, histories, and chapbooks, written by Alison Milbank at the University of Virginia.

If your work is concerned with the book trade, in particular, or print culture, generally, you will want to consult the *British Book Trade Index* (*BBTI*). Hosted by the University of Birmingham, *BBTI* provides the names of and brief biographical information for printers, publishers, and booksellers working in England and Wales before 1851. Details about individuals in related trades are also presented, such as stationers, papermakers, engravers, auctioneers, ink makers, and sellers of medicine. Following an introductory page with search advice, the index can be accessed by surname, forename, trade or biographical dates, country, county, town, book trade, and descriptor (which are related to specific book trades). For example, if you choose the book trade *bookseller*, the related descriptors will be displayed from the drop-down menu so that you can further refine your search. There are currently twenty-six bookseller trade descriptors, ranging from types of books sold (antiquarian, chapbook, Bible, music, medical, secondhand, dramatic/theatrical) to people involved (apprentice, journeyman, proprietor, assistant), and much more. Five primary book trades are represented (bookseller, bookbinder, printer, publisher, stationer) and more than seventy related trades, such as author and writer, but also fellmonger, goldbeater, hot-presser, paper marbler, parchment/vellum dealer, pen/quill maker, rag merchant, tanner/whittawer, and wood letter-maker, among others.

The advanced search interface permits searching additional nonbook trade (agriculture/horticulture to transport) and notes fields. Help buttons to the right of each search field give specific advice for searching that field, with examples. Since several terms can be used interchangeably, be sure to search all possible terms so as to not miss relevant records. If we search for booksellers trading between 1700 and 1750, in Derbyshire, thirty-two records are retrieved (with a few duplicates), listed from earliest to latest trading period. Clicking on an individual's name will retrieve the record. Mrs. Barker, for example, sold books in Chapel en le Frith, Derbyshire, in 1731. Although this is all the information we learn about her, other possible fields are address, nonbook trade, and notes. Each record also contains a link to the sources used to compile the biographical profile, listed as abbreviations.

The full bibliographical references are presented in the *BBTI* "Source List," and there is also an extensive bibliography, "The English Provincial Book Trade Before 1850: A Checklist of Secondary Sources by John Feather, with Later Additions by Paul Morgan," originally published by the Oxford Bibliographical Society in 1981. This checklist can be refined by county or category (all, general, newspapers), with seven sources specifically for studying the book trade in Derbyshire. The checklist can also be sorted alphabetically by individuals, firms, and institutions. *BBTI* is an essential tool for studying the book and book-related trades during the eighteenth century.

Further north, the **Scottish Book Trade Index (SBTI)** covers printers, publishers, booksellers, bookbinders, printmakers, stationers, and papermakers that were active in Scotland before 1850, many of which were identified through eighteenth-century Scottish imprints and newspapers. Although it isn't possible to search, you can browse the index by slightly more than fifty alphabetical divisions, beginning with the Abbotsford Club publishers and ending with Charles Ziegler, a nineteenth-century bookseller and stationer in Edinburgh. A work in progress, the latest version of the index is currently available in two A to M and N to Z PDFs, but the smaller, hyperlinked sections are still accessible on the *SBTI* website and will eventually incorporate the latest updates.

Culled from book imprints and secondary sources, the information provided for most individuals is sparse, but it includes name, trade, town(s) where they practiced their trade, address(es) with corresponding dates, and abbreviated references; some entries also have biographical or historical notes. The entry for early eighteenth-century printer William Adams is one of the fuller examples and offers details about his education, marriage, other careers as a schoolmaster and minister, imprisonment for publishing the pamphlet *Mercy, Now or Never*, date of death and age at death, and will registry. Each record also contains the abbreviated source text(s), and all secondary sources are listed in a separate document by their abbreviation, followed by a full bibliographical citation and selected annotations. *SBTI* was originally compiled by John Morris, former assistant keeper of antiquarian books at the National Library of Scotland, and the index is currently maintained by the library, which possesses a strong collection of Scottish book trade archives in its Manuscript Collections department.

Scholars can use the **Leeds Verse Database** (**BCMSV**) to search more than 6,600 English manuscript poems from the seventeenth and eighteenth centuries that comprise the Brotherton Collection at the University of Leeds. Although the digital manuscript facsimiles are only available through the Adam Matthew subscription database *Literary Manuscripts: 17th and 18th Century Poetry from the Brotherton Library, University of Leeds* (described in chapter 8), *BCMSV* still offers the ability to identify poems from this significant resource. Basic and detailed interfaces permit searching with keywords in multiple fields. The detailed search, for example, features fourteen fields, which include anywhere, start (the first three words of the poem in modernized spelling), first line, last line, attribution, author, title, date, length, verse form, content (subject), bibliographic references, manuscript number, and record number, with results sorted by first line, author, or record number. Conducting a search with the keyword *wit*, to appear anywhere in the poem, finds eighty-eight matches from anonymous authors, as well as from James Dallaway, Richard Blackmore, Joseph Browne, Alexander Pope, and others.

The results are initially displayed in brief format, with first line, author, title, date, content, and manuscript and record number. The full format illustrates additional fields, such as verse form, physical features, and compiler. The complete list of the 160 manuscripts can also be browsed. Arranged by manuscript number, each entry highlights known authors in bold text and describes the contents, for example, "Commonplace book or notebook mainly of English religious poems and prayers, c. 1715," "Commonplace book in several hands, c. 1746 to late 18th century, including English verse and prose, passages, and epitaphs in Latin and Greek, and printed poems and newspaper cuttings pasted in," and "Bifolium in a single hand, early to mid-eighteenth century, containing two poems written in response to the tale of the Rabbit Woman of Godalming."

More than 320 colored, digital page images are freely accessible to the public, mainly to provide examples of English period handwriting, and an effort was made to present every significant contributing hand in the collection. Links from these images lead to the full catalog record for each manuscript. *BCMSV* serves as a valuable entry point not only for identifying individual poems, but also for studying eighteenth-century manuscript commonplace books, miscellanies, and manuscript culture.

An exciting newcomer, when it is completed in the summer of 2013, the ***Digital Miscellanies Index*** will provide access to the contents of more than 1,000 poetic miscellanies published during the eighteenth century, representing virtually every surviving British miscellany from this period. Primarily drawn from the Harding collection at the Bodleian Library, but from other library collections as well, the database will contain first and later editions, so that approximately 1,500 miscellany volumes and 50,000 separate poems will ultimately be indexed. Scholars will be able to search the database by author, poem, genre, first line, and publisher, in addition to other fields, including composer and patron, making this an essential resource for understanding the development of popular literary taste throughout the century.

Fortunately, an online library of full-text miscellanies from Google Books is planned to accompany the index. Since many miscellanies incorporated popular musical verse, sometimes with notation or reference to the tune, the index will also feature an "Audio" section, where you can listen to a selection of pieces, for example, "Ann thou were my ain Thing," "Cold and Raw," "Intrigues of the Town," and "The Midsummer Wish." The "Performance" section illustrates how miscellanies were performed at home by recreating a house concert of *The Yorkshire Garland* with audio clips, along with the full text of this 1788 miscellany. Based on a new bibliography of eighteenth-century poetic miscellanies by Michael F. Suarez, the *Digital Miscellanies Index* project is directed by Dr. Abigail Williams at the University of Oxford and will be hosted by the Bodleian's Centre for the Study of the Book.

Sensibility was a central concept to many eighteenth-century literary endeavors, and the ***Dictionary of Sensibility*** seeks to assist students by providing multiple nuances and meanings, rather than singular definitions, for twenty-four primary "sensibilious words," as they were understood during the period. To achieve this goal, the dictionary features excerpts from selected eighteenth-century literary texts that illustrate the range of meanings for such terms as *benevolence, landscape, heart, sympathy, honor/ reputation, sublime, imagination, character, communication, education, melancholy/madness*, and *taste*. Each word entry offers a brief introduction to eighteenth-century usage, followed by links to the text excerpts. Works by more than forty authors are represented, including Addison, Cheyne, Collins, Gray, Inchbald, Mackenzie, Richardson, Swift, Williams, and Young. These excerpts are annotated with critical commentary, and related terms in the dictionary are noted, if applicable. For example, the term *compassion/pity* is defined by excerpted texts from Collins, Diderot, Goldsmith, Lewis, Richardson, Shelley, and Sterne, among others, but it has no related terms. Two bibliographies, one of primary sources and the other listing critical works, present suggested texts for further exploration.

The ***18th Century Online Encyclopedia: Enlightenment and Revolution*** is comprised of descriptions about notable figures who either contributed to the intellectual movement or were involved in the American or French revolutions, that is, people (and the role they played in the period), rather than events, are the primary emphasis. The signed entries are written by scholars in the field, and they range from one paragraph to the equivalent of several pages and conclude with recommended sources for further reading. Many British authors are covered, as well as artists, musicians, philosophers, statesmen, politicians, and theologians from Europe and North America. Like a traditional encyclopedia, the entries are arranged alphabetically, but, unfortunately, there aren't any thematic indexes, for instance, a listing by occupation or nationality, even though this information is stated in a headnote. For example, if you want to identify all of the poets, you can search *poet* as a keyword, which will retrieve entries with this occupation heading, as well as entries in which the word appears in the text. Edited by Guy Toubiana and Kevin D. Dodson, this scholarly, wiki-driven encyclopedia was last updated in August 2010.

The Bibliographical Society of America offers a valuable collection of scholarly bibliographies for literary researchers on ***BibSite***. The website's straightforward design presents guidelines for contributors, and the bibliographies are accessed through the "List of Resources" link on the right side of the page. Each bibliography is succinctly described, with earlier versions and updates noted. Scholars of eighteenth-century literature will be especially interested in James May's bibliographies, namely "Recent Studies of Censorship, Press Freedom, Libel, Obscenity, etc., in the Long Eighteenth Century" (2010), "Studies of Authorship in the Long Eighteenth-Century, c. 1988–2009" (2007; updates in 2008, 2010), and "Studies of Eighteenth-Century Journalism, Newspapers, and Periodicals, and the Periodical Press, 1988–2009" (2003; updates in 2004, 2005, 2007, 2008, 2010).

Other bibliographies addressing the eighteenth century include James Woolley's "Finding English Verse, 1650–1800: First-Line Indexes and Searchable Electronic Texts" (2004; updates in 2004, 2005, 2006, 2010), David Wallace Spielman's "Bibliographic Information for Fifty-Three Unlocated Eighteenth-Century Items in Arnott and Robinson's *English Theatrical Literature, 1559–1900*" (2009), James McLaverty's "Addenda and Corrigenda to J. D. Fleeman's 'Bibliography of the Writings of Samuel Johnson, 1731–1984'" (2003; updates in 2004, 2010, 2011), and Barbara McCorkle's "Cartobibliography of the Maps in 18th Century British and American Geography Books" (2009). *BibSite* currently offers thirty bibliographies, but since new additions are always welcome (highlighted on the left side of the page), you will want to check back not to miss potentially relevant sources for your research.

Edited by Ian Franklin, the no-frills *18th Century Bibliography* nevertheless performs a useful service by listing English, French, and selected European-language texts published between 1680 and 1810. The bibliography can be perused by decades or accessed alphabetically by author, and its strength lies in the brief description of contents and contextual notes for many entries. Unfortunately, neither the specific scope of the bibliography (how decisions were made about inclusions/exclusions) nor the publication details or annotation references are provided. Franklin states that new works are added to the bibliography; however, the lack of "last updated" date or highlighting of new entries leaves readers in the dark as to its currency.

If you are looking for eighteenth-century British literary resources on the Web, it won't be long until you run into Jack Lynch. As previously described, Lynch maintains the *Eighteenth-Century Resources* portal and a site devoted to Johnson, and he also is the general editor of *c18 Bibliographies On-Line*. This collection features commissioned bibliographies on forty-one period authors written by scholars of eighteenth-century literature, history, and culture. Figures represented here range from the canonical to the less-familiar, including Jane Barker, Lady Mary Chudleigh, Mary Hays, Eliza Haywood, Mary Leapor, and Hester Lynch Piozzi, as well as Adam Ferguson, Thomas Gray, Samuel Johnson, Bernard Mandeville, Alexander Pope, George Psalmanazar, Thomas Reid, Laurence Sterne, and Jonathan Swift.

Each bibliography is annotated and most often addresses standard editions, bibliographies, reference works, biographies, and criticism. The scope may be comprehensive for authors who have traditionally received less critical attention and selective for major figures. Written by Laura Mandell (another familiar figure on the Web), the Mary Leapor bibliography, for example, covers editions of collected works and individual works, correspondence, selected teaching editions and anthologies, biographies, and a criticism section (which lists reference works, a special journal issue, reviews, monographs, articles, and Web resources). Some bibliographies may note additional resources, including archives and depositories or dissertations. Be aware that many of the bibliographies were last revised in the early 2000s, so it is a good idea to use them as a starting point and then search *MLA International Bibliography* and *Annual Bibliography of English Language and Literature* to identify more recent works.

Representing one of several author bibliographies on the Web, the ***Swift Criticism Database*** stands out for its ability to search the Ehrenpreis Centre for Swift Studies' entire critical studies holdings by multiple fields, including author, title, keyword, and full text, and to limit by a specific date or year range. A full-text search for *satire*, for example, retrieved 456 records, which are displayed alphabetically by author. Selected records may be saved to a watchlist; however, the help instructions are available only in German, so it isn't obvious what function this feature will serve. The entire bibliography is also available as a 347-page PDF, last updated in January 2011.

Two important reference tools assist scholars with identifying unknown authors in the eighteenth-century periodicals, the *European Magazine* and the *Gentleman's Magazine*. ***Attributions of Authorship in the Gentleman's Magazine*** presents an online version of James M. Kuist's *The Nichol's File of the Gentleman's Magazine: Attributions of Authorship and Other Documentation in Editorial Papers at the Folger Library*. This database features almost 14,000 attributions that were taken from marginal annotations in the Folger Library's copy of the periodical that can be searched by keyword and limited by title or date range, or browsed by volume. Emily Lorraine de Montluzin also created two updates, "Attributions of Authorship in the Gentleman's Magazine, 1731–1868: A Supplement to Kuist," which offers 4,000 new and corrected attributions to the original list, and "A Synthesis of Finds Appearing Neither in Kuist's *Nichol's File* Nor in de Montluzin's *A Supplement to Kuist*," which contains 1,850 additional attributions. De Montluzin's updates can be searched or browsed separately, or in conjunction with Kuist's list. Be sure to consult the introductions for each database, as they contain information about the journal's publishing history, as well as important advice for searching effectively.

Attributions of Authorship in the European Magazine, 1782–1826 is also de Montluzin's work and has 2,074 "known attributions of authorship of anonymous, pseudonymous, or incompletely attributed articles, letters, reviews, and poems" from the journal. The introduction covers problems of attribution, the contributors and leading reviewers, contributions of Anna Jane Vardill, the magazine's final years, and search instructions; the database can be searched by keyword, author, title, and date range, or browsed by individual volume.

Designed as an online companion to the *Norton Anthology of English Literature*, **Norton Topics Online** offers contextual essays and other material to support studying literature throughout seven time periods, from the Middle Ages to the twentieth century. The "Restoration and 18th Century" section is concerned with literary, historical, and cultural developments in England and then Great Britain from 1660 to 1785. An introduction to the period is provided, and four topical subsections outline a typical day in eighteenth-century London, the British slave trade, a fascination with the idea of other worlds, and the creation of empire through travel and trade. Each of these subsections features related texts, study questions, a selection of annotated Web resources, and illustrations. For example, The "A Day in 18th Century London" subsection presents excerpted primary texts describing activities during the morning, afternoon, evening, and night, including the cries of London, a visit to the coffee house, and Vauxhall pleasure garden, by Addison, Boswell, Dodsley, Garretson, Jordan, Smollett, Swift, the *Female Tatler*, and the *Gentleman's Magazine*, with many illustrations by Hogarth, and others of London places and personalities. The "Plurality of Worlds" subsection has texts related to the microscope, telescope, reactions to the new philosophy, and the expanding universe, with contributions from Addison, Duck, and Sterne. For studies focused on the later eighteenth century, the "Romantic Period" section has five subsections about tourism and the Romantic landscape, the Gothic, the French revolution, orientalism, and the satanic and Byronic hero, each with related texts, questions, Web resources, and illustrations.

Complementing the contextual material is an online archive of public-domain texts from earlier editions of the *Norton Anthology of English Literature*, which can be accessed by a chronological table of contents or author's last name. Many canonical authors are represented, including works by Addison, Collins, Crabbe, Defoe, Goldsmith, Gray, Johnson, Pope, Prior, Sheridan, Steele, Sterne, Swift, and Thomson. If you are interested in tracing the popularity and canonization of texts throughout time, the "Publications Chronology" lets you identify when particular works were added or dropped from specific editions of the anthology, beginning with the first edition in 1962, through the seventh in 2000. Finally, the online archive also contains audio recordings of various works being read aloud, from Gray's "Elegy Written in a Country Churchyard" to Anna Laetitia Barbauld's "The Rights of Woman." Like the print anthology, *Norton Topics Online* is an engaging introduction to the major texts, themes, and topics of English literature during the eighteenth century.

CURRENT AWARENESS SOURCES AND ASSOCIATIONS

American Society for Eighteenth-Century Studies. Winston-Salem, NC: Wake Forest University. asecs.press.jhu.edu (accessed 28 August 2012).

Battigelli, Anna, and Eleanor Shevlin. *Early Modern Online Bibliography: EEBO, ECCO, and Burney Collection Online.* earlymodernonlinebib.word press.com (accessed 28 August 2012).

British Society for Eighteenth-Century Studies. www.bsecs.org.uk (accessed 28 August 2012).

C18-L: Resources for 18th-Century Studies across the Disciplines. www .personal.psu.edu/special/C18/c18-l.htm (accessed 28 August 2012).

cfp.english.upenn.edu: eighteenth century. Philadelphia: University of Penn-sylvania. call-for-papers.sas.upenn.edu/category/eighteenth_century (accessed 28 August 2012).

The Defoe Society. www.defoesociety.org (accessed 28 August 2012).

Early Modern Commons. commons.earlymodernweb.org (accessed 28 August 2012).

Eighteenth-Century Ireland Society/Cumann Éire san Ochtú Céad Déag. www.ecis.ie (accessed 28 August 2012).

Eighteenth-Century Scottish Studies Society. www.ecsss.org (accessed 28 August 2012).

International Gothic Association. www.iga.stir.ac.uk (accessed 28 August 2012).

International Society for Eighteenth-Century Studies. www.isecs.org (accessed 28 August 2012).

Johnson Society of London. www.johnsonsocietyoflondon.org (accessed 28 August 2012).

The Long Eighteenth. long18th.wordpress.com (accessed 28 August 2012).

Society for the Study of Early Modern Women. www.ssemw.org (accessed 1 August 2012).

It's hard to imagine how we would know what was happening in eighteenth-century literary studies without the Web. Listservs and online calls for con-ference papers and journal submissions have long been part of the academic scene. Blogs are a newer development that add another dimension to net-working between colleagues, bringing to the forefront individuals' opinions, as well as critical developments, trends, and issues pertinent to the field as a whole. Associations continue to be a vital means through which scholars connect to colleagues with similar interests and through which the field advances new scholarship by supporting conferences, seminars, grants, fellowships, and society journals and publications. The Web enables these associations to reach out to a wider audience and promote their activities and resources to existing and potential members. In addition to the current awareness sources described in this section, be sure to consult chapter 5 for advice on using table of contents alerts to stay informed about new scholarship in eighteenth-century literary studies.

One of the best ways to be cognizant of developments in the field is to subscribe to *C18-L: Resources for 18th-Century Studies across the Disciplines*. This international and interdisciplinary listserv was founded in 1990, and it continues to serve scholars interested in the long eighteenth century, from approximately 1660 to 1830. Like many academic listservs, the content may range from debates about current issues to research questions regarding specific texts or recommendations for reading or teaching. The listserv also posts notices about upcoming conferences, calls for papers, grants, and fellowships, as well as journal tables of contents. Hosted by Pennsylvania State University, the archive may be searched by keyword, subject line, author's address, or date. In addition to providing information on subscribing to the listserv, the website also features a "Selected Readings" bibliography, published as monthly and quarterly installments from 1992 to 2006, that can be searched by single keyword, as well as links to James E. May's bibliographies (described earlier in the chapter in the section about *BibSite*).

You can either browse the website or subscribe via RSS feeds to **cfp .english.upenn.edu: eighteenth century** to identify upcoming conferences, essay collections, and journal issues in which you might want to present your work. Entries are posted as received and contain the title, dates, contact person and organization, and contact email; some conference entries also list keynote or plenary speakers and their affiliations. The "Read More" link presents the full description, instructions, and assigned cfp categories. A survey of recent postings in the eighteenth-century category includes several conferences, for example, "Cannibals: Cannibalism, Consumption, and Culture," "Devils and Dolls: Dichotomous Depictions of 'The Child,'" "'By the Author of David Simple': New Approaches to Sarah Fielding," "Searching for Authority: Rebellious Readers in Early Modern Texts (1640–1740)," an essay collection on detective and mystery fiction, and calls from the *European Journal of Life Writing*. Depending on your particular research interests, you may want to examine other cfp categories as well, from "Bibliography and History of the Book" to "Cultural Studies and Historical Approaches," or "Gender Studies and Sexuality" to "Graduate Conferences," "Theatre," and "Travel Writing."

Many societies are devoted to studies of the eighteenth century or the early modern period. Rather than being focused solely on literature, these organizations often approach the period from multiple disciplinary perspectives. The **American Society for Eighteenth-Century Studies (ASECS)** was established in 1969, to cultivate interdisciplinary scholarship that addresses the late seventeenth through early nineteenth centuries. The society's website presents information about the annual meeting and calls for papers for the upcoming conference; a link to subscribe to the ASECS listserv (but no searchable archives); links to their quarterly journal, *Eighteenth-Century Studies*, and their annual publication, *Studies in Eighteenth-Century Culture*; membership information; and a list of awards, prizes, travel grants, and fellowships. A "Weekly Announcements" section keeps members and visitors up to date with information about related conferences, seminars, and other society meetings, in addition to job openings, new publications, exhibits, and prizes. Links to affiliated societies and related organizations, including the American Historical Association, Modern Language Association, and Society for French Studies, among many others, round out the resources available on this site.

The **British Society for Eighteenth-Century Studies (BSECS)** was founded a few years after ASECS, in 1971, with the aim of promoting the study of eighteenth-century history, culture, and society, not only as manifested in Britain, but worldwide. Like ASECS, they foster multidisciplinary and interdisciplinary research, ranging from art and dance history to music and literature, and from politics and medicine to science and theatre. On their website, you will find information about the general annual conference, the postgraduate conference, and related conferences and events, as well as a link to the *Journal for Eighteenth-Century Studies*, with notices on special thematic issues. BSECS sponsors the Digital Eighteenth-Century Prize for "innovative digital resources," which was awarded to *William Godwin's Diary* in 2012 (godwindiary.bodleian.ox.ac.uk/index2.html). Other prizes, fellowships, and awards are also described. An extensive "Reviews of Events" section currently features thirty-eight reviews of music, fine art, theatre, and media events, and the site also offers links to related academic institutions, societies, specialist links for literature and art, and general eighteenth-century resources.

Scholars whose work is concerned with Irish or Scottish authors, in particular, may also want to investigate the resources on these nationally focused eighteenth-century studies societies' websites. The **Eighteenth-Century Ireland Society/Cumann Éire san Ochtú Céad Déag** was founded in 1986, to promote the study of life in Ireland from 1690 to 1800. The society hosts an annual conference and publishes the journal *Eighteenth-Century Ireland/Iris* *an dá chultúr* (discussed in chapter 5). Information about membership, past conferences and upcoming events, the journal, travel fellowships, and society officers are posted on the website.

The **Eighteenth-Century Scottish Studies Society** presents similar content about membership and their annual conference on their website, including a call for papers for the 2013 joint conference with the International Adam Smith Society, entitled "Scotland, Europe, and Empire in the Age of Adam Smith and Beyond." A listing of forthcoming and past conferences back to 1988 is also provided. The "Publications" section contains an overview of titles in the *Studies in Eighteenth-Century Scotland* series, published by Bucknell University Press (volume 1 published in 1992 to the present), as well as other books and special journal issues related to period studies of Scotland.

The **International Society for Eighteenth-Century Studies** (ISECS) is affiliated with many national eighteenth-century organizations, and it encourages study and research related to all aspects of eighteenth-century cultural heritage in every country. The ISECS website offers updates about recent activities; details about the society's international congress, which is held every four years; information about national, regional, and associated societies; and information on new publications. Graduate students and recent graduates may be particularly interested in the ISECS International Seminars for early career scholars, which are held every year. Past seminars have explored "Enlightenment Liberties," "Europe and the Colonial World," and "The Body and Its Images." A "News" section provides details about forthcoming conferences, calls for articles, cultural activities, awards and grants, employment opportunities, and promotional offers from publishers. The "Research" section contains a list of English and foreign-language journals for studying the eighteenth-century, a selection of online research tools, a list of research centers in ten countries, and a link to the *C18* listserv. Together with the other society websites, the ISECS site will keep scholars well-informed about conferences, fellowships, events, and resources relevant for eighteenth-century studies.

Specialized societies, whether for specific genres, groups, or individual authors, or related disciplines, are another means to identify pertinent resources. The **Society for the Study of Early Modern Women** (SSEMW) represents scholars from a broad range of disciplines who investigate women's contributions to the "cultural, political, economic, or social spheres of the early modern period," here roughly defined as 1450 to 1750. This active society sponsors sessions at numerous professional meetings. These include the Modern Language Association; American Historical Association; Renaissance Society of America; and Sixteenth-Century Studies, where they hold their annual business meeting. Members can subscribe to the listserv, and searchable archives are posted from October 1996 to the present. The "Awards" section describes previous winners for a distinguished book, essay, or journal article; scholarly edition; translation or teaching edition; graduate student's conference presentation; collaborative project; and art and media project. SSEMW also offers travel grants for graduate students and presents calls for submissions to volume series and journals.

The scope of the **International Gothic Association (IGA)** spans from the mid-eighteenth century to the present and covers all aspects of Gothic culture, including literature, art, music, film, architecture, popular culture, and technology. The IGA website features membership information; details regarding the society's biennial conference and jointly sponsored sessions with other organizations, such as the British Society for the Study of Romanticism and the North American Society for Studies in Romanticism; a student blog; news about related conferences, symposia, and publications (with an archive from 2008–present); and a description of the journal *Gothic Studies*, with tips on writing, editing, and reviewing for the journal. An extensive directory points to related Gothic resources focused on literature, authors and texts, calls for papers, university courses (postgraduate and undergraduate), websites, journals, publishers, and miscellaneous Gothic links. Remember to consult *Literary Research and the British Romantic Era: Strategies and Sources* for additional suggestions, especially if researching later eighteenth-century authors.

The Defoe Society was founded in 2006, to foster exchanges between Defoe scholars around the world and promote the study of this author and his works. In addition to the standard information about membership and the society's biennial meeting (and related past conferences), the website presents a wealth of Defoe resources. Here you will find a brief biography with recommended reading; an extensive yearly bibliography of primary sources, as well as books, book chapters, scholarly journal articles, and dissertations and theses; descriptions of significant library collections at McMaster University and the Lilly Library, Indiana University; a list of pedagogical resources; and information about subscribing to the society's listserv. Further resources include a link to the peer-reviewed journal *Digital Defoe* and Web links of interest for studying Defoe and the eighteenth century.

In existence since 1928, the long-standing **Johnson Society of London** is comprised of international members interested in Johnson's life and works, as well as those of his circle and contemporaries, such as James Boswell, Fanny Burney, Samuel Richardson, and Richard Sheridan. The society posts programs for the seven meetings held each year on its website. Papers given at these events have addressed topics specific to Johnson (Johnson and female education; Johnson, Wesley, Cowper, and dissent; causes of Johnson's poor eyesight), in addition to more general subjects, such as the Bluestockings, books and their readers in the eighteenth century, and criminal conversation. These papers are published in the society's annual journal, the *New Rambler*, along with articles, book reviews, and tables of contents from 1967 to 2004. Other features include an annual essay competition; a bibliography of suggested reading, standard editions, biographies, journals, and bibliographies; and links to related Web sources.

Blogs are a more recent way to stay informed of current issues and developments in the eighteenth-century studies community. *The Long Eighteenth* came about when members of the *C18-L* listserv (described earlier in this section) wanted to initiate an alternative forum for discussing eighteenth-century topics. The proposition was a successful one, as the blog has been active since August 2006. In addition to browsing the posts by month and year, you can also retrieve them by subject (e.g., academic life, criticism, digital humanities, gender, history, print culture, profession, teaching, theatre, Web resources). Recent posts have addressed a closed colloquium presentation format for an upcoming ASECS conference, researching without regular access to *ECCO*, and John Locke on gay marriage. Links to other eighteenth-century resources are presented in the following categories: general eighteenth-century sites, text resources, blogs, book reviews, digital humanities, early modern links, "Fun 18th Century Stuff," philosophy and theory, Romanticism, and teaching and pedagogy.

The *Early Modern Online Bibliography: EEBO, ECCO, and Burney Collection Online* has a decidedly narrower focus: "to facilitate scholarly feedback and discussion pertaining to valuable online text-bases for the humanities," especially as it pertains to teaching and research. Created by Anna Battigelli at SUNY Plattsburgh and Eleanor Shevlin at West Chester, University of Pennsylvania, the blog archives begin in May 2009; recent discussions have considered building digital humanities networks, *18thConnect*, and National Endowment for the Humanities Digital Humanities Start-Up Grants. More than just a blog, this site offers a bibliography of articles about early modern digital bibliography and scholarship, a list of the Burney digitized periodicals with dates of coverage, James May's article about teaching with *ECCO*, and an annotated catalogue of Renaissance translations from 1473 to 1640. Additional material covers links for conferences and talks; "EEBO Interactions"; online bibliographies; digital and transcribed text collections, projects, panels, and societies; and other early modern and eighteenth-century blogs.

Finally, *Early Modern Commons* will help you to identify even more blogs, since it aggregates those concerned with the period from 1500 to 1800. Compiled into a database, the blog descriptions may be searched by keyword or browsed by broadly assigned topic areas (e.g., c18th, drama, gender, music, poetry, sources). Each blog entry provides the title, the creator(s), a brief content note, a feed of recent posts to help you in determining relevancy, a link to the blog, and assigned tags. The "c18th" category currently contains forty-five blogs, representing the cultural, historical, and social on both sides of the Atlantic, including "18th Century Blog" (fashion and culture of the 1700s), "Blog-stockings" (researching and teaching the eighteenth century), "Georgian London" (1660–1836 London, with an emphasis on immigrants and artisans), "Infamous Scribblers" (eighteenth-century female writers, artists, performers), and "The Duchess of Devonshire's Gossip Guide to the 18th Century" ("scandalous tidbits"). Whether informative or distracting, *Early Modern Commons* features a blog feast for connecting you to various eighteenth-century studies communities.

CULTURAL AND HISTORICAL SOURCES

Connected Histories: British History Sources, 1500–1900. www.connected histories.org (accessed 28 August 2012).

European History Primary Sources. primary-sources.eui.eu (accessed 28 August 2012).

Hacken, Richard, *EuroDocs: Online Sources for European History.* Provo, UT: Brigham Young University. eudocs.lib.byu.edu/index.php/Main_Page (accessed 28 August 2012).

Halsall, Paul. *Internet Modern History Sourcebook.* Bronx, NY: Fordham University. www.fordham.edu/halsall/mod/modsbook.asp (accessed 28 August 2012).

London Lives: 1690–1800—Crime, Poverty, and Social Policy in the Metropolis. www.londonlives.org (accessed 28 August 2012).

Ludwig, Katelyn. *Reinventing the Feminine: Bluestocking Women Writers in 18th-Century London.* www.katelynludwig.com/masters/index.html (accessed 28 August 2012).

Moore, Lisa L. *The Sister Arts: British Gardening, Painting, and Poetry, 1700–1832.* Austin: University of Texas at Austin. www.en.utexas.edu/Classes/Moore/index.htm (accessed 28 August 2012).

Muri, Allison, director. *The Grub Street Project: Topographies of Literature and Culture in Eighteenth-Century London.* Saskatoon, Saskatchewan, Canada: University of Saskatchewan. grubstreetproject.net (accessed 28 August 2012).

National Portrait Gallery. www.npg.org.uk (accessed 28 August 2012).

Vive la difference! The English and French Stereotype in Satirical Prints, 1720–1815. www.fitzmuseum.cam.ac.uk/gallery/viveladifference/index .html (accessed 28 August 2012).

Whether your research interests are interdisciplinary or if you want to en-hance a particular nonliterary element in your work, the Internet offers a rich selection of cultural and historical sources for placing eighteenth-century literature in context. Both primary and secondary sources are available for textual and visual investigations, covering history and social history, politics, philosophy, art, music, fashion, science, and more. This section presents a "tasting menu" of websites, rather than a comprehensive overview, to illus-trate the different types of disciplinary eighteenth-century projects available. Be sure to check the Web gateways described at the beginning of this chapter, for example, *Early Modern Resources* and *Eighteenth-Century Resources*, or watch for announcements of new projects on the listservs, blogs, and associa-tion sites, to identify additional cultural and historical materials relevant to your individual research needs.

Resources for studying British and other national histories are widely rep-resented on the Web. ***Connected Histories: British History Sources, 1500–1900*** provides an important service by enabling scholars to cross-search multiple digital resources concerned with Britain during the early modern period and nineteenth century. This website provides access to fifteen digital collections that may be searched simultaneously, including *British History Online*; *British Museum Images*; *British Newspapers, 1600–1900*; *Cause Papers in the Diocesan Courts of the Archbishopric of York, 1300–1858*; the *Charles Booth Archive*; the *Clergy of the Church of England Database, 1540–1835*; the *Convict Transportation Registers Database*; *House of Com-mons Parliamentary Papers*; *John Foxe's The Acts and Monuments Online*; the *John Johnson Collection of Printed Ephemera*; *John Strype's Survey of London Online*; *London Lives: 1690–1800*; *Nineteenth-Century British Pamphlets*; *Origins.net*; and *The Proceedings of the Old Bailey, 1674–1913*. A few of these collections are subscription only; however, you will still be able to search the content and preview the results, even if your library doesn't have access.

The "Resources" page features descriptions of each digital collection, in-cluding its scope, strengths and weaknesses, source types (e.g., maps/images, local records, books, pamphlets, printed ephemera), and access arrangement. Since the indexing emphasizes people and places, there are search fields for these categories, such as full name, given name, and family name, and users have the ability to search by keyword and date, with opportunities to filter by source type, one or more resource collections, and access. Search results are listed by individual resource, and matching entries within the collection are displayed in a snippet view. Clicking on an individual result will link to the digital resource. For example, a place search on *Suffolk* limited to the eighteenth century and freely available resources retrieved 3,945 matches in nine collections.

Numerous research guides offer detailed overviews for topical access to the collections and outline specific search strategies. They also highlight individual collections; discuss strengths and limitations for researching that topic; and list books for further reading, as well as related websites. These guides address crime and justice, family history, the history of London, imperial and colonial history, local history, Parliamentary history, poverty and poor relief, religious history, and searching for images. *Connected Histories* will be valuable to scholars investigating the political, social, and religious history of eighteenth-century Britain.

One of the most notable resources included in *Connected Histories* is ***London Lives: 1690–1800—Crime, Poverty, and Social Policy in the Metropolis***. Designed to provide insight into the lives of working and lower-class Londoners during the eighteenth century, *London Lives* is a searchable database of 240,000 digitized manuscript pages from the archival holdings of selected parishes (St. Botolph Aldgate, St. Clement Danes, St. Dionis Backchurch), sources of criminal records (Bridewell Royal Hospital, Home Office, Old Bailey Proceedings, City of London Sessions, Middlesex Sessions, Westminster Sessions), coroners (City of London, Middlesex, Westminster), and hospitals and guilds (Carpenters' Company, St. Thomas's Hospital), in addition to fifteen datasets pertaining to the period. These include directories; wills; fire insurance parish, and workhouse registers; and tax records.

Records can be searched by keyword, with limits by specific document type, individual archive, and date. A separate "Person Name Search" allows for searching of tagged surnames and forenames in the collection, with metaphone options available to account for names that sound similar. Individual archive records can also be browsed by document type and decade. Search results are displayed as brief records and link to the full transcription, as well as to the digitized document, which can be enlarged for easier reading. Before searching, it may be helpful to consult the historical background pages, which introduce the following subjects: local government, criminal justice, poor relief and charity, and guilds and hospitals. They also offer thematic research guides about interpreting an eighteenth-century manuscript and investigating apprentices, bastardy, crime, illness, poverty, and work.

The site also features guides to the thirty-nine specific types of documents included in the collection, from parish account books to biographies of executed convicts, and from coroners' inquests into suspicious deaths to parish apprenticeship indentures and registers, that discuss the material's context and offer a bibliography of recommended introductory reading. All of these resources are brought together to reconstruct the lives of thousands of individual Londoners, presented as both completed biographies and those in progress, which can be accessed alphabetically by name or by assigned keywords (e.g., beggar, coachman, gypsies, insane, pleading the belly, suicide, transportation). *London Lives* does much to vividly re-create the world of eighteenth-century London.

Aiming to understand the city as "topography and as 'social text,'" *The Grub Street Project: Topographies of Literature and Culture in Eighteenth-Century London* focuses on print culture and literary representations of London during the period. To accomplish this goal, the project features a map and image gallery of Horwood's map of London (1799), Strype's maps of London and its wards (1720), and Strype's illustrations of London's buildings and gates. Adding to these sources are several literary mapping experiments, including Pope's *The Dunciad* (1729 variorum text) and locations where Ned Ward's publications were sold, as well as where feminist and women's rights publications were sold (as identified through *ESTC* subject searches). The site also presents student mapping projects from an English class entitled "The Geography of London's Imaginary Spaces in the 18th Century," featuring texts by Boswell, Gay, Pope, Smollett, Swift, and Wilmot. This is definitely a work in progress, as several sections are without content; however, more additions are planned, and the project director, Allison Muri, welcomes submissions for digital editions of texts published or sold in London during the eighteenth century, tours of texts or events featuring eighteenth-century London, and biographies of people living and working in London during this time.

European History Primary Sources (*EHPS*) serves as a portal to scholarly digital repositories of primary source material for studying individual European countries, as well as for studying Europe as a single entity. Indexing the digital collections of major national libraries, but also smaller digitization projects, *EHPS* may be browsed by country (United Kingdom, Ireland), language, period (18th century), subject (e.g., literary, gender, cultural, political, urban, rural), and type of source (archival documents, books, cartoons, manuscripts, maps, newspapers, statistics), or searched by keyword or assigned tags. The United Kingdom collection currently contains twenty resources, including some that are part of *Connected Histories*, and others like *The First Industrial Revolution*, the William Blake Archive, *Key 17th, 18th, to 19th century Geological Literature*, and the Internet Library of Early Journals.

EuroDocs: Online Sources for European History is another gateway to freely available primary sources on the Web. Covering transcribed, facsimile, and translated historical documents, the links are arranged by broad time periods, for example, "Medieval and Renaissance Europe" and "Europe as a Supranational Region," and by country. The "History of the United Kingdom" section offers more refined period access, with a subcategory for "Britain 1689–1815," as well as subcategories for legal and government documents, as well as regional, local, and family history, whereas the "History of Scotland" section combines all resources in order based on time period. Scholars whose work focuses on Ireland will want to review this section as well. More than fifty sources are presented for eighteenth-century Britain (including England, Scotland, and Wales), and each entry notes the period covered and type of primary source available. You will find collections related to naval history, the Jacobites, Parliament and the slave trade, Sir Isaac Newton's correspondence, printed images, and more. *EuroDocs* is maintained by Richard Hacken, the European studies bibliographer at the Harold B. Lee Library at Brigham Young University.

The ***Internet Modern History Sourcebook*** features primary source texts and links to external documents to support studying European, American, and Latin American history from the time of the Reformation through the twenty-first century. Emphasis on the sourcebook as a pedagogical tool is realized by introductory sections on how to use primary sources and the nature of historiography, as well as a comprehensive overview of other sites for historical information. The main body is arranged in chronological and thematic sections; those addressing the eighteenth century span several sections, including "The Early Modern World," "Everyday Life," "Constitutionalism," "Scientific Revolution," "Enlightenment," "American Independence," "French Revolution," "Industrial Revolution," "Romanticism," "Conservative Order," "Nationalism," and "Liberalism." Each section lists relevant sources, noting the author, date, and provider within thematic subsections. For example, the "Enlightenment" section addresses precursors; the Enlightenment as propaganda; political analysis; the evaluation of the human condition; economics; philosophy; attitudes; social setting; complete digital texts; and "Religion in an Age of Reason," covering rational Christianity, evangelicalism, Catholic pietism, and Jewish responses. Although you will have to scan through potentially relevant sections to identify specifically eighteenth-century sources, the range of material available makes the hunt worthwhile.

Comprised of a series of brief, illustrated, hyperlinked essays, ***Reinventing the Feminine: Bluestocking Women Writers in 18th-Century London*** was developed as a media arts master's project by Katelyn Ludwig to portray the historical and social context of the Bluestocking movement. Five major sections cover eighteenth-century London, the development of the literary salon, the Bluestocking circle, circle members, and writing and print culture. Within these overview sections, thematic essays address such topics as monarchy and Parliament, gender roles, philanthropic activities, group meetings, and the Cultural Revolution. Biographies and images (where available) introduce twelve members of the circle, and images are also presented for many of their associates and supporters. Rounding out the site are excerpts from letters and other writings by Frances Boscawen, Catherine Graham, Elizabeth Montagu, Hannah More, Sarah Scott, Anna Seward, and Hester Thrale, in addition to a bibliography focused on multimedia design theory and sources used to create the site.

Although some of the content is available only to University of Texas at Austin students and scholars, *The Sister Arts: British Gardening, Painting, and Poetry, 1700–1832* still offers enough freely available material to provide a solid introduction to the topic. Described as sister arts because "they were considered to achieve similar effects on readers and viewers," the interrelationship between garden design, painting, and poetry is explored here through six thematic sections: "Beautiful," "Gothic," "Neoclassical," "Picturesque," "Romantic," and "Sublime." Following an overview for each section, brief introductions and accompanying images investigate architecture, painting, poetry, and landscapes and gardens, some with excerpts of garden descriptions from source texts by Jane Austen, William Gilpin, Batty Langley, William Shenstone, Horace Walpole, Joseph Warton, Thomas Whately, and others, and poetry by Addison, Blake, Coleridge, Cowley, Dalton, Darwin, Davies, Gray, Pope, Radcliffe, Seward, Taylor, Thomson, and Warton. Paintings and photographs further illustrate architectural features and buildings, garden plans, and thematic elements. Attention is also devoted to Mary Delany, the eighteenth-century garden designer and artist. *The Sister Arts* was created by Lisa L. Moore, associate professor of English and women's and gender studies.

Vive la difference! The English and French Stereotype in Satirical Prints, 1720–1815 is an online exhibit based on a 2007 show at the Fitzwilliam Museum, at the University of Cambridge. Featuring prints by artists Gatine, Gillray, Hogarth, Roehn, and Woodward, and publishers Genty, Martinet, and de La Mésangère, the exhibit explores relations between England and France during almost a century of cross-cultural influence and conflict. Introductory essays provide a historical grounding for the prints, which are displayed according to views from England and views from France. Each print or etching is presented with contextual details and can be enlarged. Some of the English prints satirize French fashion, the French revolution, and Sans-Culottes, and French prints make fun of English tourists, fashion, sensibility, and the English character. The exhibit also contains an overview of engraving, etching, aquatint, lithography, and hand-coloring techniques, as well as descriptions of selected publishers located in London and Paris.

The **National Portrait Gallery's** holdings consist of more than 175,000 portraits of well-known British men and women from the sixteenth century to the present. Paintings, drawings, sculpture, and photographs illustrate not only famous people, but also the changing nature of dress and customs throughout time, as well as the art of portraiture itself. An advanced search feature lets you explore the collections by person, with fields for role (either sitter or artist), gender, profession, professional category (e.g., individuals, literature, journalism, publishing, royalty, rulers, aristocracy), group (e.g., artist groupings, countries and counties, family tree), specific catalog, and whether living or deceased, and by portrait, with fields for title, portrait number, dates created, medium (e.g., drawing, miniature, painting, print), subjects and themes (e.g., activity, dress, genre, location), portrait set, and specific collection, and several limits, including images available on the website. With this control, you can search all media created between 1700 and 1799 (for example, that represent dancing, or female authors and publishers, active during the same period).

In addition to conducting searches, you can browse the collection highlights by time period. The "Georgian and Regency Portraits" selection covers works from 1714 to 1837, displayed in chronological order, which includes images of Fanny Burney, Robert Burns, Samuel Johnson, Alexander Pope, Mary Wollstonecraft, and many other famous artists, writers, musicians, aristocrats, scientists, explorers, and military figures. A rotating "Display" section presents online exhibits by theme. If you are interested in fashion, in particular, you can view the collections by specific dress accessory, ranging from eyeglasses and spectacles to jewelry, and from hats and head attire to masks and disguises. The National Portrait Gallery collections, consulted in conjunction with the British Museum image collections (one of the resources in the previously described *Connected Histories*), provide unparalleled access for enhancing textual research with visual material and bring eighteenth-century British literary themes and figures to life.

CONCLUSION

Although the momentum with which academic resources are transferred to an online environment seems likely only to accelerate, the majority of these resources are currently restricted by commercial subscriptions. Nevertheless, the open Web continues to gain in importance as the medium for both individual and organizational projects that enrich the study of literature, as well as countless other subjects. As illustrated by this chapter, freely available Web resources present the full text of classic literary texts, as well as many other examples of eighteenth-century print culture, from periodicals and pamphlets, to broadside ballads, miscellanies, and historical records, that can be searched in ways previously unimaginable. Standard reference tools like bibliographies, indexes, chronologies, and encyclopedias are available in electronic format to facilitate the study of select authors and works and provide historical or disciplinary context. Associations promote their mission and attract new members and serve current ones through online forums and publications, and blogs bring eighteenth-century literary scholars together in new and exciting communities.

The open Web continues to contribute in multiple and very positive ways to the development of the field, and it will likely become a more prominent player. The resources described here can help you begin your exploration of the Web's eighteenth-century studies scholarly projects and apply your search skills and evaluation criteria to identify and assess additional sources as you discover them. Subscription databases and print tools will still be the backbone of your research; however, the Web can enhance your work and be an asset by delivering complementary resources. In this regard, think of the Web as the research frontier, full of possibility.

Chapter Ten

Researching a Thorny Problem

For she was a rambling woman with very little tast of wit or humor, as appears by her writings.

> —Jonathan Swift, in a 1732 letter about Mary Davys[1]

Mrs. D. wrote several bawdy Novels, and *The Northern Heiress*.

> —*Grub-Street Journal*, July 15, 1731[2]

But I beg of such to suspend their uncharitable Opinions, till they have read what I have writ.

> —Mary Davys, in her "Preface" to *The Works of Mrs Davys*[3]

Research on a lesser-known literary figure can, in itself, be a thorny problem. Throughout this volume we have provided an overview of sources and search strategies, with advice about best practices, for advanced literary research on the eighteenth century. Traditional canonical figures are most likely to have standard editions and biographies; collected letters; and author-based bibliographies, companions, dictionaries, and encyclopedias. These resources constitute a foundation upon which scholarly inquiry can be built. When these don't exist, a literary researcher studying a lesser-known author can create his or her own knowledge base of the individual's life, works, contemporary reception, and history of scholarship in order to be able to speak and write authoritatively. Modern reprints and digital scans of eighteenth-century texts offer greater access to literary works that enhance scholarly opportunities. Many of these texts can be identified and found in library catalogs and subject-specific bibliographic databases, but a thorough, systematic process will enable a researcher to create the knowledge base as efficiently and effectively as possible. This process is not without frustrations, however, as will be seen, but it is our hope that it will be valuable as a model to follow.

Mary Davys (1674–1732) was an early eighteenth-century novelist (*The Reform'd Coquet, Familiar Letters betwixt a Gentleman and a Lady, The Accomplish'd Rake*) and playwright (*The Northern Heiress, or, the Humours of York*), contemporary with Eliza Haywood, Alexander Pope, and Jonathan Swift. She was largely forgotten until the mid-twentieth century, when her work began to be reprinted, and scholarly interest in her has increased steadily since. Probably born in Ireland, Davys was widowed by the time she was twenty-four and emigrated to London in 1700, where she began to write to support herself. In about 1704, she moved to York for a few years, where she wrote *The Northern Heiress*, and she then returned to London to see it performed in 1716. In 1718, Davys apparently earned enough money to open a coffee house in Cambridge, where she lived until she died. Although her literary output was relatively small, she is now identified as one of the authors who contributed to the development of the novel as a genre through her innovations and techniques. Davys is also studied for her themes related to gender roles, legitimacy, property, and politics, and she is appreciated for the wit and humor in her writing.[4]

The first step in creating a knowledge base for Mary Davys is to determine which research sources and strategies will contribute to the base, for example, biographies, eighteenth-century and modern editions, contemporary reception, overview of scholarship, and possibly known letters, diaries, and manuscripts. What are the titles, dates, and publishers of her works, and are modern editions available? How do we discover her reputation during her lifetime? What would a thorough literature review of scholarship related to her entail? Are there surviving letters, diaries, or manuscripts? Who are her contemporaries, and, chronologically, where does she fit in? Citations can be exported from most academic databases to bibliographic management software, such as EndNote, Zotero, or RefWorks, which can be used to generate bibliographies and keep the bibliographic data, links to electronic sources, PDFs, and any notes about and annotations for readings that are created in one location. The added value of using such software is that all the information, including the notes fields, are searchable, so that such information as names of characters and their traits and the definitions of terms can be stored in the record for the literary work. This practice enables a method for capturing and retrieving information and can function much as published author-based companions, encyclopedias, or dictionaries do for canonical figures.

Searching for resources by and about an author is generally a straightforward procedure, but there are some challenges, as we've noted throughout this volume. We looked for clues as we explored this topic to discover alternative strategies for finding relevant materials. Fortunately, the spelling of Davys's surname is relatively uncommon, so that searches by author, keyword, or subject in databases retrieve mostly relevant sources. Eighteenth-century publications, however, might be more problematic.

Jonathan Swift, who was a friend of Davys's husband, wrote her name as Davis in one letter, and we will see a different spelling found in an archive later in this chapter. It was once common not to publish the first names of women authors; therefore, a search on *mrs davys* might prove more useful at times. Her name might not be found in advertisements or contemporary commentary at all, but, instead, she may be referred to as *the author of.* In some instances from the eighteenth century, the spellings of titles were inconsistent, as with *The Reform'd Coquet*, at times spelled *Coquette*, so it would be wise to truncate *coquet**. As the long "s" in *The Northern Heiress, or, the Humours of York* offers challenges with some OCR'd text, alternative strategies could include trying *heirefs* or *heireff* ; truncating *heir**; combining other keywords from the title, like *York*, with *northern*; or searching *northern* in combination with *theatre* or the location where it was performed, Lincoln's Inn Fields. With an author who may have been little known during the first part of the century, especially for novelists who published before the Reviews came into being, searching for references in the books, periodicals, and newspapers will require patience and creative search strategies and may ultimately be fruitless.

IDENTIFYING EIGHTEENTH-CENTURY AND MODERN EDITIONS

When generating a list of eighteenth-century editions, it's best to start with the *English Short Title Catalogue, 1473–1800* (*ESTC*). Although *WorldCat* and *Copac*, the other major union catalogs to consult, contain records for both earlier, as well as modern, versions, there are many duplicate records that have to be sorted through, which can be frustrating at this early stage. An author keyword search in *ESTC* retrieves seventeen records, three for *The Amours of Alcippus and Lucippe* (1704), *The Fugitive* (1705), *The Northern Heiress* (1716), *The Reform'd Coquet* (1724, 1735, 1736, 1744, 1752, 1760, 1760?, 1763 in Dublin), *The Works of Mrs. Davys* (two imprints from 1725), *The Accomplished Rake* (1727, and two slightly different 1756 editions), and *The False Friend* (1732, a version of *The Cousins*). This is a solid initial list of her works. We will have to search elsewhere to discover the contents of *Works*, for those are not listed here. *ESTC* notes when surrogates are in the

Eighteenth Century microfilm collection (including reel number), in *Eighteenth Century Collection Online* (*ECCO*), in print, or in other formats. All but *The False Friend* and three editions of *The Reform'd Coquet* have no surrogates, but the records do indicate which libraries own copies. At present, *ESTC* does not have the option to export citations to a bibliographic management system, so the data from these records will need to be manually added or exported from *WorldCat* or *Copac*.

An author search in *WorldCat* retrieves more than 200 records, while *Copac* offers more than 170, for eighteenth-century and modern editions, anthologies, and microform and digital facsimiles. As *ESTC* didn't include the table of contents for *Works*, you can browse through the full records for that title to find items that contain the information. *WorldCat* has a record for a microfilm copy of *The False Friend*, which had no surrogates listed in *ESTC*, and might be available for borrowing via interlibrary loan. Frans De Bruyn's 1985 entry on Davys in the *British Novelists, 1660–1800* volume of the *Dictionary of Literary Biography*, discussed further later in this chapter, provides a list of titles, dates when first published or revised, and the modern editions available, including *The Accomplished Rake, The Reform'd Coquet,* and *Familiar Letters betwixt a Gentleman and a Lady*.[5] The last title, originally part of *Works* and reprinted in 1955, by the Augustan Reprint Society, was the first modern edition of any of Davys's writing. To complete the search for all available information about her works, you can check the *New Cambridge Bibliography of English Literatures*, the standard bibliography to works by and about authors; it does not, however, list Davys.

BIOGRAPHICAL INFORMATION

As no full biography was found in *WorldCat* or *Copac*, we turned to two standard biographical sources: *Oxford Dictionary of National Biography* (*ODNB*) and *Dictionary of Literary Biography* (*DLB*). *WorldCat* did have a record for Frans De Bruyn's essay in *British Novelists, 1660–1800*, mentioned earlier. Because Davys came from Ireland, we also consulted the *Dictionary of Irish Biography* (*DIB*). The brief entry in the earlier *Dictionary of National Biography* incorrectly places her as active in the mid-1750s, probably because the second edition of *The Accomplished Rake* was published then.[6] Although general English literary companions will offer basic biographical information, the lengthier discussions found in these three sources will give more detail, along with bibliographies to mine, the location of personal papers, and, if any exist, images of the individual. Davys is found in all three, but as there are no references to images or personal papers, it is unlikely that any exist.

These sources indicate that there are letters in which she is mentioned written by Jonathan Swift: he knew Davys's husband in Ireland, he was acquainted with her, and he sent her money. Both De Bruyn and *DIB* cite Swift's collected letters as sources. The only other contemporary accounts of her life are found in the prefaces she wrote for her literary works, where she included personal details.

If they exist, letters, diaries, and other personal papers would provide important insights. As already mentioned, none of the three biographical sources consulted referred to manuscripts or personal papers. Searching further, she is not listed in the *Location Register of English Literary Manuscripts and Letters: Eighteenth and Nineteenth Centuries*, or in the *National Register of Archives*, or *Archive Finder*, nor are there records to archives or manuscripts in *WorldCat* or the British Library manuscript collection. It is possible that there are unknown documents in libraries in York or Cambridge, where she spent most of her adult life, but, as she has become a source of scholarly inquiry, it is likely that other researchers have tried and failed to locate surviving documents.

In his early study on Davys, William H. McBurney undertook to discover anything he could about her coffee house. "According to the records of licenses issued by the vice chancellor of Cambridge University . . . a 'Widow Davies' received a license in 1718. Thereafter the name of 'Mary Davies' appears frequently in the registries."[7] Note that another possible spelling of her name comes to light in this description of the archival research on the author. Depending upon the research project, it might be useful to consult the *The Account Books of Jonathan Swift*, edited by Paul V. Thompson and Dorothy J. Thompson (1984), to locate the archives holding the account books, or to look for the archives for the Lincoln's Inn Fields, where *The Northern Heiress* was performed.

As little is known about Davys's life, to gain the fullest possible picture about her, the next steps in this quest would be to review Swift's letters and Davys's prefaces, and to read the items cited in the bibliographies found in the biographical essays. There are two editions of Swift's collected letters, both arranged chronologically: *The Correspondence of Jonathan Swift*, edited by Harold Williams, and *The Correspondence of Jonathan Swift, D. D.*, edited by David Woolley. Two editions of *Journal to Stella*, which also has letters from Swift and which is also edited by Williams, were published by Clarendon Press in 1948 and 1963.[8] It might be worth checking the *Journal to Stella* website, discussed in chapter 9, to see if Swift's letters with references to Davys are there as well. We'll discuss two of Swift's letters concerning Davys's death below; these two letters are also in *Electronic Enlightenment*. (Be aware that Swift actually received a letter after Mary Davys's death from another M. Davys.) After consulting Swift's letters, the next step will be to read the prefaces in the modern and facsimile editions identified earlier in the process and scour them for any additional autobiographical details.

CONTEMPORARY RECEPTION

Davys's prefaces and dedications also provide clues about the contemporary response to her work and her hopes for their reception. *The Fugitive* is dedicated to Mrs. Esther Johnson in Dublin, the woman also known as Swift's Stella; Isobel Grundy interprets "regular, professional dedicators" like Davys as evidence that they were "obviously interested in building brand-name recognition for themselves." She further notes that Davys, "who began by addressing useful contacts," including Esther Johnson and Queen Anne, later reached out more broadly when she dedicated her work "To the Ladies of Great Britain" and "To the Beaus of Great-Britain."[9]

Starting with her third publication, the 1716 printing of *The Northern Heiress*, Davys identifies herself as the author. In the preface to this play, she tells her audience of the "success it met with the third night, was (considering the Time of Year, and my own want of acquaintance), infinitely above what I had reason to expect; and as the town and the ladies in particular, have been pleas'd to favour my first attempt, it will make me more industrious to promote their diversion at a more convenient season." About opening night, she reports, "the first night, in which lay all the Danger, was attended with only two single hisses," and she goes on to describe her detractors.[10] *The London Stage*, a calendar of plays performed in London between 1660 and 1800, notes the receipts of her plays found in the archival records for Lincoln's Inn Fields; more research would need to be done to determine if the receipts reflect well upon the play's performance.[11]

Her second play, *The Self Rival*, never reached the stage. Although Mc-Burney notes that she suffered the "general prejudice against the works of 'female wits'; and in the prologue to the play, 'as it should have been acted at the Theatre-Royal in Drury Lane,' . . . she made the conventional but justified lament: When Women write, the Criticks, now-a-days Are ready, e'er they see, to damn their Plays," but in his opinion the play had "slight merit."[12]

In *The Reform'd Coquet*'s preface, where she is listed by name, but also, oddly, as the author of *The Humours of York* rather than *The Northern Heiress*, Davys explains that she was advised by two male friends to publish it by subscription, another form of patronage and promotion, which McBurney says was rarely the practice for novels. "The printed list of 169 subscribers at three shillings a copy includes 107 students, three duchesses (of Rutland, Richmond, and Albemarle), and the interesting trio of Mr. Gay, Mrs. Mar.

Blount, and Alexander Pope, Esq."[13] What this list says about her literary reputation is open to interpretation, but it is intriguing that she accomplished this attention with her fourth work, written several years after *The Northern Heiress*. The novel went on to be reprinted seven times after her death.

Scholars have found two contemporary commentators about Davys: Swift's letters and a *Grub-Street Journal* article. Looking up "Davys" in the index to Williams's multivolume *The Correspondence of Jonathan Swift* permits us to find the letters easily without knowing the dates. In his two letters to Benjamin Motte, a bookseller, referring to Davys death, Swift is engaging Motte's help with a problem that arose. Motte received a letter from Mr. Ewen, a brewer in Cambridge.[14] Ewen claimed to have inherited Davys's wealth and that he had in his possession several letters from Swift to Davys's husband and to her. Ewen subtly threatened to publish the letters, which angered Swift. Ewen subsequently wrote to Swift, stating that Davys had "pretended to have many years ago writ a book or part of a book," which the world attributed to Swift. Swift told Mott that it was more than thirty years since Davys's husband died and that he had only met the widow once or twice in London, and once in Cambridge. The letters to her husband "were common letters of friendship among young people" and were written to a man Swift "loved very well, but marryd very indiscreetly." He concludes "that either Ewen lyes, or the Printers would be much disappointed, for she was a rambling woman with very little tast of wit or humor, as appears by her writings."[15] Perhaps this response about her writing could be the result of anger at the situation in which he found himself, but as he didn't appear to esteem her in any of his letters, it is likely that he didn't appreciate her writing.

The other piece of contemporary perspective on Davys is an article published in the deliberately offensive *Grub-Street Journal*, on July 15, 1731, with a response from Davys in the next issue, on July 22, 1731. References to these articles were found in secondary sources but were difficult to find digitally. Although the *Grub-Street Journal* is available via *British Periodicals*, no search to find it by keywords proved successful. A combination of poor-quality typeface and images, in the case of Davys's reply so light as to be unreadable, plus the fact that most references to Davys were oblique, except referring to her as "Mrs. D. wrote several bawdy Novels, and *The Northern Heiress*," made searching challenging. We were able to find both articles by using the citations found in secondary sources to go directly to the issues. Because the *Grub-Street Journal* writer used innuendo and cultural references well known at the time, online OCR'd text cannot penetrate the language to retrieve relevant materials.

We conducted a wide variety of searches, using various techniques, to determine if we could identify undiscovered references to Davys in *ECCO, 17th and 18th Century Burney Collection Newspapers* (*Burney*), and *British Periodicals*. No death notice was found in *Gentleman's Magazine*, either through a keyword search or browsing the death notices at the time of her death. Most items retrieved were advertisements for her books and announcements for the performance of *The Northern Heiress*. Searches in *Burney*, which carries advertisements and announcements that appeared in such newspapers such as the *Daily Courant* and *Daily Post*, were more successful; searching *mrs davys* retrieved advertisements for *Works*, but because of the nature of promoting books at the time, this title was also listed in advertisements for books that were published later. The last ad was in 1736. Announcements for *The Northern Heiress* were finally found by searching *northern* and *theatre* in *Burney*, and limiting to the dates it had been performed in late April and early May 1716.

It takes a great deal of work to prove a negative, but we tentatively concluded that there are no other contemporary references to Davys's reputation in the literature from the time, tentatively because we don't know if we missed sources because of the poor quality of the typeface and images, and because of the use of opaque cultural references typical at that time. Searches in Google Books, Internet Archive, and HathiTrust Digital Library were no more fruitful, and she is not in *UK RED: The Experience of Reading in Britain, from 1450 to 1945*. The notes in the reprinted Pickering & Chatto *Grub-Street Journal, 1730–1733*, edited by Bertrand A. Goldgar, does indicate that the July 22 letter "is supposedly from Mrs. Mary Davys, in response to one pretending to be hers."[16] Unfortunately, no index is provided in this modern edition that would allow scholars to access the text and notes; online versions of these types of compilations would benefit researchers if the notes were searchable. Perhaps publishers of *ECCO*, *Burney*, and *British Periodicals* could partner with the Modern Language Association and Modern Humanities Research Association to develop scholarly projects that would add invaluable information, formerly the purview of scholarly editions, to digital collections.

REVIEW OF THE SCHOLARLY LITERATURE

A literature review serves two purposes: It can be part of a larger study, providing a foundation for the argument to be made and demonstrating understanding of the academic conversation to be entered, or it can be a freestanding article that can indicate future avenues of study by pointing out gaps in the literature, highlighting central or unresolved themes, bridging related or disparate areas, or identifying new perspectives.[17] A literature search is a crucial step in the literature review process, whereby a research question is formulated, relevant databases selected, keywords brainstormed, key scholars and works identified, and bibliographies mined. If working on a literary figure, genre, or theme that has been well studied, the scholarly output may be overwhelming, so it is best to focus on some aspect of the topic, for example, film adaptations of eighteenth-century novels. Our purpose here, however, is to build a knowledge base about Davys; we will use the literature review process as a means of systematically retrieving all secondary academic sources we can find on her and export the citations into a bibliographic management system where we can delete duplicates, keep links to online books and articles, and store PDFs. Our keywords will be *mary davys*, and we will search in the library catalog, union catalogs, and bibliographic reference books and databases.

We started the search in the literary bibliographic databases. Searching *mary dayvs* in both *MLA International Bibliography* (*MLAIB*) and *Annual Bibliography of English Language and Literature* (*ABELL*) retrieved several dozen references on the author, including the academic studies by Robert Day and William McBurney from the 1950s, and the first dissertations written on her from the early 1970s, Peter S. Stephenson's *Three Playwright-Novelists: The Contribution of Dramatic Techniques to Restoration and Early Eighteenth-Century Prose Fiction* and Donald H. Stefanson's *The Works of Mary Davys: A Critical Edition*. Both full-text dissertations are available online from *Dissertations and Theses Full Text*. To find useful information in *ABELL*, it is important to search either Davys's name both first-name-first and last-name-first, or use the *near* proximity operator to retrieve both at once: *mary near davys*.

Although *MLAIB* and *ABELL* generally index the literary articles found in full-text academic journal collections, new discoveries can be made by searching *Project Muse*, *JSTOR*, and *Periodicals Archives Online* directly, including book reviews, review essays, and articles in journals that are not indexed by the bibliographic databases. Searching *Dissertations and Theses Full Text* directly will also retrieve items that might not be found in the main literary databases, where Davys may be discussed as part of a larger study but is not mentioned in the title of the dissertation or abstract.

Because *WorldCat* and *Copac* have primary, as well as secondary, sources on Davys, we combined *mary davys* with *criticism* to narrow the results. This search in *WorldCat* retrieved a promising bibliographic reference resource, Robert Ignatius Letellier's *The English Novel, 1700–1740: An Annotated Bibliography*, which could have references not found elsewhere. For full-text searches in books, Google Books and HathiTrust are useful resources for finding references to Davys in monographs.

In the process of conducting a literature review search, it is helpful to see if any literature reviews have already been written on the topic. The *Year's Work in English Studies* may not identify any new sources, but the annual overview and analysis of scholarly works on authors, eras, and themes, found in this resource and in review articles generally, assist scholars in keeping abreast of trends in scholarly inquiry on the topic.

After this initial literature search, the next step is to evaluate the results and select the sources based on focus and coverage. As your research proceeds, it is important to continue to mine bibliographies to find additional relevant materials. To keep up with new scholarship, see if e-mail alert options, which generate automatic notifications of new content, are available. In some library catalogs and bibliographic databases, searches can be saved and alerts sent when new materials that meet the criteria of the search are added. Journal websites with alerts will send out notifications of new issues, including tables of contents, for those who register.

Even though scholars have proven that the works of Mary Davys deserve study and comparison with her contemporaries, there are large gaps in what we know about her and her reception during her lifetime. We are fortunate that her works were collected in the 1725 volume, for, as we have seen, nothing remains of her personal papers and manuscripts. Her books were available and advertised during her lifetime and in the decades after her death, but then largely forgotten for two centuries. She was a businesswoman, an educated woman, and a creative woman, who must have either had a library of her own or a community that shared their books, newspapers, and periodicals. As coffee houses were a source of communal sharing of such publications, we can speculate that such a venue provided her with access to the writings of her day.

Through the process we have described, of systematically creating an author-centered knowledge base, we learned a great deal about what is known of Davys. We have also identified editions of her works and begun to build a bibliography of her critical heritage. We have exhausted the resources covered in this volume in an attempt to identify manuscripts, archives, and contemporary perceptions. We have captured the data from our research in a central bibliographic management system, where we can store the citations we have discovered thus far and add to them in the future, and where we can keep notes and personal annotations on readings. We have built a foundation that will enable us to confidently move ahead with our research on Mary Davys and her literary works.

CONCLUSION

Throughout this volume, we introduce and discuss a wide range of research sources that are invaluable to the eighteenth-century literary scholar, from the standard, literary bibliographic databases *MLAIB* and *ABELL*, to author-, period-, and genre-specific reference sources, journals, and websites, and from digital collections of eighteenth-century books, periodicals, newspapers, and manuscripts, to library collections and archives and manuscript reposi- tories. There is a wealth of primary-source digital content for materials once solely available to those with access to large eighteenth-century collections. Effective research skills and strategies are core to successful searching, and standard research techniques will stand you in good stead, but with the wealth of eighteenth-century digital collections of primary sources come some chal- lenges. Although realizing why both the eighteenth-century publishing indus- try and the twenty-first digital surrogates of primary sources offer obstacles does not always make the research process easier, such knowledge can make the sometimes frustrating struggle more comprehensible. You aren't alone, so turn to your reference librarian when you need help. Nonetheless, we hope that this volume has given you insights into and an understanding of the re- search process and provided you with clear explanations of strategies that will benefit you as an eighteenth-century literary scholar.

NOTES

1. Harold Williams, ed., "Swift to Benjamin Motte, Dublin, 4 November 1732," in *The Correspondence of Jonathan Swift*, vol. 4 (Oxford, UK: Clarendon Press, 1965), 84.

2. Bertrand A. Goldgar, ed., *The Grub-Street Journal, 1730–1733* (Brookfield, VT: Pickering & Chatto, 2002), 3.

3. Mary Davys, "Preface," *The Works of Mrs. Davis* (London: H. Woodfall, 1725), ESTC T202035, in *Eighteenth Century Collections Online*, find.galegroup.com/ecco/ infomark.do?&source=gale&prodId=ECCO&userGroupName=udenver&tabID=T00 1&docId=CB129000874&type=multipage&contentSet=ECCOArticles&version=1.0 &docLevel=FASCIMILE.

4. Details of Davys's life from were taken from Paula R. Backscheider, "Davys, Mary (1674–1732)," in *Oxford Dictionary of National Biography*, online edition ed. Lawrence Goldman (Oxford, UK: Oxford University Press, 2004), www.oxforddnb .com/view/article/7327; Frans De Bruyn, "Davys, Mary (1674–1732)," in *British Novelists, 1660–1800*, ed. Philip Breed Dematteis and Leemon B. McHenry, 131–38, *Dictionary of Literary Biography*, vol. 39 (Detroit, MI: Gale Research, 1985); Wil- liam H. McBurney, "Mrs. Mary Davys: Forerunner of Fielding," *PMLA* 74, no. 4 (September 1959): 348–55; Sinéad Sturgeon, "Davys, Mary," in *Dictionary of Irish Biography*, ed. James McGuire and James Quinn (Cambridge, UK: Cambridge Uni- versity Press, 2009), dib.cambridge.org.

5. De Bruyn, "Davys, Mary (1674–1732)," 131.

6. McBurney, "Mrs. Mary Davys: Forerunner of Fielding," 348.

7. McBurney, "Mrs. Mary Davys: Forerunner of Fielding," 350n–51n.

8. In addition, Woolley provides this information in a note, in which he writes, "Some Money: recorded (in part) in Account Books between 1704 and 1718." David Woolley, ed., *The Correspondence of Jonathan Swift, D. D.*, vol. 3 (New York: Peter Lang, 2003), 559n.

9. Isobel Grundy, "Women and Print: Readers, Writers, and the Market," in *The Cambridge History of the Book in Britain*, vol. 5, 1695–1830, ed. Michael F. Suarez and Michael L. Turner (New York: Cambridge University Press, 2009), 155–56.

10. Mary Davys, "Preface," *The Northern Heiress, or, the Humours of York* (London: H. Meere, 1716), ESTC T009578, in *Eighteenth Century Collections Online* (Detroit, MI: Gale Cengage, 2003–), find.galegroup.com/ecco/.

11. *The London Stage, 1660–1800: A Calendar of Plays, Entertainments, and Afterpieces, Together with Casts, Box-Receipts, and Contemporary Comment*, Part 2, vol. 1, 1770–1729 (Carbondale: Southern Illinois University Press, 1960–1968), 400.

12. McBurney, "Mrs. Mary Davys: Forerunner of Fielding," 349.

13. McBurney, "Mrs. Mary Davys: Forerunner of Fielding," 350n.

14. In their respective collected letters, both Williams and Woolley provide information in their notes about Mr. Ewen. The information is similar to what Goodwin and Shore wrote in the *Oxford Dictionary of National Biography* entry for William Howell Ewin (also spelled Ewen), born in 1731: his father was "Thomas Ewin, formerly a grocer, and later a brewer in partnership with a Mr Sparks," and a contemporary report that "my friend, Dr. Ewin, by being much of his father's turn, busy and meddling in other people's concerns." Gordon Goodwin, "Ewin, William Howell (*bap.* 1731, *d.* 1804)," rev. Heather Shore, in *Oxford Dictionary of National Biography*, edited by H. C. G. Matthew and Brian Harrison (Oxford, UK: Oxford University Press, 2004), online edition, ed. Lawrence Goldman, www.oxforddnb. comview/article/9017.

15. Williams, "Swift to Benjamin Motte," 83–84.

16. Goldgar, *The Grub-Street Journal, 1730–1733*, 224.

17. Susan Imel, "Writing a Literature Review," in *The Handbook of Scholarly Writing and Publishing*, ed. Tonette S. Rocco and Tim Hatcher (Hoboken, NJ: Jossey-Bass, 2011), 145–60.

Appendix

Since many literary research projects incorporate elements from other disciplines or are driven by interdisciplinary inquiry, this appendix presents a selection of additional disciplinary resources to consult as a starting point for further investigation. Examples of general, multidisciplinary sources, as well as standard reference tools in art, garden history and design, historical atlases and geographical resources, history, music, philosophy, religion, sciences and medicine, social sciences, and theater, are described. Like the field of literary studies, each discipline (or disciplinary grouping) has a similar range of reference sources: guides to the literature, dictionaries, encyclopedias, companions, indexes, and bibliographies. We have chosen to highlight these primary tools and a representative sample of other sources unique to that discipline. You will most likely have access to these titles either at your university library or through interlibrary loan, or, in the case of subscription databases, access to a resource with similar coverage. You can search for reference works in the library catalog by following the tips provided throughout this volume, or consult library disciplinary research guides for other suggestions. Your reference librarian can also direct you to recommended resources for your specific project. Finally, look to the guides described here for fuller treatments of core and specialized research tools available in other disciplines.

GENERAL RESOURCES

Guides

Balzek, Ron, and Elizabeth Aversa. *The Humanities: A Selective Guide to Information Resources*, 5th ed. Englewood, CO: Libraries Unlimited, 2000.

Although dated, this book lists important sources and provides helpful evaluative annotations for print and electronic research tools in the general humanities, philosophy, religion, visual arts, performing arts, and languages and literatures.

Kieft, Robert, ed. *Guide to Reference*. Chicago: American Library Association. www.guidetoreference.org.
Based on the standard reference tool *Guide to Reference Books*, which was edited for many years by Robert Balay, this online edition, entitled *Guide to Reference*, contains approximately 16,000 annotated print and Web-based reference sources selected by librarians and subject specialists. This guide may be searched by keyword in multiple fields, or browsed by the seven main subject categories, which include general reference works, humanities, social and behavioral sciences, history and area studies, science, technology and medicine, and interdisciplinary fields.

Lester, Ray, ed. *The New Walford: Guide to Reference Resources*. 3 vols. London: Facet Publishing, 2005– .
This is the British standard version of *Guide to Reference* (see the previous entry), published in three volumes devoted to science, technology, and medicine (volume 1); the social sciences (volume 2); and the humanities (volume 3). Each volume provides annotations for the selected sources arranged by discipline and subject. Volume 3 is forthcoming.

Indexes and Bibliographies

Academic Search Complete. Ipswich, MA: EBSCO Publishing. www.ebscohost.com.
This interdisciplinary article database indexes almost 13,000 general and scholarly journals. It includes full text of articles when available and coverage for some titles back to the late nineteenth century.

Expanded Academic ASAP. Farmington Hills, MI: Thomson Gale. infotrac.galegroup.com.
This database surveys general and scholarly journals across multiple disciplines, with full text available for many titles. Since the coverage of this database and *Academic Search Complete* varies, and the full-text content available online can differ, it is valuable to search both databases if possible.

ProQuest Dissertations and Theses: Full Text. Ann Arbor, MI: ProQuest. www.proquest.com.

Both *MLA International Bibliography* (*MLAIB*) and *Annual Bibliography of English Language and Literature* (*ABELL*) (see chapter 4) index dissertations on literary topics, but coverage is limited to the period of time addressed in each, and the records don't have abstracts. This database supplements *MLAIB* and *ABELL* and gives abstracts for the dissertations found in those two resources. *ProQuest Dissertations and Theses* contains dissertations from other disciplines and includes more than 2.7 million citations to dissertations written worldwide from 1861 to the present. It also offers full text for most titles written after 1997.

ART

Dictionaries, Encyclopedias, and Handbooks

Brigstocke, Hugh, ed. *The Oxford Companion to Western Art*. New York: Oxford University Press, 2001.
Featuring more than 2,600 entries, this companion covers all aspects of Western art, from biographical sketches of 1,700 individual artists and their works to art movements, theory, regional surveys, and more. It excludes architecture, as well as non-Western subjects. It is also available as part of *Oxford Art Online* (see the *Oxford Art Online* entry in this section).

Chilvers, Ian, ed. *The Oxford Dictionary of Art*, 3rd ed. New York: Oxford University Press, 2004.
This edition is primarily concerned with Western art and offers definitions about painting, drawing, sculpture, and the applied arts. Coverage spans from arts of the classical period through the twenty-first century.

Oxford Art Online. Oxford, UK: Oxford University Press. www.oxfordart online.com.
This premium art resource enables cross-searching of several standard reference tools, including *Grove Art Online*, *The Benezit Dictionary of Artists*, *The Oxford Companion to Western Art*, *The Concise Dictionary of Art Terms*, and *The Encyclopedia of Aesthetics*. Searches may be refined by category, such as time periods, people, themes and subjects, art and art forms, and geography. The signed essays contain bibliographies and link to related images and content. Those without access to *Oxford Art Online* can obtain much of the *Grove Art Online* content from the thirty-four-volume *The Dictionary of Art* (1996), with extracts collected in *The Grove Dictionary of Art: From Renaissance to Impressionism*, edited by Jane Turner (2000).

Guides

Arntzen, Etta, and Robert Rainwater. *Guide to the Literature of Art History*. Chicago: American Library Association, 1980.
Marmor, Max, and Alex Ross, eds. *Guide to the Literature of Art History 2*. Chicago: American Library Association, 2005.
These two guides provide annotations describing key reference sources for the study of architecture, sculpture, drawings, paintings, prints, photography, and decorative and applied arts. General art bibliographies, dictionaries, encyclopedias, histories, and handbooks are also addressed. Geographic subcategories within sections identify sources about Great Britain and Ireland.

Jones, Lois Swan. *Art Information: Research Methods and Resources*, 3rd ed. Dubuque, IA: Kendall/Hunt, 1990.
As the title indicates, this source presents research methods for studying art and art history and also describes specific resources to support that research.

Jones, Lois Swan. *Art Information and the Internet: How to Find It, How to Use It*. Phoenix, AZ: Oryx Press, 1999.
Although a bit dated, this guide offers useful advice for finding art information on the Internet and features selected websites for art history research. These include websites for museums; academic institutions; cultural, civic, and professional organizations; and foundations.

Indexes and Bibliographies

Art & Architecture Complete. Ipswich, MA: EBSCO. www.ebsco.com.
Addressing art worldwide, from the earliest times to the present, this database provides indexing and abstracts for more than 780 scholarly journals, trade publications, and magazines, as well as books and 63,000 images. Full-text coverage of 380 journals and 220 books is included. The databank covers such subjects as antiques, archaeology, architecture, costume design, decorative and graphic arts, interior and landscape design, painting, photography, printmaking, and sculpture.

Bibliography of the History of Art. Santa Monica, CA: J. Paul Getty Trust, Getty Art History Program. library.getty.edu/bha.
Available through the Getty Research Institute website, *Bibliography of the History of Art (BHA)*, together with *International Repertory of the Literature of Art* (1975–1989), covers more than 4,000 journals, as well as books, dissertations, and exhibition catalogs published from 1975 through 2007.

Concerned with European and American (post-European arrival) visual arts from their beginnings to the early twenty-first century, the databases can be searched individually or simultaneously, or browsed by Library of Congress subject headings. Although *BHA* ceased indexing new material in 2008, the subscription database *International Bibliography of Art* (ProQuest, 2008–) continues in its place and includes global coverage of art post-1945.

International Bibliography of Art. Ann Arbor, MI. ProQuest. www.proquest
    .com.
Focused on European and American art from the earliest times to the present, the *International Bibliography of Art* indexes books, journal articles, conference proceedings, dissertations, and exhibition and dealer's catalogs. It also incorporates *Bibliography of the History of Art* and *International Repertory of the Literature of Art.*

GARDEN HISTORY AND DESIGN

Dictionaries, Encyclopedias, and Companions

Charlesworth, Michael, ed. *The English Garden: Literary Sources and Documents.* 3 vols. Robertsbridge, UK: Helm Information, 1993.
This three-volume compilation of source documents is concerned with English gardens and gardening primarily during the period from 1700 to 1830. As indicated by the title, excerpts from literary works, as well as other contemporary writing (manuscripts and publications), describe individual gardens, theories, and aesthetic judgments.

Desmond, Ray. *Dictionary of British and Irish Botanists and Horticulturalists: Including Plant Collectors, Flower Painters, and Garden Designers.* London: Natural History Museum, 1994.
Brief entries on more than 1,500 gardeners, 1,800 nurserymen, 1,400 botanical artists, and more are presented in this biographical dictionary. The alphabetical arrangement facilitates finding information about known individuals, and the professions index lists names in chronological order and is therefore helpful for identifying eighteenth-century figures.

Shoemaker, Candace A., ed. *Encyclopedia of Gardens: History and Design.* 3 vols. Chicago, IL: Fitzroy Dearborn Publishers, 2001.
This reference work examines garden history worldwide through signed essays about individuals, public and private gardens, places, and subjects, with an emphasis on European and North American developments. Entries

related to the eighteenth century cover author and garden theorist Alexander Pope, Scottish gardener William Aiton, English landscape gardener Lancelot Brown, architect painter and garden designer William Kent, the Georgian period, landscape garden style, the garden in literature and poetry, and London parks, among many others. Most entries include a biography and selected publications (for individuals) and a list for further reading. The encyclopedia is enhanced with many color plates, as well as black-and-white garden plans, illustrations, and photographs.

Taylor, Patrick, ed. *The Oxford Companion to the Garden.* New York: Oxford University Press, 2006.

This compilation addresses all aspects of the garden, from ancient to modern, in more than 1,750 entries that cover topics ranging from individual gardens; designers, architects, landowners, naturalists, nurserymen, and plant collectors; historical, scientific, and social perspectives; and garden features, terms, and styles. Although this companion is concerned with gardens around the world, England, Scotland, Wales, and Ireland are well represented. The main entry, "British Isles," presents a historical survey, with nearly two pages devoted to the eighteenth century. Numerous color photos and illustrations enhance the text, as well as a select bibliography arranged by country.

Indexes and Bibliographies

See the major art, literature, history, and science databases for different perspectives on the role of garden and landscape design during the eighteenth century.

HISTORICAL ATLASES AND GEOGRAPHICAL RESOURCES

Buisseret, David, ed. *The Oxford Companion to World Exploration.* 2 vols. New York: Oxford University Press, 2007.

This companion is comprised of approximately 700 entries on such topics as explorers, regions and places, expeditions, wars, ships and navigation, organizations, maps, and film, among others. A topical outline guides the reader to sections of interest and includes a listing of extracts from primary sources.

Cohen, Saul B., ed. *The Columbia Gazetteer of the World*, 2nd ed. 3 vols. New York: Columbia University Press, 2008.

Referring to itself as an "encyclopedia of geographical places and features," this standard reference source provides concise information on the political (e.g., geographic regions, states, capitals, neighborhoods) and physical world (e.g., continents, oceans, lakes, rivers, islands, mountains, deserts, volcanoes), as well as special places (e.g., national parks, historic and archaeological sites, mines, mythic places).

Cunliffe, Barry, Robert Bartlett, John Morrill, Asa Briggs, and Joanna Bourke, eds. *The Penguin Atlas of British and Irish History: From Earliest Times to the Present Day*. New York: Penguin, 2002.
Using overview and small-scale colored maps, photographs, illustrations, and essays, this atlas explores British and Irish history in five chronological periods: ancient, medieval, early modern, nineteenth century, and modern. Thematic sections within these periods focus on such narrower topics as "Colonial Expansion to 1707," "Eighteenth-Century Dublin," "The Jacobite Rebellions," "Agricultural Change," "Country Estates," "Enlightenment Edinburgh," and "The Eighteenth-Century Empire." This resource also includes a detailed chronological table, a listing of rulers of Britain and Ireland, and a bibliography.

Edwards, Ruth Dudley, with Bridget Hourican. *An Atlas of Irish History*, 3rd ed. New York: Routledge, 2005.
Arranged thematically, this atlas features black-and-white maps, graphs, and charts on the subjects of cartography, military developments, politics, religion, the Irish abroad, land, infrastructure, economy, social change, Northern Ireland, and literature from antiquity to the present. Scholars of the eighteenth century will find relevant sections on the 1798 rising, Dissenters, the transfer of land ownership, eighteenth-century trade, and the Irish Parliament. This reference concludes with a selected bibliography.

Gilbert, Martin. *The Routledge Atlas of British History*, 5th ed. New York: Routledge, 2011.
This atlas comprises 214 black-and-white thematic maps arranged chronologically from 50 B.C. to the 2012 Olympic Games in London. Maps about the eighteenth century address Jacobite risings in 1715 and 1745; the European powers in India; agriculture, trade, and transport; the War of the Spanish Succession; and the revolt of the American colonies, among others.

Hemming, John. *Atlas of Exploration*, 2nd ed. New York: Oxford University Press, 2008.
This colorful and visually appealing atlas is organized by the following regions and topics: early exploration, Asia, Africa, Central America and South America, North America, the Pacific, Australia and New Zealand, the

Arctic, the Antarctic, oceanography, and twenty-first century exploration. A concluding section provides brief biographical sketches of explorers, geographers, and cartographers and a timeline of exploration (2300 B.C. to 2007).

Mills, A. D. *A Dictionary of British Place-Names*. New York: Oxford University Press, 2004.
This dictionary provides the origin and meaning of place-names for 17,000 towns, cities, villages and hamlets, counties, districts, rivers, and coastal features, including those from England, Scotland, the Scottish islands, Wales, Northern Ireland, the Republic of Ireland, the Channel Islands, and the Isle of Man. A glossary of selected common elements in British place-names (e.g., baile, eski, sceaga, weald, ynys) and a bibliography of works for further reading enhance this resource.

Porter, A. N., ed. *Atlas of British Overseas Expansion*. New York: Simon & Schuster, 1991.
Approximately fourteen of the 140 black-and-white maps in this collection cover aspects of British settlement, trade, and emigration during the eighteenth century, from European rivalries in the New World to the British North Atlantic trading system, from the conquest of Canada to the War of the American Revolution, and from British exports from West Africa to the British expansion in India. Each map is accompanied by a narrative description, and the book concludes with brief subject bibliographies and an index.

Ryhiner Map Collection. Canton of Berne, Switzerland: University of Bern. www.ub.unibe.ch/content/bibliotheken_sammlungen/sondersammlungen/ the_ryhiner_map_collection/index_ger.html.
This impressive map collection contains more than 16,000 maps, charts, plans, and views dating from the sixteenth through eighteenth centuries. The link to worldwide sources includes maps of the heavens, hemispheres, Europe, and individual countries and regions from around the world. Each digital map is offered in high resolution and can be enlarged, and the bibliographical record provides details about title, publication information, and subject headings (in German).

HISTORY

Chronology

Mellersh, H. E. L., and Neville Williams, eds. *Chronology of World History*. 4 vols. Santa Barbara, CA: ABC-CLIO, 1999.

This general chronology provides brief entries covering annual events in politics, government, economics, science, technology, medicine, arts, education, culture, religion, sports, and births and deaths. For more detailed entries about chronological developments in science, consult that corresponding section in this appendix.

Dictionaries, Encyclopedias, and Companions

Arnold-Baker, Charles. *The Companion to British History*, 2nd ed. New York: Routledge, 2001.
This hefty encyclopedia provides entries on all aspects of English, Scottish, Welsh, and Irish history, including their relationships with other countries, from 55 B.C. to 2000. It also includes three appendixes, "English Regnal Years," "Selected Warlike Events," and "Genealogies and Diagrams."

Brumwell, Stephen, and W. A. Speck, eds. *Cassell's Companion to Eighteenth-Century Britain*. New York: Cassell and Co., 2001.
Featuring both longer essays and brief entries arranged alphabetically, this companion examines British history from the Glorious Revolution in 1688 through the Battle of Waterloo in 1815. Such topics as the Augustan age, children, dueling, industry, the reformation of manners, textiles, and the Grand Tour are presented, in addition to entries on significant individuals, places, and historical events.

Cannon, John, ed. *The Oxford Companion to British History*, rev. ed. New York: Oxford University Press, 2002.
Like other Oxford companions, this source presents brief entries for people, places, institutions, events, and concepts of English, Irish, Welsh, and Scottish history. "Local history" is emphasized by entries for counties, provinces, ancient kingdoms, modern regions, and important towns. There are also entries on the Declaratory Act, stagecoaches, the Grand Tour, fairs, and major figures from the monarchy and government. This resource also includes maps, genealogies, and a subject index.

Connolly, S. J., ed. *The Oxford Companion to Irish History*, 2nd ed. New York: Oxford University Press, 2002.
This companion covers Irish individuals (none living), events, and institutions through the twentieth century. The second edition expands the treatment of Irish prehistory, the arts, and literary figures. Entries range from longer essays on agriculture, Dublin, overseas trade, and painting to shorter entries on calendar custom, ballads, the Northern Star, and the Society of Friends. This compilation also includes historical maps and a subject index.

Dewald, Jonathon, ed. *Europe 1450 to 1789: Encyclopedia of the Early Modern World.* 6 vols. New York: Charles Scribner's Sons, 2004.
Embracing a broad definition of Europe, this encyclopedia examines not only Western Europe, but also Russia, Eastern Europe, and the Ottoman Empire, and it also places events within a worldwide context. Likewise, the editors aimed to include many cultural groups, with essays addressing Muslims, Jews, and Orthodox Christians, as well as Catholics and Protestants. This compilation has entries on advice and etiquette books, archaeology, class, status and order, food and drink, the ghetto, Huguenots, marriage, old age, public health, scientific revolution, and tobacco, in addition to entries on specific people, countries, places, and topics. It also features maps of Europe from 1453 to 1795; a chronology (1450–1789) covering social, scientific, and cultural events; black-and-white illustrations and some color plates; a thematic outline; and an index.

Hornblower, Simon, and Antony Spawforth. *The Oxford Classical Dictionary*, 3rd rev. ed. New York: Oxford University Press, 2003.
This dictionary is a standard reference work for ancient Greek and Roman history and culture. The third edition is more interdisciplinary and introduces and expands coverage of ancient sexuality, the history of women, and the Near Eastern world. It also includes additional thematic entries. Use this source for information on classical historical and mythological figures and events.

Loades, David, ed. *Reader's Guide to British History.* 2 vols. New York: Fitzroy Dearborn, 2003.
This guide aims to introduce readers to recommended works of secondary scholarship, to trace the "main themes, changes, [and] controversies in interpretation and presentation" (vii) in the history of the British Isles from the earliest times to the present, excluding the republic of Ireland since 1922. Beginning with a bibliography, each entry then proceeds to discuss the selected works within the context of the topic. Sample topics related to the eighteenth century address individuals (e.g., James Cook, George II); events (e.g., Jacobite rebellions, Seven Years' War); poetry, fiction, and drama of the period; and topical essays on the sugar trade, the Bluestockings, coffee house culture, poverty and social control, and the Whigs, among others. There is a complete list of thematic topics for the early modern period, 1485–1783 (xxi–xxii) and modern period, 1783–1914 (xxii–xxiii). This compilation also includes alphabetical and thematic lists of entries, as well as a comprehensive bibliography.

Lynch, Michael, ed. *The Oxford Companion to Scottish History*. New York: Oxford University Press, 2001.
This companion provides entries on the following themes and elements of Scottish history: events; biographies; politics; government; economic life; social life; religion; peoples and families; demographics; physical environment and material culture; places; culture; relations with Britain, Ireland, Europe, and the world; ethnographies; and historians, historical sources, and heritage. See, for example, the essay on Scottish culture during the Enlightenment (1660–1843), which discusses philosophy, art, language, literature, poetry, music, the novel, and medicine.

Panton, Kenneth J. *Historical Dictionary of London*. Lanham, MD: Scarecrow Press, 2001.
Following an introductory overview of London's history, this dictionary presents brief entries on the "people, institutions, political forces, economic trends, and social values that gave the metropolitan area its shape and focus" (xiii), as well as entries for the city's districts (e.g., boroughs, hamlets, suburbs). Additional maps, chronologies, London government contact information, organization Web addresses, and an extensive bibliography complete this handy reference work.

Guides

Fritze, Ronald H., Brian E. Coutts, and Louis A. Vyhnanek. *Reference Sources in History: An Introductory Guide*, 2nd ed. Santa Barbara, CA: ABC-CLIO, 2004.
Arranged in fourteen chapters by type of resource, this guide provides annotations for 930 print and electronic historical reference works, covering all time periods and geographical areas. Resources discussed include standard reference sources (e.g., guides, bibliographies, periodical guides and core journals, periodical indexes and abstracts, dissertations), in addition to geographical sources and atlases, historical statistical sources, archives, and microforms. Sources specifically for British history are presented in the relevant categories throughout this source.

Indexes and Bibliographies

Bibliography of British and Irish History. Turnhout, Belgium: Brepols, 2010– . www.brepols.net.

This is the subscription version of the previously freely available Royal Historical Society Bibliography, which contains more than 4,600 records for books, chapters, and journal articles covering British history from the Roman occupation to the present.

Davies, Godfrey, ed. (1st ed.), and Mary Frear Keeler, ed. (2nd ed.). *Bibliography of British History: Stuart Period, 1603–1714*, 2nd ed. Oxford, UK: Clarendon Press, 1970.
This annotated bibliography of contemporary through mid-twentieth-century publications covers the following subjects: general reference works; political, constitutional, legal, ecclesiastical, military, naval, economic, social, and cultural history; local history for counties, cities, and towns; colonial history; Wales; Scotland; and Ireland.

Hirst, Derek M. "British Isles, 1450–1800." In *The American Historical Association's Guide to Historical Literature*, 3rd ed. 2 vols. Edited by Mary Beth Norton. New York: Oxford University Press, 1995.
This is a selective annotated bibliography of the "best contemporary historical scholarship" (xi) published primarily from 1961 to 1992. It includes entries organized under the following headings: "English Political History"; "Political Thought"; "Foreign Relations and Military History"; "Economic, Religious, Intellectual, Social, and Legal History"; "Women, Family, and Household"; "History of Science"; "The Arts"; "Scotland"; "Ireland"; and "Wales." Scholars may wish to consult other national and period bibliographies in the guide, depending on specific research projects.

Historical Abstracts Online. Santa Barbara, CA: ABC-CLIO, 1954– . Available online at www.ebscohost.com.
This is a principal bibliographic database for historical research that indexes books, journal articles, and dissertations published from 1954 to the present addressing the history of the world after 1449, excluding the United States and Canada, which are covered in the database *America: History and Life*. It presents international coverage of key historical journals, in addition to selected journals in the social sciences and humanities. The advanced search permits limiting by decade(s) or century and subject terms (e.g., Great Britain, satire, gender, families, social life and customs, insanity). This database is especially useful in researching a wide range of subjects within a historical period, including popular culture, science, medicine, and so forth.

Pargellis, Stanley, and D. J. Medley, eds. *Bibliography of British History: The Eighteenth Century, 1714–1789*, 2nd ed. Totowa, NJ: Rowman & Littlefield, 1977.

Like Davies's *Bibliography of British History: Stuart Period, 1603–1714,* this annotated source briefly describes contemporary through mid-twentieth-century publications about the following subjects: general reference works; political, constitutional, legal, ecclesiastical, military, naval, economic, social, and cultural history; local history for counties, cities, and towns; colonial history; Wales; Scotland; and Ireland. Both bibliographies were issued under the direction of the American Historical Association and the Royal Historical Society of Great Britain.

Historical Sources

Douglass, David C., ed. *English Historical Documents.* New York: Oxford University Press, 1953– .
This collection presents documents from 500 to 1914, including laws, speeches, letters, diary entries, debates, treaties, reports, and statistical tables. Several volumes cover the eighteenth century. Volume VIII (1660–1714) surveys the monarchy, Parliament, public finance, the church, local government and social life, trade and plantations, Scotland, Ireland, the armed forces, foreign affairs, and sovereigns and politicians. Volume X (1714–1783) addresses similar topics, in addition to the colonies in America, India, and Africa; agriculture; and industry. Volume XI (1783–1832) features the cabinet and royal prerogative, Parliament, the legal system, poor law administration, economic development, social and religious life, the Empire, and foreign policy. And Volume IX is solely concerned with American colonial documents to 1776. Each section begins with an introduction and bibliography.

MUSIC

Dictionaries, Encyclopedias, and Handbooks

Latham, Alison, ed. *The Oxford Companion to Music.* New York: Oxford University Press, 2002.
With an emphasis on the Western classical tradition, this authoritative source covers definitions of musical terms, forms, and styles, and provides entries on people, works, instruments, movements, and many other musical subjects, spanning from the medieval period to the present. It is also available as part of *Oxford Music Online* (see the *Oxford Music Online* entry in this section).

Randel, Don Michael, ed. *The Harvard Dictionary of Music,* 4th ed. Cambridge, MA: Belknap Press of Harvard University Press, 2003.

Now available in a revised edition, this source gives an international perspective on all aspects of musical genres and history, from Afro-Cuban jazz to allemande, and from harpsichord to zarzuelas.

Oxford Music Online. Oxford, UK: Oxford University Press. www.oxford
  musiconline.com.
Oxford Music Online provides access to *Grove Music Online* (the primary dictionary for the discipline), *The Oxford Companion to Music*, *The Oxford Dictionary of Music*, and *The Encyclopedia of Popular Music*. Users can browse by subject or biography sections, or search all content, just biographies (with options for name, occupation, nationality), or only bibliographies.

Guides

Duckles, Vincent H., Ida Reed, and Michael A. Keller, eds. *Music Reference
  and Research Materials: An Annotated Bibliography*, 5th ed. New York:
  Schirmer Books, 1997.
This standard guide features descriptions of more than 3,500 important bibliographies, indexes, dictionaries, encyclopedias, companions, chronologies, histories, catalogs, discographies, yearbooks, and Web resources for music research. It contains sources published through 1995.

Sampsel, Laurie J. *Music Research: A Handbook*. New York: Oxford University Press, 2009.
With an emphasis on the research process, this guide covers the major music research tools, in English and selected European languages, for a graduate audience. Sources addressed include general and specialized encyclopedias and dictionaries, library catalogs, periodical indexes, indexes to other materials (e.g., dissertations, theses, conference papers, festschriften, complete works, historical sets, musical monuments, anthologies), thematic catalogs, histories, bibliographies, discographies, iconographies, directories, and Internet sources. It also presents writing, style, and citation sources.

Indexes and Bibliographies

The Music Index: A Subject-Author Guide to Music Periodical Literature.
  Warren, MI: Harmonie Park Press. www.hppmusicindex.com.
Covering popular and classical music periodicals, this index also includes review articles, as well as scholarship. The print index begins in 1949 and spans to the present; the online version addresses 1979 to the present.

RILM Abstracts of Music Literature. New York: RILM. www.rilm.org.
This international index for scholarly music literature in any language includes abstracts in English. It covers books, journals, dissertations, reviews, films and videos, and commentaries published from 1969 to the present.

Sources and History

Grout, Donald Jay, J. Peter Burkholder, and Claude V. Palisca. *A History of Western Music*, 8th ed. New York: Norton, 2010.
This compilation surveys the development of Western musical traditions from the ancient and medieval periods through the twentieth century. "The Eighteenth Century" section addresses Italy and France during the early century, German late-Baroque composers, Enlightenment musical taste and style, opera and vocal music, instrumental music, and classical music in the late eighteenth century.

PHILOSOPHY

Dictionaries, Encyclopedias, and Handbooks

Audi, Robert. *The Cambridge Dictionary of Philosophy*, 2nd ed. New York: Cambridge University Press, 1999.
This dictionary contains more than 4,400 entries on individual philosophers (including non-European figures), terms, concepts, and philosophical movements.

Craig, Edward, ed. *Routledge Encyclopedia of Philosophy*. 10 vols. New York: Routledge, 1998. www.rep.routledge.com.
This substantial work offers more than 2,000 signed essays about different philosophical movements and figures, including Anglo-American and continental philosophy. The last volume in the print edition gives a detailed index; the online version allows for searching by philosophical themes, world philosophies, periods, and world religions, as well as by full text.

Dematteis, Philip B., and Peter S. Fosl, eds. *British Philosophers: 1500–1799.* Vol. 252, *Dictionary of Literary Biography*. Detroit: Gale Group, 2002.
Part of the *Dictionary of Literary Biography*, this volume presents essays about the writings of early modern British philosophers, including such eighteenth-century figures as Mary Astell, Jeremy Bentham, Richard Bentley, George Berkeley, Edmund Burke, Joseph Butler, Samuel Clarke, Anthony

Collins, Damaris Cudworth (Lady Masham), David Hartley, David Hume, Francis Hutcheson, John Locke, Sir Isaac Newton, John Norris, William Paley, Joseph Priestly, Thomas Reid, Adam Smith, John Toland, Catharine Trotter, and Mary Wollstonecraft.

Honderich, Ted, ed. *The Oxford Companion to Philosophy*, 2nd ed. New York: Oxford University Press, 2005.
Spanning from antiquity to the present, this companion contains brief, signed entries about individual philosophers, movements, and ideas worldwide.

Horowitz, Maryanne Cline, ed. *New Dictionary of the History of Ideas*. 6 vols. New York: Charles Scribner's Sons, 2005.
This compilation covers intellectual history from the earliest times to the twenty-first century in more than 700 signed essays that fall within four main themes, "Communication of Ideas," "Geographical Areas," "Chronological Periods," and "Liberal Arts Disciplines and Professions." The bibliographies lead to both primary and secondary sources.

Guides

Bynagle, Hans E. *Philosophy: A Guide to the Reference Literature*, 3rd ed. Westport, CT: Libraries Unlimited, 2006.
Following general chapters about other research guides, bibliographies, indexes, handbooks, encyclopedias, dictionaries, Web resources, and history sources, this annotated bibliography for scholarly research describes sources for Western philosophies by time period, non-Western philosophy, and specific subjects (e.g., philosophy of education, religion, art, ethics, logic, metaphysics).

Indexes and Bibliographies

Dillon, Martin, ed. in chief, and Shannon Graff Hysell, assoc. ed. *ARBA In-Depth: Philosophy and Religion*. Westport, CT: Libraries Unlimited, 2004.
This is a compilation of 436 *ARBA* (*American Reference Books Annual*) reviews selected from the 1997 to 2003 volumes that pertain to philosophy and religion. This source is useful in identifying relevant dictionaries, encyclopedias, directories, bibliographies, indexes, guides, and other reference tools. The "Religion" section covers Baha'I faith, Bible studies, Buddhism, Christianity, Hinduism, Islam, Judaism, Native American religions, occult-

ism and witchcraft, Shinto, Sikhism, and Taoism, whereas the "Philosophy" section addresses resources for the discipline in general.

The Philosopher's Index: An International Index to Philosophical Periodicals and Books. Bowling Green, OH: Philosopher's Information Center. Available online through various vendors.
With an emphasis on international scholarship, this index covers journals, books, and book reviews from 1940 to the present, with select coverage extending back to 1902. Fifteen subfields of philosophy comprise the subject matter. These include aesthetics; axiology; epistemology; ethics; logic; metaphilosophy; metaphysics; philosophical anthropology; and the philosophies of education, history, language, religion, and science, as well as political and social philosophy.

RELIGION

Dictionaries, Encyclopedias, and Handbooks

Jones, Lindsay, ed. *Encyclopedia of Religion*, 2nd ed. 15 vols. New York: Macmillan, 2005.
This standard reference work presents more than 3,000 entries about religion in everyday life as experienced around the world, highlighting both cross-cultural and cultural-specific surveys.

Guides

Balzek, Ron, and Elizabeth Aversa. *The Humanities: A Selective Guide to Information Resources*, 5th ed. Englewood, CO: Libraries Unlimited, 2000.
Although dated, this book lists important sources and provides helpful evaluative annotations for print and electronic research tools in the general humanities, philosophy, religion, visual arts, performing arts, and languages and literatures.

Johnston, William M. *Recent Reference Books in Religion: A Guide for Students, Scholars, Researchers, Buyers, and Readers*, rev. ed. Chicago: Fitzroy Dearborn, 1998.
Although the "recent" in the title is no longer accurate, this source still provides a solid guide to print reference sources published between 1970 and 1997 concerned with major world religions, mythology, the philosophy of religion, and religion and the social sciences.

Indexes and Bibliographies

Religion and literature are covered by *MLA International Bibliography* and *Annual Bibliography of English Language and Literature*. The history of religion is included in *Historical Abstracts Online*.

ATLA Religion. Chicago: American Theological Library Association. Available online via various vendors.
ATLA Religion indexes journal articles, book reviews, essays, and dissertations from 1949 to the present, with selected coverage before 1949, on all aspects of religion and theology. The print versions of this database are entitled *Religion One* (periodicals) and *Religion Two* (multiauthor works).

Dillon, Martin, ed. in chief, and Shannon Graff Hysell, assoc. ed. *ARBA In-Depth: Philosophy and Religion*. Westport, CT: Libraries Unlimited, 2004.
This is a compilation of 436 *ARBA* (*American Reference Books Annual*) reviews selected from the 1997 to 2003 volumes that pertain to philosophy and religion. This source is useful in identifying relevant dictionaries, encyclopedias, directories, bibliographies, indexes, guides, and other reference tools. The "Religion" section covers Baha'I faith, Bible studies, Buddhism, Christianity, Hinduism, Islam, Judaism, Native American religions, occultism and witchcraft, Shinto, Sikhism, and Taoism, whereas the "Philosophy" section addresses resources for the discipline in general.

SCIENCES AND MEDICINE

Dictionaries, Encyclopedias, and Handbooks

Burns, William E. *Science in the Enlightenment: An Encyclopedia*. Santa Barbara, CA: ABC-CLIO, 2003.
This source examines eighteenth-century science in entries about instruments and devices, language and communication, people, science and society, scientific disciplines and institutions, theories and ideologies, and topics of investigation. Twenty-one noted British individuals are included, as well as such topics as comets, natural theology, medicine, ballooning, popularization, industrialization, and zoology. The encyclopedia concludes with a chronology (1699–1830), bibliography, and list of recommended websites.

Burns, William E. *The Scientific Revolution: An Encyclopedia*. Santa Barbara, CA: ABC-CLIO, 2001.

Burns provides entries on the "leading personalities, ideas, instruments, and institutions that created early modern science, as well as the scientific disciplines themselves" (xvii), here defined as ranging from the later sixteenth through the early eighteenth centuries. This encyclopedia includes entries on such topics as the circulation of blood, geology, religion and science, literature, midwives, and mechanics, with additional listings on Bernard Le Bouvier de Fontenelle and Antoni van Leeuwenhoek. A chronology covers events from 1503 to 1727, and the bibliography presents information on books, journal articles, and websites.

Bynum, William F., E. Janet Browne, and Roy Porter. *Dictionary of the History of Science*. Princeton, NJ: Princeton University Press, 1981.
This dictionary contains information on the ideas of science throughout the history of Western science. There is a useful bibliography, divided by broad science subject categories, at the beginning of the book.

Bynum, William F., and Roy Porter, eds. *Companion Encyclopedia of the History of Medicine*. 2 vols. New York: Routledge, 1993.
This compilation of seventy-two essays covers all aspects of the history of medicine, including theories of life, health, and disease; medicine and society and culture; diagnosis; education; nursing; and the hospital. It also has a chapter on medicine and literature.

Gossin, Pamela, ed. *Encyclopedia of Literature and Science*. Westport, CT: Greenwood Press, 2002.
This encyclopedia features more than 650 entries on writers and scientists and their works and theories, as well as relevant subjects pertaining to the interdisciplinary study of science and literature. The essay "Literature and Science (Chronological Periods)" is a good starting point in identifying relevant figures of the eighteenth century, and entries on Jonathan Swift, Voltaire, John Locke, William Derham, Lawrence Sterne, and others, or topical entries on the Enlightenment, natural philosophy, popularizations, the telescope, imagination, and the scientific method provide additional information. Each entry concludes with references, and the encyclopedia contains a selected bibliography for further reading.

Heilbron, J. L., ed. *The Oxford Companion to the History of Modern Science*. New York: Oxford University Press, 2003.
This companion features entries on historiography, scientific institutions and organizations, the body of scientific knowledge, apparatus and instruments, applied sciences, and biographies from 1550 to the early twenty-first century.

Indexes and Bibliographies

For articles on the history of the sciences and medicine during the eighteenth century, use *Historical Abstracts Online* or *America: History and Life* for topics related to the colonies. The interdisciplinary coverage of both *Academic Search Complete* and *Expanded Academic ASAP* make them valuable starting points as well.

Web of Science. Philadelphia, PA: Institute for Scientific Information. isiknow ledge.com.
This is an interdisciplinary index to articles in more than 9,000 international science, social science, and humanities journals. If available, the years of coverage depend on the library's subscription.

Sources and History

Hessenbruch, Arne, ed. *Reader's Guide to the History of Science.* Chicago: Fitzroy Dearborn, 2000.
This is a guide to recommended and important readings about individuals, disciplines and institutions, and themes relevant to the history of science, technology, and medicine. The list of sources are reviewed and compared in one- to two-page essays. It includes entries on the Royal Society of London, music and science since 1700, the Enlightenment, and madness, among many other topics pertinent to the eighteenth century.

Kiple, Kenneth F., ed. *The Cambridge World History of Human Disease.* New York: Cambridge University Press, 1993.
This compilation of essays and statistical data provides historical overviews of medical practices, public health concerns, and major diseases from around the world and throughout the ages.

Lindberg, David C., and Ronald L. Numbers. *The Cambridge History of Science.* 8 vols. New York: Cambridge University Press, 2003– .
Volume 4 of this series, *Eighteenth-Century Science*, provides readable, scholarly essays about the role of science during the period. Thematic sections address "Science and Society," "Disciplines," "Special Themes," "Non-Western Traditions," and "Ramifications and Impacts." Within these sections are essays on women and gender in science, natural philosophy, scientific instruments, India, print and public science, and the intersection of science with trade and empire, as just a few examples.

SOCIAL SCIENCES

Dictionaries, Encyclopedias, and Handbooks

Darity, William A., ed. *International Encyclopedia of the Social Sciences*, 2nd ed. 9 vols. Detroit, MI: MacMillan Reference USA, 2008. www.gale .cengage.com.
The second edition of this standard reference work presents almost 3,000 entries that reflect current scholarship and theoretical trends regarding the social sciences and their historical development, including race, gender, and queer studies. This volume covers all of the major social science disciplines, as well as interdisciplinary studies.

Smelser, Neil J., and Paul B. Baltes, eds. *International Encyclopedia of the Social and Behavioral Sciences*. 26 vols. New York: Elsevier, 2001. www .sciencedirect.com.
This impressive and significant multivolume work features 4,000 articles about the social and behavioral science disciplines, including economics, sociology, linguistics, archaeology, area studies, law, gender studies, anthropology, ge-ography, demography, philosophy, statistics, public policy, history, religious studies, psychology, political science, education, and more. Biographical en-tries for important figures within the disciplines are also addressed. Due to the size of this work, it is highly recommended to consult the subject and name indexes so as not to miss relevant information in related essays.

Guides

Herron, Nancy L., ed. *The Social Sciences: A Cross-Disciplinary Guide to Selected Sources*, 3rd ed. Englewood, CO: Libraries Unlimited, 2002.
This compilation lists relevant print and electronic sources and provides evaluative annotations for research in the general social sciences, political science, economics, business, history, law, anthropology, sociology, educa-tion, psychology, geography, and communication.

Indexes and Bibliographies

For articles about some of the social sciences during the eighteenth century, including education, government, or law, or such social topics as poverty or population, use *Historical Abstracts Online* or *America: History and Life* for topics related to the colonies. The interdisciplinary coverage of both *Aca-demic Search Complete* and *Expanded Academic ASAP* make them valuable starting points as well.

SocINDEX with Full Text. Ispwich, MA: EBSCO. www.ebscohost.com.
This database covers sociology and related fields, and indexes journals, books, and conference papers. Although *Historical Abstracts Online* is more comprehensive for historical topics, *SocINDEX* includes some articles with a historical focus, such as those about poor relief or crime.

Web of Science. Philadelphia, PA: Institute for Scientific Information. Available online at isiknowledge.com.
This is an interdisciplinary index to articles in more than 9,000 international science, social science, and humanities journals. If available, the years of coverage depend on the library's subscription.

Sources and History

Lindberg, David C., and Ronald L. Numbers. *The Cambridge History of Science.* 8 vols. New York: Cambridge University Press, 2003– .
Volume 7 of this series, *Modern Social Sciences*, provides valuable scholarly essays about the history of various social sciences, including economic theory, education, psychology, ethnography, and political science. Issues addressed include ideas of class, the invention of race, and utopian socialism. Part 1 concentrates on social sciences to the end of the nineteenth century and offers chapters of interest to the eighteenth-century literary scholar, for example, "British Economic Theory from Locke to Marshall," "Scientific Ethnography and Travel, 1750–1850," and "History and Historicism." See the "Sciences and Medicine" section in this appendix for information on another volume in this series.

THEATER

Literary research tools often include drama and dramatists. The following represent some conventional as well as some unique types of resources available to researchers in theater.

Dictionaries, Encyclopedias, and Handbooks

Dictionary of Literary Biography. Gale Cengage, 1978– . www.gale.cengage .com.
This resource is described at length in chapter 2. For volumes pertinent to theater, see *Restoration and Eighteenth-Century Dramatists* (volumes 80, 84, and 89).

Hartnoll, Phyllis, ed. *The Oxford Companion to the Theatre*, 4th ed. New York: Oxford University Press, 1983.
Although the contents in this compilation do not represent current scholarship, this is still a useful source for concise, factual information about actors, playwrights, directors, theaters, and other subjects regarding the theatre and its history.

Mann, David, and Susan Garland Mann. *Women Playwrights in England, Ireland, and Scotland, 1660–1823*. Bloomington: Indiana University Press, 1996.
Covering the long eighteenth century, this source provides biographical entries for approximately 600 women playwrights and their works.

Moody, Jane, and Daniel O'Quinn, eds. *The Cambridge Companion to British Theatre, 1730–1830*. New York: Cambridge University Press, 2007.
This companion features 17 essays about various aspects of the theatre from the eighteenth century through the Romantic period. Topics addressed include the genres of comedy, tragedy, pantomime, and melodrama; female playwrights and actresses; spectatorship; private theatricals; race and profit; Irish theatre; and scenography.

Guides

Simons, Linda Keir. *The Performing Arts: A Guide to the Reference Literature*. Englewood, CO: Libraries Unlimited, 1994.
Like other guides to the literature, this annotated bibliography covers standard reference tools for researching theater, dance, and other performing arts, except music, including dictionaries and encyclopedias, bibliographies, indexes, catalogs, biographical sources, and archival resources.

Indexes and Bibliographies

MLA International Bibliography and *Annual Bibliography of English Language and Literature* are both excellent indexes for scholarly research about theater during the eighteenth century.

International Bibliography of Theatre and Dance with Full Text. Boulder, CO: American Society for Theatre Research and Theatre Research Data Center, 1982–present. www.ebscohost.com.
This extensive bibliography provides citations and some abstracts for more than 60,000 journal articles, books, book chapters, and dissertations related to studying ballet, cinema, comedy, dance, drama, film, mime, opera, puppetry,

and theatre in 126 countries. It also includes full text for 170 selected journals and 360 books.

Stratman, Carl J. *A Bibliography of British Dramatic Periodicals, 1720–1960*. New York: New York Public Library, 1962.
This slim volume offers a chronological list of 674 periodicals concerned with the theater, beginning in 1720, with *The Anti-Theatre* and *The Theatre*, which were published in London and throughout England, Scotland, and Ireland. Twenty-seven titles have their origins in the eighteenth century.

Sources and History

Langhans, Edward A. *Eighteenth-Century British and Irish Promptbooks: A Descriptive Bibliography*. New York: Greenwood, 1987.
Langhans describes more than 350 promptbooks and related documents, including marked copies, preparation copies, rehearsal copies, and partbooks, arranged by author.

Thomson, Peter, ed. *The Cambridge History of British Theatre*. 3 vols. New York: Cambridge University Press, 2004.
This set surveys British theatre from its origins through the twentieth century. The entire eighteenth century is addressed in volume 2, which spans the period from the Restoration in 1660 to 1895.

Van Lennep, William, Emmett L. Avery, Arthur H. Scouten, George Winchester Stone, and Charles Beecer Hogan, eds. *The London Stage: 1660–1800: A Calendar of Plays, Entertainments, and Afterpieces, Together with Casts, Box-Receipts, and Contemporary Comment. Compiled from the Playbills, Newspapers, and Theatrical Diaries of the Period*. 6 pts. in 12 vols. Carbondale: Southern Illinois University Press, 1966–1979.
Organized by season, year, month, and day, this source outlines daily theatrical entertainment in London and provides information about the venue, title, author, cast (if known), and contemporary commentary. Parts 2 through 5 cover the eighteenth century, as follows: part 2, 1700–1729; part 3, 1729–1747; part 4, 1747–1776; part 5, 1776–1800.

Bibliography

Auburn, Mark S. "Sheridan, Richard Brinsley (1751–7 July 1816)." In *Restoration and Eighteenth-Century Dramatists, Third Series*. Edited by Paula R. Backscheider, 289–322. *Dictionary of Literary Biography*, Vol. 89. Detroit, MI: Gale Research, 1989.

Backscheider, Paula R. "Davys, Mary (1674–1732)." In *Oxford Dictionary of National Biography*, online ed. Edited by Lawrence Goldman. Oxford, UK: Oxford University Press, 2004. Accessed 28 July 2012, from www.oxforddnb.com/view/article/7327.

———. "Defoe, Daniel (1660?–1731)." In *Oxford Dictionary of National Biography*, online ed. Edited by Lawrence Goldman. Oxford, UK: Oxford University Press, 2004. Accessed 28 July 2012, from www.oxforddnb.com/view/article/7421.

Beall, Jeffrey, and Karen Kafadar. "The Proportion of *NUC Pre-1956* Titles Represented in OCLC WorldCat." *College and Research Libraries* 66, no. 5 (September 2005): 431–35.

Bevis, Richard. "Goldsmith, Oliver (10 November 1730?–4 April 1774)." In *Restoration and Eighteenth-Century Dramatists, Third Series*. Edited by Paula R. Backscheider, 148–71. *Dictionary of Literary Biography*, Vol. 89. Detroit, MI: Gale Research, 1989.

Bouché, Nicole. *Digitization for Scholarly Use: The Boswell Papers Project at the Beinecke Rare Book and Manuscript Library*. Washington, DC: Council on Library and Information Resources, 1999. Accessed 28 July 2012, from www.clir.org/pubs/reports/pub81-bouche/pub81.pdf.

British Library. "History of the British Library." *British Library*. Accessed 20 August 2012, from www.bl.uk/aboutus/quickinfo/facts/history.

Burke, Frank G. *Research and the Manuscript Tradition*. Lanham, MD: Scarecrow Press, 1997.

Cooper, Thompson. "Davys, Mary (fl. 1756)." In *Oxford Dictionary of National Biography*, online ed. (Dictionary of National Biography Archive). Edited by Lawrence Goldman. Oxford, UK: Oxford University Press, 1888. www.oxforddnb.com/view/olddnb/7327.

Davys, Mary. "Preface." *The Northern Heiress: Or the Humours of York*. London: H. Meere, 1716. ESTC T009578. In *Eighteenth Century Collections Online*. Detroit, MI: Gale Cengage, 2003– . find.galegroup.com/ecco/.

———. "Preface." *The Works of Mrs. Davis*. London: H. Woodfall, 1725. ESTC T202035. In *Eighteenth Century Collections Online*. Detroit, MI: Gale Cengage, 2003– .

Deacon, David. "Yesterday's Papers and Today's Technology: Digital Newspaper Archives and 'Push Button' Content Analysis." *European Journal of Communication* 22, no. 5 (2007): 5–25.

De Bruyn, Frans. "Davys, Mary (1674–1732)." In *British Novelists, 1660–1800*. Edited by Philip Breed Dematteis and Leemon B. McHenry, 131–38. *Dictionary of Literary Biography*, Vol. 39. Detroit, MI: Gale Research, 1985.

DeZelar-Tiedman, Christine. "The Proportion of *NUC Pre-56* Titles Represented in *RLIN* and OCLC Databases Compared: A Follow-up to the Beall/Kafadar Study." *College and Research Libraries* 69, no. 5 (September 2008): 401–6.

Donoghue, Frank. *The Fame Machine: Book Reviewing and Eighteenth-Century Literary Careers*. Stanford, CA: Stanford University Press, 1996.

Early English Books Online. "The Early Chronology of UMI and the *Early English Books* Microfilm Collections." Ann Arbor, MI: ProQuest/Chadwyck-Healey. eebo .chadwyck.com/about/about.htm#chron.

Forster, Antonia. "Book Reviewing." In *The Cambridge History of the Book in Britain*, Vol. 5, 1695–1830. Edited by Michael F. Suarez and Michael L. Turner, 631–48. New York: Cambridge University Press, 2009.

Foster, Janet, and Julia Sheppard, eds. *British Archives: A Guide to Archive Resources in the United Kingdom*, 4th ed. New York: Palgrave, 2002.

Fowler, Bridget. *The Obituary as Collective Memory*. New York: Routledge, 2007.

Furrie, Betty. "What Is a MARC Record, and Why Is It Important?" In *Understanding MARC Bibliographic: Machine-Readable Cataloging*. Washington, DC: Library of Congress, 2009. www.loc.gov/marc/umb/um01to06.html.

Gillespie, Stuart. "Leapor, Mary (1722–1746)." In *Oxford Dictionary of National Biography*, online ed. Edited by Lawrence Goldman. Oxford, UK: Oxford University Press, 2004. www.oxforddnb.com/view/article/16246.

Goldgar, Bertrand A., ed. *The Grub-Street Journal, 1730–1733*. Brookfield, VT: Pickering & Chatto, 2002.

Goodwin, Gordon. "Ewin, William Howell (bap. 1731, d. 1804)." In *Oxford Dictionary of National Biography*. Edited by H. C. G. Matthew and Brian Harrison. Oxford, UK: Oxford University Press, 2004. Online edition edited by Lawrence Goldman. www.oxforddnb.comview/article/9017.

Gregory, Jeremy, and John Stevenson. *The Longman Companion to Britain in the Eighteenth Century, 1688–1820*. New York: Longman, 2000.

Griffin, Dustin. "The Rise of the Professional Author?" In *The Cambridge History of the Book in Britain*, Vol. 5, 1695–1830. Edited by Michael F. Suarez and Michael L. Turner, 132–45. New York: Cambridge University Press, 2009.

Grundy, Isobel. "Women and Print: Readers, Writers, and the Market." In *The Cambridge History of the Book in Britain*, Vol. 5, 1695–1830. Edited by Michael F.

Suarez and Michael L. Turner, 146–59. New York: Cambridge University Press, 2009.

Harris, Bob. "Print Culture." In *A Companion to Eighteenth-Century Britain*. Edited by H. T. Dickinson, 283–93. Malden, MA: Blackwell, 2002.

Hemlow, Joyce. *A Catalogue of the Burney Family Correspondence, 1749–1878*. New York: New York Public Library, 1971.

Heyd, Uriel. *Reading Newspapers: Press and Public in Eighteenth-Century Britain and America*. Oxford, UK: Voltaire Foundation, 2012.

Imel, Susan. "Writing a Literature Review." In *The Handbook of Scholarly Writing and Publishing*. Edited by Tonette S. Rocco and Tim Hatcher, 145–60. Hoboken, NJ: Jossey-Bass, 2011.

Italia, Iona. *The Rise of Literary Journalism in the Eighteenth Century: Anxious Employment*. New York: Routledge, 2005.

Jackson, Ian. "Approaches to the History of Readers and Reading in Eighteenth-Century Britain." *Historical Journal* 47, no. 4 (2004): 1,041–54.

Langford, Paul. *A Polite and Commercial People: England, 1727–1783*. New York: Oxford University Press, 1989.

Lohr, Steve. "Google Schools Its Algorithm." *New York Times*, March 6, 2011, p. 4. www.nytimes.com/2011/03/06/weekinreview/06lohr.html?pagewanted=all&_r=0.

The London Stage, 1660–1800: A Calendar of Plays, Entertainments, and Afterpieces, Together with Casts, Box-Receipts, and Contemporary Comment, Part 2, Vol. 1, 1770–1729. Carbondale: Southern Illinois University Press, 1960–1968.

Londry, Michael. "On the Use of First-Line Indices for Researching English Poetry of the Long Eighteenth Century, c. 1660–1830, with Special Reference to Women Poets." *Library* 5, no. 1 (2004): 12–38.

McBurney, William H. "Mrs. Mary Davys: Forerunner of Fielding." *PMLA* 74, no. 4 (September 1959): 348–55.

Melton, James Van Horn. *The Rise of the Public in Enlightenment Europe*. New York: Cambridge University Press, 2001.

Murphy, J. Stephen. "The Death of the Editor." *Essays in Criticism: A Quarterly Journal Founded by F. W. Bateson* 58, no. 4 (October 2008): 289–304.

Pearson, Jayn, and Keith Soothill. "Using an Old Search Engine: The Value of the *Times Index*." *Sociology* 37, no. 4 (November 2003): 781–90.

Philo-Grubaea. "From the Pegasus in Grub-Street." *Grub-Street Journal*, July 15, 1731, p. 3. *British Periodicals*, search.proquest.com/docview/5639084?accoun tid=14608.

Raven, James. "The Book as a Commodity." In *The Cambridge History of the Book in Britain*, Vol. 5, 1695–1830. Edited by Michael F. Suarez and Michael L. Turner, 85–117. New York: Cambridge University Press, 2009.

Richetti, John. "Introduction." In *The Cambridge Companion to the Eighteenth-Century Novel*. Edited by John Richetti, 1–7. Cambridge, UK: Cambridge University Press, 1996.

Rogers, Pat. *Defoe, the Critical Heritage*. Boston: Routledge and Kegan Paul, 1972.

Roper, Derek. *Reviewing before the Edinburgh, 1788–1802*. Newark: University of Delaware Press, 1978.

Rose, Mark. "Copyright, Authors, and Censorship." In *The Cambridge History of the Book in Britain*, Vol. 5, 1695–1830. Edited by Michael F. Suarez and Michael L. Turner, 118–31. New York: Cambridge University Press, 2009.

Smith, Margaret M., and Alexander Lindsay, comps. *Index of English Literary Manuscripts: Volume III, 1700–1800*, pt. 2 (London: Mansell, 1986–1997).

Spedding, Patrick. "'The New Machine': Discovering the Limits of *ECCO*." *Eighteenth-Century Studies* 44, no. 4 (2011): 437–53.

Sturgeon, Sinéad. "Davys, Mary." In *Dictionary of Irish Biography*. Edited by James McGuire and James Quinn. Cambridge, UK: Cambridge University Press, 2009. dib.cambridge.org.

Suarez, Michael F. "Introduction." In *The Cambridge History of the Book in Britain*, Vol. 5, 1695–1830. Edited by Michael F. Suarez and Michael L. Turner, 1–35. New York: Cambridge University Press, 2009.

———. "Publishing Contemporary English Literature, 1695–1774." In *The Cambridge History of the Book in Britain*, Vol. 5, 1695–1830. Edited by Michael F. Suarez and Michael L. Turner, 649–66. New York: Cambridge University Press, 2009.

———. "Towards a Bibliometric Analysis of the Surviving Record, 1701–1800." In *The Cambridge History of the Book in Britain*, Vol. 5, 1695–1830. Edited by Michael F. Suarez and Michael L. Turner, 39–65. New York: Cambridge University Press, 2009.

Sullivan, Alvin, ed. *British Literary Magazines.* Vol. 1, *The Augustan Age and the Age of Johnson, 1698–1788.* Westport, CT: Greenwood, 1983.

Tanner, Simon, Trevor Muñoz, and Pich Hemy Ros. "Measuring Mass Text Digitization Quality and Usefulness: Lessons Learned from Assessing the OCR Accuracy of the British Library's *19th Century Online Newspaper Archive*." *D-Lib Magazine* 15, no. 7/8 (July/August 2009). www.dlib.org/dlib/july09/munoz/07munoz.html.

Troide, Lars. "Burney, Charles (1757–1817)." In *Oxford Dictionary of National Biography*. Edited by H. C. G. Matthew and Brian Harrison. Oxford, UK: Oxford University Press, 2004. Online edition edited by Lawrence Goldman. www.oxforddnb.com/view/article/4079.

Williams, Harold, ed. *The Correspondence of Jonathan Swift.* 5 vols. Oxford, UK: Clarendon Press, 1963–1965.

Woolley, David, ed. *The Correspondence of Jonathan Swift, D. D.* 4 vols. New York: Peter Lang, 1999–2007.

Woolley, James. *Finding English Verse, 1650–1800: First-Line Indexes and Searchable Electronic Texts.* New York: Bibliographical Society of America. www.bibsocamer.org/bibsite/woolley/index.pdf.

Index

AAAJ. See British Literary Magazines: The Augustan Age and the Age of Johnson, 1698–1788

ABELL. See Annual Bibliography of English Language and Literature

Access to Archives, 186, 193

Adam Matthew Publications, 139, 142

Addison, Joseph, *The Spectator*, 154, 159–60

The Age of Johnson: A Scholarly Annual, 115, 119–20

The Alexander Pope Encyclopedia (Rogers), 45, 47

American Society for Eighteenth-Century Studies (ASECS), 240, 242

"and" (Boolean operator), 8–10, 9*f*

"Anna Laetitia Aikin Barbauld (1743–1825)" (Ockerbloom) in *(A Celebration of Women Writers) (CWW)*, 225, 227

Ann Radcliffe: A Bio-Bibliography (Rogers), 105, 108

Annual Bibliography of English Language and Literature (ABELL), 83, 87–89, 89*f*

annual reviews, 82, 91–92

Archive Finder, 187, 194

archives, 181–205; definition of, 181–82; digital and microform collections of, 199–204; locating, 186–95; repositories and collections of, 196–99; research in, best practices for, 183–85; Web resources of, period and general electronic, 213–22; Web resources of, specialized electronic text, 222–25

Archives Wales/Archifau Cymru, 187, 193

ARCHON Directory, 187, 195

art, resources on, 269–71

ASECS. *See* American Society for Eighteenth-Century Studies

Ash, Lee, *Subject Collections: A Guide to Special Book Collections and Subject Emphases as Reported by University, College, Public, and Special Libraries and Museums in the United States and Canada*, 187, 195

Attributions of Authorship in the European Magazine, 1782–1826 (de Montluzin), 230, 238–39

Attributions of Authorship in the Gentleman's Magazine (de Montluzin), 230, 238

authors: catalog searches on, 55–60, 56*f*, 58*f*; contemporary reviews on specific, 169–73; eighteenth-century bibliographies on, 105–9; sources on individual, 45–51; Web sources on specific, 225–29

Backgrounds to Restoration and Eighteenth-Century English Literature: An Annotated Bibliographical Guide to Modern Scholarship (Spector), 95, 105

Backscheider, Paula R., *A Companion to the Eighteenth-Century English Novel and Culture*, 23, 28

Balay, Robert, *Early Periodical Indexes: Bibliographies and Indexes of Literature Published in Periodicals before 1900*, 154, 157

Barbauld, Anna Laetitia: "Anna Laetitia Aikin Barbauld (1743–1825)" (Ockerbloom) in *(A Celebration of Women Writers) (CWW)*, 225, 227

Bateson, F. W., *Cambridge Bibliography of English Literature*, 83, 91

Battestin, Martin C., *A Henry Fielding Companion*, 45, 48

Battigelli, Anna, *Early Modern Online Bibliography: EEBO, ECCO, and Burney Collection Online*, 240, 245

BBTI. See British Book Trade Index

BCMSV. See Leeds Verse Database

Bear, Risa, *Renascence Editions*, 213, 216

Beasley, Jerry C., *A Check List of Prose Fiction Published in England, 1740–1749*, 94, 99

Berry, Reginald, *A Pope Chronology*, 45, 48

bibliographies, 81–112; compiling your own author-centered, 109–11; eighteenth-century, 94–105; eighteenth-century author, 105–9; general literary, 83–94. *See also* indexes

Bibliographies and Guides, 139, 141

A Bibliography of Eliza Haywood (Spedding) 105, 106–7, 170, 171

A Bibliography of the Works of Samuel Johnson: Treating His Published Works from the Beginnings to 1984 (Fleeman), 105, 107

BibSite, 229, 236–37

A Biographical Dictionary of Actors, Actresses, Musicians, Dancers, Managers and Other Stage Personnel in London, 1660–1800 (Highfill & Burnim & Langhans), 38, 45

biographical sources, 38–45

Birch, Dinah, *The Oxford Companion to English Literature*, 31, 34

Black, Jeremy, *Eighteenth-Century Britain, 1688–1783*, 23, 30

The Blackwell Companion to the Enlightenment, (Yolton & Porter & Rogers & Stafford), 24, 31

Bodleian Library Broadside Ballads, 222, 223

Bomarito, Jessica, *Gothic Literature: A Gale Critical Companion*, 32, 33–34

books: print, microform, and digital formats, 136–39; printed matter and, finding 143–47

Boolean searching, search strategies, 7–10, 8*f*

Boswell, James: *The Boswell Collection*, 199, 201; *Boswellian Studies: A Bibliography* (Brown), 105, 109

The Boswell Collection, 199, 201

Boswellian Studies: A Bibliography (Brown), 105, 109

Bracken, James K., *Reference Works in British and American Literature*, 20, 22

Brackett, Virginia, *The Facts on File Companion to British Poetry: 17th and 18th Centuries*, 23, 29–30

Brady, Corey, *Dictionary of Sensibility*, 229, 236

British Archives: A Guide to Archive Resources in the United Kingdom (Foster & Sheppard), 187, 194–95

British Book Trade Index (BBTI), 229, 232–33

British Fiction, 1750–1770: A Chronological Check-List of Prose Fiction Printed in Britain and Ireland (Raven), 94, 99

British Library: *Index of Manuscripts in the British Library*, 196, 197; *Main Catalogue*, 75, 76, 147, 150; Manuscripts Reading Room, 185–86; *Search Our Catalogue, Archives and Manuscripts*, 75, 76–77, 196–97

British Literary Magazines: The Augustan Age and the Age of Johnson, 1698–1788 (AAAJ) (Sullivan), 155–56

British Literary Manuscripts Online, c. 1660–1900, 199, 200–201

British Periodicals, 154, 157–58, 173, 174–75, 175*f*

British Society for Eighteenth-Century Studies (BSECS), 240, 242

British Women Playwrights around 1800 (Crochunis & Eberle-Sinatra), 213, 219

British Women Romantic Poets, 1789–1832, 213, 218–19

British Women Writers, 1700–1850: An Annotated Bibliography of Their Works and Works about Them (Horwitz), 94, 102

Brown, Anthony E., *Boswellian Studies: A Bibliography*, 105, 109

BSECS. *See* British Society for Eighteenth-Century Studies

Bullard, Paddy, *Journal to Stella*, 225, 227–28

Bulletin de la Société d'Etudes Anglo-Américaines des XVIIe et XVIIIe Siècles, 121, 126

Burling, William J., *A Checklist of New Plays and Entertainments on the London Stage, 1700–1737*, 94, 101

Burney, Frances: *The Cambridge Companion to Frances Burney* (Sabor), 46, 49

Burney. See 17th and 18th Century Burney Collection Newspapers

Burnham, Anne Mullen, *A Guide to Irish Fiction, 1650–1900*, 32, 36

Burnim, Kalman A., *A Biographical Dictionary of Actors, Actresses, Musicians, Dancers, Managers and Other Stage Personnel in London, 1660–1800*, 38, 45

call numbers, Library of Congress, browsing, 67–68

Cambridge Bibliography of English Literature (Bateson), 83, 91

The Cambridge Bibliography of English Literature (Shattock), 84, 91

Cambridge Collections Online, 23, 27

The Cambridge Companion to British Theatre, 1730–1830 (Moody & O'Quinn), 24, 27

The Cambridge Companion to Eighteenth-Century Poetry (Sitter), 24, 26–27

The Cambridge Companion to English Literature, 1650–1740 (Zwicker), 24, 25–26

The Cambridge Companion to English Literature, 1740–1830 (Keymer & Mee), 24, 26

The Cambridge Companion to Frances Burney (Sabor), 46, 49

The Cambridge Companion to Gothic Fiction (Hogle), 32, 33

The Cambridge Companion to the Eighteenth-Century Novel (Richetti), 24, 26

The Cambridge Guide to Literature in English (Head), 32, 34–35

The Cambridge History of English Literature, 1660–1780 (Richetti), 24, 25
catalogs, library, 53–79
catalog searches: author, 55–60, 56*f*, 58*f*; subject, 63–67, 67*f*; title, 60–63, 61*f*, 62*f*
Catalogue (National Library of Ireland/ Leabharlann Náisiúnta na hÉierann), 75, 78
"A Catalogue of Magazine Novels and Novelettes, 1740–1815" (Mayo), in *(The English Novel in the Magazines: 1740–1815)*, 155, 157
c18 Bibliographies On-Line (Lynch), 230, 237–38
C18-L: Resources for 18th-Century Studies across the Disciplines, 240, 241
A Celebration of Women Writers (CWW) (Ockerbloom), 209, 211–12; "Anna Laetitia Aikin Barbauld (1743–1825)," 225, 227
Center for Research Libraries (CRL): description of, 68, 75
cfp.english.upenn.edu: eighteenth century, 240, 241
A Check List of English Prose Fiction, 1700–1739 (McBurney), 94, 98–99
A Checklist of New Plays and Entertainments on the London Stage, 1700–1737 (Burling), 94, 101
A Check List of Prose Fiction Published in England, 1740–1749 (Beasley), 94, 99
Chisick, Harvey, *Historical Dictionary of the Enlightenment*, 23, 31
chronologies, 37–38
companions, 23–31; genre, 31–37
A Companion to Eighteenth-Century Poetry (Gerrard), 24, 28
A Companion to Literature from Milton to Blake (Womersley), 24, 28

A Companion to the Eighteenth-Century English Novel and Culture (Backscheider & Ingrassia), 23, 28
A Companion to the Gothic (Punter), 32, 33
Complete Hanoverian State Papers Domestic, 1714–1782, 199, 202
Concise History of the British Newspaper in the Eighteenth Century, 147, 148
A Concordance to the Poems of Jonathan Swift (Shinagel), 46, 50–51
Connected Histories: British History Sources, 1500–1900, 246, 247–48
contemporary reviews, 163–79; letters, diaries, verse, and more, 176–78; modern indexes to eighteenth century, 167–69
Copac, 68, 73–74
Cope, Virginia, *Dictionary of Sensibility*, 229, 236
Cox, Michael, *The Oxford Chronology of English Literature*, 37–38
Critical Companion to Jonathan Swift: A Literary Reference to His Life and Works (Degategno & Stubblefield), 45, 49
CRL. *See* Center for Research Libraries
Crochunis, Thomas C., *British Women Playwrights around 1800*, 213, 219
CWW. *See A Celebration of Women Writers*

databases, 15–16; vs. interface platforms, 15–16; vs. vendors, 15–16
Davys, Mary, 255–64; biographical information on, finding, 258–60; contemporary reception to, 260–62; scholarly literature about, review of, 262–64; works by, identifying eighteenth-century and modern editions of, 257–58
Defoe, Daniel: *Defoe: The Critical Heritage* (Rogers), 170–71; *The*

Defoe Society, 240, 244; *Digital Defoe: Studies in Defoe and His Contemporaries*, 116, 120–21
Defoe: The Critical Heritage (Rogers), 170–71
The Defoe Society, 240, 244
Degategno, Paul J., *Critical Companion to Jonathan Swift: A Literary Reference to His Life and Works*, 45, 49
Delon, Michel, *Encyclopedia of the Enlightenment*, 24, 31
de Montluzin, Emily Lorraine: *Attributions of Authorship in the European Magazine, 1782–1826*, 230, 238–39; *Attributions of Authorship in the Gentleman's Magazine*, 230, 238
Diaries and Papers of Elizabeth Inchbald, from the Folger Shakespeare Library and the London Library, 199, 201
DIB. See Dictionary of Irish Biography from the Earliest Times to the Year 2002
dictionaries, 23–31
A Dictionary of British and American Women Writers, 1660–1800 (Todd), 39, 44
Dictionary of Irish Biography from the Earliest Times to the Year 2002 (McGuire & Quinn), 39, 41–42
Dictionary of Literary Biography (DLB), 38, 42–44, 187, 190–91
Dictionary of Sensibility (Brady & Cope & Millner & Mitric & Puckett & Siegel), 229, 236
digital collections, finding, 139–43
Digital Defoe: Studies in Defoe and His Contemporaries, 116, 120–21
Digital Miscellanies Index, 230, 235
DLB. See Dictionary of Literary Biography
DocumentsOnline, 196, 197

Dodson, Kevin, D., *18th Century Online Encyclopedia: Enlightenment and Revolution*, 230, 236
Dodson, Suzanne Cates, *Microform Research Collections: A Guide*, 139, 140

Early British Periodicals, 154, 157–58
Early English Newspapers, 147, 149–50
Early Modern Commons, 240, 245–46
Early Modern Online Bibliography: EEBO, ECCO, and Burney Collection Online (Battigelli & Shevlin), 240, 245
Early Modern Resources (Howard), 209, 211
Early Periodical Indexes: Bibliographies and Indexes of Literature Published in Periodicals before 1900 (Balay), 154, 157
Eberle-Sinatra, Michael, *British Women Playwrights around 1800*, 213, 219
ECCB: The Eighteenth-Century Current Bibliography, 94, 96–97
ECCO. See Eighteenth-Century Collections Online, Part I and Part II
ECS. See Eighteenth-Century Studies (ECS), 121, 123
EHPS. See European History Primary Sources
EIC. See Essays in Criticism: A Quarterly Journal of Literary Criticism
The Eighteenth Century, 1688–1815 (Langford), 24, 30
Eighteenth-Century Anglo-American Women Novelists: A Critical Reference Guide (Saar & Schofield), 95, 101–2
18th Century Bibliography (Franklin), 230, 237
Eighteenth-Century Book Tracker (Pauley), 214, 215–16

Eighteenth-Century Britain, 1688–1783 (Black), 23, 30

eighteenth-century British literature: books, periodicals, and newspapers on, 135–62; definition of, x; encyclopedias, dictionaries, and companions to, 23–31; scholarly journals on, 115–21

Eighteenth-Century Collections Online, Part I and Part II (ECCO), 143–44, 145*f*, 173, 176

Eighteenth-Century English Microform Holdings, 139, 140–41

Eighteenth Century English Provincial Newspapers, 147, 149

Eighteenth-Century E-Texts (Lynch), 214, 217

Eighteenth-Century Fiction (ProQuest/ Chadwyck-Healy), 143, 144–145

Eighteenth-Century Fiction (University of Toronto Press), 116, 118

Eighteenth-Century Ireland/Iris an dá chultúr, 121, 125

Eighteenth-Century Ireland Society/ Cumann Éire san Ochtú Céad Déag, 240, 242–43

Eighteenth Century Journals: A Portal to Newspapers and Periodicals, c. 1685–1815, 155, 159

Eighteenth-Century Life, 121, 123

The Eighteenth-Century Novel, 116, 117–18

18th Century Online Encyclopedia: Enlightenment and Revolution (Toubiana & Dodson), 230, 236

Eighteenth-Century Resources (Lynch), 209, 210

Eighteenth-Century Scottish Studies Society, 240, 243

Eighteenth-Century Studies (ECS), 121, 123

Eighteenth-Century Studies (Sauer), 209, 212

Eighteenth-Century: Theory and Interpretation, 121, 124

Eighteenth-Century Thought, 121, 124–25

Eighteenth-Century Women: Studies in Their Lives, Work, and Culture, 121, 124

18thConnect: Eighteenth-Century Scholarship Online, 213, 215

Éire-Ireland: A Journal of Irish Studies, 127, 132

Electronic Enlightenment, 176, 177, 199, 203–4

electronic records, 3–7

ELH: English Literary History, 128, 130

ELN. See English Language Notes

Encyclopedia of British Writers (Hager), 38, 44–45

Encyclopedia of the Enlightenment (Delon), 24, 31

Encyclopedia of the Enlightenment (Kors), 24, 30–31

encyclopedias, 23–31; genre, 31–37

English Drama, 143, 145–46

English Fiction of the Eighteenth Century, 1700–1789 (Probyn), 24, 29

The English Gothic: A Bibliographic Guide to Writers from Horace Walpole to Mary Shelley (Spector), 95, 102–3

English Language Notes (ELN), 128, 133

English Literary Periodicals, 155, 157–58

The English Novel, 1700–1740: An Annotated Bibliography (Letellier), 94, 97–98

The English Novel, 1770–1829: A Bibliographical Survey of Prose Fiction Published in the British Isles (Garside & Raven & Schöwerling), 94, 100

The English Novel in the Magazines: 1740–1815, "A Catalogue of Magazine Novels and Novelettes, 1740–1815" (Mayo), 155, 157

English Short Title Catalogue, 1473–1800 (ESTC), 94, 95–96, 147, 148–49, 149*f*, 155, 156

English Verse, 1701–1750: A Catalogue of Separately Printed Poems with Notes on Contemporary Collected Editions (Foxon), 94, 100–101

Essays in Criticism: A Quarterly Journal of Literary Criticism (EIC), 128, 133

ESTC. See English Short Title Catalogue, 1473–1800

EuroDocs: Online Sources for European History (Hacken), 246, 249–50

European History Primary Sources (EHPS), 246, 249

The Facts on File Companion to British Poetry: 17th and 18th Centuries (Brackett), 23, 29–30

Fielding, Henry: *A Henry Fielding Companion* (Battestin), 45, 48

field searching, search strategy, 7

The First Gothics: A Critical Guide to the English Gothic Novel (Frank), 94, 103

Fleeman, J. D., *A Bibliography of the Works of Samuel Johnson: Treating His Published Works from the Beginnings to 1984*, 105, 107

Forster, Antonia: *Index to Book Reviews in England, 1749–1774*, 167–68; *Index to Book Reviews in England, 1775–1800*, 167–68

Foster, Janet, *British Archives: A Guide to Archive Resources in the United Kingdom*, 187, 194–95

Foxon, D. F., *English Verse, 1701–1750: A Catalogue of Separately Printed Poems with Notes on Contemporary Collected Editions*, 94, 100–101

Fraistat, Neil, *Romantic Circles*, 209, 212–13

Frank, Frederick S.: *The First Gothics: A Critical Guide to the English Gothic Novel*, 94, 103; *Gothic Writers: A Critical and Bibliographical Guide*, 95, 104–5; *Guide to the Gothic: An Annotated Bibliography of Criticism*, 94, 103–104; *Guide to the Gothic II: An Annotated Bibliography of Criticism, 1983–1993*, 94, 104; *Guide to the Gothic III: An Annotated Bibliography of Criticism, 1994–2003*, 94, 104

Franklin, Ian, *18th Century Bibliography*, 230, 237

Full Catalogue (National Library of Wales/Llyfrgell Genedlaethol Cymru), 75, 77

fuzzy searching, search strategy, 11–12

Gale Cengage Learning, 139, 141–42

garden design, resources on, 271–72

garden history, resources on, 271–72

Garside, Peter, *The English Novel, 1770–1829: A Bibliographical Survey of Prose Fiction Published in the British Isles*, 94, 100

general research, resources on, 267–69

genre resources, encyclopedias, and companions, 31–37

Gentleman's Magazine, 155, 160

geography, resources on, 272–74

Gerrard, Christine, *A Companion to Eighteenth-Century Poetry*, 24, 28

Google, search strategies, 16

Google Art Project (Google), 16

Google Books (Google), 16, 143, 146, 213, 221–22

Google Scholar (Google), 16

A Gothic Chronology, 230, 232

Gothic Literature: A Gale Critical Companion (Bomarito), 32, 33–34

Gothic Studies, 121, 127

Gothic Writers: A Critical and Bibliographical Guide (Thomson & Voller & Frank) 95, 104–5

Gray, Thomas: *Thomas Gray Archive* (Huber), 225, 226–27

The Grub Street Project: Topographies of Literature and Culture in Eighteenth-Century London (Muri), 246, 249

The Guardian (1821–2003) and The Observer (1791–2003), 147, 154

A Guide to Irish Fiction, 1650–1900 (Loeber & Loeber & Burnham), 32

Guide to the Gothic: An Annotated Bibliography of Criticism (Frank), 94, 103–104

Guide to the Gothic II: An Annotated Bibliography of Criticism, 1983–1993 (Frank), 94, 104

Guide to the Gothic III: An Annotated Bibliography of Criticism, 1994–2003 (Frank), 94, 104

A Guide to Welsh Literature c. 1700–1800 (Jarvis), 32, 36

Hacken, Richard, *EuroDocs: Online Sources for European History*, 246, 249–50

Hager, Alan, *Encyclopedia of British Writers*, 38, 44–45

Hahn Daniel, *The Oxford Guide to Literary Britain and Ireland*, 32, 36–37

Halsall, Paul, *Internet Modern History Sourcebook*, 246, 250

The Handbook to Gothic Literature (Mulvey-Roberts), 32, 33

Hannaford, Richard Gordon, *Samuel Richardson: An Annotated Bibliography of Critical Studies*, 105, 108–9, 169, 172

Harner, James L., *Literary Research Guide: An Annotated Listing of Reference Sources in English Literary Studies*, 20–22

Harrison, Brian, *Oxford Dictionary of National Biography (ODNB)*, 39–41, 187, 191

HathiTrust Digital Library, 143, 146, 213, 222

Haywood, Eliza: *A Bibliography of Eliza Haywood* (Spedding) 105, 106–7, 170, 171

Head, Dominic, *The Cambridge Guide to Literature in English*, 32, 34–35

A Henry Fielding Companion (Battestin), 45, 48

Highfill, Philip H., Jr., *A Biographical Dictionary of Actors, Actresses, Musicians, Dancers, Managers and Other Stage Personnel in London, 1660–1800*, 38, 45

historical atlases, resources on, 272–74

Historical Dictionary of the Enlightenment (Chisick), 23, 31

Historical Outline of Restoration and 18th Century British Literature (Yadav), 230, 231

history, resources on, 274–79

Hogle, Jerrold E., *The Cambridge Companion to Gothic Fiction*, 32, 33

Home Office Papers and Records: Order and Authority in England: Series One, Home Office Class HO 42 (George III, Correspondence, 1782–1820), 199, 202

Horwitz, Barbara Joan, *British Women Writers, 1700–1850: An Annotated Bibliography of Their Works and Works about Them*, 94, 102

Howard, Sharon, *Early Modern Resources*, 209, 211

Huber, Alexander, *Thomas Gray Archive*, 225, 226–27

Huntington Library Quarterly: Studies in English and American History and Literature, 121, 126–27

IGA. *See* International Gothic Association

Inchbald, Elizabeth: *Diaries and Papers of Elizabeth Inchbald, from the Folger Shakespeare Library and the London Library*, 199, 201

indexes, 81–112. *See also* bibliographies

Index of English Literary Manuscripts: Volume III, 1700–1800 (Smith & Lindsay), 187, 188–89

Index of Manuscripts in the British Library, 196, 197

Index to Book Reviews in England, 1749–1774 (Forster), 167–68

Index to Book Reviews in England, 1775–1800 (Forster), 167–68

Ingrassia, Catherine, *A Companion to the Eighteenth-Century English Novel and Culture*, 23, 28

International Gothic Association (IGA), 240, 244

International Society for Eighteenth-Century Studies (ISECS), 240, 243

Internet Archive, 143, 146–47

Internet Modern History Sourcebook (Halsall), 246, 250

Irish Newspaper Archives, 147, 154

Irish Newspapers in Dublin Libraries, 1685–1754, 147, 150

ISECS. *See* International Society for Eighteenth-Century Studies

Jarvis, Branwen, *A Guide to Welsh Literature c. 1700–1800*, 32, 36

JECS. *See Journal for Eighteenth-Century Studies*

JEMCS. *See Journal for Early Modern Cultural Studies*

The John Johnson Collection: An Archive of Printed Ephemera, 200, 202–203

Johnson, Clifford R., *Plots and Characters in the Fiction of Eighteenth-Century English Authors*, 24, 29

Johnson, Samuel: *The Age of Johnson: A Scholarly Annual*, 115, 119–20; *A Bibliography of the Works of Samuel Johnson: Treating His Published Works from the Beginnings to 1984* (Fleeman), 105, 107; *Johnsonian News Letter*, 116, 120; Johnson Society of London, 240, 244–45; *New Rambler: Journal of the Johnson Society of London*, 116, 120; *Samuel Johnson* (Lynch), 225, 228–29; *Samuel Johnson in Context* (Lynch), 45, 49–50

Johnsonian News Letter, 116, 120

Johnson Society of London, 240, 244–45

Jokinen, Anniina, *Luminarium: Anthology of English Literature*, 213, 216–17

"Jonathan Swift, 1667–1745" (Landow), in *(Victorian Web)*, 225, 228

Jones, Steven E., *Romantic Circles*, 209, 212–13

Journal for Early Modern Cultural Studies (JEMCS), 122, 126

Journal for Eighteenth-Century Studies (JECS), 122–23

journals. *See* scholarly journals

Journal to Stella (Bullard), 225, 227–28

JSTOR: The Scholarly Journal Archive, 83, 92–93

Keymer, Thomas, *The Cambridge Companion to English Literature, 1740–1830*, 24, 26

keywords: brainstorming, 2–3, 3*t*; vs. subject searches, 13–14

Kors, Alan Charles, *Encyclopedia of the Enlightenment*, 24, 30–31

Lancashire, Ian, *Representative Poetry Online (RPO)*, 214, 219–20

Landow, George P., "Jonathan Swift, 1667–1745" in *(Victorian Web)*, 225, 228

Langford, Paul, *The Eighteenth Century, 1688–1815*, 24, 30

Langhans, Edward A., *A Biographical Dictionary of Actors, Actresses, Musicians, Dancers, Managers and Other Stage Personnel in London, 1660–1800*, 38, 45

Laurence Sterne in Cyberspace (Uchida), 225, 229

Leeds Verse Database (BCMSV), 230, 234–35

Letellier, Robert I., *The English Novel, 1700–1740: An Annotated Bibliography*, 94, 97–98

The Lewis Walpole Library, 196, 198–99

library catalogs, 53–79

Library of Congress (LOC): *Library of Congress Online Catalog*, 75, 77; *National Union Catalog, Pre-1956 Imprints: A Cumulative Author List Representing Library of Congress Printed Cards and Titles Reported by Other American Libraries (NUC)*, 69, 74–75; *National Union Catalog of Manuscript Collections (NUCMC)*, 187, 192

Library of Congress Online Catalog, 75, 77

limiting, search strategy, 14–15

Lindsay, Alexander, *Index of English Literary Manuscripts: Volume III, 1700–1800*, 187, 188–89

The Literary Gothic (Voller), 223, 224–25

Literary Manuscripts: 17th and 18th Century Poetry from the Brotherton Library, University of Leeds, 200, 201

literary reference sources, general, 19–52

Literary Research Guide: An Annotated Listing of Reference Sources in English Literary Studies (Harner), 20–22

Literary Reviews in British Periodicals, 1789–1797: A Bibliography with a Supplementary List of General (Non-Review) Articles on Literary Subjects (Ward), 167, 168–69

Literary Reviews in British Periodicals, 1798–1820: A Bibliography with a Supplementary List of General (Non-Review) Articles on Literary Subjects (Ward), 167, 168–69

Literature Compass, 116, 117

Liu, Alan: "Restoration and 18th Century" in *(Voice of the Shuttle) (VOS)*, 209, 210–11; *Romantic Chronology*, 230, 231–32

LOC. *See* Library of Congress

Location Register of English Literary Manuscripts and Letters: Eighteenth and Nineteenth Centuries (Sutton), 187, 189–90

Loeber, Magda, *A Guide to Irish Fiction, 1650–1900*, 32, 36

Loeber, Rolf, *A Guide to Irish Fiction, 1650–1900*, 32, 36

London Lives: 1690–1800–Crime, Poverty, and Social Policy in the Metropolis, 246, 248–49

The Long Eighteenth, 240, 245

Ludwig, Katelyn, *Reinventing the Feminine: Bluestocking Women Writers in 18th-Century London*, 246, 250–51

Lumen: Selected Proceedings from the Canadian Society for Eighteenth-Century Studies/Travaux de la Société Canadienne d'Etude du Dix-Huitième Siècle, 122, 125

Luminarium: Anthology of English Literature (Jokinen), 213, 216–17

Lynch, Jack: *c18 Bibliographies On-Line*, 230, 237–38; *Eighteenth-Century E-Texts*, 214, 217; *Eighteenth-Century Resources*, 209, 210; *Samuel Johnson*, 225, 228–29; *amuel Johnson in Context*, 45, 49–50

Machine Readable Cataloging. *See*
MARC records
Magazines for Libraries (MFL), 114,
115
Main Catalogue (British Library), 75,
76, 147, 150
Main Catalogue (National Library of
Scotland/Leabharlann Nàiseanta na
hAlba), 75, 78
*The Mainstream Companion to Scottish
Literature* (Royle), 32, 35
Mandell, Laura, *Romantic Chronology*,
230, 231–32
manuscripts, 181–205; digital and
microform collections of, 199–204;
locating, 186–95; repositories and
collections of, 196–99; research in,
best practices for, 183–85
Mapping the Republic of Letters, 200,
204
MARC records, 3–7; structure of, 3–7,
5*f*, 5*t*, 6*f*
Marcuse, Michael J., *A Reference Guide
for English Studies*, 20, 22–23
*Mary Wollstonecraft Godwin,
1759–1797: A Bibliography of
the First and Early Editions, with
Briefer Notes on Later Editions and
Translations* (Windle), 105, 107–8
Matthew, Henry C. G., *Oxford
Dictionary of National Biography
(ODNB)*, 39–41, 187, 191
Mayo, Robert D., "A Catalogue of
Magazine Novels and Novelettes,
1740–1815" in *(The English Novel
in the Magazines: 1740–1815)*, 155,
157
McBurney, William H., *A Check List of
English Prose Fiction, 1700–1739*,
94, 98–99
McEvoy, Emma, *The Routledge
Companion to the Gothic*, 32–33
McGuire, James, *Dictionary of Irish
Biography from the Earliest Times to
the Year 2002 (DIB)*, 39, 41–42

medicine, resources on, 284–86
Mee, John, *The Cambridge Companion
to English Literature, 1740–1830*,
24, 26
MFL. See Magazines for Libraries
*Microform Research Collections: A
Guide* (Dodson), 139, 140
microforms collections, finding,
139–43
Miller, William G., *Subject Collections:
A Guide to Special Book Collections
and Subject Emphases as Reported
by University, College, Public, and
Special Libraries and Museums in
the United States and Canada*, 187,
195
Millner, Mike, *Dictionary of Sensibility*,
229, 236
Mitric, Ana, *Dictionary of Sensibility*,
229, 236
MLA Directory of Periodicals, 114–15
*MLAIB. See MLA International
Bibliography of Books and Articles
on the Modern Languages and
Literatures*
*MLA International Bibliography of
Books and Articles on the Modern
Languages and Literatures (MLAIB)*,
83, 84–89, 87*f*
*MLQ. See Modern Language Quarterly:
A Journal of Literary History*
Modern English Collection, 214,
220–21
*Modern Language Quarterly: A Journal
of Literary History (MLQ)*, 128, 130
Modern Language Review, 128, 129–30
modifying, search strategy, 14–15
Moody, Jane, *The Cambridge
Companion to British Theatre, 1730–
1830*, 24, 27
Moore, Lisa L., *The Sister Arts: British
Gardening, Painting, and Poetry,
1700–1832*, 246, 251
Mulvey-Roberts, Marie, *The Handbook
to Gothic Literature*, 32, 33

Muri, Allison, *The Grub Street Project:*
Topographies of Literature and
Culture in Eighteenth-Century
London, 246, 249
music, resources on, 279–81

The National Archives (TNA), 196,
197
The National Archives of Ireland/
Chartlann Náisiúnta na hÉierann,
196, 198
national library catalogs, 75–78
National Library of Ireland/Leabharlann
Náisiúnta na hÉierann (NLI):
Catalogue, 75, 78, 196, 198
National Library of Scotland/
Leabharlann Nàiseanta na hAlba:
Main Catalogue, 75, 78, 196, 198
National Library of Wales/Llyfrgell
Genedlaethol Cymru, 196, 198; *Full*
Catalogue, 75, 77
National Portrait Gallery, 246, 251–52
The National Records of Scotland, 196,
198
National Register of Archives, 187,
192–93
National Union Catalog, Pre-1956
Imprints: A Cumulative Author List
Representing Library of Congress
Printed Cards and Titles Reported
by Other American Libraries (NUC),
69, 74–75
National Union Catalog of Manuscript
Collections (NUCMC), 187, 192
NCBEL. *See The New Cambridge*
Bibliography of English Literature
Nelson, Carolyn, *Union First Line Index*
of English Verse, 13th–19th Century
(Bulk 1500–1800), 176, 178, 187,
190
nesting, search strategy, 12
The New Cambridge Bibliography
of English Literature (NCBEL)
(Watson), 84, 89–91, 148, 155, 156,
167, 169

New Literary History: A Journal of
Theory and Interpretation, 128, 131
New Rambler: Journal of the Johnson
Society of London, 116, 120
newspapers: contemporary reviews in
eighteenth-century, 173–76; finding,
147–54; print, microform, and digital
formats of, 136–39
NLI. *See* National Library of Ireland/
Leabharlann Náisiúnta na hÉierann
Norton Topics Online, 230, 239–40
"not" (Boolean operator), 10, 9*f*
Novels-On-Line, 214, 217–18
NUC. *See National Union Catalog,*
Pre-1956 Imprints: A Cumulative
Author List Representing Library
of Congress Printed Cards and
Titles Reported by Other American
Libraries
NUCMC. *See National Union Catalog*
of Manuscript Collections

Ockerbloom, Mary Mark, *A Celebration*
of Women Writers (CWW), 209, 211–
12; "Anna Laetitia Aikin Barbauld
(1743–1825)," 225, 227
OCR searches, search strategy, 11–12,
151
ODNB. *See Oxford Dictionary of*
National Biography
online searching, basics of, 1–17
Optical Character Recognition. *See*
OCR
O'Quinn, Daniel, *The Cambridge*
Companion to British Theatre, 1730–
1830, 24, 27
"or" (Boolean operator), 10, 9*f*
OTA. *See University of Oxford Text*
Archive
The Oxford Chronology of English
Literature (Cox), 37–38
The Oxford Companion to English
Literature (Birch), 31, 34
The Oxford Companion to Irish
Literature (Welch), 32, 35–36

Oxford Dictionary of National Biography (ODNB) (Matthew & Harrison), 39–41, 187, 191
The Oxford Guide to Literary Britain and Ireland (Hahn & Robins), 32, 36–37

Palmer's Index to the Times Newspaper, 147, 150
PAO. See Periodicals Archive Online
Pauley, Benjamin, *Eighteenth-Century Book Tracker,* 214, 215–16
periodicals: contemporary reviews in eighteenth-century, 173–76; finding, 154–60; print, microform, and digital formats of, 136–39. *See also* scholarly journals
Periodicals Archive Online (PAO), 83, 93, 155, 158
Periodicals Index Online (PIO), 83, 93–94, 155, 158
Philological Quarterly (PQ), 128, 133
philosophy, resources on, 281–83
phrase searching, search strategy, 12–13
Pickering & Chatto, 139, 142
PIO. See Periodicals Index Online
Plots and Characters in the Fiction of Eighteenth-Century English Authors (Johnson), 24, 29
PMLA: Publications of the Modern Language Association of America, 128, 129
Pope, Alexander: *The Alexander Pope Encyclopedia* (Rogers), 45, 47; *A Pope Chronology* (Berry), 45, 48
A Pope Chronology (Berry), 45, 48
Porter, Roy, *The Blackwell Companion to the Enlightenment,* 24, 31
PQ. See Philological Quarterly
Probyn, Clive T., *English Fiction of the Eighteenth Century, 1700–1789,* 24, 29
The Proceedings of the Old Bailey, 1674–1913, 223, 224
Project Gutenberg, 214, 221

Project Muse, 84, 93
proximity operators, search strategy, 13
Puckett, Kent, *Dictionary of Sensibility,* 229, 236
Punter, David, *A Companion to the Gothic,* 32, 33

Quinn, James, *Dictionary of Irish Biography from the Earliest Times to the Year 2002 (DIB),* 39, 41–42

Radcliffe, Ann: *Ann Radcliffe: A Bio-Bibliography* (Rogers), 105, 108
Raven, James: *British Fiction, 1750–1770: A Chronological Check-List of Prose Fiction Printed in Britain and Ireland,* 94, 99; *The English Novel, 1770–1829: A Bibliographical Survey of Prose Fiction Published in the British Isles,* 94, 100
"Recent Studies in the Restoration and Eighteenth Century" *(SEL: Studies in English Literature, 1500–1900),* 95, 97
A Reference Guide for English Studies (Marcuse), 20, 22–23
Reference Works in British and American Literature (Bracken), 20, 22
Reinventing the Feminine: Bluestocking Women Writers in 18th-Century London (Ludwig), 246, 250–51
relevancy searching, search strategies, 14
religion, resources on, 283–84
Renascence Editions (Bear), 213, 216
Representative Poetry Online (RPO) (Lancashire), 214, 219–20
reprints, finding, 139–43
research guides, 20–23
"Restoration and 18th Century" *(Voice of the Shuttle) (VOS)* (Liu), 209, 210–11
Restoration and Eighteenth-Century Theatre Research, 116, 118

Review of English Studies, 128, 132–33
Richardson, Samuel: *Samuel Richardson: An Annotated Bibliography of Critical Studies* (Hannaford), 105, 108–9, 169, 172; *Samuel Richardson: A Reference Guide* (Smith), 170, 172–73
Richetti, John: *The Cambridge Companion to the Eighteenth-Century Novel*, 24, 26; *The Cambridge History of English Literature, 1660–1780*, 24, 25
Robins, Nicolas, *The Oxford Guide to Literary Britain and Ireland*, 32, 36–37
Rogers, Deborah D., *Ann Radcliffe: A Bio-Bibliography*, 105, 108
Rogers, Pat: *The Alexander Pope Encyclopedia*, 45, 47; *The Blackwell Companion to the Enlightenment*, 24, 31; *Defoe: The Critical Heritage*, 170–71
Romantic Chronology (Mandell & Liu), 230, 231–32
Romantic Circles (Fraistat & Jones), 209, 212–13
The Routledge Companion to the Gothic (Spooner & McEvoy), 32–33
Royle, Trevor, *The Mainstream Companion to Scottish Literature*, 32, 35
RPO. See Representative Poetry Online

Saar, Doreen Alvarez, *Eighteenth-Century Anglo-American Women Novelists: A Critical Reference Guide*, 95, 101–2
Sabor, Peter, *The Cambridge Companion to Frances Burney*, 46, 49
Samuel Johnson (Lynch), 225, 228–29
Samuel Johnson in Context (Lynch), 45, 49–50
Samuel Richardson: An Annotated Bibliography of Critical Studies (Hannaford), 105, 108–9, 169, 172

Samuel Richardson: A Reference Guide (Smith), 170, 172–73
Sauer, Geoffrey, *Eighteenth-Century Studies*, 209, 212
SBTI. See Scottish Book Trade Index
SCAN. See Scottish Archive Network
Schofield, Mary Anne, *Eighteenth-Century Anglo-American Women Novelists: A Critical Reference Guide*, 95, 101–2
scholarly journals, 113–34; eighteenth-century culture, 121–27; eighteenth-century literature, 115–21; general, 127–34; periodical research resources for, 114–15. *See also* periodicals
Schöwerling, Rainer, *The English Novel, 1770–1829: A Bibliographical Survey of Prose Fiction Published in the British Isles*, 94, 100
sciences, resources on, 284–86
Scottish Archive Network (SCAN), 187, 193
Scottish Book Trade Index (SBTI), 230, 233–34
Scottish Literary Review, 128, 132
Scriblerian and the Kit-Cats, 116, 118–19
Search Our Catalogue, Archives and Manuscripts (British Library), 75, 76–77, 196–97
search strategies, creating, 7–15
SEL: Studies in English Literature, 1500–1900, 116, 117; "Recent Studies in the Restoration and Eighteenth Century," 95, 97
17th and 18th Century Burney Collection Newspapers (Burney), 147, 151–54, 153*f*, 173, 175–76
Shattock, Joanne, *The Cambridge Bibliography of English Literature*, 84, 91
Sheppard, Julia, *British Archives: A Guide to Archive Resources in the United Kingdom*, 187, 194–95

Shevlin, Eleanor, *Early Modern Online Bibliography: EEBO, ECCO, and Burney Collection Online*, 240, 245

Shinagel, Michael, *A Concordance to the Poems of Jonathan Swift*, 46, 50–51

Siegel, Danny, *Dictionary of Sensibility*, 229, 236

The Sister Arts: British Gardening, Painting, and Poetry, 1700–1832 (Moore), 246, 251

Sitter, John, *The Cambridge Companion to Eighteenth-Century Poetry*, 24, 26–27

1650–1850: Ideas, Aesthetics, and Inquiries in the Early Modern Era, 121, 125–26

Smith, Margaret M., *Index of English Literary Manuscripts: Volume III, 1700–1800*, 187, 188–89

Smith, Sarah W. R., *Samuel Richardson: A Reference Guide*, 170, 172–73

social science, resources on, 287–88

Society for the Study of Early Modern Women (SSEMW), 240, 243–44

The Spectator (Addison & Steele), 154, 159–60

Spector, Robert D.: *Backgrounds to Restoration and Eighteenth-Century English Literature: An Annotated Bibliographical Guide to Modern Scholarship*, 95, 105; *The English Gothic: A Bibliographic Guide to Writers from Horace Walpole to Mary Shelley*, 95, 102–3

Spedding, Patrick, *A Bibliography of Eliza Haywood*, 105, 106–7, 170, 171

Spooner, Catherine, *The Routledge Companion to the Gothic*, 32–33

SSEMW. *See* Society for the Study of Early Modern Women

Stafford, Barbara Maria, *The Blackwell Companion to the Enlightenment*, 24, 31

State Papers Online: The Government of Britain, 1509–1714, 200, 202

Steele, Richard, *The Spectator*, 154, 159–60

Sterne, Laurence: *Laurence Sterne in Cyberspace* (Uchida), 225, 229

Stubblefield, R. Jay, *Critical Companion to Jonathan Swift: A Literary Reference to His Life and Works*, 45, 49

Studies in Eighteenth-Century Culture, 122, 123–24

Studies in the Novel, 128, 131–32

Subject Collections: A Guide to Special Book Collections and Subject Emphases as Reported by University, College, Public, and Special Libraries and Museums in the United States and Canada (Ash & Miller), 187, 195

subjects, catalog searches on, 63–67, 67*f*

subject searches, search strategy, 13–14

Sullivan, Alvin, *British Literary Magazines: The Augustan Age and the Age of Johnson, 1698–1788 (AAAJ)*, 155–56

Sutton, David C., *Location Register of English Literary Manuscripts and Letters: Eighteenth and Nineteenth Centuries*, 187, 189–90

Swift, Jonathan: *A Concordance to the Poems of Jonathan Swift* (Shinagel), 46, 50–51; *Critical Companion to Jonathan Swift: A Literary Reference to His Life and Works* (Degategno & Stubblefield), 45, 49; "Jonathan Swift, 1667–1745" (Landow), in *(Victorian Web)*, 225, 228; *Journal to Stella* (Bullard), 225, 227–28; *Swift Criticism Database*, 230, 238; *Swift Studies*, 116, 119

Swift Criticism Database, 230, 238

Swift Studies, 116, 119

theater, resources on, 288–90
Thomas Gray Archive (Huber), 225, 226–27
Thomson, Douglass H., *Gothic Writers: A Critical and Bibliographical Guide*, 95, 104–5
Times Digital Archive, 1785–2006, 147, 154
titles, catalog searches on, 60–63, 61*f*, 62*f*
TNA. *See* The National Archives
Todd, Janet, *A Dictionary of British and American Women Writers, 1660–1800*, 39, 44
Topic Guide: Great Britain, 139, 141
Toubiana, Guy, *18th Century Online Encyclopedia: Enlightenment and Revolution*, 230, 236
truncation searches, search strategy, 10–11

Uchida, Masaru, *Laurence Sterne in Cyberspace*, 225, 229
UK RED: The Experience of Reading in Britain, from 1450 to 1945, 177
Ulrich's Periodicals Directory, 114, 115
union catalogs, 68–75
Union First Line Index of English Verse, 13th–19th Century (Bulk 1500–1800) (Nelson), 176, 178, 187, 190
University of Oxford Text Archive (OTA), 214, 220

Victorian Web, "Jonathan Swift, 1667–1745" (Landow), 225, 228
Vive la difference! The English and French Stereotype in Satirical Prints, 1720–1815, 246, 251
Voice of the Shuttle (VOS), "Restoration and 18th Century" (Liu), 209, 210–11
Voller, Jack G.: *Gothic Writers: A Critical and Bibliographical Guide*, 95, 104–5; *The Literary Gothic*, 223, 224–25
VOS. See Voice of the Shuttle

Ward, William S.: *Literary Reviews in British Periodicals, 1789–1797: A Bibliography with a Supplementary List of General (Non-Review) Articles on Literary Subjects*, 167, 168–69; *Literary Reviews in British Periodicals, 1798–1820: A Bibliography with a Supplementary List of General (Non-Review) Articles on Literary Subjects*, 167, 168–69
Watson, George, *The New Cambridge Bibliography of English Literature (NCBEL)*, 84, 89–91, 148, 155, 156, 167, 169
Web resources, 207–53; author sites as, 225–29; cultural and historical societies as, 246–52; current awareness sources and associations as, 240–46; evaluation of, 208–9; period and general electronic text archives as, 213–22; reference tools for, 229–40; scholarly gateways as, 209–13; specialized electronic text archives as, 222–25
Welch, Robert, *The Oxford Companion to Irish Literature*, 32, 35–36
wildcard searches, search strategy, 10–11
Windle, John, *Mary Wollstonecraft Godwin, 1759–1797: A Bibliography of the First and Early Editions, with Briefer Notes on Later Editions and Translations*, 105, 107–8
Wollstonecraft Godwin, Mary: *Mary Wollstonecraft Godwin, 1759–1797: A Bibliography of the First and Early Editions, with Briefer Notes on Later Editions and Translations* (Windle), 105, 107–8
Women's Writing, 128, 131
Womersley, David, *A Companion to Literature from Milton to Blake*, 24, 28
The Word on the Street, 223–24

WorldCat, 69–72, 71*f*, 139, 142–43, 148, 150, 155, 156–57, 187, 192
WorldCat.org, 69, 72–73, 72*f*, 139, 142–43, 148, 187, 192

Yadav, Alok, *Historical Outline of Restoration and 18th Century British Literature*, 230, 231
Yale University: Lewis Walpole Library, 196, 198–99
Yearbook of English Studies, 128, 130

Year's Work in English Studies (YWES), 84, 91–92
Yolton, John W., *The Blackwell Companion to the Enlightenment*, 24, 31
YWES. See Year's Work in English Studies

Zwicker, Steven N., *The Cambridge Companion to English Literature, 1650–1740*, 24, 25–26

About the Authors

Peggy Keeran is a professor and the arts and humanities reference librarian at the University of Denver Penrose Library.

Jennifer Bowers is an associate professor and the social sciences reference librarian at the University of Denver Penrose Library.

The authors are coeditors of the Scarecrow Press series Literary Research: Strategies and Sources and the authors of *Literary Research and the British Romantic Era: Strategies and Sources* (No. 1) and *Literary Research and the British Renaissance and Early Modern Period: Strategies and Sources* (No. 8).